Expectations, Uncertainty and the Term Structure of Interest Rates

Expectations, Uncertainty and the Term Structure of Interest Rates

J. C. DODDS
Esmée Fairbairn Research Fellow in Economics

J. L. FORD
Professor of Economics, University of Sheffield

Martin Robertson

First published 1974 by Martin Robertson and Company Ltd., 17 Quick Street, London NI 8HL

ISBN 0 85520 036 7

Typeset in Britain by Preface Limited, Salisbury and printed in Britain by The Pitman Press, Bath

Contents

This book is dedicated to
CAROL and MARGARET

Preface

Our objective in writing this book has been to set out critically the analytical base of the major theories, considered to be theories, on the term structure of interest rates. We see this as a useful exercise in itself, but wish also to map out guidelines by which each of the theories, or strictly speaking its hypotheses or propositions, could be subjected to empirical evaluation, and to accompany the discussion on the procedural aspects of that evaluation by a critical survey of the existing evidence, and of new evidence compiled by ourselves, on each of the theories of the term structure. The evidence we have advanced is largely new evidence, not only because we have used our own newly constructed data on bond yields on which to test the theories, but also because we have produced new tests of some of them, though some of those tests are refinements of the existing tests in this field.

We hoped to be able to come to some definite conclusions on the value of this or that theory on or approach to the relationship between bond yields in the real world. We believe that we have been able to produce some pointers in that direction, and to provide avenues for further research in this area. But what has been illustrated again is that in Economics there is 'many a slip 'twixt theory and practice'; in particular, the difficulties of carrying out applied econometric studies are often formidable! As a profession we tend to be eternally optimistic, and we never learn from experience, even though we often impute error-learning behaviour to economic agents! Once we endeavour to concretise an hypothesis and put it into a mathematical form suitable for econometric testing, all kinds of difficulties arise. And the lid of Pandora's box is really opened wide when the econometric testing *per se* is being undertaken. There are problems connected with the definition of variables, their measurement, and the interpretation of the statistical attempts at testing the hypotheses.

We have to accept the fact, for fact it is, that in our particular discipline it is not possible to get a 'knock-down' answer on the value of an hypothesis and hence upon the question of the relative value of this or that hypothesis on, in our case, the determination of the structure of interest rates. We can go so far, and only so far.

This has been demonstrated here, and at times we have deliberately set out to show this. This is why on the odd occasions the text might appear to be pretentious, such as in chapter 4, where details are given of how the theory might be tested by using certain distributed lag schemes, yet the results are inconclusive. For our endeavour has been to experiment as much as possible and to say so. Though it is rarely possible in a text of this size to give anything more than cursory details of those experiments, at times it is advisable to say something about them, for they indicate how the work outlined here could be further developed; and it partly indicates which experiments — though perhaps all, intuitively speaking, worth while — are, in fact, worth expending time and effort on.

The avenues of research followed here, and those areas where we have suggested that further work should be undertaken (some of which, as we state in later chapters, we ourselves have already embarked upon), are not the only ones that can or have been pursued in this area. We have not attempted to touch on the work that has been concerned, for example, with applying spectral analysis to the term structure. Because of the scope and nature of this book, neither have we touched on other similar work in this area, such as that of Richard Roll on *The Behaviour of Interest Rates.* This is an excellent piece of research and the fact that we have not referred to it in no way reflects what we think of it. Nor have we been able to include details of the promising approach recently taken by Charles Nelson (reference (63) in the References), which came to hand when this book was initially completed.

About the specific contents of the book we need say little here. We might note just one other thing. The last chapter we have kept deliberately short, even though some of the other chapters in the book are very lengthy. This is because, where necessary, the chapters themselves contain a summary of the empirical results contained within them. There was nothing extra that could be achieved by repeating these summaries, even in an alternative form, in the final chapter. We have tried as far as we were able to take what we might call a scholarly stance in writing the major chapters of the book. That is to say, we have sought to portray the essence of each of the theories in as straightforward, as full and as unpretentious a way as we could accomplish in the time and space available. The discussion is, therefore, critical: it is not meant to be disparaging. We are well aware of the difficulties of carrying out research in this area; and what we ourselves have said will no doubt be critically evaluated. But as has been said before, the nature of the social sciences is such that, if a piece of empirical research is not worth criticising, then it does not have much value.

J. C. DODDS
J. L. FORD

Sheffield, October 1973

Acknowledgements

This book has been in manuscript form in one stage or another since the beginning of 1972 and we have been extremely fortunate in the help and encouragement we have had from a number of friends and colleagues who have read the manuscript for us. Without this it is doubtful if the book would ever have been completed. They have expended time and effort on the manuscript far beyond the call of duty.

We wish to record our gratitude to: Mr John F. Richards; Charles F. Carter, Vice-Chancellor of the University of Lancaster; Professor George Shackle and Professor Jack C. Gilbert; who commented on all or most of the book. John Richards, in particular, with his vast practical knowledge of the bond market was able to bring us down to earth, so to speak. We have not always been able to take account of their comments in full because of limitations of space, and Professor Shackle would have preferred a more expanded treatment of the theme of Time and Knowledge. Only they will know how much the book as now written owes to their comments and suggestions. But we must, of course, exonerate them from any commissions and omissions that have occurred.

We are grateful too for the computer programs made available to us by Jon Stewart, of the University of Manchester, who also, together with our colleague Professor John Nicholson, kindly made suggestions as to how we might estimate our under-sized sample model in chapter 6. He is involved with our research team in the Economics Research Section at the University of Sheffield in developing the model for a book on model-building which is to be completed early in 1974. That work, and the research on financial institutions referred to in chapter 6, arises out of a project that was initiated two years ago to examine the role of financial intermediaries in the U.K., under the direction of our colleague Professor George Clayton. We are grateful for the financial support given by the S.S.R.C. and the Esmée Fairbairn Charitable Trust for our work in this area and on the financial model; and to George Clayton for enabling us to divert our energies in the last few months to the writing of this book.

Though they have not seen the full details of the model summarised and used in chapter 6, we are also indebted to the encouragement we have had on our attempts to construct a model from Professor Jim Ball of the London Graduate School of Business Studies, and especially from Professor Lawrence Klein of the Wharton School of Finance and Commerce, who made suggestions for the expansion and development of our first pilot model.

The production of this book has involved an herculean effort by our secretary, Miss Linda Henderson, who has had to type several versions of the manuscript from often indecipherable drafts. The final draft had to be completed in a very short space of time and she worked like a Trojan to see that we met our deadline. For all of this we express our warmest thanks to her. A thank-you is also due to Mrs Muriel Burton, who helped us with the data collection, the computer work and the proof-reading.

Finally, and by no means least of all, we must say a special thanks to our wives and to J.L.F.'s family, who had much to endure, particularly when the work on the book moved into its final stages.

J. C. DODDS
J. L. FORD

Foreword

The Stock Exchange and other financial markets provide a splendid challenge to the economist. Here are numerous 'commodities', defined with precision, which are traded in markets which — even if not strictly 'perfect' — are free and quick-reacting. The consequent prices are recorded from day to day, or even from hour to hour. They trace out patterns which at first seem to be like the random wanderings of a flock of sheep, but on examination show repetitions of typical characteristics, such as those studied by the chartists. How can this unrivalled mass of data be related to theories about the actions and motivations of the individuals operating in the market?

If anyone succeeded in discovering a great unifying principle, like the law of gravity, behind all these disorderly data, he would no doubt swiftly be corrupted by the immense wealth he could command. But, as this book shows, the problem of understanding human actions is not as simple as understanding the fall of an apple. Mr. Dodds and Professor Ford have taken an apparently simple section of the market, in which safe bonds are traded and yield a rate of interest. These bonds are distinguishable by their terms to maturity. What sense can be made of the resultant pattern of interest rates? On this matter various theories have been propounded. Is it possible to say that some are wrong, or that some are nearer to being right than others?

Mr. Dodds and Professor Ford, after extensive, scholarly and original work, do indeed come up with some answers. What they reveal, however, is that all the theories are over-simplified. In fact, they provide a remarkable example of the difficulty of finding order in the results of the actions of differing individuals: the way of progress may have to be to go back to the study of the actions of individual investors or of reasonably homogeneous groups. Maynard Keynes' analysis, in the *Treatise on Money*, of the balance between Bulls and Bears, is still an example to be followed.

Those interested in theories of the rate of interest, in financial markets, and in econometric method, will all find value in this book. It will provide a point of reference for all future work in this difficult area.

CHARLES F. CARTER

Lancaster, November 1973

1 An Overview of Yield-to-Maturity Curves and Theories of the Term Structure

1.1

In this book we shall be concerned with the relationships (in advanced countries) between the interest rates on various financial assets — assets that can be distinguished from each other, as far as possible, solely by their length of life, that is their term-to-maturity. Our analytical and empirical discussion will either explicitly or implicitly cover a number of important questions relating to the relationships between interest rates, namely the term structure of interest rates, and the forces that determine and shape those relationships, such as:

(i) At any moment in time, short- and long-term rates of interest prevail side by side. What constraints in logic and in practice govern their mutual relationships?

(ii) Do the relations between interest rates on financial claims of different lengths all emanate from a common source in the inherent nature of interest rates?

(iii) Are interest rates influenced by the particular situations, 'endowments', commitments, preferences and expectations of individuals on the financial markets? This question itself admits of several separate ones, three of which are of some importance:

(a) Do differences in the commitments, where these may be loosely described as their financial obligations to others, of the different participants on the market influence the structure of interest rates?

(b) Can differences in the preferences of the individuals on the market have any appreciable effect on the relationship between the yields on long-term and short-term bonds (and other relevant claims), where we think of preferences in terms of the desire to borrow and to lend in different parts of the market for reasons that are innate, and depend upon the 'utility function' of the individual? For example, borrowers may desire, *ceteris paribus*, to borrow long whilst investors may continually prefer to lend short — given their commitments, expectations, etc., and to do so because they prefer not to have to accept too much risk: they are 'security-preferrers'.

(c) Is it possible for differences among individuals in respect of their expectations (about the movement of prices and of yields in the market) to play an essential role in the formation of the structure of interest rates? Here what immediately springs to mind is the 'two poles' view, or the two views (Bulls-Bears) theory of Lord Keynes's *Treatise on Money* (7).

(iv) If expectations (of market prices and hence of market yields) are deemed to be important in determining the term structure of interest rates, can the investigation of their role in influencing the market be aided by the introduction of the concept of a (market) normal rate or range of interest rates of the kind used by Keynes (81) in his Liquidity-Preference Theory of the Rate of Interest? If so, how? Additionally, how can such a concept be quantified to make it operational in econometric investigation, bearing in mind the enormous changes that have occurred in the structure of interest rates and in what would be regarded as a 'normal' long-term rate of interest between the 1940s and the 1970s in the U.K., and in the capital markets of other advanced countries?

Some of these questions are answered in different ways, theoretically as well as empirically, in the following pages: most are answered in the context of this or that 'theory' which has been advanced to account for the nature of the term structure at points in time and for changes in that structure between various moments. Others are dealt with explicitly in the course of our discussions, question (iv), for example, in chapter 4. One or two, whether treated explicitly or implicitly in our discussion, are not dealt with in as great a depth as they could be; this is true, for instance, of question (iii) (c).

All are considered not as questions *per se* but as part of our discussions of the major theories that are contained in the literature on the term structure of interest rates. For the purposes of this book we have chosen to concentrate on four major theories. Three of these, the Expectations or Traditional Theory, the Liquidity (or Risk) Premium Theory and the Hedging Pressure Theory, are well established and are generally regarded as being important. We hold the fourth theory, that advanced by Malkiel (11), in the same light, even though it is developed out of the work of others, especially of Lord Keynes. Of recent origin, though not much younger than the Hedging Pressure Theory, the Malkiel Theory has a close affinity to the Expectations Theory and will be presented and analysed after we have considered the latter. Discussions of the Liquidity Premium Theory and the Hedging Pressure Theory follow thereafter.

We shall see how each theory attempts to tackle the question of the determination of the term structure in slightly different ways, and that as a result they tend to ask different sets of the questions outlined earlier; and that even where they ask the same questions, such as those concerned with the role of expectations, they do not give the same answers. Our object will be to discover, with the help of empirical investigations of the theories analysed, if answers can be given to the kind of questions listed previously taken collectively, so that we can reach some overall conclusions on the variables, and perhaps on their quantitative importance, which influence the relationship between the yields on long-term and short-term financial claims.

If such a position could be attained it would have direct relevance for many groups in the economy, of which not the least important are the monetary authorities. For they have to administer the Government's borrowing requirement and they will be concerned with its composition and the terms on which government debt must be issued if it is to be taken up by investors. They may wish, as they have in the U.S.A. (see Modigliani and Sutch (93)) and the U.K. (see Goodhart (69)), to 'twist' the structure of interest rates, in which case they will have to know if it will be possible for them to twist the structure by altering the stock on the market of the various maturities of debt it issues. They will also have to know, or at least to have some rough indication of, the extent to which they will have to change the composition of the outstanding debt if they are to succeed in their policy. All of this will necessitate their having some idea of the determinants of the term structure. For these determinants may be such, because of the behaviour of investors (lenders) on the government debt market, that *ceteris paribus* changing debt supplies has no influence, or only imperceptible effect, on the term structure.

Let us now begin our story. In the remainder of this chapter we shall discuss some preliminary matters on the yield-to-maturity data that are used to test alternative theories of the term structure, and thus to seek answers to the key questions on that structure. The nature of these data is outlined, and nothing more than that, in section 1.2 which, though it does seem to start us off in an abrupt manner, is a necessary commentary on those data. This is followed in section 1.3 by a consideration of the derivation of those data. Finally, section 1.4 provides a brief synopsis of the theories we shall analyse in the book.

1.2

It is self-evident that if any attempt is to be made to judge the value of a given theory in explaining, or accounting for, the structure of interest rates at, say, a point in time, suitable data must be to hand. These data concern the yields on assets having 1, 2, 3, ... , n years to run before they mature. The data normally used to represent those yields for government bonds (or, in Durand's case, for prime corporate bonds (40), (41)) are their *gross yields-to-maturity*. As we shall see in chapter 2, these are not always the kind of data we are seeking. For except in special circumstances, the yield-to-maturity of an n-year bond will not equal *the rate of interest* on that bond.

The conventional yield-to-maturity formula for an asset with a life of n years is as follows:

$$P = \frac{C}{(1+y)} + \frac{C}{(1+y)^2} + \ldots + \frac{C}{(1+y)^n} + \frac{F}{(1+y)^n} \qquad (1.2.1)$$

where P is the present price of the bond (its 'present value'), C is the coupon payment on it, F is the face value of the bond, payable on redemption, and y is the yield-to-maturity. It is assumed, *inter alia*, that the coupon payments do not vary from year to year; that they are made annually (and not semi-annually as often happens in practice); that the bond is redeemed at a given point in time, namely n years from the present moment, so that it does not have a range of dates at which it may be redeemed by the issuing authority. The yield-to-maturity is therefore an 'internal rate of return'.

The situation portrayed by equation (1.2.1) can be regarded then as one wherein an investor who buys an n-year bond and holds it till maturity has made a number of separate loans, a one-year loan of C pounds sterling, a two-year loan of the same amount, . . . , and an n-year loan of $C + F$ pounds sterling. The rate that makes the discounted values of these loans just equal to the present price of the n-year bond is the yield-to-maturity on that bond.

To examine the relationship between the calculated yield-to-maturity on an n-year bond and the return or rate of interest on that n-year bond (held until redemption) in a way that is directly relevant to our discussion in this book, and particularly to the discussions in chapters 2 and 3, we shall have to jump ahead of our story somewhat.[1] In chapters 2 and 3, which are devoted to the Expectations or Traditional Theory of the term structure, we shall see that the cornerstone of that theory is the view that for any investor (all are alike in the confines of the theory) the return that he expects to receive from investing a sum of money P in an n-year bond by holding it until it matures should equal the return he expects to receive from investing P successively in n *one*-year bonds. Strictly speaking, the present value of the returns expected from these two alternative investments should be identical.

Thus, if we consider the n-year bond we have to discount the n coupons plus the capital gain or loss $(F-P)$ by the appropriate rates of interest. The present value of the returns from investing in the n-year bond are therefore:

$$\frac{C}{(1+r_1)} + \frac{C}{(1+r_1)(1+r_2)} + \ldots + \frac{C+(F-P)}{(1+r_1)(1+r_2)\ldots(1+r_n)}. \tag{1.2.2}$$

Here $r_1, r_2, \ldots$ are the one-year rates of interest (discount) expected to rule at the outset of periods 1 to n. Technically r_1 is known and is usually written in capital letter form to denote that fact. To obtain the present value of the returns expected from investing the amount of money P successively in one-year bonds, we only have to replace the numerator of each of the terms in equation (1.2.2) by $Pr_1, Pr_2, \ldots, Pr_n$, respectively. Setting the two present values equal to each other enables us to write this alternative expression for P:

$$P = \frac{C}{(1+r_1)} + \frac{C}{(1+r_1)(1+r_2)} + \ldots + \frac{C+F}{(1+r_1)(1+r_2)\ldots(1+r_n)}. \tag{1.2.3}$$

We may now consider equations (1.2.1) and (1.2.3) together. In doing so we may note that following Sir John Hicks (1) — and we shall discuss this in later chapters — we can regard the actual rate of interest on the n-year bond (R_n) as being made up of a series of expected one-year rates such that:

$$(1+R_n)^n = (1+r_1)(1+r_2)\ldots(1+r_n). \tag{1.2.4}$$

It is possible, from equations (1.2.1), (1.2.3) and (1.2.4), to make deductions as to the conditions that would produce a situation in which the yield-to-maturity on the n-year bond was equal to the rate of interest on that bond:

(i) All expected future one-year rates of interest are equal and are equal to the current spot one-year rate (in which case we have static expectations of the Hicksian kind for all relevant future years). But this makes the actual rate of interest the same on all bonds no matter what their length of life happens to be.

(ii) The bond pays no coupons at all. This, of course, is another peculiar situation, for it means that any length-of-life bond must always sell below par, otherwise there would be no return from purchasing it. If C is zero we are left with only the discounted face value terms in equations (1.2.1) and (1.2.4), from which it must follow that yield-to-maturity equals the rate of interest.

(iii) Coupons are paid but are given in a lump sum of nC at the date when the bond is redeemed.

In circumstances such as these, if n is say, twenty years, so that we may regard it as a 'long-term' bond, the calculated yield-to-maturity will be the long-term rate of interest. Where the kind of conditions laid down in (i)—(iii) do not hold, the use of yield-to-maturity data for actual interest rate data will not be entirely appropriate.

1.3

We may leave the concept of the yield-to-maturity at this stage; for the purposes of the present book we have noted all the salient points relating to it. We can now proceed to look at the construction of the yield-to-maturity data themselves.

It is almost certain that at every instant in time when we require those data they will not be immediately available: they will have to be calculated. Thus if we take, say, a point of time in any year, such as 31 March 1950, we will have on the U.K. market for government debt a number of bonds with varying lengths of life from which we can calculate the yield-to-maturity. But at the time, stock for every integer length of life from 1 to n years will not be available (that is, it is extremely unlikely that they would all be available). So it becomes necessary to *interpolate* from the data that do exist, by one method or another, the yields on the remaining bonds. These estimated yields will be a better or a less good approximation to the 'true' yields, if those yields could only be observed, depending upon whether the interpolation procedure adopted is a better or a less good one.

The interpolation procedures are intrinsically concerned with finding means of connecting up the observed data points relating yield-to-maturity with years (or time)-to-maturity. They are basically of two types. One approach involves the inherent calculation of a yield curve via an equation built up from the observed data. These equations can be developed in an *ad hoc* or a rigorous fashion, and they can be used to cleanse the observed data of 'extraneous' influences such as those arising out of the existence of bonds with different coupons. The other main approach is to plot the observed data on yields- and time-to-maturity and then fit a 'curve' to them by hand. This can involve the drawing of a free-hand smooth curve through the observation points; it can take the form of a 'curve' that interpolates linearly between points without the use of any weighting system, so that the observed points are connected by straight lines as we proceed along the maturity spectrum; it can also take the form of weighted interpolation between points. This last is not exactly free-hand curve fitting but it is nearer in spirit to that method than it is to the equation-fitting method. We shall discuss these various ways in which we can estimate yield-to-maturity data later in this section. It is those kind of data, and hence the yield-to-maturity curve that lies behind their derivation, which provide the foundations for many stockbroking and nearly all theoretical studies of the term structure (though stockbrokers often also use a curve based on a 'volatility' term index and redemption yields);[2] for not only does it provide the raw material on which to test existing theories of that structure, but it also provides us with phenomena that have to be explained by a 'good' theory of the term structure.

Thus, to consider this point, let us illustrate the main characteristics of yield-to-maturity curves. These curves might apply at a point in time (based on any kind of data period, that is, monthly data, quarterly data . . .) or as a composite curve for a whole period of time such as 1952–72. In figure 1.3.1 we have drawn: an ascending curve; a descending curve; a static horizontal curve; and a humped curve. The ascending curve, for example, tells us that the yield gap is positive, that 'the' long-rate stands above the short-rate. What causes the gap to be positive has to be explained by a satisfactory theory of the term structure: equally, of course, the theory has to be able to account for a negative yield gap and the existence of no yield gap at all.

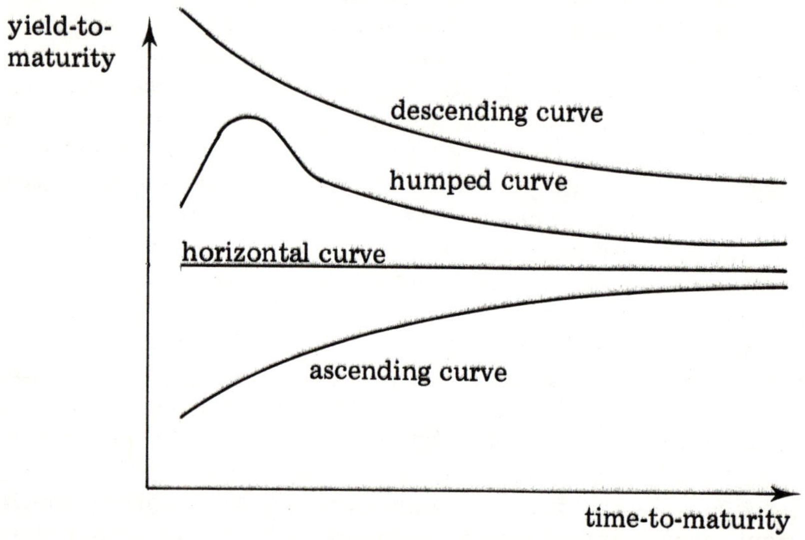

Figure 1.3.1

The composite curve does perhaps need a little explanation. If we were to take a period of time, say a twenty year period, and aggregate curves for points within each year, say 31 March, we would obtain a composite relationship. This would indicate the normal or average yield-to-maturity over the period. The alternative procedure for assessing curves over time is to examine individual curves for each year. The normal relationship we would find over, say, the period since early 1950s would be for an ascending curve: there would be a few each of the descending and horizontal types and probably only one or two with pronounced humps in the shorter end of the maturity spectrum. These relationships averaged out would produce an ascending composite curve. This pattern of the yield-to-maturity relationship over time is true for the available U.S.A. and U.K. data (see for example Durand (40), (41), Malkiel (11); Grant (39)).

Since these yield-to-maturity curves are normally drawn on a Cartesian diagram, i.e. they are two-dimensional, the implication is that the relationship portrayed in one such curve is solely one between yield and years-to-maturity (or time-to-maturity). No other variables are supposed to enter the relationship between a group of bond yields from which a yield-to-maturity curve is to be derived. Ideally this would mean that the bonds have to be alike in all respects save their lives-to-maturity. But we know that in a real-world environment bonds are differentiated in some respects. They may have flexible redemption dates; there may be sinking fund provisions; and, more particularly, bonds do not carry a uniform coupon. The first two special features can usually be accommodated by excluding those stocks from the sample, but the issue of coupon is more difficult because it is not just differences in the size of coupons *per se* but how investors assess coupons with regard to their tax liability. To put it more simply, if current yields are high, a low-coupon stock will be selling at a discount compared with a higher coupon stock of the same maturity, but coupon payments *vis-à-vis* capital gain from the selling of bonds may not be valued one for one by some investors.

In their study of yield-to-maturity curves in the U.K. Burman and White for instance state that:

> A fundamental feature of the market for British government-securities is the distinction which persons and most companies draw between the investment return obtained as income (dividends), which is liable to tax, and the return received as capital gains, which is tax free if the stock is held for more than one year.[1] Investors for whom this distinction is important are called net investors. Other investors for whom dividends and capital gains are equivalent are described as gross investors . . . .
>
> These tax considerations give rise to differences in gross yields between high and low-coupon stocks, the latter having greater appeal for net investors because they offer a larger capital gain at redemption.
>
> [1] Except between April 1965 and April 1969.
>
> [(80) pp. 473–4]

How individual researchers have taken account of coupon differences in the compilation of their data we shall comment on later in this section when we examine the data available for empirical tests. One other factor that may affect the differentiation of bonds is the size of the issue and, in the use of corporate bonds as utilised by Durand ((40), (41)), the credit worthiness of the borrower.

In summary, then, we are saying that differences in bonds themselves and how investors regard them make it difficult to isolate a group of homogeneous assets. Unless these factors are taken into account or discounted in some way the supposition must be that those features do not exist, or if they do they are insignificant in their effect. Not only are there the difficulties of obtaining a group of securities perfectly homogeneous in all respects apart from term-to-maturity; but a continuous yield curve has to be produced from the finite number of actual observed yields, so that a narrow band about the resultant yield-to-maturity curve may contain both *estimated* and true yields. Thus the curves actually produced are almost certain to be only approximations. This is evidenced from the changes that the Bank of England have made in their curve fitting ((80), (117)).[3] It will be impossible to assess the degree of approximation objectively with any accuracy, but at least to gain some insight into how the various series of data have been compiled as a likely guide to their accuracy or reliability we can give an *overview*, and nothing more than that, of the possible methods that can be employed to interpolate yield estimates from data or observed yields.[4] We do so because we feel such a procedure will be of some value *per se*.

We may begin with the data that have been used most often, namely, those for the U.S.A. produced by David Durand ((40), (41)). Consider then the set of data he first produced, which were on an annual basis, for the period 1900—1942, related to high quality corporate bonds in the New York market for the whole maturity range from zero to ninety years. The yearly yield was derived from observation of bond prices during the first quarter of each year. An average yield was derived from six distinct price quotations of a representative group of bonds (over fifty were chosen from nearly two thousand) — the choice being aimed at eliminating special features of certain securities, including redemption, and those securities that were generally non-active, in normal trading conditions. A general point of some importance here is that, by not taking account of such securities, not only is the sample size reduced but observed yields that *are* part of the market, and therefore should also be explained, are being eliminated.[5] Durand limited his study still further by restricting himself to only three of the four shapes of the curves presented in figure 1.3.1, eliminating the humped curve, though he also allowed for a rising yield curve which, over the short maturities, ascended at a constant rate, thereafter taking the normal ascending slope. From the original data *smoothed* free-hand curves were drawn. The fitting of such curves clearly rests heavily on the *subjective* assessment of the individual compiler. The possible existence of 'errors' in Durand's data is further enhanced when it is noted that Durand seems not to have adequately handled the problems of coupons, etc. His data are particularly suspect at the short-end of the curve.[6]

However, although others have rushed in with great alacrity to use Durand's data for testing theories of the term structure, he himself was very much aware of their deficiencies, particularly for such an exercise:

> . . . the basic yield curves are designed to create a quick and crude impression of the term structure of high grade yields at a moment in time; and for this they are adequate . . . [but they] may err badly for any particular maturity [and a] type of refined analysis for which the basic yields are not entirely appropriate is the calculation of implied forecasts of future short-term bond yields . . . .
>
> [(41), pp. 348, 351, 353]

This last point is very apposite in regard to the Meiselman (8) model.

The yield estimates for the U.K. that have figured prominently in tests of the term structure, especially of the Meiselman model on the Expectations Theory, are those compiled by J. A. G. Grant (39). He collected quarterly yield data for British government securities from the end quarter 1924 to the third quarter 1962. Like Durand, he drew up a representative list of stocks omitting those that had special redemption features, but he also omitted those where coupon rates were 'markedly higher or lower than that of the majority of stocks outstanding at that time' ((39), p. 69). Tax considerations were ignored and, apart from the inclusion of Consols as a long-term stock, undated securities were of course excluded. Grant naturally had to employ interpolation to estimate yields at the various maturities for which no stocks were outstanding at that time. Unlike Durand, he used *linear interpolation*, to the effect that these hypothetical yields were derived from the actual market yields on securities either side of the maturity in question, appropriately weighted:

> Thus for instance, had the yield of an actual ten-year security been 5 per cent, and that of an actual 11½ year bond next longest in term been 6.50 per cent the yield of a hypothetical 11 year bond would have been an average of the two, weighted inversely to their term difference from it; 6 per cent.
>
> [(39), p. 69]

The estimated yields then quoted by Grant are for one to six years, ten, eleven, fifteen years and Consols.

Grant's data, just like Durand's, are particularly suspect in the early maturities. Where no data exist on one-year rates Grant uses a weighted average allotment rate on 91-day Treasury bills. The data as a whole suffer from the inherent weaknesses noted hitherto that the securities included are not strictly a homogeneous set, apart from the possible errors embodied in the interpolation procedure.

Grant's data came in for some heavy censure, from, for example, D. Fisher (55). One of his criticisms concerns the choice for 1932–51 of the rate of the U.K. Government's Treasury bills as a proxy for that on one-year bonds. His major objections centred however, on the kind of linear interpolation Grant used and particularly on the fact that in his view Grant did not pay enough attention to the adjustment of the data for coupon effects. In his 'Reply' to Fisher, Grant (64) successfully dealt with some of these criticisms and, as the work of Neil Wallace (70) has shown, the coupon effect *could* be of only minor proportions, as Grant noted. Fisher and others and we ourselves have however attempted to take account of coupons directly. It is for example interesting to note that up to 1972 the Bank of England excluded stocks with coupons less than 5% (see (117)) but now takes account of them in a more explicit way [see (80), and note 13)]. Grant's data therefore are suspect particularly on this count; on the other issues raised by Fisher, particularly on the 1932–51 period, we have taken account of these by omitting that period, using data for the 1952–62 period.

Fisher's own series of yield estimates ((55), (56)) cover the period 1951–63 on a quarterly basis. The data consist of twenty observations covering the range of maturities for each quarter. To derive the 'unobserved' yields, and therefore to provide a basis for the drawing of yield-to-maturity curves should there be a desire to draw them, he fitted an equation to the observed yields, rather than use Grant's or Durand's methods of interpolation. The equation, fitted for each quarter, is:

$$Y = \alpha_1 + \beta_1 M + \beta_2 M^2 + \beta_3 M^3 + \beta_4 \log M + \beta_5 C + \beta_6 C^2 + \beta_7 \log C \tag{1.3.1}$$

where Y stands for yield, M for term-to-maturity and C for the coupon rate.

Fisher argued that application of equation (1.3.1) released compilers of yield curves from the assumption that they must be *monotonic*, which, as noted, those produced by Durand happen to be. It also represented an explicit, and more rigorous, attempt to remove biases in the resulting set of data that might arise especially from the coupon effect, which, in Fisher's impression, '[is] a factor which is not only statistically significant but also the source of spurious "errors" in the representative yields' ((56), p. 323). Yet (in a footnote) he then recognises that the evidence (e.g. of Neil Wallace's (70) unpublished work) available on coupon effects suggests that their net effect may indeed be imperceptible. However he is adamant in his conclusion that: 'The empirical effect in the

British data is strongly positive' ((56), p. 323 n. 2). It must be said, however, that in ten out of the fifty-two quarterly yield curves fitted via equation (1.3.1) he found that the coupon effect was, statistically speaking, zero at the 10% level of significance, and he therefore omitted it. In his review and critique of methods of fitting yield-to-maturity curves R. S. Masera (9) observed that to suggest as Fisher does that *a priori* the coupon effect *is* significant, and then to drop it out of ten of the yield curves, seems somewhat inconsistent and illogical.

We have already referred in this section to the work of Burman and White (80) done at the Bank of England. They argue that in one sense the coupon effect may be easily identified — for instance, stocks with high coupons will often lie above the fitted yield curve and this systematic effect can easily be taken into account — but if the purpose of deriving a yield curve is to assess, say, the terms for government lending within the public sector or government borrowing itself, then explicit account must be taken of the coupon:

> When interest rates are historically high, the coupon which the Government must offer on an issue to sell at par will also have to be historically high. Existing stocks in the same maturity range with lower coupons will then promise some capital gain on maturity. As a result, a curve statistically fitted to the existing scatter of yields, without an explicit estimate of the coupon effect, will significantly under-estimate the coupon which will have to be offered by the Government on a new issue to be priced at par.
>
> [(80), p. 470]

This is perhaps a more specialised reason for the need to take account of coupon payments, but it is significant that the Bank of England's economists are very conscious that observed yields may be biased in this way.

Another approach to the construction of yield-to-maturity curves is that of Masera (9). He has produced an extremely extensive and thoroughly masterly survey of the alternative methods, and their advantages and disadvantages, of constructing yield-to-maturity curves, and therefore of yield-to-maturity data. In the process he has produced (although, in the nature of things, this has to be more of a subjective evaluation than an objective one) probably the best set of yield-to-maturity curve data published to date.

Masera's data are for Italy on a monthly basis for the period 1957—67. They do suffer from the limitation that the maturity range covered is only for one to nine years. Masera points out that the Italian bond market is rather different from, and less 'sophisticated' than, that of the U.S.A. or the U.K., yet he was able to study a homogeneous group of securities which were an important part of the whole market and which were actively traded, these securities being known as B.T.P. (Buoni Tesero Poliennali), all of which effectively had a 5% coupon. Unfortunately the actual number of observations for each of the months over the data period were quite small, being of the order of six to nine; but they are well spread over the (restricted) maturity spectrum.

As a result of errors and biases which he felt were contained within the methods of Durand, Grant and Fisher, Masera proposed his own scheme by which to fit yield curves to the observed data. He fitted these three equations to each month's data:

$$Y = \alpha_1 + \beta_1 M \tag{1.3.2}$$

$$Y = \alpha_2 + \beta_2 M + g_2(\log M)^2 \tag{1.3.3}$$

$$Y = \alpha_3 + \beta_3 M + g_3(\log M)^2 + \delta_3 M^3 \tag{1.3.4}$$

where Y and M are as defined for Fisher's equation (1.3.1). The best equation was chosen out of these three for each month, the choice being made in terms of the performance of the equations as measured by their goodness-of-fit (the coefficient of determination, adjusted for degrees of freedom, namely, $\bar{R}^2$) and the significance (judged by reference to the 10% level) of the individual regression coefficients. This means that if we consider three consecutive monthly periods, for example, for each one the yield curve could well be estimated by a different equation, as happened for months 8—10, 1967.

We have compiled our own set of data on yields-to-maturity for the U.K. bond market for the period 1953—71. The data are on an annual basis as of the 31 March (or the nearest market day to that date) of each year. With most years we have a large number of observations over the whole maturity spectrum, with the number exceeding twenty for most of our data points. From these observations we constructed yield curves from which we derive yields for bonds with one to twenty-six years of life.

We constructed the yield curves for each year by using both the free-hand curve fitting method and the equations method. If we consider the free-hand method first of all we followed the smoothing technique by using French curves; we also made use of the weighted linear interpolation method of Grant and we also drew yield curves by straightforward unweighted linear interpolations between the points of observations on actual yields and maturities. Because we had a fair number of observations on yields and maturities the unweighted and weighted series (which is how we shall refer to them in the rest of the book) are not very different from each other for most of the years of our sample period. But for several years in the period the smoothed data (which is how we shall identify this set of data in the book from this point on) are very different from those produced by linear interpolations. This is especially true of the late 1960s.

In fitting equations to our observed data points we employed the Fisher equation and the Masera equations together with equations of our own design. Since the fitting of curves to the data is a mathematical exercise, one of finding an equation with enough bends in it or whatever is appropriate for any given set of observed data points, the number of possible equation forms that can be tried is large. We experimented with several types of equations but the best one consistently was one where Y was a linear function of M, M^2, M^3 and of log M. We cannot possibly reproduce the full details of each of the five equations for each of the nineteen years of our sample period. For this book anyway we have not relied on data derived from these equations; we have relied only on the 'free-hand' data. This is because, where we felt that we could select a good equation out of the five equations that produced yields that look sensible when plotted alongside the actually observed yields, the results we obtained on the term structure, on which we report in the following chapter, from using the data provided by the equations, were intrinsically no different from those obtained by using the smoothed data. On a number of occasions, however, the equations performed very badly, if we measure performance by $\bar{R}^2$. This is particularly true of the years 1957, 1965—70; for 1966—9 inclusive; in fact, statistically speaking, the equations exhibited zero relationships between yield-to-maturity and the selected explanatory variables. Also, even where some of the equations produced extremely high $\bar{R}^2$s it was not always possible to use them for 'predicting' the missing yields, because the degree of multicollinearity in them, especially in the Fisher equation, was excessive: on most occasions that collinearity was almost perfect, with the determinant of the zero-order correlation matrix of the explanatory variables being in the order of 'zero point ten zeros'. The existence of such multicollinearity, of course, does not cause the slope coefficients in the equations to be biased in the technical (statistical) meaning of that term, but they will not have their 'true' values because of the rounding error that will follow from the multicollinearity. We found that this 'bias' was such as to produce yield curves that seemed to us to depart too far from the observed data. For all these reasons we decided to abandon the attempt to use data generated from formal equation-fitting; it would have been possible to combine the data obtained from equations for a few years in the sample period with those obtained from the 'free-hand' methods. But we have not pooled the data in this way, and in any case we are against such a procedure in practice.

There is then no point in our quoting our results on equation-fitting even if we had the space to do so. But it may be of some interest to the reader to make some brief observations on the chief characteristics of those results. We may think of the five equations as: (1.3.2) to (1.3.4) above, (1.3.1) above, and Y is a function of M, M^2, M^3 and log M. For the vast majority of the years for which the curves were fitted, the $\bar{R}^2$s rose as we went through the equations from (1.3.2) to (1.3.1). There were several occasions, however, when our own equation just outshot equation (1.3.1), the Fisher equation. The results showed that coupon effects were significant only for three of the years in our sample period. Even then, though the values of the Durbin—Watson statistic — used to test for the presence of serial correlation in the residuals — are satisfactory, there is some doubt about the significance of the coupon effects because of multicollinearity.

Let us now summarise the discussion in this section. There are two main problems in collating a set of yield data for a given point in time. The first is that only some of the whole maturity spectrum of 'bonds' are traded, so observed yields are not comprehensive. The other problem follows from the fact that the observed yields that are used should, as far as is feasible, be cleaned of all influences other than time-to-maturity.

The first problem is possibly the greater, for it means that some procedure or other has to be relied upon to generate the missing yields. Of the methods available, the most sophisticated would appear to be those that fit equations of one kind or another to the observed data as a means of estimating the missing data. The use of free-hand 'curves' perhaps seems *prima facie* to be a rather unscientific and rough-and-ready means by which the yield-to-maturity data can be obtained. But it is not possible to say *a priori* which method is the better one, nor is it an easy matter to judge which equation is best when the formal equation-fitting method is being used. The choice of method will depend upon the nature of the raw (observed) data. It is possible, however, that the free-hand methods can lead to the calculation of a set of 'inaccurate' yield data, since these methods depend so much, given the nature of the raw data, on the judgement of the person processing the data into a yield-to-maturity curve.

Equation-fitting can be a useful exercise because it might be of some help in cleansing the raw data of the influence of coupons, if there is any such influence in them. But there are dangers in using such curves even if equations can be selected for all observation points in the sample period that have extremely high $\bar{R}^2$s. For the nature of the curves fitted, for example second- and third-order polynomicals in, say, maturity, will mean that there is high multicollinearity in the statistical equations. So it may not be possible for us to 'predict' the unobserved yields that well, and neither may it be possible for us to single out such things as 'coupon effects'.

Even bearing these points in mind it is difficult to be dogmatic about the absolute and relative quality of each of the sets of data referred to in this sector, all of which will figure in the empirical tests of the term structure discussed in this book. However, we can perhaps remark that Durand's data are the most suspect.

1.4

It is now in order for us to say a little about the theories of the term structure discussed in this book, in the testing of which we require to avail ourselves of the kind of data discussed in the previous sections of this chapter. As we do so we shall take the opportunity to comment on the lay-out of the following chapters in the book.

The Expectations Theory, as its name would suggest, is a theory of the term structure that is founded upon the notion of 'expectations'. It contains the view that, at a point in time, the yield-gap depends *exclusively* upon the expectations of the capital *market* about (future) interest rates. Those expectations relate specifically to future *one*-year rates. The yield-gap becomes dependent solely upon expectations about these, *short*, rates because of the assumptions upon which the theory is built, which make it possible to consider all investors collectively, that is as a market, and which suggest that investors take a long view of their investment strategy. The theory leads to a very straightforward explanation of the term structure, and it produces a series of important observations on what, for given states of expectations, will be the actual yield-gap at a point in time, and how it might change from one point in time to another, *ceteris paribus*. The full import of this comment will be appreciated from our discussions of the theory; therefore it provides information on how the term structure might be *changed*. In effect, it states implicitly that if the monetary authorities desire to change the yield-gap they can do so only by, somehow or other, affecting expectations of short, or one-year, interest rates. This is a theory that is built upon 'perfectly competitive' conditions, with the participants in the market for financial assets either having, or believing that they have, perfect knowledge of all future rates of interest. As a result demand conditions are produced that mean that the prices of and returns on assets are independent of supplies, unless changes in supplies affect expectations.

The Expectations Theory is laid out in detail in chapter 2, where its testable predictions are discussed and evaluated. The last part of the chapter contains observations on existing empirical tests of the theory which are, we might say, pre-Meiselman (8) in their tenor.

Chapter 3 then follows up the discussion of the Expectations Theory *per se* with a thorough theoretical and empirical evaluation of the researches of David Meiselman (8). The latter's work, in fact, is directly related to the Expectations Theory. Because of the kind of data problems that arise in any attempt to subject the theory to empirical testing, and because, for the reasons we have enunciated in chapter 2, he too dismissed the existing tests of the theory, he suggested an alternative method of testing it. His method relies very much on the spirit, and indeed the acceptance, of the theory he was implicitly trying to assess; for it basically proposes an hypothesis by which *expectations* are *revised* over time. These revisions of expectations concerning the short rates are fundamental to the theory. Clearly, *ceteris paribus*, if a powerful and reliable means can be found for unearthing those factors that cause expectations to be adjusted, then, following on from the expectations theory itself, we shall have a method by which we can assess how the yield-gap will change since it is held to be based on levels of expected short rates.

A close relation of the Expectations Theory is that of Malkiel (11) which forms the subject of the discussion in chapter 4, though this theory is based on a view of investors' behaviour that is contrary to that of the Expectations Theory (for investors are assumed to have a short-term investment horizon). As a consequence of studying the bond market Malkiel came to the conclusion that investors generally speaking do have a *short* period planning horizon, which is a characteristic that he has incorporated in his own theory. But the basic motivation of investors in the Expectations Theory is retained. Also, expectations, either explicitly or implicitly, form a part of his theory. The centrepiece of the theory, in fact, is the Keynesesque[7] construct, the normal range of interest rates, specifically in his theory of the normal range of long-term interest rates. It is by investors' views of how interest rates will move within the normal range that expectations can enter the Malkiel Theory; and it is by reference to such 'expected' movements that investors will switch between the long and the short ends of the market, and so influence, or determine, the observed yield-gap. This kind of argument can be epitomised, with certain simplifying assumptions, in an equation which does have as its dependent variable 'the' yield-gap. In this respect the Malkiel Theory is more operational and tangible than the Expectations Theory, even though it contains within it the very essence of that theory.

The movement away from the influence of the Expectations Theory really begins with the Liquidity Premium or Risk Premium Theory, which forms the substance of the discussion in chapter 5. However, that theory cannot divest itself completely of expectational influences. For it is built upon virtually the same assumptions and same investor motivation as is the Traditional Theory. One assumption is different, however: in contradistinction to the Traditional Theory, the Liquidity Premium Theory assumes that investors will not have, or behave as though they have, perfect information of the (expected) returns to be received from investing in the future in short (or long) bonds. Rather there is an element of risk involved in investing in bonds that will mature in the future, and indeed in estimating any kind of future returns on bonds. Additionally, investors react to that risk, in that they are hypothesised to be risk-averters: in the Traditional Theory even if risk, or we should say uncertainty, were present it would never enter into investors' calculations at all, and so would in no way influence their choice of securities to purchase, and hence the yield-gap. The allowance for risk is made by adjusting the expected one-year, or short-term, rates of interest by the appropriate 'risk premium'. The term structure that emerges is influenced, in some circumstances predominantly so, by expectations.

But in taking due note of, and making allowance for, risk the Liquidity Premium Theory is one remove from the Expectations or Traditional Theory. This movement away from the latter is complete when we come to the Hedging Pressure Theory. In its extreme form the latter has no place for expectations to influence the term structure, for the demands by the various investors in the financial market are held not to be dependent upon the expected returns that can be obtained from investing in them and in other assets. All the securities available on the maturity continuum are supposed to be regarded by potential investors as distinct securities; in no way is any one security regarded as being a substitute for any other. This means that, for example in general terms, the market for short-term bonds cannot influence the market for long-term bonds, therefore expectations of 'short' rates have no influence on 'long' rates, and consequently on the yield-gap. The price, and hence return, on each kind of stock is determined by supply and demand in that market alone. In suggesting that for investors the financial market is 'segmented' in this way, the theory is saying fundamentally that an extreme version of risk aversion provokes investors into attempting to match their assets with their liabilities. Given the market's demand function for financial assets, the consequence of the Hedging Pressure Theory is that changes in the relative *supplies* of the assets change the term structure.

There is a weaker form of the Hedging Pressure Theory which does allow for expectations to influence behaviour somewhat, but where the dominant influence on investor behaviour is to match assets and liabilities. This form of the theory still ascribes a strong role, therefore, to asset supplies in determining the term structure.

In chapter 6 we shall set out the essence of the Hedging Pressure Theory and discuss the ways by which it might be tested. We shall provide a critical review of the work of others and of our own that has been undertaken to test the theory. This will involve our giving details of a pilot general equilibrium model of the U.K. financial sector that we have been working on which can be used to test theories of the term structure including the Hedging Pressure Theory.

There then follows a brief final chapter which will include broad suggestions for further research in this area. For though others have been suggesting other avenues by which to look at the term structure (here we think of the spectral analysis studies), there is still a great deal of very important work to be done on some of the topics discussed or raised in this book, which will not be superseded by the recent statistical researches of the term structure.

Before we proceed to our task, some general points. It is self-evident that, if we are looking at the term structure of interest rates at a point in time, that structure has emerged from, and will change because of, the nature of the demand and supply functions for all of the assets on the financial market. To determine the factors that affect the price of an asset, and hence its return, all we need know are details of the (market) demand function and supply function for it. The theories of the term structure that we shall be concerned with in the main in the following pages make different assumptions from each other about either side or both sides of the market.

Though we cannot spell this out at this stage without putting the whole of the book into this chapter, this point is worth bearing in mind for the task ahead; for it helps to put the theories into perspective and to see why they reach such divergent conclusions on the variables that determine the term structure.

What emerges is that, at one end of the spectrum there is the Expectations Theory, where the term structure is determined solely by expectations, but where *speculative* activity cannot in fact exist. In this theory there is no role for risk or uncertainty, nor is there any role for asset supplies in affecting the term structure. At the other end of the spectrum is the Hedging Pressure Theory which (in its extreme form) assigns a zero role to expectations and to speculative behaviour, and which places the whole burden of accounting for changes in the term structure on to changes in the relative supplies of the various financial assets. Halfway along the spectrum, there is the Risk Premium Theory. This theory has a role for expectation, a role for risk and a partial role for relative asset supplies. If it had given no role to risk it would have reverted to the Expectations Theory; likewise, had it given a full role to risk it would have become the Hedging Pressure Theory. The Malkiel Theory comes somewhere between the Expectations Theory and the Risk Premium Theory.

Notes to Chapter 1

1. These matters are handled in this same way by A. Buse (10) and D. Fisher (56).
2. The measure of volatility used by stockbrokers is often referred to by them as a 'term index'. This they define as:

> the percentage change in price for a £1 change in yield either side of the present gross redemption yield, i.e. if the present gross redemption yield of Funding 3½% 1999/2004 is 8.5%, then the term index is:

$$\frac{\text{Price to yield } 7\tfrac{1}{2}\% - \text{Price to yield } 9\tfrac{1}{2}\%}{\text{Price to yield } 8\tfrac{1}{2}\% \text{ to redemption}} \times 100$$

This quote is taken from the publication *Gilt-Edged Securities* issued by the firm of stockbrokers, Phillips and Drew. We are grateful to Mr David A. Crofts of that firm for making this publication available to us and for allowing us to refer to it. In that book will be found some data for the U.K. on term indices and a critique of them. But the publication concludes that: 'the term index is a useful concept and one that should replace term as the measure of the liability of a stock to fluctuate, but like the concept of the redemption yield it should be used with care'. Unfortunately, we cannot discuss the volatility index in depth here, nor can we discuss the reasons why stockbrokers did, in fact, introduce it.

3. After this chapter was completed another paper was published by J. P. Burman (118) on the yield-to-maturity curve, revising the earlier work of Burman and White (80): as a consequence the Bank of England's yield-to-maturity curves are to be estimated on yet another new basis. This latest paper by Burman is a fascinating one on the coupon-effect.

4. On the construction of yield-to-maturity curves, see for example R. S. Masera (9). For examples of alternatives to the equation-fitting forms discussed in this chapter see J. M. Brew (119) and G. T. Pepper (120) and the discussion that follows the latter's paper.

5. In some ways it is possible to support those who would take the line here that all the raw data should be used, and that to discard some of it is to ignore what must be explained. For the question is: how do we decide precisely what data to discard? The temptation will be to reject observations that look odd or are 'out of line' with the main body of observations. But not only is it possible that such a procedure is an arbitrary one, for which there is no scheme that can be applied systematically to all time-points for which data are being obtained; it is also one that can affect the conclusions that we might draw from the data that remain. For suppose some of the stock that is discarded is so discarded because the coupons on them are higher than those on the retained stock. The yields on the latter, however, could well have been influenced by the presence of those high-coupon stocks; and they may not have been influenced systematically across the maturity range. We can be biasing the results of tests of the term structure in unknown ways by manipulating the market-given data.

6. The assumption that there are no humped curves, coupled with the free-hand smoothing of the observed data to produce the yield curve, will in fact bias the testing of term structure theories which are based on that kind of data in favour of the Expectations Theory and will consequently lend support to Meiselman's (8) hypothesis based on that theory, as we shall see in later chapters. There are occasions when it is appropriate to use free-hand smoothing techniques on the raw yield data (see, for example, G. L. S. Shackle (50), which is one of the first attempts to draw yield-curves for the U.K. and to analyse movements in them between different points in time).

7. We borrow the adjective 'Keynesesque' from G. L. S. Shackle (71), where he so describes models that have been constructed with Keynesian components. Malkiel's normal range depends upon Keynes's normal interest rate level.

2 The Traditional or Expectations Theory of the Term Structure of Interest Rates

2.1

The 'Expectations Theory', or what, because of its relatively long history, we may label the 'Traditional Theory', should perhaps be regarded as the classic theory of the term structure. It is a theory that suggests that at a (present) moment in time the actual relationship between the yield on long-term (financial) assets *vis-à-vis* the yield on short-term assets can be adequately accounted for by knowledge of the *market's expectations* as to the yields on very short-term assets. Those expectations may also enable predictions to be made concerning future relationships between long-term and short-term yields.

In the following pages we shall elaborate on this theory. In section 2.2 we portray the essentials of the theory. Section 2.3 proves, and discusses, 'the fundamental theorem' that emerges from the theory, from which ensue various propositions on the yield structure. It also gives some illustrations of how that theorem is or can be altered if the framework (i.e. assumptions) of the theory is altered in such ways that it assumes a guise somewhat similar to that of the Risk Premium and Hedging Pressure Theories; and it gives some discussion of the consequences for the theory of a situation in which the *modus operandi* of the investors is not what the theory implicitly assumes it to be.

As a corollary of section 2.3, section 2.4 extracts from the fundamental theorem of the Expectations Theory the notion of how and why expectations become the prime, indeed, *ceteris paribus*, the sole determinant of the yield structure. The result is a series of propositions concerning the term structure at a moment of time and at future points in time. Section 2.4 also evaluates these propositions in respect of their empirical testability and shows how they could be tested if adequate data are available. Section 2.5 follows up this empirical discussion with some brief comments on actual, pre-Meiselman (8), empirical tests of the Expectations Theory.

2.2

The Expectations Theory is frequently, indeed almost invariably, referred to as the Hicks—Lutz theory ((1), (2)). However, as has been pointed out elsewhere (e.g. Luckett (3), Ford and Stark (4), Ford and Dodds (5)), it is not strictly correct to refer to it in this way. For example, one could argue that, although Hicks's work contains the essentials of the Expectations Theory, it ultimately lays the foundation of, and comes down in favour of, the so-called Risk Premium/Liquidity Premium Theory of the term structure. Also, although Lutz's work leans heavily in favour of the Expectations Theory *per se* (2), in view of the earlier work of Irving Fisher (6) and especially of Lord Keynes (7) it would not be unfair to suggest that these last named should be regarded as originators of the theory. But because of his extensive work on the theory much credit is due to Lutz. Perhaps, therefore, it might have been better had the theory been called the Keynes—Lutz or the Fisher—Keynes—Lutz theory.

However, let us put this rather narrow doctrinal question behind us and take a brief look at the framework of the Traditional Theory. That theory rests on the three basic assumptions detailed at the outset of Lutz's classic paper (2). These assumptions are, in Lutz's own words:

> (1) everybody concerned knows what the future short-term rates will be, i.e. there is accurate forecasting in the market;
> (2) there are no costs of investment, either for lenders or for borrowers;
> (3) there is complete shiftability for lenders as well as for borrowers. The lender who wants to invest for, say, ten years is equally well prepared to buy a ten-year bond or to lend on a one-year contract and to re-lend ten times. Similarly, a lender who wants to invest for only one year is in principle prepared to buy a ten-year bond or a bond of any other maturity and to sell it again after the first year. The same shiftability is assumed for the borrower.
>
> [(2), pp. 499—500]

Assumption (3) directly rules out the Hedging Pressure hypothesis, while assumption (2) means that in choosing their optimum portfolios investors need only be concerned with the *on-the-market* yield of assets. Assumption (1) is, however, probably the most vital of these three assumptions; and it is one that we must discuss, if only briefly.

There are two ways in which we could interpret assumption (1). First, we could take it at its face value. This means that the statement is to be taken in its *objective* sense. Investors know today what tomorrow's rate of interest is on a one-year bond because they have a time machine which allows them to propel themselves forward and to take a sight of the bond market as it will be when 'tomorrow' has moved along the axis of time and become 'today'. Each and every investor has *complete information* on future short-term bond prices and yields. Therefore, in an *ex ante* sense each investor knows beyond any doubt what the *ex post* position will be tomorrow, the day after tomorrow, and so on. In this sense there must be accurate forecasting: but each investor, and hence 'the' market, is not indulging in forecasting in the literal sense of that word. For each investor has *full information* about the future movement of short-term rates at each actual moment in time. Under these circumstances no forecasting *per se* can exist.

We shall refer to this interpretation of assumption (1) as the 'strong' interpretation of it. This is the interpretation given by Lutz himself; and when we refer to the 'strong version' of the Expectations Theory we shall mean that version of it which relies on the 'strong' interpretation of assumption (1). This 'objective perfect foresight'[1] assumption raises some difficulties, as we shall see later, not the least of which is that the Meiselman hypothesis, allegedly based on the Expectations Theory, cannot exist.

For that hypothesis to exist, and indeed one could argue for the Expectations Theory to command any support, we should abandon this (objective) perfect knowledge assumption. There is clearly a limit as to how far we can transgress from the Lutzian conception of assumption (1): we cannot for example state that, since we are dealing with *time*, and are unavoidably concerned with future time, we should, in looking at expected short-term interest rates, introduce uncertainty elements. To do so takes us out of a world in which expectations alone determine the term structure. But we can interpret assumption (1) and not have to go that far. The second way of looking at the assumption is in terms of *subjective certainty*, a concept entirely different from *objective certainty*. Considering assumption (1) in this light, we say that every investor *believes* he knows with complete certainty what future short-term rates of interest will be. In such a situation each investor believes that he has an accurate forecast of those interest rates. Additionally, we assume that all investors hold the same view about future rates of interest; then there is such a thing as a market view covering those rates.

When we refer to the 'weak' form of the Expectations Theory, we mean the theory built on the three Lutzian assumptions, with assumption (1) being cast in terms of *subjective* certainty. The theory only requires assumption (1) to be looked at in this manner: all the predictions that emerge from the 'strong' form of the theory about expectations and the term structure hold on this interpretation of the assumption, though it is not always an easy matter to prove those predictions once we remove objective certainty from the analysis. The Meiselman (8) hypothesis can exist only if the 'weak' form of the Expectations Theory is adopted.

In view of assumptions (2) and (3) investors and borrowers will be willing to shift from the long end of the market to the short end, and vice-versa, *as the opportunity presents itself*. Clearly, an opportunity to switch from one end of the market to the other will present itself if the expected returns from investing a unit of money in these two types of assets should be different for a given investment period. For example, arbitrage will be induced if the expected return on a given short-term bond exceeds that on a given long-term bond; for then a *rational investor* will purchase the short-term in preference to the long-term bond; the absence of 'transaction costs' enables him to realise this expected interest differential in full. Similarly, for an investor already in long bonds there will be an incentive to move out of them and into short bonds. *In toto* the direction of these asset-switches will be known, given either interpretation of assumption (1), for all investors will act in the same way. So this kind of asset-switching must result in an adjustment in the prices, and hence in the returns, on the two types of bonds such that their (expected) returns become equivalent: this is the *equilibrium situation*.

The Traditional approach then, although having comparatively few basic assumptions, produces a straightforward and easily managed framework of analysis. From that analysis follows a very powerful theorem, which we may label the *equalisation theorem*. It states that (expected) returns from investing a unit of money, for any given length of time (the 'holding period'), should be the same no matter what length-of-life assets are purchased by the given investors in the financial market.

In terms of propositions or hypotheses that can be developed from the framework of the Traditional Theory about the structure of interest rates, and in terms of the Meiselman (8) kind of hypothesis, what is crucial is the way in which the equalisation theorem can be and has been expressed. In that regard let us then consider the investment of *a unit* of money under the assumptions of the Traditional Theory. If we ignore the coupon payments on the bonds that could be purchased, so that in effect no interest is paid until any given bond actually held is redeemed on maturity, then we can derive the *Hicksian* formula expressing the equalisation theorem ((1), pp. 144-5). This formula is equivalent to the Fisherian (6) formula, which has become the centrepiece of the Traditional Theory, although an alternative, Lutzian (2), formula exists for representing the equalisation theorem, and we shall refer to it towards the end of this section.

In advancing his formula Hicks argued as follows:

> A contract to deliver goods at monthly intervals over a period of six months is equivalent to a spot transaction and a series of forward transactions; similarly, a loan for six months is equivalent to a loan for one month, combined with a series of forward loan transactions, each renewing the loan (re-lending the principal, or principal and interest) for a successive month. If we decide upon some minimum period of time, loans for less than which time we shall be prepared to disregard, every loan of every duration can be reduced to a standard pattern — a loan for a minimum period, combined with a given number of renewals for subsequent periods of the same length, contracted forward ... we take as the minimum period one 'week'.
>
> ... the rate of interest for loans of two weeks, running from our first Monday, is compounded out of the 'spot' rate of interest for loans of one week and the 'forward' rate of interest, also for one-week loans, but for loans to be executed in the second week. If no interest is paid until the conclusion of the whole transaction, then the same capital sum must be arrived at by accumulating for two weeks at the two-week rate of interest, or alternatively by accumulating for one week at the one week rate, and then accumulating for a second week at the 'forward' rate. The two transactions are ultimately identical. Thus, if we write $R_2, R_3, \ldots$ for the current two-weeks, three-weeks, ... rates (the 'long' rates), $r_2, r_3, \ldots$ for the 'forward' short rates, r_1 (or R_1), for the current short rate (it belongs to both systems), we shall have:[2]

$$
\begin{aligned}
1+R_1 &= 1+R_1 \\
(1+R_2)^2 &= (1+r_1)(1+r_2) \\
(1+R_3)^3 &= (1+r_1)(1+r_2)(1+r_3)
\end{aligned}
$$

[(1), pp 144—5]

The above formulae can be generalised for *n*-periods (be it weeks, months, years . . .) as follows:

$$(1 + R_n)^n = (1 + R_1)(1 + r_2)(1 + r_3) \ldots (1 + r_n). \qquad (2.2.1)$$

Here we have substituted R_1 for r_1; and we find that 'the' long-term rate of interest is a geometric average of the current spot one-period rate and all relevant 'forward', 'expected', one-period rates.

Thus, suppose we consider investment over a three-unit period. Then the essence of what Hicks said is that that investment can be considered from two *extreme* points of view. On the one hand, it can be regarded as an investment in a three-period bond, for the whole of the period, the bond being redeemed at the end of the period; on the other hand, it can be envisaged as a series of smallest possible loans, by way of a series of purchases of successive one-period bonds (three in all). Any other combination of length-of-life bonds is permissible for the rational investor. But his investment strategy can be conveniently, and simply, expressed by reference to two points on the maturity spectrum of available financial assets; for the (expected) return from investing at the one end of the market (in the three-period bond) must be the same as that from investing at the other extreme end of the market (successively in one-period bonds).

The return expected from investing in the three-period bond for the whole of the investment — or holding — period is *known*, in fact, at the outset of the holding period. For on the threshold of that period there will be on the market an actual rate of interest, and an actual price for a three-period bond. From this, given the par value of the bond, the return from investing a unit of money in the three-period bond until it matures can be calculated and it is a value that is known with complete certainty. However it is clear that, apart from R_1, all future expected rates on *one*-period bonds are uncertain. Therefore the market has to make some estimates about those rates — these are r_2 and r_3 in the Hicksian formula quoted above. These estimates in the Traditional model are assumed, by assumption (1) in fact also to be 'known'.

Should we have data on the holding-period returns (the R_2 to R_n) for the outset of the given period, we could calculate a set of 'expected' future one-period rates from the Hicksian formula. Thus, from equation (2.2.1):

$$(1 + R_{n-1})^{n-1} = (1 + R_1)(1 + r_2)(1 + r_3) \ldots (1 + r_{n-1}) \qquad (2.2.2)$$

$$\therefore r_n = \frac{(1 + R_n)^n}{(1 + R_{n-1})^{n-1}} - 1. \qquad (2.2.3)$$

The Hicks—Lutz theory is preoccupied with expected one-period rates, as can be judged from an equation such as (2.2.1), and as will be seen later on in this chapter. In thinking about the empirical properties of the theory *per se*, and of the Meiselman Hypothesis (see chapter 3) related to that theory, we shall naturally be led to investigate the ways and means by which we can deduce a set of expected one-period rates for any point in time — when those rates are not *explicitly* provided for us by the market.

We come, therefore, to an important matter about which we should say something at this point even though it involves our repeating some of the remarks we made in chapter 1. Where empirical evidence has been assembled by investigators of the determination of the term structure of interest rates, that evidence has almost invariably been based on data on bond yields derived from *yield-to-maturity* data, which have been read off yield-to-maturity curves.

We may leave on one side the possibility that, because yield-to-maturity curves have to be fitted to allow yields to be estimated for whatever length-of-life bond does not actually exist on the market, those curves may produce erroneous estimates of those yields. The main point is that, if yield-to-maturity data are being used to represent (known) holding-period returns on two- to *n*-year bonds, only in special circumstances will the yields-to-maturity be equivalent to the holding-period returns. One of those circumstances arises when all the coupon payments due on any bond are paid only when the bond matures: this condition is met in the Hicksian formula, equation (2.2.1) (which is also consistent with the payment of no coupons). Another situation that will make the yields and the returns synonymous is when coupons can be paid to the bond-holder year by year but where he immediately reinvests those coupons in a situation where all future expected one-year rates of interest are equal to the current spot one-year rate.

Both of these *are* special circumstances; and it follows, therefore, that in a real-world situation using yield-to-maturity data will produce biased, or inaccurate, estimates of (true) expected future one-year returns if the Hicksian formula is applied to the yield-curve data in order to calculate these expected returns. In other words, the Hicksian equalisation of expected returns formula is a correct specification of the equalisation theorem only under the assumption that all coupon payments are made in a lump sum at the time that any given bond matures. The yield-to-maturity curve data will therefore not be equivalent to the (known) 'long-period' returns in the Hicksian formula if coupons are paid periodically. So in using that formula to calculate forward expected one-year returns we shall not be calculating the true values of these rates.

Also, the general point remains that, even if we produce a formula to epitomise the equalisation theorem, it must be based on holding-period returns for two- to *n*-year bonds; and, almost invariably, proxying those returns by yields-to-maturity will indeed produce only proximate estimates of future expected short-term rates of interest at any moment in time. The degree of 'bias' in the expected short-term rates is incalculable; it will also be affected by the way that the yield curves have been derived.

For the most part the Hicksian equation (2.2.3) has been applied to yield-to-maturity curve data to provide estimates of forward expected one-year rates of interest. However, A. Buse (10), and we ourselves (see chapter 3), have made use of an alternative representation of the equalisation theorem to arrive at a set of forward one-year rates. This representation is due to Lutz (2). The Lutzian formula differs from the Hicksian in its treatment of coupon or interest payments. To be precise, it is: 'based on the assumption that long term interest payments are made regularly at the same intervals as those at which the short rate is paid' ((2) footnote 2, p. 500).

The Lutzian formula, using the notation he adopted to enable a ready comparison to be made with the Hicksian formula in equation (2.2.1), is:[3]

$$R_n = \frac{(1+r_1)(1+r_2)\ldots(1+r_n)-1}{(1+r_n)(1+r_3)\ldots(1+r_n)+(1+r_3)\ldots(1+r_n)+\ldots+(1+r_n)+1}\,. \tag{2.2.4}$$

From the formula for R_{n-1} etc. it is possible, as with the Hicksian formula, to calculate a set of Lutzian forward rates.[4] This formula, however, provides us with long-term rates of interest that are equivalent to yields-to-maturity only when bonds are *selling at par* (see note 3 to this chapter). So even though Lutz makes a somewhat more realistic assumption than Hicks does, the former's version of the equalisation theorem will calculate expected short-term rates of interest accurately from yield-to-maturity data only in one special instance.

2.3

The assumptions of the Traditional Theory then enable us to formulate a simple, though elemental rather than elementary, theorem about the equalisation of (expected) returns for any investor from any conceivable investment strategy over any particular investment, or holding, period. It is instructive to utilise a (very) simple portfolio model to demonstrate the theorem. Such an approach, epitomising as it does the decision-making process of individuals, separately or collectively, on the financial market, can be readily manipulated to illustrate how adjusting the assumptions of the traditional model can rescind the equalisation theorem or amend it, to a lesser or greater degree.

It follows, as we already know, from the assumptions of the Hicks—Lutz theory that each and every investor need concern himself only with the *return he expects* to receive from a unit of investment in a given bond for the length of his holding period. Following the conventional micro approach we may hypothesise that an individual investor will have a 'utility function' such that:

$$U_{\bar{t}} = f(W_{\bar{t}}): f' > 0, f'' < 0 \qquad (2.3.1)$$

where U is utility; W is wealth; and t is time, with $\bar{t}$ indicating 'end-of-period' t. So (2.3.1) states that an investor's utility at the end of period t, or if we like the beginning of period $t + 1$, will depend solely upon his wealth position at the end of period t. For it is that wealth position, *ceteris paribus*, that determines the consumption possibilities open to him in period $t + 1$ and later periods, and in traditional fashion utility depends upon present and future consumption. Therefore the (rational) investor's objective is clear. He should endeavour to maximise the actual return from his investment in financial assets so that from his initial endowment of investable wealth he will have maximised his end-of-period wealth.

In the context of the Hicks—Lutz model our investor has no need to allow the choice of his investment strategy to be influenced by uncertainty. For him, by assumption, there is none: in the 'weak' version of the theory he *believes* he knows with complete certainty the return, or yield, he will receive from investment of a unit of money in a given asset for the length of his holding period. This means that he can calculate, without error, the *actual* returns he would obtain from any investment strategy. But technically speaking, we should say that our investor will be seeking to maximise, under given constraints, the *expected return* from his investable wealth. In the 'strong' version of the theory he does not know what returns each and every asset will give him.

Thus let us denote the (total) expected return from investing wealth in financial assets by E. Let us also suppose for convenience that there are, at the time our individual is deciding on his ideal investment strategy, only two assets available for him to purchase. Call these securities 1 and 2; and denote by x_1 and x_2 the amount of (nominal) money invested in those assets. Furthermore let: e_1 and e_2 represent the expected returns, or yields, from investing one unit of investable wealth (W) in assets 1 and 2, respectively. Then we may write the investor's one-period decision process in this familiar, and straightforward, manner:

$$\max.\ E = e_1x_1 + e_2x_2 \tag{2.3.2}$$

subject to

$$W = x_1 + x_2. \tag{2.3.3}$$

Letting λ be the Lagrangean multiplier we have:

$$E = e_1x_1 + e_2x_2 + \lambda\,(W - x_1 - x_2). \tag{2.3.4}$$

Therefore, the first-order conditions for a maximum E are that $e_1 = e_2$. Thus, *if both* assets 1 and 2 are to be held then it will be *necessary* for the yields on these two assets to be identical for the duration of the investment period.

Though we might seem to have used a steamroller to crack a walnut, this mathematical proof enables us to reach the very important, if obvious, conclusion that a single investor, and hence the market as a whole, will not be *willing to hold*, for a given investment period, all of the particular securities placed on the market by suppliers unless they all promise to yield the same return per unit of investment. Otherwise, we have the classic Bernoullian situation,[5] where the optimum policy for an investor is to choose that security which offers the highest yield and invest all his money in it for the length of his holding period.

Given the nature of the choice of investment strategy in the Hicks—Lutz model, and this applies outside our one-period model, it follows that for an individual it is not possible for us to deduce how investable wealth will be divided amongst the securities that could be purchased (that is those that have equivalent expected yields). For the demand curve for each asset by each investor is perfectly elastic at the given expected return. So too is the demand curve for the market for each asset. Therefore asset supplies, and hence *relative supplies* of assets, have no part to play in determining the term structure — *unless* changes in those supplies affect expectations.

Let us now move outside the framework of the Hicks—Lutz theory by altering its assumptions, in order to examine the effect on the equalisation theorem. Assumption (2) of the theory detailed in section 2.2 stated that there are no transaction costs involved in the sale or purchase of any asset for any investor on the market. Lutz himself made some extensive comments on the effects of transaction costs for the equalisation theorem in his original paper; and he has recently (15) reiterated those points. Also the work of Malkiel (11) in particular and of Hicks (12) contains detailed analysis of transaction costs. Our aim here however is far more modest: we wish merely to indicate the possible importance of the existence of such costs on the equalisation theorem. Accordingly our discussion is very brief: in it we assume that transaction costs can exist, while assumptions (1) and (3) of the traditional approach remain intact.

In the circumstances the *net* (i.e. gross return less transaction costs) expected return from investing in any one asset must equal that from any other asset. This carries with it the obvious implication that the *gross* expected returns from given assets over the holding period need not be equal. In effect, they can be equal only if *the marginal transaction costs* for a given asset equal those for any other asset. Thus, if we consider only two assets again, assets 1 and 2, the gross return of asset 1 (the e_1) can equal that of asset e_2 in equilibrium only if the cost of buying/selling one extra unit of asset 1 equals that cost for asset 2. Given that there exist transaction costs it is likely that investors will tend to choose to invest in those assets that best correspond to their holding period.[6]

To illustrate the effect of transaction costs on the equalisation theorem we may consider two simple examples. The first example supposes that an investor purchases assets 1 and 2 at the outset of his investment period, asset 1 being an asset that matures at the end of the one-unit length investment period, while asset 2 happens to be an asset with two periods remaining before it is redeemable. It further supposes that there are purchase costs for assets 1 and 2, but that there are selling costs only for asset 2. Then let the purchase costs (PC_i) be represented by this function:

$$PC_i = ax_i,\ i = 1, 2; \quad a > 0. \tag{2.3.5}$$

Selling costs (SC_i) we may posit are somehow related to initial holdings of asset 2, therefore:

$$SC_i = bx_i,\ i = 2; \quad b > 0. \tag{2.3.6}$$

The relevant equations for the marginal expected returns from assets 1 and 2 (ME_1 and ME_2) are now:

$$ME_1 = (e_1 - a) \quad (2.3.7)$$

$$ME_2 = (e_2 - a - b). \quad (2.3.8)$$

Since in the optimum portfolio $ME_1 = ME_2$, it follows at once from these last two equations that $e_1 \neq e_2$. The net yields on the assets must be equal: but the gross yields, the yields-on-the-market, cannot be equal. Here the marginal transaction costs for the two assets (or the marginal addition to total costs of an extra unit of investment in asset 1 or 2) are not the same (being a and $a + b$). So the equalisation theorem no longer holds.

As a second simple example relating to transaction costs, we may postulate that there are no selling costs for asset 2. Then the marginal transaction costs of investing in assets 1 and 2 are equivalent, so that the equalisation theorem still holds.

Now let us turn to the more interesting, and complex, situation where again we have no transaction costs and perfect mobility of funds between the various assets existing in the maturity continuum, but where no longer do investors feel absolutely certain about the returns they expect from any given assets. We are therefore removing assumption (1) of the Hicks—Lutz model; again for simplicity we shall keep to a one-period model (in which there are still only two assets).

For the sake of argument we shall follow the probabilistic[7] approach to the question of uncertainty, thereby rendering it equivalent to 'risk'. Then e_1, for example, will be 'the mathematical expectation' of return from a unit of investment in asset 1. We shall assume that e_1 and e_2 are accompanied by only one risk factor, namely s_1 and s_2, their standard deviations.

Under conditions of risk, Von Neumann and Morgenstern (16) have shown that an individual can be regarded as making his choice of optimum strategy (here optimum portfolio) on the basis of *maximisation* of his *expected utility*. The latter is here given as $E(U)$: but to avoid a confusion over the symbols E for expected value and E for expected return, we shall denote $E(U)$ by U_e. Let us now assume the existence of a general expected utility function which conditions the behaviour of our investor, of this form[8]:

$$U_e = F(E, S). \quad (2.3.9)$$

We then merely make these two observations:

$$\frac{\partial U_e}{\partial E} > 0; \quad \frac{\partial U_e}{\partial S} < 0. \tag{2.3.10}$$

That is, our investor is a risk-averter.

His decision now is to be epitomised as: maximise U_e, equation (2.3.9), subject to:

$$W = x_1 + x_2. \tag{2.3.11}$$

Letting λ once more be the Langrangean multiplier we find that:

$$\frac{\partial U_e}{\partial x_i} = \frac{\partial U_e}{\partial E}\frac{\partial E}{\partial x_i} - \frac{\partial U_e}{\partial S}\frac{\partial S}{\partial x_i} - \lambda = 0, \; i = 1, 2. \tag{2.3.12}$$

The equilibrium position for an investor is now epitomised by the equality of 'the marginal utility' of investing in assets 1 and 2. If we divide $\partial U_e/\partial x_i$ by $\partial U_e/\partial E$, ignoring λ, we have what Hicks (12) has recently called the *marginal advantage curve*, as opposed to the marginal utility curve, from investment in asset *i*. All of the marginal advantages (MA_i) must, of course, be equal for an optimum portfolio to have been selected.

In the present context:

$$MA_i = e_i - A\frac{\partial S}{\partial x_i} \tag{2.3.13}$$

where $A = \partial U_e/\partial E/\partial U_e/\partial S$. It then materialises that when the optimum portfolio *is* selected:

$$e_1 - e_2 = A\left(\frac{\partial S}{\partial x_1} - \frac{\partial S}{\partial x_2}\right) \tag{2.3.14}$$

So now, unless the marginal addition to (total) risk from investing in the two assets is identical, the expected on-the-market yields of the two assets will *not* have to be equal to make it sensible for an investor to hold quantities of either asset.

The demand curves for assets 1 and 2, derived from equation (2.3.12) and the budget restraint are, on the for-convenience supposition that e_1 and e_2 are independent[9]:

$$x_1 = \frac{1}{\Delta}(e_1 - e_2) + \left(\frac{s_2^2}{s_1^2 + s_2^2}\right)W \tag{2.3.15}$$

$$x_2 = \frac{1}{\Delta}(e_2 - e_1) + \left(\frac{s_1^2}{s_1^2 + s_2^2}\right)W \tag{2.3.16}$$

where $\Delta = (A/S)(s_1^2 + s_2^2)$, which is a positive expression since we have already taken account of the negative sign of A in equation

(2.3.12). The coefficients in equations (2.3.15) and (2.3.16) also have their correct signs. As they must be in any two-asset demand model, assets 1 and 2 are therefore seen to be gross substitutes for each other: the wealth effect for both assets is also as it should be.

There will now be a demand curve for the individual investor for each asset which on the *ceteris paribus* assumption will not be perfectly elastic with respect to e_i. In fact, the demand curves will be of the conventional type, downward sloping to the right, so that as e_i falls so too does x_i. On the supposition that all investors have the same expectations, the same degree of uncertainty about any particular expected future return and the same objective function, we can derive a market demand curve for each asset by aggregation of the demand curves of individual investors. That demand curve will have the same characteristics, of course, as any individual's demand curve.

Therefore, the actual yield structure on the market will depend, *ceteris paribus*, upon the supplies of assets. The supply functions for all assets under the present conditions (assuming that all the conditions exist to enable suppliers of bonds — the borrowers — to be treated as a homogeneous group) will be upward sloping to the right.

Therefore, as would be expected, altering the assumptions of the Traditional model alters, or can alter, its basic conclusion. Although we have employed a simple one-period, two-asset model to illustrate our points, the model can easily be expanded to *n* assets (and not so easily to more than one period), leaving our conclusions unaffected. However, although the portfolio approach allows the theory to be set in perspective — and its basic theorem readily proved — it can be used further to show that, again as we would imagine, there can be instances when changing, for example, the first two assumptions of the Hicks—Lutz model leaves its theorem unaffected, because the *net* effect of changing the assumptions is zero.

It is quite easy to appreciate how critics might seize upon the assumptions of the Traditional Theory as a means of attacking the theory itself, ignoring in the process the protestations of M. Friedman (24) against a methodology that attempts to discredit a theory solely by pointing out the 'real world weaknesses' in its assumptions, thereafter altering those assumptions to 'more realistic' ones, and subsequently rendering the theory otiose. Other criticisms on similar lines to those we have just considered have been voiced against the Traditional Theory. These largely concern the implications in Lutzian assumption (1), that: (a) *all* investors have the same expectations; and (b) it is (expected) *short*-term interest rates that govern the yield structure.

The former point is by far the lesser one. It has, however, been made much of by D. G. Luckett (3), though it can be located in earlier writings than his, for example in those of Joan Robinson (65). As Meiselman (8) for one has suggested, the existence of *diverse* expectations poses no real threat to the essence of the Traditional Theory provided the market is *dominated*, in terms of funds to be traded, by market practitioners who do have the same expectations, and who act upon those expectations.

Point (b), however, is not easily dismissed or glossed over. *Ceteris paribus*, it can be a factor of overwhelming importance for the feasibility of the Hicks—Lutz theory. Again, although in this regard Luckett's remarks were anticipated by Robinson, it is Luckett who has really expressed concern at this implied behaviouristic postulate of the theory. But in doing so he has only hinged on a remark that was, in fact, actually made by Lutz himself in his original enunciation of the theory:

> An investor's personal expectations about the future course of short rates do not necessarily commit him as to his expectations about the long rate, since the latter depends, not on what *he* thinks about the future short rates, but what the 'market,' i.e., other people, think about them. The individual investor, therefore, may quite reasonably form an opinion about the future long rate which is inconsistent with his opinion about future short rates.
>
> [(2) p. 414: italics in original]

From the discussion in section 2.2 it follows that such a situation is untenable: it would rescind the Expectations Theory. Long-rate expectations must be consistent with short-rate expectations: this is the basis of, and follows from, the equalisation theorem. The formation of expectations regarding future one-year interest rates necessarily implies the existence of future expected long-term rates of interest (see section 2.5 below and section 3.7 in chapter 3). The strong interpretation of Lutz's assumption (1), concerning the knowledge of the future that the market participants have, would itself rule out anything other than a situation where the market's views of expected long rates were consistent with its view of expected short rates. Lutz concedes in his later work (15) that he did err on this issue in his earlier presentation of the Traditional Theory.

If long- and short-rate expectations are not consistent a simple example, such as that devised by Luckett himself, will illustrate explicitly the consequences for the Expectations Theory:

> Let us suppose . . . that *everyone* . . . comes to believe that long rates will rise, even though they also believe that short rates will remain constant. What effect will this have on the structure of rates? Patently, it will cause a shift out of the long market and into the short to avoid the capital loss attendant on the rising long rate. The effect of this shift will be that short-term yields will fall while rates in the long market will rise. An upsweeping curve will result . . . which is *not* the result of any changes in the expectations about the future course of short-term interest rates. It is the result solely of changed expectations about future *long* rates. . . . . The long rate is thus not an average of expected future short rates . . . .
>
> [(3) pp. 139—40: italics in original]

This then raises the whole question, which is central to the Traditional Theory, of the value of the postulate that the market forms its view of the interest rate structure, and therefore of whether it should invest in the long or the short end of the market, on the basis of expected *short*-term interest rates. In a footnote which must have been referred to as often as some of the most learned papers in the journals (although it is usually misquoted or misrepresented!), Joan Robinson puts the issue in this way:

> . . . . The view that the long rate can be determined solely from expectations about the short rate is untenable.
>
> It is true in a world in which expectations are definite and unanimous, that when we know today's bond rate and today's bill rate, we can reckon what change in the price of bonds is expected over the life of the bills. Then, looking into a further future, we can assume that the bill rate then expected to rule is known, and that by then the expected price of bonds is expected to obtain. Then we can reckon the expected changes in bond prices over the further future, and so to Kingdom Come. Then the whole pattern of expectations could be described in terms of the expected short rates alone. But all this means is that rational expectations must be self consistent. It certainly does not detach the rate of interest from dependence on its boot straps for, in such a world, the only reason for a difference between short and long rates is the expectation of a change in the long rate . . . .
>
> In real life it would be perfectly rational for a man to expect . . . that, for example, over the next year or two the bill rate will continue to be held steady at a low value while the bond rate fluctuates round, say, 3%. But it would not be rational for him to think that he knows exactly what the rates of interest will be every day from today till Kingdom Come.
>
> [(65) p. 102 n. 20]

What Joan Robinson is in the main challenging is the idea that investors form expectations of short rates for indefinite periods ahead; but she is really implying that such a notion is not appropriate because it is not possible for investors to have any clear opinion on future short-term rates except for points in time very close to the present. They form near-term expectations: but that is all. Though she is interpreting Lutz's assumption (1) in its weaker form (at the end of the above-quoted remarks), she is calling into question the whole ethos of the Hicks—Lutz theory. If it is accepted that investors do not form other than very near-term expectations, then there is not much left of the Traditional Theory. To dispute Lutz's assumption (1) it is really necessary to view it in the weaker form, that 'every investor believes he knows . . .'. But if we accept that form of it, it does become pertinent to ask: how far into the future will investors be bothered to predict short-term rates of interest? For the theory to have any significant value the answer to this question must be 'a considerable number of years ahead'. It cannot be a period as short as that suggested by Mrs Robinson, neither does it need to be as (indefinitely) long as she intimates. But it must be many, many years ahead of each present moment in time.

Mrs Robinson then sees short-rate expectations as not (solely) determining the long rate, changes in expectations concerning the *long*-rate causing the interest rate differential between 'shorts' and 'longs'. Since Lord Keynes was instrumental in setting the Traditional Theory on to the lines sketched earlier — via his analysis of forward markets — it comes as no surprise that *he* finds the link between (expected) short rates and long rates acceptable. Indeed he puts forward an extremely convincing argument in support of the view that changes in actual short-term rates will cause changes in actual long-term rates — or that the current short rate should influence current long-term rates (see (7) pp. 352—62). At the outset of his discussion on that issue he states in forthright fashion that: '. . . it is reasonable that long-term rates should bear a definite relation to the prospective short-term rates, quarter by quarter, over the years to come . . .'. It might be significant to note that this impression comes from someone who was not only a shrewd, careful observer and analyst of the 'stock market', but who was also an extremely successful participant in the market! (even if, as current gossip would have it, he was aided by more than a small share of luck in making the fortune he did make for King's College).

In the 1930s Keynes advanced his Liquidity Preference Theory of Interest, a theory that was meant to explain the *level* of 'the' long-term rate. But that theory can be used to explain the term structure of interest rates; indeed, the whole conception that there exists a preference for liquidity, on a conventional interpretation of liquidity, is at the very heart one of the rival theories to the Traditional Theory, namely the Liquidity Premium or Risk Premium Theory. One of the earliest publications to realise that Keynes's theory of interest could be construed as shedding light on the term structure is the paper by N. Kaldor (67) in which he was attempting to interpret the theory *per se.* His conclusion, expressed in the words of Sir Dennis Robertson, who, acting in his familiar role as 'unraveller *par excellence*' has disentangled what Kaldor said, was one that is entirely consistent with the view of the Keynes of the *Treatise*, noted above:

> Thus according to Kaldor there is one-way traffic along the causeway between the two rates, the short rate determining the long, but the long exerting no influence on the short.
>
> [(66) pp. 218–19]

Because:

> . . . he finds in the current and expected short rates a solid pedestal for the whole system, these governing the normal and so also the current long rate. . . . [ibid.]

Robertson himself thereafter did not share this viewpoint and set out to demolish Kaldor (and therefore, Kaldor *et al.*), and he concluded with this sally, which epitomises his standpoint:

> Thus acceptance of the ordinary theory of arbitrage between the long and short markets does not compel us to posit a one-way traffic along the causeway from short to long. Nor indeed does it prevent us from holding, with Marshall and (I think) Fisher, that in a free enterprise economy, . . . it is . . . the long rate which is the senior partner.
>
> [(66) p. 221]

The position is clear: it can be demonstrated in a simple manner that the Traditional Theory, based on the Hicksian equalisation theorem, is destroyed if short rates do not determine the long rates, if investors can simultaneously hold expectations about the short rates that are inconsistent with those they hold about long rates. All this without reference to the Pandora's box that is opened if we allow *diverse* expectations to exist throughout the length and breadth of the capital market. Doubts can be raised concerning the wisdom of Lutz's assumption (1), however evaluated, and the logical outcome of an acceptance of those doubts is that we must seek another explanation of the term structure. The wisdom of accepting such an assumption might be judged by investigation of the actions of investors on the bond market: such evidence as does exist (see for example, Malkiel (11)] tends to indicate that many investors have a short-period planning horizon and therefore might be expected to be more myopic than the Traditional Theory would suggest; and therefore, the theory might be resting on unsure foundations.

If we do not dispute Lutz's assumptions concerning the *modus operandi* of investors, the theory remains untarnished. If we do alter the spirit of Lutz's assumption (1), the theory, *ceteris paribus*, evaporates into thin air, for it is deprived of its *point d'appui.*

2.4

The point we have now reached is this: arbitrage in the market will see to it, in the theory, that no matter what any individual's holding period is, he can choose to invest his wealth in bonds of any length of life. The investment strategy selected will yield — must yield — him the same (expected) rate of return as any other that might have been chosen, which conclusion can be epitomised in the kind of formulae developed by Hicks and Lutz. Should one of the assumptions not hold that render n-year holding-period returns synonymous with yields-to-maturity, then use of the Hicksian formula will mean, *inter alia*, that we have an inaccurate set of expected rates if we calculate those rates from yield-to-maturity data. Use of the Lutzian formula will likewise produce only 'estimates' of forward rates.

Nevertheless it is the Hicksian formula that has been employed in the literature in most discussions of the Traditional Theory. So let us now accept that formula with its possible weaknesses and turn to consider what it can tell us about the structure of interest rates (market yields) and about the movement of interest rates over time.

The Hicksian equation, written in the Meiselman (8) notation, is:

$$(1 + R_{nt}) = [(1 + R_{1t})\,(1 + {}_{t+1}r_t) \ldots (1 + {}_{t+n-1}r_t)]^{1/n} \qquad (2.4.1)$$

Here ${}_{t+i}r_t$ with one-year rate expected at t to hold at $t + c$, and R_{jt} is the actual j-year rate at t. Equation (2.4.1) tells us straghtaway that 'the', or any, 'long-term' rate of interest is a geometric average of the actual (spot) one-year rate and all relevant expected one-year rates less unity. Hence the obvious name, the Expectations Theory, and the commonplace observation that the long-term rate of interest depends upon future expectations about 'the' short-term rate of interest.

Some important and well-established propositions can be deduced from equation (2.4.1). Consider first of all the term structure of yields *at a moment in time*, *t*. Then we can derive these propositions:

Proposition 1 (a) Should it happen that the market expects one-year rates to rise *monotonically* in the future, then at *t* the long-term rate of interest will exceed the short-term rate of interest.[10] The yield-to-maturity curve is, therefore, upward sloping to the right.[11]

(b) A weaker form of (a). If it happens that the market expects all future short-term (that is, one-year) rates to be higher than the current spot one-year rate, then, even if there is no systematic relationship between the future, expected, one-year rates, the actual long-term rate will here also exceed the short-term rate.

There are two corollaries to 1a and 1b:

Proposition 2 (a) If instead of monotonically rising expected one-year rates we should have monotonically falling expected one-year rates, the yield curve must be downward sloping to the right.

(b) Likewise, if for rising rates in 1b we substitute falling rates, the short-term rate will exceed the long-term rate.

By implication we have a third major proposition, already noted on an earlier occasion:

Proposition 3 If the market expects all the future one-year rates to be equal to the current spot one-year rate, the market effectively has static expectations in the Hicksian sense, and it follows that the yield-to-maturity curve will be horizontal. There will be no yield gap.[12]

These three propositions relate to the term structure of interest rates at a point in time. The theory, approximated as it is by equation (2.4.1), however, allows some deductions to be made covering interest rates over time. In effect, we can make observations, with lesser or greater ease, about: (i) the term structure of interest rates *over time*; and, (ii) the courses of interest rates, also over time.

Let us take (ii) first, by which we mean that it is (or could be) possible to make pronouncements on the relationship between the interest rate on one type of bond, say of *n* years' life at time *t* with the rate on it at time $t-1$. Once more, to enable us to elaborate on statement (ii) we must focus our attention on equation (2.4.1).

The first proposition we may take note of is this:

Proposition 4 (a) If at a moment in time, say point t, the market's anticipations respecting future one-year rates are such that for a given length of time from t it expects rates to be higher now than they were viewed from the vantage point of time $t-1$, and the actual spot rate on a one-year bond at t happens to be higher than at $t-1$ (i.e., $R_{1t} > R_{1t-1}$), then we may conclude that the long-term rate at t, R_{nt}, will exceed R_{nt-1}. All actual rates at t will exceed those at $t-1$ for given length-of-life bonds.[13] Should these conditions be maintained for several time periods we may obviously conclude that rates on given bonds can be fairly well described as 'rising over time'.

These kinds of conditions could be produced, or perhaps we should more accurately say be reinforced, by the existence in reality (or in theory) of the Meiselman Hypothesis, which we shall discuss in the next chapter.

(b) The opposite of proposition 4a. If at a moment in time, say point t, the market's anticipations relating to future one-year rates are such that for a given length of time from t it expects rates to be lower now than when they were viewed from the vantage point of time $t-1$, and the actual spot rate on a one-year bond at t happens to be lower than at $t-1$ (i.e. $R_{1t} < R_{1t-1}$), then we may conclude that the long-term rate at t, R_{nt}, will be lower than R_{nt-1}. All actual rates at t will be lower than those at $t-1$ for given length-of-life bonds.

Proposition 5 In the words of Lutz, 'the long rate can never fluctuate as widely as the short rate' ((2) p. 501).. To prove this contention for the sake of simplicity Lutz uses the arithmetic version of the Fisherian formula, which with a slight change of notation is the Hicksian formula. So if we return for the moment to the Hicksian presentation of his formula we have:

$$(1+R_{nt})^n = (1+r_1)(1+r_2)\ldots(1+r_n) \qquad (2.4.2)$$

where $R_1 = r_1$. When this geometric average is replaced by the arithmetic average we are left with this alternative formula:

$$R_{nt} = \frac{r_1 + r_2 + \ldots + r_n}{n}. \qquad (2.4.3)$$

Lutz's proof is based upon equation (2.4.3), upgraded for $t+1$:

$$R_{nt+1} = \frac{r_2 + r_3 + \ldots + r_{n+1}}{n}. \qquad (2.4.4)$$

But to upgrade equation (2.4.3) in this manner is to suppose that *expectations never change*: here is the strong interpretation of his assumption (1). Here the actual one-year rate in t is r_1 and r_2 is the actual rate in period $t + 1$. If the interest rate on an n-year bond is to change by the same amount between t and $t + 1$ as is the short rate from equation (2.4.3) and (2.4.4), we can arrive at the equations at the centre of Lutz's proof of proposition (5), namely:

$$r_1 - r_2 = \frac{r_1 + r_2 + \ldots + r_n}{n} - \frac{r_2 + r_3 + \ldots + r_{n+1}}{n} \qquad (2.4.5a)$$

or:

$$n(r_1 - r_2) = r_1 - r_{n+1}. \qquad (2.4.5b)$$

Equation (2.4.5b) tells us the conditions under which long and short rates will change by the same amount. Lutz makes this deduction on the basis of it:

> [that the equation will hold] is the more improbable, the longer is the term to maturity of the bond [n], and for very long terms it is practically impossible. Hence long rates fluctuate less than short rates.
>
> [(15) pp. 213—14]

The proof is valid, as it stands — but it is as simple as it is because of the assumption of perfect knowledge concerning future short-term rates of interest. Such a state of affairs means that a rate of interest expected to rule on a one-year bond in the future never changes, and when the passage of time has taken us to the actual point for which the 'forecast' was made it *is* seen to be the ruling spot rate. This is indeed a very strong line to take;[14] and since the market never has to revise its expectations of any single future expected one-year rate because it makes no errors at all, the Meiselman Hypothesis, founded as it is on the market revising its expectations on the basis of past forecast errors, is made otiose.

But in view of our foregoing remarks we should ask ourselves this question: would proposition 5 follow (at all, or as easily) if we took the Hicksian formula and did not interpret it in the 'strong' manner that Lutz did? The answer to this question happens to be yes! but the proof that the answer is in the affirmative is not as straightforward as the Lutzian proof of proposition 5, nor is it as clear-cut as it might be. It seems appropriate to include a (heuristic) proof of proposition 5 without Lutz's 'strong' assumption, but to bury it, in the circumstances, in a footnote.[15]

It might be further argued in relation to proposition 5 that over a stretch of time, and indeed over two consecutive time periods, it might be appropriate in the context of the real world to judge the relative fluctuations in the rates on short and long bonds by their standard deviation or coefficient of variation. It can be shown that, in the Hicks—Lutz model, using the strong Lutzian assumption in the Fisherian or Hicksian formula produces results on these measures of fluctuation consistent with the arguments and points noted above.

The final group of propositions, or deductions, from the Traditional Theory relates to the term structure of interest rates over time. On this matter J. W. Conard ((23) pp. 301—2) has stated that:

> .... since this theory does not describe how expectations are formed, there is room for any influence that may change them to alter the value of any or all future short rates, and hence to produce a wholly new rate structure. Thus it is possible to make any pattern of change in the structure of rates compatible with the . . . theory by merely assuming the appropriate changes in the sets of expected short rates.

This is undoubtedly a correct evaluation of the situation, as will be gathered from what we say below. Because it is, we shall advance only two propositions regarding the term structure over time. These are relatively simple propositions but they do demonstrate that the theory can offer observations on such an important empirical matter. So we now look at propositions (6) and (7).

Proposition 6 As a corollary of proposition 1 we may argue as follows. If, over a certain time period (i.e. two or more consecutive periods), all future rates should be continually rising, then at a moment in time we know from proposition 1 that $R_{nt} > R_{1t}$, but we may also deduce that $(R_n - R_1)_t < (R_n - R_1)_{t+i}$, where $i = 2 \ldots n$, if for n periods (years) 'given' expected one year rates are rising. Just to clarify the explicit assumptions in the statement we are, in fact, assuming that these kinds of conditions hold:

$$_{t+1}r_t < {}_{t+2}r_t < \ldots < {}_{t+n-1}r_t \qquad (2.4.6)$$

and

$$_{t+1}r_{t+1} > {}_{t+1}r_t; \quad {}_{t+2}r_{t+1} > {}_{t+2}r_t; \quad \ldots; \quad {}_{t+2}r_{t+2} > {}_{t+2}r_{t+1}; \quad {}_{t+3}r_{t+2} > {}_{t+3}r_{t+1} \ldots \qquad (2.4.7)$$

The relationships contained in equation (2.4.7) merely inform us that the one-year rate expected to be determined on the market for a stated date in the future is continually revised upward, period by period, until we reach the date concerned. In equation (2.4.6) we find the strong conditions for the existence of a rising yield-to-maturity curve at a point in time. A possible proof of proposition 6 is given in the accompanying footnote.[16]

The concomitant proposition in respect of proposition 6 is one where the signs in equations (2.4.6) and (2.4.7) are reversed, etc., so giving us proposition 7. Conditions opposite to those in proposition 6 will result in a situation wherein *the yield-gap declines over time.*

Since in proposition 7 we have conditions that are the opposite of those in proposition 6 we have: $R_{1t+1} < R_{1t}$, $R_{nt+1} < R_{nt}$, $R_{nt} < R_{1t}$ and $R_{nt+1} < R_{1t+1}$. Thus, since in period t the yield-gap is negative the fact that at t+1 it has declined means that, although still negative it is approaching zero, with the long rate moving upwards towards the value attained by the short rate.

This is as far as it seems sensible, and practical, to consider the kinds of propositions that can be deduced from the Hicks—Lutz theory when the latter is epitomised in the Hicksian/Fisherian equation. However, we might add one additional proposition, since it was formulated by Lutz (2) in his original paper on the term structure, and since that proposition can be used as a qualification to some of those we have chosen to list and discuss above.

This proposition we may simply call L, after Lutz:

Proposition L To quote Lutz himself on this proposition:

> It is possible that the long rate may move temporarily contrariwise to the short rate. The long rate would rise, in spite of a simultaneous fall in the short rate, if the preceding short rate was lower than the average of the succeeding short rates, and *vice versa.* If we use the arithmetic averages as a first approximation, it can easily be seen that this is so. If, for instance, the short rates in three successive years are four per cent, three per cent, and eight per cent, respectively, the yield on a bond redeemable at the end of the third year will be five per cent in the first year and will rise to five and one-half per cent in the second year, in spite of the fall in the short rate from the first to the second year.
>
> [(2) p. 502]

This proposition, despite the fact that it is couched in terms of Lutz's employment of the strong interpretation of the first basic assumption of the Traditional model, is important for propositions 1 to 7. For instance, in discussing propositions related to movements in interest rates *over time*, we have made an *assumption* about changes in the short rate. Even if, to take as a point of illustration proposition 4. all expected one-year rates in t are higher than in $t-1$, even if it should happen that $R_{1t-1} > R_{1t}$, it is still possible for

$R_{nt} > R_{nt-1}$. In other words, in proposition 4 the supposition that $R_{1t} > R_{1t-1}$, is, under the given conditions in respect of one-year expected rates, an additional sufficiency condition, not a necessary condition, for the occurrence on the financial market of the relationship $R_{nt} > R_{nt-1}$. This can be appreciated from our discussion and proof of proposition 4 above: it is also accurately portrayed by Lutz's own example under perfect forecasting, using the proxy for the geometric average.

The Traditional approach, though a very simple model built on rather sweeping assumptions, offers a rich fund of ideas on the yield structure both at a point in time and over time. The predictions that follow from the approach have direct relevance to real-world questions, but it is when we come to the actual testing of these predictions against the empirical data that we find the fund somewhat illusory.

The propositions that we have derived from the Traditional Theory are not all couched in a form suitable for statistical or econometric testing, but they are major hypotheses and also are empirically orientated. Propositions 1 to 3 concern the structure of yields at a point in time, and it is necessary for the validity of the theory that it should satisfy *all* three propositions. The movement of the yield structure over time is contained in propositions 4 to 7 and here also the theory can be verified on the basis of each proposition and all four propositions as a group. Again, it is necessary for the theory to satisfy *all* conditions.

To state a platitude, a prerequisite of any empirical test of any theory is the existence of appropriate data; if these data are not available the theory is (at that time anyway) an empty empirical box. But let us assume that we have appropriate data at hand. How then should we go about the task of testing propositions 1—7? To answer this query we shall take the propositions *seriatim*.

We would test proposition 1 by grouping together all those years for which at the beginning of each the market's expected rates of interest on one-year bonds, given to us as data somehow by the market (as true evidence about expectations), were in excess of the ruling spot rate of one-year bonds. Having done this the difference between long and short rates for those periods would be calculated. We should then find that these yield-gaps are *all* positive and there should be no exception to this if the theory is to pass this test. Propositions 1a, 2a and 2b would have to be tested in the same manner by a simple grouping together of similar observations over the data period. No econometrics *per se* is called for in testing these hypotheses. Proposition 3 will be tested in the same way. So the given data period can be divided into three sub-periods (if all should exist) according to the expectations of the market concerning future one-year bond rates.

To test proposition 4 we can use precisely the same method as with the earlier propositions, but we can also call to our aid some econometric analysis. Thus suppose (we are considering, it will be recalled, the movement of interest rates over time) that we discover in a given data period that the conditions detailed in proposition 4a are upheld. Then for that block of (preferably consecutive) data we can compare R_{jt} and $R_{j(t-i)}$, where $j = 2, 3 \ldots, n$, and $i = 1, 2 \ldots, K$. We must find, for example, that $R_{nt} > R_{nt-1}$. But the quite detailed assumptions or conditions behind proposition 4a enable us to concentrate our attention on two 'variables' and to formulate a simple equation.

Thus, it is legitimate for us to argue from proposition 4a that:

$$(R_{nt} - R_{nt-1}) = a_1 + b_1({}_t r_{t-1} - R_{1t-1}) \qquad (2.4.8a)$$

or

$$\frac{R_{nt}}{R_{nt-1}} = a_2 + b_2 \left(\frac{{}_t r_{t-1}}{R_{1t-1}} \right). \qquad (2.4.8b)$$

Alternatively:

$$(R_{nt} - R_{nt-1}) = a_3 + b_3(R_{1t} - R_{1t-1}) \qquad (2.4.9a)$$

or,

$$\left(\frac{R_{nt}}{R_{nt-1}} \right) = a_4 + b_4 \left(\frac{R_{1t}}{R_{1t-1}} \right). \qquad (2.4.9b)$$

It must be remembered that we are using these equations on the basis of the conditions that hold in proposition 4a and hence in the block of data for which we shall test these equations. In the equations, n can take any value in excess of one, as usual. We might make a few comments about these equations.

Equation (2.4.8a) indicates that in the Hicks–Lutz theory, given the *ceteris paribus* clause, we should be able to determine the direction of change in the rate on any bond with a life of at least two years, from a knowledge of the difference between the one-year rate expected at $t - 1$ to rule at t and the actual spot one-year rate at $t - 1$. We would expect that $b_1 > 0$ if, on this count, the theory is to be supported by the facts.

But, furthermore, under the assumptions made about expected one-year rates, we could expect, given the market data on expected rates, that $a_1 = 0$. For should ${}_t r_{t-1} = R_{1t-1}$, given the assumptions made,

R_{nt} should equal R_{nt-1}. If we consider, in the context of the present framework, the companion equation (2.4.8b) we would expect from the theory that the slope coefficient was positive again, but that there exists this restriction on the coefficients in the equation: $a_2 + b_2 = 1$. Thus, should ${}_tr_{t-1} = R_{1t-1}$, *ceteris paribus*, $R_{nt} = R_{nt-1}$; that is R_{nt}/R_{nt-1} should equal unity. Therefore, the restriction $a_2 + b_2 = 1$ should hold if the theory is valid, and hence if proposition 4a is empirically sound. Even though that proposition is basically formulated to handle situations where $({}_tr_{t-1} - R_{1t-1})$ is positive, in an econometric test of it, of course, we would be including tests of proposition 4b (and of periods where ${}_tr_{t-1} - R_{1t-1}$, is zero).

Having estimated the equations: (a) we would want the signs of the slope coefficients to be positive and, of course, significantly different from zero; (b) we would want significantly different from zero, $\bar{R}^2$s; (c) we would wish restrictions on the coefficients to be supported by the facts; an F-test based on a comparison of the residuals from the equations in the ordinary least squares case and those arising out of restricted least squares estimates would have to be performed.

It is not necessary to say much about proposition 5 except that in testing the proposition we could, for a whole data period, as well as taking the differences between ΔR_{nt} and ΔR_{1t} for given ts, evaluate the empirical worth of the Hicks—Lutz theory via this proposition by means of a comparison of the standard deviations, or the coefficients of variation of the long and short rate series.

Propositions 6 and 7 can naturally be empirically assessed in the same way. For example, if we take proposition (6), given that we have classified our data according to its assumptions, we can test it by taking the differences between $(R_n - R_1)_t$ and $(R_n - R_1)_{t+1}$, $i = 2 \ldots n$. They should be negative if the theory is a true description of reality (assuming it has fulfilled all the other tests). We have no need here for anything other than a straightforward 'arithmetic' test of the real-world value of the theory; nothing of much import can be attained by attempts at econometric formulations of this proposition, although some such formulations can actually be made.

We have now, in effect, established a reasonably exhaustive framework for the empirical testing of the Hicks—Lutz theory. But none of the various aspects of that framework are actually testable *unless* the data we use on the expected one-year rates or yields are what we might call observed, or market-given, or independently-given. However, as we already noted in section 2.2, most researchers[17] into the term structure have used data on expected one-year rates that have been derived from yield-to-maturity curves, and these are the type of data, for the most part, we shall utilise in this book. These curves by definition, at any moment of time, contain within them a set of implied forward one-year rates; so from given yields-to-maturity, employing the basic Hicksian equation (2.2.1) and replacing the expected one-year rates (the *r*s) by one-year 'expected forward' rates (the ϕs), we arrive again at a familiar equation:

$$_{t+n-1}\phi_t = \frac{(1 + R_{nt})^n}{(1 + R_{(n-1)t})^{n-1}} - 1. \qquad (2.4.10)$$

Largely as a consequence of the work of Meiselman (8) it is these forward rates that have been adopted as (*unbiased*) measures of the required expected one-year rates. But these forward rates have two very important characteristics: (i) they are *implied* rates, and are not independently given to us by the participants in the financial market; and (ii) they are subject to *error*.

This error has two sources. The first arises out of the lack of accuracy in the construction of the yield-to-maturity curves themselves. The other, more crucial, error is due to the fact, already noted, that except in certain peculiar circumstances yields-to-maturity will not be synonymous with true *n*-year holding-period returns and in consequence will not accurately portray the market's views about expected one-year (holding period) yields.

In any test of the Traditional Theory it is data on *n*-year holding-period returns, independently given, that are required, and therefore, except for proposition 5, which concerns the relative fluctuations of the long and short rate, none of the propositions that are essential to the full and rigorous testing of the theory can in fact be tested using as a basis yield-to-maturity curve data. This is a point well made by a number of researchers in the field (see for example Meiselman (8)) and we shall only consider one proposition to demonstrate its validity.

Thus let us examine proposition 1a. If we should 'observe' from the existing structure of rates at point *t* that all forward one-year rates, $_{t+1}\phi_t$ to $_{t+n-1}\phi_t$, are in excess of R_{1t}, it will also be 'observed' that $R_{1t} < R_{2t} < \ldots < R_{nt}$. Via proposition 1a we might then be tempted to conclude that the Expectations Theory has scored one point in its favour. However, we are not entitled to make such an inference — for this reason: when $_{t+1}\phi_t$ to $_{t+n-1}\phi_t$ all exceed R_{1t} at the beginning of period *t*, it *must* be observed that the yield curve slopes upward to the right.

If it is assumed that the implied one-year rates at our disposal are a correct indication of the market's own views about expected interest rates, and we assume that the market acts rationally on the basis of those expectations, then we could test the Expectations Theory by reference to the above-discussed propositions, beginning with 1a. But, effectively, such a test would be worthless — or pointless: for the theory would, indeed must, always pass such a test.

2.5

The existence of *independent* evidence on market-expected one-year yields would clearly be sufficient to enable testing of the Hicks—Lutz theory to be undertaken. Any such testing should assume the form outlined in the previous section, whether the theory is being assessed at a point in time or over time. For the propositions detailed hitherto provide a framework for empirically evaluating the Traditional Theory.

However, so far no such exhaustive testing of the theory exists. It is usually argued that the only substantial testing of the theory is that executed by D. Meiselman (8), whose work we shall consider and develop in the next chapter. All other tests of the Hicks—Lutz theory to date have tended to be of very limited scope and to suffer from a basic methodological weakness. To be precise, these tests performed by individuals such as W. B. Hickman (27) and C. Walker (29), and, of more recent vintage, those undertaken by J. M. Culbertson (28a and b), have been founded on the notion that the Traditional Theory relies for its validity on the accurate prediction of expected one-year rate of interest or yields. The bulk of their empirical testing of the theory relies heavily on examining data on market yields to see if expectations were 'fulfilled'.

Their thesis was a simple (indeed naive) one: unless expectations *were* fulfilled, the Hicks—Lutz theory must necessarily be erroneous. This view found its way into the basic literature on the term structure and has only now been challenged, largely as a result of Meiselman's (8) work. For, to refer to a remark that is often quoted, no less an authority than J. W. Conard ((23), p. 290) argued that: '. . . to build a theory whose predictions can be meaningfully tested' was possible only if it was supposed that the market made accurate predictions. *But*, the crucial point is that so long as expectations once formed actually *influence* the term structure, it does not matter whether those expectations turn out to have been optimistic or pessimistic. As Meiselman for one has rightly argued: 'Anticipations may not be realised yet still determine the structure of rates in the manner asserted by the theory' ((8), p. 12).

At this juncture it seems opportune to state that, given relevant data, the tests we have suggested for assessing the Traditional Theory do not depend upon expectations being realised. They depend solely upon the market behaving in the way predicted by the theory, given the market's expected one-year rates: if they do so behave then at a point in time, for example, a term structure will emerge that fits that laid down in the Traditional approach. Investors are assumed to act only on the basis of their expectations.

Every test of the Traditional Theory made by Hickman (27), for example, relies on the view that the market must be seen to forecast accurately. In effect, there are three tests of the Traditional Theory described in Hickman (27). The results of the two major tests, which for simplicity, following Kessel (30), we have labelled Hickman Test One and Two, are reported in tables 2.5.1 and 2.5.2, respectively.

In table 2.5.1 we have the results from a comparison of yield-to-maturity curves in the U.S.A. For each of the years 1936 to 1942 three such curves are referred to: (1) the actual, observed, curve for the given year; (2) the yield curve that would apply in that year if the previous year's yield curve were to hold in that year; (3) forecasts of yield curves for the given year made in previous years, when the forecasts are made on the basis of the Hicks—Lutz theory.

A word or two should be said in order to elaborate on curves of type 3. Consider then, as an illustration, the year 1937. In view of the fact that the data period only begins in 1935 there are only two forecast curves for 1937. The one is derived from the term structure in 1935, and the other is derived from the term structure in 1936. On the basis of the Traditional Theory, and with the employment of yield-to-maturity curve data, the expectations of the market in 1935 for the year 1937 can be obtained from that data, *ceteris paribus*, by means of the now familiar Hicksian formula. Thus, supposing that the longest life bond has a term-to-maturity of thirty years (i.e. $n = 30$), we may write for 1935:

$$(1 + R_{30,1935}) = (1 + R_{1,1935})(1 + {}_{1936}r_{1935}) \ldots (1 + {}_{1964}r_{1935}). \quad (2.5.1)$$

So that the actual thirty-year bond rate in 1935 carries within it a

Table 2.5.1 Results of Hickman 'test one' on the Hicks–Lutz theory

Year	Type of curve		Area under curve	Difference in area between actual and forecast curve
1935	Actual		56.47	
1936	Actual		48.45	
	Projection of 1935		56.47	8.02
	Theoretical forecast from:	1935	62.92	14.47
1937	Actual		45.14	
	Projection of 1936		48.45	3.31
	Theoretical forecast from:	1936	55.00	9.86
		1935	67.30	22.16
1938	Actual		48.42	
	Projection of 1937		45.14	−3.28
	Theoretical forecast from:	1937	50.85	2.43
		1936	60.20	11.78
		1935	70.00	21.58
1939	Actual		41.29	
	Projection of 1938		48.42	7.13
	Theoretical forecast from:	1938	54.08	12.79
		1937	55.39	14.10
		1936	64.07	22.78
		1935	71.97	30.68
1940	Actual		37.42	
	Projection of 1939		41.29	3.87
	Theoretical forecast from:	1939	46.73	9.31
		1938	58.19	20.77
		1937	59.01	21.59
		1936	66.74	29.32
		1935	73.20	35.78
1941	Actual		36.25	
	Projection of 1940		37.42	1.17
	Theoretical forecast from:	1940	42.76	6.51
		1939	51.02	14.77
		1938	61.10	24.85
		1937	61.83	25.58
		1936	68.21	31.96
		1935	74.01	31.76
1942	Actual		41.28	
	Projection of 1941		36.25	−5.03
	Theoretical forecast from:	1941	41.38	0.10
		1940	47.13	5.85
		1939	54.31	13.03
		1938	62.98	21.70
		1937	64.13	22.85
		1936	68.88	27.60
		1935	74.28	33.00

Source: W. B. Hickman (27), table 1, pp 111–5. This table is also reproduced in R. A. Kessel (30), appendix A.

series of expected one-year rates up to the year 1964. Given that the yield-to-maturity curves provide us with information on R_{1t} to R_{nt}, for the year 1935 we can calculate those one-year rates the market 'expects' to hold on the market at the beginning of years 1935 to 1966 inclusive by invoking equation (2.4.10).

This information on expected rates of interest will enable us to calculate the rates that the market expects in 1935 will obtain at the outset of 1937 on bonds with lengths of life of 1 to $(n-2)$ years inclusive; that is, in symbolic form, the market's view in 1935 of the values of R_1 to R_{n-2} in 1937 can be assessed. We cannot give the market's 1935 expectation of n or of $n-1$ length-of-life bonds for 1937, because if $n = 30$, we require in 1935 details of the expected one-year rates for 1965 and 1966, which we do not have. So in deriving the predicted values for 1937, two years ahead of 1935, we shall be short of two observations on one-year expected rates.

On the supposition that the Hicks—Lutz theory's forward rates are true estimates of expected one-year rates, and so on, from both 1935 and 1936, for example, we can calculate the market's expectations of R_1 to R_{n-2} and of R_1 to R_{n-1}, respectively, for 1937. We then have *expected yield curves* for 1937 based on 1935 and 1936. Likewise, for all years there will be expected yield curves (covering nearly the whole range of that curve, save the furthermost segment of it) derived from the yield structure in all previous years.

These expected yield curves are founded on the existence of the Traditional Theory. In 'test one' of that theory Hickman compared the relevant segments of the actual yield curves (curves (1)), for the years 1936—42, with the prediction of the term structure by the theory (curves (3)). He maintained that the theory must be an accurate predictor; so that the 'area under the curves' (1) and (3) for a given year should be identical, or very close. As can be seen from the 'area difference' column in table 2.5.1, expectations were not fulfilled for all the years of Hickman's inquiry, though as the present period is approached expectations become 'more accurate'.

In 'test one' Hickman also tested the Hicks—Lutz theory in another way, by seeing how it compared with a simple static expectations hypothesis. That hypothesis (which is also assessed in terms of its predictability) is what we would now call an 'inertia hypothesis'. To be specific, the supposition is that the market expects the term structure in period t to hold in period $t+1$, and that such an hypothesis can account for the *observed* term structure better than can the Hicks—Lutz theory. Again, except for 1938 and 1942, this behaviouristic postulate succeeds better than the Hicks—Lutz

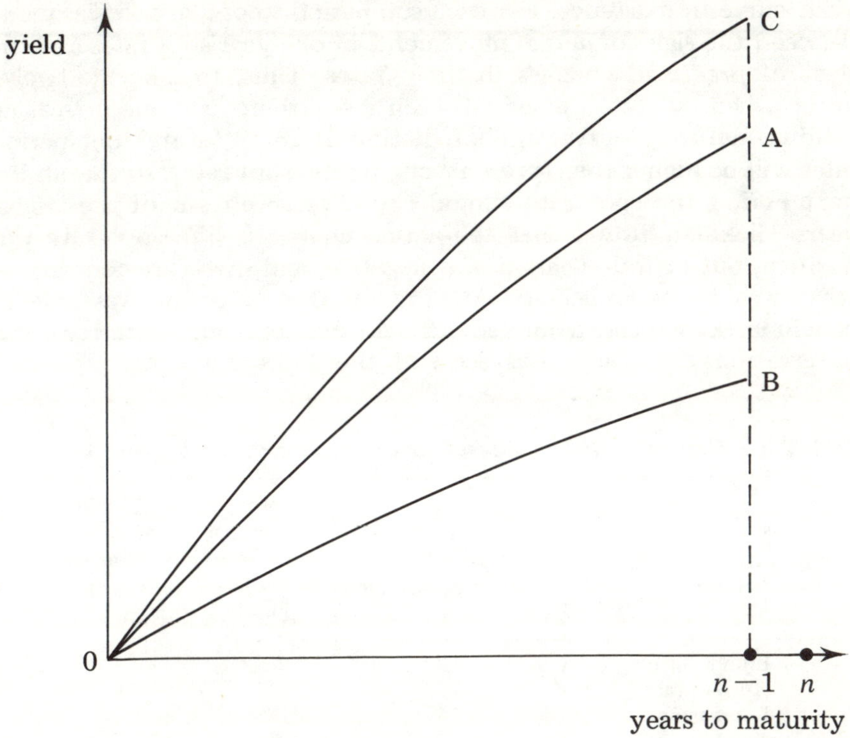

Figure 2.5.1

thesis, the first item in the 'area difference' column for 1936, 1937 and 1939—41 being lower than that of any other.

'Test one' can be demonstrated pictorially. Thus consider figure 2.5.1. Curve A represents the actual yield-to-maturity given for a given year t. Curve B represents the curve predicted for t by the Expectations Theory in $t-1$, while curve C is the actual yield curve in period $t-1$. All three curves cover at least $n-1$ years to maturity. A comparison of the curves reveals that the difference between the areas under A and C is less than that between the areas under A and B. The curve C is 'nearer' to curve A; therefore the inertia hypothesis is a better forecaster of the term structure in t than is the Expectations Theory.

We may now say a few words about 'test two'. This is based on thirty-seven years selected out of the period 1900—42, the selected period being divided into three parts depending upon the type of yield curve in existence. For each sub-period a comparison was made between the signs of *actual* movements in one-year spot rates and the signs of *predicted* changes in those rates. Thus, to take the twelve years when at the outset of each year there was an increasing yield-to-maturity curve, the prediction is that 'future' one-period rates will be higher than 'present' one-period spot rates, so that in the next period the spot rate should rise. For seven out of the twelve years Hickman found that the actual change in the spot rate was positive; but in four years it was negative, and therefore contrary to what was to be expected. Arguing on these lines he was able to conclude, as we see from table 2.5.2, that ten out of thirty-seven observations definitely disagreed with the Hicks—Lutz theory.

Table 2.5.2 Results of Hickman 'test two' of the Hicks—Lutz theory

Type of term structure at beginning of year	No. of years in which prevailing	No. of years in which change in short-term rate to next year was		
		plus	minus	zero
Increasing	12	7	4	1
Horizontal	10	6*	4*	
Decreasing	15	6**	9	
Total	37	19	17	1

*Partial disagreement of historical pattern of term structure with H.—L. theory.
**Definite disagreement of historical pattern of term structure with H.—L. theory.

Source: Hickman (27) and Kessel (30).

Hickman's 'test three' was again based on accurate forecasting in Lutz's sense. Using the strong Lutzian interpretation of assumption (1) of the Traditional Theory he argued, as we have seen in section 2.4 that Lutz did, that the change in the long-term rate from one year to the next should be determined solely by the effect of dropping the previous year's one-year spot rate and adding a one-year forward rate at the long end. This can be seen from equations (2.4.3) and (2.4.4). Hickman found, in fact, that only eighteen out of the forty years of his data period met this requirement. Apart from the other deficiencies in Hickman's 'test three' (See Kessel (30)[18]), it suffers from the same drawback as his other two tests in that, in accepting the strong Lutzian view about 'foresight', it assumed that the market always holds a given view about a one-year rate expected at a given date in the future. If this is so it could only conceivably happen if the market always found that its forecasts were correct: but we have discussed this earlier on in this chapter.

These tests by Hickman highlight the need to be careful about subjecting the Traditional Theory to empirical investigation and demonstrate the necessity to have in mind the kind of framework established in section 2.4 by which to attempt to assess the theory — given appropriate data, of course.

Yet the empirical tests by Hickman, Walker (29) and Macaulay (45) were important, for, being first tests of the theory, they made the obvious point that it *should* be tested and they made it possible for others to reflect on the systematic basis by which the theory should be assessed. They also stimulated further theoretical work in the field, once it was fully grasped that their tests of the Hicks—Lutz theory were controversial.

Notes to Chapter 2

1. We have chosen to make the distinction between the two interpretations of the first Lutzian assumption explicit, and to do so by using the terminology 'objective' and 'subjective' certainty, as a result of comments we have had, particularly from Charles Carter and George Shackle. Professor Shackle suggested implicitly that we should label the 'strong' version, as we have called it, of assumption (1) the perfect foresight version, and the 'weak' interpretation as the subjective certainty view. Perfect foresight and objective certainty stand for the same thing, but the pairing of subjective certainty with objective certainty makes clearer the distinction we need to make in the text.

Professor Shackle also writes as follows:

> Does not assumption (1) really abolish any problem? From this assumption, we need only say that if people's behaviour is internally consistent, arithmetic dictates the structure of rates; or it may be that only one structure of rates is consistent both with itself or with rationality and perfect foresight on the part of the members of the market.

This is true, whichever way we look at assumption (1), for any point in time. But using the assumption of perfect foresight or of objective certainty concerning all expected one-year rates in the future, the expectations model of the term structure has an even simpler look, and it becomes about as far removed from 'reality' as it can be. Given the objective certainty assumption the term structure falls into place virtually automatically. But we still produce a theory of the term structure out of the Lutzian model, and we can deduce some statements on the effect of short-term expectations on that structure. Those statements have to be couched in a slightly different way from those propositions listed in the main text below; that is all.

The assumptions behind the Expectations Theory certainly make it a theory from which the conclusions flow more easily than they do from most theories. Nonetheless it is a theory, and one from which, by the simple arithmetic into which it can be translated, allows deductions that are potentially testable to be made about the term structure.

The question of 'perfect foresight' poses many difficulties in economics, as well as in other disciplines (in the social sciences in particular); and it can lead to many paradoxes. In the latter regard we call to mind the textbook example of Sherlock Holmes pursuing Moriarty: they cannot *both* have perfect foresight. The only solution to the problem would be the *status quo* — neither can gain by making a move, since the move is known beforehand by the other.

The greatest difficulties are confronted where we are concerned with situations which, like the above example, are similar to those discussed in game theory. Where we are analysing contests or bargaining between individuals or groups of individuals then the assumption of perfect foresight raises almost insuperable obstacles. In the present context, of the Expectations Theory of the term structure, that assumption does not carry with it quite the degree of difficulty and indecisiveness that it does in 'conflict' situations. Here we are more concerned with a game against nature. Both sides of the market know what prices and yields will obtain on the market at stated dates in the future before the market has actually met to trade bonds that will cause these prices and yields to be registered. These are *data* for both suppliers (lenders) and demanders (borrowers). It is true that each side of the market can work out the optimum strategy for the other side: but these strategies will be consistent with each other and they will produce a *solution*, and an equilibrium one; and, *ex definitione*, that solution can only produce a set of yields that show that 'accurate forecasting' obtains.

There are many interesting and intricate issues raised by the assumption of perfect foresight which have occupied philosophers and economists alike. Perhaps we may permit ourselves a few observations on this remark, even though we shall have to leave this topic here. The philosophers have been concerned, *inter alia*, with the possibility and meaning of precognition, and of the whole question of 'knowledge' and its relationship to 'information'. (In this context we might mention, as an illustration, the work of Sir Alfred J. Ayer (110). The works of Sir Karl R. Popper, familiar enough to social scientists, are also of relevance here.) For economists these issues open up the role of 'time', and hence of knowledge, in economic theories. Professor Shackle has written at great length in numerous places on these matters, but we might mention here his latest, and perhaps most elegant, penetrating writings on them, namely his *Epistemics and Economics* (109).

2. To which Hicks has this important footnote: 'All rates taken per week, and measured in fractions rather than percentages; a rate of 1/10 per cent per week is thus written 0.001'. We are concerned with the return from investing a unit of money.

3. The Lutzian equation can be proved in the following way. Let P be the principal to be invested, which will equal the present price of the long-term bond; R represent the long-term rate of interest; r_1, r_2, . . . , are the expected future one-year rates. From the equality of returns from investing long and of

expected returns from investing the principal in successive short bonds we can write (where PR is the coupon):

$$P = \frac{PR}{(1+r_1)} + \frac{PR}{(1+r_1)(1+r_2)} + \ldots + \frac{PR+P}{(1+r_1)(1+r_2)\ldots(1+r_n)}. \quad (1)$$

If we divide equation (1) through by P and multiply by the least common denominator we obtain:

$$\begin{aligned}(1+r_1)(1+r_2)(1+r_3)\ldots(1+r_n) = {} & R(1+r_2)(1+r_3)\ldots(1+r_n) \\ & + R(1+r_3)(1+r_4)\ldots(1+r_n) \quad (2) \\ & + \ldots + R(1+r_n) + R + 1.\end{aligned}$$

Having transposed 1 to the other side and solved for R we have the Lutzian equation for the long-term rate. Notice that we have assumed that the long-term bond *is* selling *at par* — otherwise the P terms on the right-hand side of equation (1) would have to be replaced by F, the face value of the bond (see Conard (23) p. 205 and Buse (10) p. 396).

4. See Buse (10) and chapter 3 below.

5. On the Bernoullian principle of investment strategy, which really deals with risky situations, see for example Hicks (12), essay 6; Borch (13), chapter III; Champernowne (14), chapter 20.

6. In this simple way it is possible to see that transaction costs could perhaps be a factor influencing an investor to choose a portfolio that is closely related to his holding period. If we are thinking of the investor as a financial institution then the holding period may be determined by the size and structure of its liabilities. Transaction costs could then be a factor making for a situation in which the institution matches its assets and liabilities. So the institution appears to behave in the way that the Hedging Pressure Theory suggests — though for different reasons. But transaction costs are only one out of many items involved in the portfolio decision.

7. On this see, for example: Borch (13); Hicks (12); Champernowne (14).

8. This is the procedure adopted for example by Markowitz (17) and Hicks (12): a procedure that is not followed, however, by Tobin in his classic paper (18). Tobin starts from this particular function:

$$U(R) = (1+b)\,R + b\,R^2 \quad (1)$$

where U is actual utility and R is actual return from investing wealth in the the available securities. From equation (1) we then have, taking expected values:

$$E(U) = (1+b)\,E(R) + bE\,(R^2) \quad (2)$$

in our notation:

$$U_e = (1+b)\,E + bE^2 + bS^2. \quad (3)$$

Certain restrictions are placed on the ratio $(1+b)/2b$ in equations (1) and (3). Even so, this kind of utility function has been severely criticised by Pratt (20) and by Arrow (19): for there to be risk aversion on the part of an investor $b < 0$ (as can be seen directly from equation (3)). But according to Arrow, for example, equation (1) violates the 'principle of decreasing absolute risk-aversion' ((19), p. 35). He argues that the utility function should contain within it that principle; that is, as R increases (effectively, the wealthier an individual investor becomes), we should expect him, risk-averter as he is, to demand or hold (proportionately) more risky assets than he demanded or held at the lower level of wealth. For Arrow absolute risk aversion is given by:

$$\frac{-U''(R)}{U'(R)} \tag{4}$$

where the prime represents the first derivative of $U(R)$, and double prime the second derivative of that function. With the present utility function, which differs only by a constant from that used by Arrow (and by Hicks (22) in his earlier critique of the quadratic utility function), we find that equation (4) becomes:

$$\frac{1}{-\left(\frac{1+b}{2b}\right)-R}. \tag{5}$$

$U(R)$ reaches a maximum at $U' = 0$, that is where $R = (1 + b)/2b$. In the range zero to the latter U' is positive, as required. But, when R is within that range, as R itself increases the expression in equation (5) must become numerically larger; thus absolute risk aversion is an increasing function of R.

Further criticisms of the quadratic utility function, especially in the confines of a multi-period model, can be found in Mossin (21).

9. That is: $S^2 = s^2x_1 + s_2^2x_2^2 + 2\ \text{cov}_{12}\ x_1x_2$. If the returns on assets 1 and 2 are completely independent of one another $\text{cov}_{12} = 0$. Then differentiating S^2 partially, for example, with respect to x_1 yields:

$$\frac{2S\,\partial S}{\partial x_1} = 2s_1^2\, x_1$$

therefore

$$\frac{\partial S}{\partial x_1} = \frac{s_1^2}{S}\, x_1.$$

10. Proof: Let ${}_{t+1}r_t = a_1R_{1t}$; ${}_{t+2}r_t = a_2R_{1t}$ . . . ; ${}_{t+n-1}r_t = a_nR_{1t}$. We are postulating that $a_n > a_{n-1} > \ldots > a_2 > a_1 > 1$. Then expanding the product term in the right-hand side of equation (2.4.1) will result in each R_{1t} term having a coefficient greater than that on each comparable R_{nt} term. Therefore, R_{nt} must exceed R_{1t}.

11. Following the convention noted in chapter 1 of measuring yield-to-maturity on the vertical axis and time-to-maturity on the horizontal axis of a Cartesian diagram.

12. The proof of this is trivial. In equation (2.2.1) or (2.4.1) we have all ${}_{t+k}r_t(k = 1 \text{ to } n-1) = R_{1t}$. Therefore, $(1 + R_{nt})^n = (1 + R_{1t})^n$.

13. Proof:

$$(1 + R_{nt-1})^n = (1 + R_{1t-1})\,(1 + {}_tr_{t-1})\,(1 + {}_{t+1}r_{t-1}) \ldots (1 + {}_{t+n-2}r_{t-1}) \tag{1}$$

$$\left(\frac{1 + R_{nt-1}}{1 + R_{nt}}\right)^n = \frac{(1+R_{1t-1})\,(1+{}_tr_{t-1})\,(1+{}_{t+1}r_{t-1}) \ldots (1+{}_{t+n-2}r_{t-1})}{(1+R_{1t})\,(1+{}_{t+1}r_t)\,(1+{}_{t+2}r_t) \ldots (1+{}_{r+n-1}r_t)}. \tag{2}$$

The imagined conditions entail these relationships:

$$R_{1t} > R_{1t-1};\ (1 + {}_{t+1}r_t) > (1 + {}_t r_{t-1});\ (1 + {}_{t+2}r_t) > (1 + {}_{t+1}r_{t-1}) \quad (3)$$

etc. These last inequalities concern the forecasts of one-year bond rates for one, two, three . . . , years ahead of the beginning of $t-1$ *and* t. Given equation (3) it follows from (2) that $R_{nt} > R_{nt-1}$.

14. It seems that Conard ((23), chapter 13) has also *implicitly* criticised Lutz on these grounds.

15. We might begin with the arithmetic average version of the Hicksian equation, since Lutz adopted that average. This *is* a procedure followed merely for convenience. Then:

$$R_{nt} = \frac{R_{1t} + {}_{t+1}r_t + \ldots + {}_{t+n-1}r_t}{n} \quad (1)$$

$$R_{nt+1} = \frac{R_{1t+1} + {}_{t+2}r_{t+1} + \ldots + {}_{t+n}r_{t+1}}{n} \quad (2)$$

or:

$$R_{nt} - R_{nt+1} = \frac{R_{1t} - R_{1t+1}}{n} + \frac{A}{n} \quad (3)$$

where:

$$A = ({}_{t+1}r_t - {}_{t+2}r_{t+1}) + ({}_{t+2}r_t - {}_{t+3}r_{t+1}) + \ldots + ({}_{t+n-1}r_t - {}_{t+n}r_{t+1}). \quad (4)$$

Should A be very small, because rates for given future periods, *although revised* period by period, are not revised significantly and/or (as would be unacceptable to the Meiselman hypothesis) in opposite directions, then we are in a situation which approximates that Lutz utilised. Therefore we see from equation (3) that long rates will change by less then short rates will. If $A < 0$, and $R_{1t+1} > R_{1t}$, we know, although we need the geometric average Hicksian formula to prove this point, that via proposition 4a of the Hicks–Lutz model, $R_{nt+1} > R_{nt}$, With $A < 0$ it is then obvious from equation (3) that proposition 5 of the Hicks–Lutz model is a valid one in that model.

Consider now the Hicksian equation:

$$(1 + R_{nt})^n = (1 + R_{1t})(1 + {}_{t+1}r_t) \ldots (1 + {}_{t+n-1}r_t). \quad (5)$$

Then it follows immediately that:

$$(R_{nt} - R_{nt+1}) = [(1 + R_{1t})A]^{1/n} - [(1 + R_{1t+1})B]^{1/n} \quad (6)$$

where:

$$A = \prod_{k=1}^{n-1} (1 + {}_{t+k}r_t) \text{ and } B = \prod_{k=1}^{n-1} (1 + {}_{(t+1)+k}r_{t+1}).$$

Suppose, for a variety of possible reasons, A should equal B; then equation (6) can be simplified to read as follows:

$$(R_{nt} - R_{nt+1}) = [(R_{1t} - R_{1t+1})A]^{1/n}. \quad (7)$$

Given that all expected rates are positive A itself must be greater than unity. Therefore $(R_{nt} - R_{nt+1})$ cannot equal $(R_{1t} - R_{1t+1})$: the former must be lower than the latter.

16. From the Hicksian equation:

$$R_{nt+1} - R_{nt} = [(1 + R_{1t+1})(B)]^{1/n} - [(1 + R_{1t})(A)]^{1/n} \qquad (1)$$

where:

$$A = \prod_{k=1}^{n-1} (1 + {}_{t+k}r_t) \quad \text{and} \quad B = \prod_{k=1}^{n-1} (1 + {}_{(t+1)+k}r_{t+1}). \qquad (2)$$

Also,

$$R_{1t+1} - R_{1t} = \frac{(1 + R_{nt+1})^n}{B} - \frac{(1 + R_{nt})^n}{A} \qquad (3)$$

But it follows from equation (1) and expression (2) that:

$$(R_{nt+1} - R_{nt})^n = (B - A) + BR_{1t+1} - AR_{1t}. \qquad (4)$$

Under the assumptions explicitly contained within proposition 6 it must be the case that (with non-zero and non-negative future rates of interest) both A and B exceed zero; also the proposition assumes $B > A$. From equation (4) we have:

$$(R_{nt+1} - R_{nt}) = [(B - A) + BR_{1t+1} - AR_{1t}]^{1/n}. \qquad (5)$$

Given the absolute and relative values of A and B it follows from equation (5) that, since $(R_{nt+1} - R_{nt})$ must be as defined there, that difference must be less than $R_{1t+1} - R_{1t}$: therefore $(R_{nt+1} - R_{1t+1}) > (R_{nt} - R_{1t})$.
For if

$$(R_{nt+1} - R_{nt}) = (R_{1t+1} - R_{1t}) \qquad (6)$$

then, from equation (5):

$$R_{1t+1} - R_{1t} = [(B - A) + BR_{1t+1} - AR_{1t}]^{1/n} \qquad (7)$$

this equality can hold only if $A = B = 1$ and $n = 1$, conditions which either are not contained within proposition 6 or are nonsensical ($n = 1$). The alternative expression to equation (7) is:

$$(R_{1t+1} - R_{1t})^n = [(B - A) + BR_{1t+1} - AR_{1t}]. \qquad (8)$$

Since R_{1t} and R_{1t+1} will be in decimals (e.g. 0.04, not 4%, as we are considering the return per unit of money invested) we have:

$$(R_{1t+1} - R_{1t})^n \to 0 \text{ as } n \to \infty \qquad (9)$$

(with $R_{1t+1} > R_{1t}$). For the given values of A and B, therefore, the left-hand side of equation (8) will be lower than the right-hand side. Therefore, the change in the long rate, $R_{nt+1} - R_{nt}$, will exceed the (also positive) change in the short rate, $R_{1t+1} - R_{1t}$, so that proposition 6 is valid.

17. Although Culbertson (28), for example, uses (*ex post*) holding-period returns data.

18. See Kessel (30), appendix A. In chapter 1 there is an excellent summary of the work of Walker, Macaulay, etc. . . .

3 The Meiselman Hypothesis in Theory and Practice

3.1

In the previous chapter we have seen, and have constantly stressed, the need for (true) information on expected one-year market returns as a requisite for substantial empirical evaluation of the Hicks–Lutz term structure theory. Realising the crucial role that such expectations play in the Traditional Theory, Meiselman (8), in his inquiries into that theory, concentrated on 'expectations'. However he did not formulate hypotheses concerning the determination of expectations *per se*: rather, he set himself the somewhat different, but *ceteris paribus* related, task of accounting for (and, hopefully, explaining) *changes* in expectations. His work is founded on a 'revision of expectations', or 'adaptive expectations' type 'model'.

In section 3.2 we describe the ideas advanced by Meiselman on 'revision of expectations', comparing them *en passant* with previous work on the Traditional Theory. Section 3.3 is a general discussion of the nature and limitations of adaptive expectations, error-learning, hypotheses which is germane to the arguments advanced in other chapters as well as to those contained in section 3.2 itself. This is followed in section 3.4 by the results of some of our own empirical tests of the basic Meiselman Hypothesis set out in section 3.2. Section 3.5 details and discusses some of the already existing results on the Meiselman hypothesis and compares them with those noted in section 3.4. Section 3.6 discusses the implications of the Meiselman Hypothesis and of its validity for the Liquidity Premium Theory of the term structure. Then section 3.7 considers Meiselman's alternative expression of his hypothesis.

3.2

In establishing his particular test of the Expectations Theory Meiselman (8) argued as follows:

> Independent evidence of interest rate expectations is virtually unobtainable; and behaviour based on those expectations is revealed only by the phenomena we seek to explain. How then can the theory be tested?
>
> The expectations hypothesis need not be tested by relating yield curves to contemporaneous expectations. Instead *changes* in, rather than *levels* of interest rates can be related to factors which systematically cause *revisions of expectations*. . . .
>
> [(8) p. 18: italics in original]

We shall have occasion to refer to the first sentence of the second paragraph of this quotation later on. Meanwhile, given that the work of Meiselman *is* for the most part focused on examining changes in, or revisions of, previously held expectations, it is pertinent to seek an answer to this question: from whence do the *levels* of expected returns (rates) themselves materialise? For it is self-evident that those levels provide the material essential to any exercise designed to explain *changes* in expected returns. As far as Meiselman is concerned the answer does not lie in, for example, some kind of scheme based on previous *observed* market one-year rates, such as a distributed lag function of the type referred to below and in other chapters of the book; nor does it lie in the collection of information from 'the market' itself about its expectations by way of some kind of questionnaire. Rather the answer lies nearer at hand, as it were:

> . . . In some respects the task of estimating expectations for purposes of testing the expectations hypothesis is made easier because, according to the theory we seek to test, expectations are already impounded and discounted in the term structure.
>
> [(8) p. 19]

That is to say, Meiselman takes as indicators of the market's expected one-year rates, at any point in time, the 'forward', one-year rates revealed by the market itself and embodied in the *yield-to-maturity curve.* This procedure suffers from the disadvantage discussed in chapter 2, in that yield-to-maturity curves do not, in general, provide us with data on *n*-year holding-period returns. But, leaving that consideration on one side, such a step carries with it the implication, explicitly noted, of course, by Meiselman, that the 'derived forward' one-year rates are to be regarded as the *true, unbiased*, estimates of the market's expected one-year rates. This means that the forward rates, which will be calculated, if the Hicksian formula is adopted, by equation (2.2.1) (the ϕs, as we have labelled them) for given dates in the future from a particular t, are regarded as being equivalent to the expected one-year rate (the rs, as we have denoted them).

Thus, as we have already indicated in section 2.4, equation (2.2.3) becomes equivalent to equation (2.4.10). Therefore, to recapitulate, we may write, using Meiselman's notation:

$$_{t+n-1}r_t = {}_{t+n-1}\phi_t = \frac{(1+R_{nt})^n}{(1+R_{(n-1)t})^{n-1}}. \qquad (3.2.1)$$

For $n \geqslant 2$ we have from the yield-to-maturity curve a set of forward, *implied*, one-year rates, which now are to be regarded as providing us with a set of one-year *expected* rates. We shall return later in this chapter (in section 3.6) to examine the significance of this assumption that forward and expected rates are synonymous.

Having obtained 'information' on expected one-year rates in this manner, since these cannot, as we have seen, be employed to test the Hicks—Lutz theory as it should be tested, Meiselman attempted to test the theory indirectly, by setting up an hypothesis on the method by which the market revises the given levels of expected one-year rates. The method proposed by Meiselman is similar to the adaptive-expectations, error-learning models of the Cagan—Friedman ((47), (24)) type: but it differs from them in at least one very important way, namely that it starts with 'knowledge' of the level of expected rates for any period. Thus, in summary of Meiselman's approach Telser (46) has made the poignant remark that:

> I wish to emphasise that although Meiselman's model belongs to the same family of adaptive expectations as the Cagan and Friedman models, he introduces a new feature that exploits the special fact of the market revealing its expectations in the forward rates. Meiselman correctly asserts that this model can say nothing about the *level* of expected interest rates but can only tell how expectations change. Meiselman's expected rates are . . . not weighted averages of past spot rates. . . .
>
> [(46) p. 551]

As to those changes in expectations, Meiselman tells us that since we are given the data on expected interest rates in the yield-to-maturity curve we therefore need not concern ourselves with those rates:

> Rather we can observe the responses of expectations to errors which have been made in forecasting actual market rates, again within the context of the theory being tested.
>
> [ibid.]

The basic Meiselman Hypothesis can, in effect, be expressed in the ensuing fashion. From the yield curve at a given moment of time we may 'read off' a set of forward (now equal to expected) one-year rates. Thus, at time t there will be such a rate for (the beginning of) periods $t+1$, $t+2$ . . . , $t+n-1$. Or, expressing the matter in Meiselman-like terminology, we may say that there will be revealed on the market at t one-year rates expected to be in evidence, 1, 2, . . . , $n-1$, periods ahead of time t itself. Likewise, let us go backwards in time to, for our present purposes, $t-1$. At that point the yield-to-maturity curve will tell us what one-year rates the market expects will hold for periods $t-1+1$, $t-1+2$ . . .; that is, for periods t, $t+1$, . . . , $t+n-2$. Thus to put the issue in more tangible form, in, say, 1968 ($= t-1$) and 1969 ($= t$) the market will have formed expectations of one-year rates to hold at the beginning of 1970 onwards. The Meiselman Hypothesis compares the rate for a given future period expected in 1969 *vis-à-vis* the rate expected in 1968.

From such a comparison of adjacent given-period one-year expected rates we have the changes in expectations; these are the dependent variables in Meiselman's study, while the one independent variable is, in fact, the *error* in forecasting the current period one-year rate. For in period $t-1$ the market will have an expectation of the one-year rate that will obtain at the outset of period t, i.e., one period ahead. At the start of period t there will be an actual spot, observed, one-year rate, R_{1t}. Meiselman's contention is that the error-variable, causing revision to all future one-year expected rates at a point in time, t, is the difference between the actual (one-year) rate at t and the market's expected rate for t: that is, $(R_{1t} - {}_tr_{t-1})$.

Therefore, the general form of Meiselman's Hypothesis is:

$$ {}_{t+n}r_t - {}_{t+n}r_{t-1} = f(R_{1t} - {}_tr_{t-1}). \tag{3.2.2} $$

The Meiselman *a priori* expectation is that $f' > 0$. The sole cause of revision to expected one-year rates is the error-term, so that upon linearising (3.2.2), as Meiselman does, we have:

$$ {}_{t+n}r_t - {}_{t+n}r_{t-1} = a + b\,E_t \tag{3.2.3} $$

or in 'first difference' form:

$$ \Delta_{t+n}r_t = a + b\,E_t \tag{3.2.4} $$

with the additional expectation that $a = 0$. That is, if, and only if, E_t differs from zero will expected rates be revised in period t. It is equation (3.2.4), once a random error term is added to it, that forms the basis of the econometric testing of the Meiselman Hypothesis.

The Meiselman test of the Expectations Theory differs then in one fundamental respect from the previous tests, briefly commented upon in chapter 2, of the theory. It does not rely in any way on the market correctly predicting future one-year rates of interest. But it is a test that relies on yield-to-maturity curve data *and*, additionally and importantly, it is one which, again similarly to previous tests, relies on the supposition that the implied, the forward, one-year rates of interest are the market's expected rates.

It is also a test that would be ruled out *ex hypothesi* by the Lutzian interpretation of 'perfect foresight', as noted already in chapter 2. For, in such circumstances, ${}_{t+j}r_t = {}_{t+j}r_{t-1}$, for $j = 1, 2, \ldots n$. An expected one-year rate of interest for a given future period once formed is never altered.

As Telser has noted in the remark quoted earlier, the hypothesis contained in equation (3.2.4) is not exactly the same as an adaptive expectations hypothesis. The latter allows us to examine changes in expectations but, furthermore, it is initially an hypothesis about how *levels* of expectations are formed — even though conceptually it is a close relation of Meiselman's own hypothesis.

Thus consider, for illustration, Cagan's own (47) representation of an adaptive expectations hypothesis. In his study, which incidentally is unquestionably a major and scholarly contribution to the literature on money and economic activity, it will be remembered that Cagan was interested in hyperinflation and in that regard with how we might envisage measuring the *expected* rate of inflation — or the rate of change of the general price level. From the data he compiled for Austria, Germany, Greece, Hungary, Poland and Russia, he was struck by a certain pattern that emerged from them all which led him to advance one of the earliest ever *formal* statements of an adaptive expectations hypothesis:

> The expected rate of change in prices seems to depend in some way on what the actual rates of change were in the past. One way is implied by the following assumption . . . *The expected rate of change in prices is revised per period of time in proportion to the difference between the actual rate of changes in prices and the rate of change that was expected.*
>
> [(47), p. 37: italics in original]

A symbolic expression of this notion would be:

$$g_t^* - g_{t-1}^* = \lambda(g_t - g_{t-1}^*) \qquad (3.2.5)$$

where g denotes rate of inflation; the time subscripts have their usual interpretation; and an asterisk by a rate of inflation indicates an expected, as opposed to an actual, value. So, at time t the market will form a different idea of the expected rate of inflation from the one it formed at time $t - 1$ if, and only if, that view turns out to be incorrect, in that it does not exactly equal the actual rate of inflation in period t. Here is an error variable. But, unlike the Meiselman Hypothesis, an hypothesis such as equation (3.2.5) tells us something about the *level* of expectations. It can explicitly provide information on dg_t^* only if data on the levels of expectations are available beforehand. The Meiselman Hypothesis employs data on levels of expected magnitudes as we have seen; the Cagan-type hypothesis is a scheme by which those levels can be generated.

From equation (3.2.5) we can then derive this expression for g_t^*, the expected level of the rate of inflation:

$$g_t^* = \sum_{i=0}^{n} \lambda(1-\lambda)^i g_{t-i}. \tag{3.2.6}$$

If we define $\lambda \in (0, 1)$, then equation (3.2.6) states that the expected value of g is a geometrically declining weighted average of previous actual values of g (with all weights positive) — recall, in this connection, the prior quotation from Cagan.[1] As formulated in equation (3.2.6), one obvious objection that could be raised against such a suggestion is that, logically speaking, unless the time aspect of the subscripts is made more explicit (e.g. by separating them out into indicators of say, beginning-period, during-period and end-period variables), it should not include g_t, since then the present period's actual rate of inflation is being used in the computation of the present period's expected rate of inflation.

Solving the integral in (3.2.6) we end up with equation (3.2.5). This can be seen more easily in long-hand fashion if we write (3.2.6) more fully and apply to it the Koyck (32) transformation, as it is frequently called. Then, we may write:

$$g_t^* = \lambda g_t + \lambda(1-\lambda) g_{t-1} + \lambda(1-\lambda)^2 g_{t-2} + \ldots + \lambda(1-\lambda)^n g_{t-n}. \tag{3.2.7}$$

To carry out the suggested transformation we multiply equation (3.2.7) by $(1 - \lambda)$; lag it one period; take the resulting expression from (3.2.7) itself. Thus:

$$(1-\lambda)g_{t-1}^* = \lambda(1-\lambda)g_{t-1} + \lambda(1-\lambda)^2 g_{t-2} + \ldots + \lambda(1-\lambda)^{n+1} g_{t-n+1} \tag{3.2.8}$$

$$\therefore g_t^* - (1-\lambda)g_{t-1}^* = \lambda g_t, \text{ as } n \to \infty. \tag{3.2.9}$$

From whence it follows that:

$$g_t^* - g_{t-1}^* = \lambda(g_t - g_{t-1}^*) \tag{3.2.10}$$

namely, expression (3.2.5).

From the view that errors in forecasting cause the market to revise their expectations, we have a means of determining the level of expectations. From the same assumption, *given* data on expectations, the Meiselman study tests the *error-learning* hypothesis *per se.* But in that the Meiselman hypothesis concerns revisions of a whole vector of expected one-year rates as a result of *a* forecast error, it makes it impossible to devise a distributed lag scheme from it that will explain levels of expected rates.

In evaluating the kind of hypothesis advanced by Meiselman, it seems appropriate to return to the quotation from his work given at the outset of section 3.2. To repeat the second paragraph of it:

> The expectations hypothesis need not be tested by relating yield curves to contemporaneous expectations. Instead *changes* in, rather than *levels* of interest rates can be related to factors which systematically cause *revisions of expectations*. . . .
>
> [(8), p. 18]

Meiselman's view expressed in the paragraph prior to this statement, that the difficulty in testing the Traditional Theory by using data on levels of expected interest rates is that those data are invariably given to us by 'the phenomena we seek to explain', is not in dispute. It is a summary of the position we have outlined in chapter 2. However, it is not possible to support the view that the Traditional Theory can be assessed solely by examining the reasons why expectations are changed.

It cannot be denied that *if* the Expectations Theory is valid, *and* if we have to hand adequate data on expected one-year rates of interest, then if a scheme can be discovered by which those expected rates are revised period by period we have at our disposal a means by which we can forecast if, and how, the term structure of interest rates will change from one period to another. The validity of this suggestion can be proved from the discussion in chapter 2.

The essential point about the Meiselman Hypothesis is that it does rest on those two predications — that the theory is correct, and that we have access to adequate data on expected one-year rates. But even then, besides not being a direct test of the theory, the Meiselman Hypothesis is only *an hypothesis, an idea* of how expectations might change. It is one possible hypothesis — which must be evaluated empirically, and theoretically — and the Hicks—Lutz theory will not be repudiated if the Meiselman Hypothesis fails to pass an empirical test:

> . . . it does not matter for the expectational theory if the basic Meiselman hypothesis is not supported by the facts. For it is only an hypothesis — of how expectations are revised. The forward rates may well be unbiased estimates of expected rates, and also may well determine the rate structure as the Hicks–Lutz theory suggests, . . . even though expectations are not revised in line with Meiselman's hypothesis.
>
> [Ford and Dodds (5), p. 99]

One important problem with ideas of the Meiselman kind, which we shall meet again in our discussion of the Malkiel Theory in chapter 4, is that, even if they were to be direct tests of the theory under review, they are also tests of the assumptions that have been made, or hypotheses that have been advanced, to allow the theory to be tested:

> In order to carry the matter further [proper testing of the Traditional Theory], it is necessary to introduce a theory of the determination of expectations, or of changes in expectations. (This itself introduces fresh uncertainty about the results, since any consequent test becomes a joint test of the term structure theory and expectations theory).
>
> [Johnson (48), p. xiii]

What is ideally needed is a method by which levels of expectations can be generated, thereby allowing a direct test of the theory to be undertaken on the basis of the propositions or predictions that follow from the theory.[2] But if the expectations data are generated, and not market-given, then we do come up against the problem of '*jointness*'. With an hypothesis of the Meiselman kind, however, we are further removed from the theory itself and one could dispute whether or not the hypothesis is good enough ever to be classed as involving a joint test of the theory. For even if the Meiselman Hypothesis is an empirically successful one it can only tell us something about the term structure *if* the traditional theory is valid, or is accepted as being so *a priori.*

3.3

Although, to repeat the point, the Meiselman Hypothesis is not a pure adaptive expectations hypothesis, so not making it possible to generate (more useful) data on levels of expected rates, it is of that kind, and it is, therefore, an error-learning hypothesis. So, *inter alia*, it contains the advantages and disadvantages inherent in the latter. Error-learning hypotheses play an essential part nowadays in applied econometric work on expectational factors. We shall return to their role in this respect in chapter 4. At this juncture, although we have only presented scheme (3.2.6) and the Meiselman scheme (3.2.4), it seems worth our while to break off from our main task in this chapter and digress a little on the concept of error-learning models in economics.

One of the basic premises embodied in error-learning hypotheses is that the actors or agents in a given situation or experiment learn from experience. Their conception of the future is derived (almost) exclusively from history. Their search for knowledge to help them to peer into the future to try to see what it will bring sends them back in time. *Memory*, rather than *imagination*, conditions their expectations of the future; uncertainty, it is felt, can be reduced by delving into the security of the past.

Out of these ways of looking at things emerges the view that what should be foremost in the decision-maker's mind about the 'outcome' in the future is the very recent past. In that regard, how near to or far from the actual 'outcome' was the individual's *last* guess at that 'outcome'? If it was not on target, the error-learning model suggests that he will revise his expectations regarding future outcomes. More dogmatically than this, it states that the individual (or 'the market') will definitely revise his expectations if they prove to have been bad forecasts of the present. Yet further: expectations will automatically, *mechanically*, be revised downwards/upwards if they were perceived to have been too high/low. In some respects error-learning models might well be judged to be 'robot models' of human behaviour — something like the textbook classical macro-model, which when pieced together cannot prevent itself from zooming off to full employment

The individual automatically adjusts his expectations about the future if they have been found wanting by immediate experience. In this respect error-learning models are very restricting. They carry with them the obvious implications that no kind of allowance is made for the nature of the circumstances connected with the error in forecasting. It inevitably leads to the following kind of contention, which, it is a platitude to say, would gain a measure of support from a little introspection:

> It may well happen that when the market realises its error it will leave its expected rate unchanged — or even increase it — for the market will surely investigate, no matter how superficially or expeditiously this may be done, the circumstances that might have brought about the error. These economic and/or political factors will be seen by the market as providing it with information or knowledge, on which to evaluate the future: they will be as much a part of its experience and 'factual-equipment' as the error in forecasting itself. It may make the judgement that the circumstances that caused it to err at the given time were of an ephemeral nature.
>
> [(5), p. 85]

Expectations then might *not* be adjusted. Yet it is perfectly legitimate to suggest that they might be:

> For example, it could be contended that no matter how the market assesses the factors that caused it to make an error of judgement, it will fear the worst, or if we like, play for safety and make the appropriate . . . adjustment to its previous expected market rates in the belief that although it feels with certainty that the given factors have played themselves out, it had better make an allowance just in case it just might be proved wrong again.
>
> [ibid.][3]

In utilising these deterministic models we are getting close to the approach in modern psychology to decision-making and human behaviour adopted by the so-called Behaviourist School.

The latter purged:

> . . . psychology of all 'intangibles and unapproachables'. The terms 'consciousness', 'mind', 'imagination' and 'purpose', together with a score of them, were declared to be unscientific . . . and banned from the vocabulary.
>
> [(51), p. 20]

> . . . Behaviourism did away with the concept of mind and put in its place the conditioned-reflex chain. [ibid.]

That chain can be summarised in the phrase 'stimulant — response nexus'. Presented with a particular stimulus, some individuals make a particular response, such as in the mechanistic—deterministic adaptive expectations model.

We cannot push the analogy with Behaviourism too far: but it is there, and the error-learning models we employ in economics suffer from some of the weaknesses, and limitations, inherent in the doctrine of the Behaviourists. We have almost removed the mind from the participants in the financial market, either viewed separately as individuals or collectively as a market. A reflex action mechanism is postulated: there appears to be no room for thought, or imagination, to enter into the formation of expectations at any juncture.

Yet, despite their denial of the crucial mental evaluation of a given situation, and the substitution for it of an automatic adjustment process, error-learning models have played a large part in economic theory and in applied economics. They have even found their way into the psychologically based, and more introspective, non-deterministic expectational theory devised by G. L. S. Shackle (see for example (52), (53)) as a rival to the probabilistic approach to expectations and uncertainty in economics.

Inevitably, much more can be said about the nature of, and the rationale of using, error-learning models, but we shall have to let the matter rest here. But it is worth making ourselves more fully aware of the assumptions implicit in those kinds of models, whilst at the same time also acknowledging that it would be well-nigh impossible to reformulate them in a way that would still render them suitable for econometric work. Apart from the fact that they facilitate the latter, their use could be further justified by suggesting that perhaps they are appropriate expressions of changes in expectations *on the average.* On this kind of interpretation, in fact, they can be assimilated into the framework of econometric analysis.

In his work on expected rates of inflation, R. M. Solow (54), like Cagan, has adopted a simple adaptive expectations hypothesis. His remarks concerning the justification of using it have been put very succinctly, and since they are particularly germane at this point they are worth recording here:

> For analytical purposes it is natural to suppose that the currently expected rate of inflation depends systematically on past observed rates of inflation. Obviously, current expectations depend also on current events, gossip, policy announcements and political prejudices. The only way to handle such features in theory is to regard them as irregular disturbances to a systematic relation. [(54), pp. 3–4]

In other words, we can try to circumvent the problems we have noted about accepting an error-learning hypothesis by adding a random error term, u_t, to it, a term that is, in effect, an umbrella term for all the non-mechanical, impossible-to-concretise variables which, in addition to the 'error-learning variable', cause expectations to be reconsidered. This interpretation of the error-learning hypothesis is convenient for econometric purposes when we are supposing that, on the *average*, the basic error-learning mechanism is appropriate, and when any irregular, relatively minor, outside factors can be discounted on the average and subsumed in the 'error' term. On this note let us indeed pass on to considering the econometric testing of the Meiselman Hypothesis, which can now be represented as:

$$\Delta_{t+n}r_t = a_n + b_nE_t + {}_{t+n}u_t. \tag{3.3.1}$$

3.4

In the following paragraphs we shall discuss the results we ourselves have obtained from applying the Meiselman Hypothesis to data for government bonds in the U.K. and to data on government sector bonds in Italy. But before proceeding it seems appropriate to consider just what we would expect our empirical inquiries to reveal if the Meiselman Hypothesis is to be supported by the data.

To recapitulate on observations made in section 3.2, we may state immediately that the *a priori* expectation is that: (i) all the *a*s in equation (3.3.1) will be, statistically speaking, zero; and (ii) all the *b*s will be positive and statistically in excess of zero. Expectation (i) follows from two considerations: (1) we would expect that, if E_t is zero, no single expected one-year rate is revised; (2) Meiselman himself held the view that the *a*s should be zero because, given (1), his argument was that, assuming his hypothesis has good general explanatory power, in such conditions only expectations determine the term structure of interest rates. So, in his opinion the notion that the *a*s are zero rules out the existence of liquidity premiums and hence of the Liquidity Premium Theory. For his hypothesis was advanced with the dual purpose of testing the Traditional Theory *per se* and of testing it, simultaneously, against one of its major rivals, the Liquidity/Risk Premium Theory. We shall have something detailed to say on the relationship between the numerical value of the *a*s and the existence of liquidity premiums in section 3.6. For the present we take cognizance of the fact that Meiselman's hope was that the *a*s would be effectively zero.

We would expect intuitively that the *b*s would decline systematically with n, so that a given percentage change in the forecast error provokes a smaller percentage response in expected rates on behalf of the market, the further into the future are the points in time for which they are making predictions of one-year rates. L. G. Telser (46) has attempted to prove that the *b*s must follow this pattern if the Meiselman Hypothesis is to be logically internally consistent: he has suggested that, given this relationship, and the assumption that $b_1<1$, there is also a systematic relationship between the *a*s and n. That relationship is an increasing one; and in the limit the value of the constant term should be $a_1/(1-b_1)$. However, his proof seems to rest on the sufficient conditions rather than on the necessary conditions for the Meiselman Hypothesis to be internally consistent.[4]

With these kind of guidelines in mind let us now examine the empirical results of tests of the hypothesis that we have undertaken. These results come from three sets of data: (i) those constructed by J. A. G. Grant (39) for the U.K.; (ii) those compiled for the Italian bond market by R. S. Masera (9); and (iii) those that we have processed ourselves for the U.K. which are used in the three forms discussed in chapter 1 above, namely, unweighted, weighted and smoothed.

Grant's data have come in for some censure from D. Fisher (55), but it is by no means certain that Fisher's own data (56) are superior to those of Grant. But, in any case, rather than use the whole of Grant's data (stretching back to 1924) as, for example, Malkiel (11) and Buse (57) have done, we have used his data only from 1952 onwards. These data seem to be virtually free of the strictures raised against them by Fisher: they are quarterly data and they terminate in the third quarter of 1962. As we have observed in chapter 1 there are numerous difficulties with the construction of yield-to-maturity curves upon which the expected rates of interest rely, and it is almost impossible to be dogmatic about the quality of such data, but of the data published to date those of Durand [(40), (41)] for company bonds in the U.S.A., used by Meiselman himself (extended by Homer (42)), seem to be the most dubious, while those of Masera (9) for Italy are perhaps the most reliable (although they are very special and very limited data for one- to nine-year bonds). The Italian data are on a monthly basis for 1957—67 inclusive. Our own data are on an annual basis for the years 1953—71.

We shall consider the results we obtained from Grant's and Masera's data first of all. Since we have only relatively recently published these results in detail (see (5)) we shall confine ourselves to providing a summary of those results in the text, without going into the elaborate length of quoting the equations themselves.

Two sets of forward (expected) rates were calculated for both sets of data, the one based on the Hicksian, the other based on the Lutzian method.[5] Also the inertia variant of the Meiselman Hypothesis was tested for both countries using both sets of forward rates. The inertia hypothesis is of the Hickman kind mentioned in chapter 2, and it simply means that for ${}_tr_{t-1}$ we substitute R_{1t-1} in the Meiselman Hypothesis, summarised in equation (3.3.1). We may refer to this inertia 'error-term' as E'_t.

We may catalogue our findings as follows:

(1) *Grant's data for the U.K.*

(a) *Meiselman hypothesis: Hicksian forward rates.* Here n took the values 1 to 4. The simple correlation coefficient for all equations was low; and $\bar{R}^2$ was almost zero for all equations. The bs showed no pattern, though where they were significantly different from zero — they were positive and less than one. The intercept came out as zero statistically speaking, but all equations exhibited strong positive serial correlation in the residuals.

(a′) *Inertia hypothesis: Hicksian forward rates.* For $n = 1$ and $n = 2$ the results were reasonable, and considerably better than for the pure Meiselman Hypothesis (i.e. with E_t as the error-term). But the goodness-of-fit was approximately 30% for $n = 1$ and 20% for $n = 2$. Both values of b were significantly different from zero: they were positive and less than one (in neither equation was there evidence of serial correlation in the residuals). Although the constant terms were negative they were effectively zero.

(b) *Meiselman hypothesis: Lutzian forward rates.* These results were of no value: they gave no support to the hypothesis, neither did they exhibit any pattern in the parameters.

(b′) *Inertia hypothesis: Lutzian forward rates.* The outcome here was very similar to that under (b), except that for $n = 1$ a good result was obtained: but in terms of goodness-of-fit this was very much inferior to the equation for $n = 1$ where Hicksian forward rates were used (a′).

(2) *The Italian data*

(i) *Meiselman hypothesis: Hicksian forward rates.* To keep the results comparable with those for the U.K. we just let n take the values 1 to 4. For $n = 1$, 2, and 3 correlation coefficients of around 0.30 were found. But in terms of $\bar{R}^2$ the results were very poor, though they were marginally better than the equivalent results for the U.K. ((a) above). There was evidence of serial correlation in the residuals but even so, taken at their face value, the slope coefficients (except for b_4) were highly significant; *but* two of them were *negative*, contrary to expectations.

(i′) *Inertia hypothesis: Hicksian forward rates.* The results obtained gave no support worth speaking of to the hypothesis.

(ii) *Meiselman hypothesis: Lutzian forward rates.* For $n = 1$ and $n = 2$ the equations produced correlation coefficients of 0.38 and 0.61, respectively ($\bar{R}^2$s of 0.14 and 0.37); but these were *negative* correlations. The intercepts came out at zero, and the slope coefficients were significantly different from zero, but were negative.

(ii′) *Inertia hypothesis: Lutzian forward rates.* Again for $n = 3$ and $n = 4$ the results were worthless. However, for $n = 1$ and $n = 2$ the results were similar to those under (ii). The slope coefficients came out as negative (they had high t values, though there was evidence of positive auto-correlation of the residuals). The intercepts were positive now, however; and the relationship between goodness-of-fit of the two equations was the reverse of that in (ii). Here for $n = 1$ the correlation coefficient was 0.55 ($\bar{R}^2$ of 0.30) whilst for $n = 2$ it was 0.36 ($\bar{R}^2$ of 0.12).

These results speak for themselves: considered *in toto*, in the light of the remarks we made at the outset of this section, they offer no support for the Meiselman Hypothesis *per se*, neither do they suggest it is a superior specification to the inertia hypothesis. The results appear to be sensitive to the type of forward rate employed; but they do not show any evidence that they are *systematically* affected by the length of data period being used.

There still remains in the background the question of how the original data have been compiled and how sensitive the results are to the methods that have been adopted to calculate the yield-to-maturity data. A striking illustration of just how important the choice of method can be is provided by the statistical results we found for the Meiselman Hypothesis and the inertia variant of it from our own data for the U.K. Since these results have not appeared elsewhere we have provided them in full in the tables 3.4.1 to 3.4.4 below. We have omitted the equations that were based on Lutzian forward rates; and we have also not quoted the findings that emerged from using the weighted data. The latter produced results almost identical with, though very marginally better than, those produced by using the unweighted data.

In presenting the econometric results in this book we have followed our normal practice. So the standard errors of given parameter estimates appear under those estimates, and the statistical significance of the estimates is indicated by the following system of asterisks: one indicates that the estimate is significant at the one per cent level and better; two that it is significant at the five per cent level and better; and three related to the ten per cent level. R^2 is the coefficient of determination; $\bar{R}^2$ is that coefficient adjusted for degrees of freedom; r is the simple correlation coefficient; d is the Durbin—Watson statistic used to test for serial correlation in the residuals; and ρ is Orcutt's coefficient being the value of ρ in a first order auto-regressive scheme of the actual residuals u_t in the equation $u_t = \rho u_{t-1} + \epsilon_t$, where ϵ_t is a random error term.

In table 3.4.1 we have presented the results for the Meiselman Hypothesis on the unweighted data. These results speak for themselves. They exhibit no systematic, coherent support for the hypothesis; there is, in fact, only one equation of any substance, that for $n = 1$. Even there the power of the hypothesis is not very high. We have not quoted here the F-statistic which indicates the significance of the goodness-of-fit of each equation: but it is apparent from the table that the only equation where that fit was significantly different from zero is that for $n = 1$.

Table 3.4.2 is the companion to table 3.4.1, containing the results for the inertia hypothesis. The latter did not prove very successful,

Table 3.4.1 Meiselman hypothesis: unweighted annual U.K. data, Hicksian rates

Equation no.	Value of n	Intercept	Slope coefficient	r	$\bar{R}^2$	d	ρ
3.4.1	1	0.*4295 (0.211)	0.*4630 (0.231)	0.4593	0.158	1.634	0.167
3.4.2	2	0.*5081 (0.248)	0.3209 (0.272)	0.2915	0.024	1.316	0.256
3.4.3	3	−0.0414 (0.362)	0.4870 (0.397)	0.3016	0.031	2.194	−0.439
3.4.4	4	0.0464 (0.407)	0.6197 (0.447)	0.3376	0.055	1.538	−0.199
3.4.5	5	0.3431 (0.531)	0.5015 (0.581)	0.2167	−0.016	0.825	0.798
3.4.6	6	0.0999 (0.522)	0.0789 (0.572)	0.0316	−0.065	1.645	0.123
3.4.7	7	0.8913 (0.484)	0.6377 (0.530)	0.2966	0.027	1.520	0.208
3.4.8	8	0.2823 (0.281)	0.0245 (0.308)	0.02	−0.066	1.802	0.019
3.4.9	9	0.4872 (0.355)	0.3099 (0.389)	0.2024	−0.023	1.717	0.094

Table 3.4.2 Inertia hypothesis: Unweighted annual U.K. data, Hicksian rates

Equation no.	Value of n	Intercept	Slope coefficient	r	$\bar{R}^2$	d	ρ
3.4.10	1	0.1932	0*.4340	0.5357	0.240	2.281	−0.153
		(0.201)	(0.177)				
3.4.11	2	0.3466	0.2933	0.3316	0.051	1.841	−0.073
		(0.245)	(0.215)				
3.4.12	3	−0.3730	0*.7334	0.5656	0.275	1.931	−0.275
		(0.314)	(0.276)				
3.4.13	4	−0.2875	0.6397	0.4335	0.134	0.877	0.656
		(0.391)	(0.343)				
3.4.14	5	0.1308	0.3246	0.1760	−0.034	1.202	0.160
		(0.537)	(0.471)				
3.4.15	6	0.0383	0.1454	0.0836	−0.060	1.605	0.149
		(0.522)	(0.458)				
3.4.16	7	0.5958	0.4980	0.2880	0.022	1.719	0.099
		(0.486)	(0.427)				
3.4.17	8	0.1398	0*.4937	0.5157	0.217	1.934	−0.013
		(0.241)	(0.212)				
3.4.18	9	0.2691	0.4904	0.3962	0.101	1.988	−0.097
		(0.334)	(0.293)				

but we can observe that it turned out to be better than the Meiselman Hypothesis. There were significant relationships for n equals 1, 3, 4, 8, 9; in all those equations the constant term was effectively zero, and the slope coefficient was positive. There is no pattern to the slope coefficients or the simple correlation coefficients.

When we move to tables 3.4.3 and 3.4.4, which are based on the smoothed data, the results take on an entirely new appearance and the situation changes dramatically. The Meiselman Hypothesis now looks quite powerful, and it has the edge, albeit only slightly, over the inertia hypothesis. For both hypotheses the slope coefficients are all less than one, positive, and decline as n increases. For the Meiselman Hypothesis; save for $n = 1$, all the intercepts are positive, and significantly different from zero, statistically speaking; while they also increase with n, as Telser (46) believed they should. In the inertia equation, however, the intercepts are all statistically speaking zero.

In the light of these empirical observations, which at best, save for the U.K. smoothed data results, could be described as agnostic, and which, bearing in mind those results, raise a query about the susceptibility of the hypotheses to the nature of the data used, a reasonable conclusion would seem to concur with the suggestion of

Table 3.4.3 Meiselman hypothesis: smoothed annual U.K. data, Hicksian rates

Equation no.	Value of n	Intercept	Slope coefficient	r	$\bar{R}^2$	d	ρ
3.4.19	1	0.1574 (0.099)	0*.7685 (0.097)	0.8921	0.783	1.897	0.040
3.4.20	2	0*.2400 (0.109)	0.6671 (0.107)	0.8420	0.691	2.796	−0.410
3.4.21	3	0*.2591 (0.108)	0*.6209 (0.106)	0.8264	0.663	2.512	−0.279
3.4.22	4	0.1920 (0.099)	0*.5748 (0.097)	0.8282	0.666	1.883	0.022
3.4.23	5	0*.2641 (0.097)	0*.5660 (0.095)	0.8300	0.669	1.921	−0.098
3.4.24	6	0*.2303 (0.104)	0*.5156 (0.102)	0.7842	0.591	1.642	0.096
3.4.25	7	0*.2875 (0.101)	0*.5026 (0.099)	0.7842	0.590	1.441	0.136
3.4.26	8	0*.2914 (0.108)	0*.4469 (0.106)	0.7259	0.498	1.620	0.104
3.4.27	9	0*.3047 (0.114)	0*.4235 (0.112)	0.6884	0.441	1.481	0.203

Table 3.4.4 Inertia hypothesis: smoothed annual U.K. data, Hicksian rates

Equation no.	Value of n	Intercept	Slope coefficient	r	$\bar{R}^2$	d	ρ
3.4.28	1	−0.1032 (0.107)	0.7622 (0.105)	0.8757	0.752	2.621	−0.329
3.4.29	2	0.0227 (0.130)	0*.6150 (0.128)	0.9687	0.565	2.694	−0.363
3.4.30	3	0.0566 (0.126)	0*.5734 (0.124)	0.7556	0.544	2.480	−0.277
3.4.31	4	−0.0016 (0.106)	0*.5634 (0.104)	0.8037	0.623	2.256	−0.155
3.4.32	5	0.0756 (0.108)	0*.5433 (0.106)	0.7886	0.599	1.996	−0.093
3.4.33	6	0.0555 (0.107)	0*.5116 (0.106)	0.7707	0.568	1.904	−0.009
3.4.34	7	0.1216 (0.112)	0*.4746 (0.110)	0.7328	0.508	1.544	0.136
3.4.35	8	0.1410 (0.112)	0*.4370 (0.111)	0.7028	0.462	1.758	0.055
3.4.36	9	0.1639 (0.120)	0*.4052 (0.118)	0.6519	0.389	1.556	0.186

A. Buse (10), that Telser (46) is 'somewhat premature' in making this kind of judgement on the Meiselman Hypothesis:

> The most challenging task for future research on the term structure of rates is the extension of the expectations model so as to incorporate the effects of other variables that might affect expectations in addition to the forecast error . . . . A preliminary approach would examine the residuals of the existing Meiselman regressions with a view to finding hints on left-out expectational variables.
>
> [(46) p. 560]

The kind of evidence on which Telser was basing this conclusion will be the subject of the next section of this chapter. It does offer much more support for the Meiselman Hypothesis than we have found, except in table 3.4.3. But our evidence indicates that the hypothesis might well have very little to offer us, so that in examining the residuals we are looking for an entirely new set of explanatory variables, and not just for some variables that can be employed in addition to the Meiselman 'error-term'. But the success of the hypothesis could well depend crucially upon the kind of yield data used, and the way the forward rates are calculated. There is an added difficulty, of course, that should always be borne in mind, namely that those forward rates, even on the assumption that expected rates equal forward rates, are only approximations to those expected rates when they are calculated by the Hicksian and Lutzian methods.

3.5

We turn our attention now to the empirical results on Meiselman's hypothesis that have been obtained by other researchers. In discussing these results we feel that it will be easier for the reader to follow if we provide details of them in tabulated form, largely as they were presented by the researchers themselves, together with our comments on them, rather than just giving a synopsis of them.

We begin, appropriately, with Meiselman's tests of his own hypothesis. These were based mainly on the data compiled by David Durand (40) on U.S. corporate bonds on an annual basis — and from those data the one-year forward rates were derived via the Hicksian formula only. The results of these tests are catalogued in table 3.5.1 (see (8), table 1, p. 22).

Table 3.5.1 The results of Meiselman's tests of his hypothesis on annual U.S.A. corporate bond yield data (1901–54)

n	a*	b	r
1	0.00 (0.02)	0.703	0.952
2	0.00 (0.03)	0.526	0.867
3	-0.01 (0.04)	0.403	0.768
4	-0.02 (0.04)	0.326	0.682
5	-0.02 (0.04)	0.277	0.642
6	-0.01 (0.03)	0.233	0.625
7	-0.02 (0.03)	0.239	0.631
8	0.01 (0.03)	0.208	0.590

*Standard errors of a are in parentheses.
Source: (8), p. 22.

The overall picture that can be gathered from table 3.5.1 is of a better set of results than those we have found for U.K. and Italian government bond data using Hicksian forward rates. The b coefficients are all positive; while the values of a are all absolutely small and are statistically speaking zero at the 1% level of confidence or better. The values of b are a declining function of n; so likewise are the correlation coefficients. All these correlation coefficients of Meiselman are significantly different from zero.

However, because of this, even the *prima facie* excellent results achieved by Meiselman himself lose some, if not much, of their claim to our attention when we contemplate fully the nature of these characteristics that they exhibit. For unless the hypothesis can account for a substantial percentage of the revisions that occur in given expected one-year rates then it cannot be of much help in telling us how and by how much the yield curve will alter period by period — even if the Expectations Theory is regarded as being inviolate. We perceive from table 3.5.1 that the Meiselman Hypothesis accounts for only 36–50% of the changes that occur in the one-year expected rates for $n \geqslant 3$.

All these observations have been made without any reference to the data employed by Meiselman, which are probably the weakest that exist in the literature on the term structure. Durand himself was fully aware, as we have indicated in chapter 1 above, of the quality of his data and never intended them to be employed in the present kind of inquiry. Nevertheless, Meiselman's results prompted a good deal of discussion of his data as well as of his methodology. Of those who challenged his data two at least were motivated to produce their own sets of observations on the term structure. These commentators were A. Buse (57) and J. A. G. Grant (39).

Buse's criticism of Meiselman's own tests is one which is general in that, in Buse's opinion, it applies to all Meiselman-type tests if the data being employed are of a special form. In effect, Buse argued that since the yield-curve data presented by Durand were obtained by smoothing the yield curves they bias the empirical results in favour of the hypothesis.[6] His conclusion was that the Meiselman results reported in table 3.5.1 above (i.e. the pattern of the *b*s, *r*s, etc.):

> . . . are implied by any set of smoothed yield curves in which short-term interest rates have shown a greater variability than long-term rates.
>
> [(57), p. 49]

Thus:

> For any given yield curve, there is a set of associated forward rates which can be graphed in conjunction with that yield curve. The dependent variable of the Meiselman model . . . is the difference between two such sets of forward rates, one of which has been moved one unit along the horizontal axis of the yield-time co-ordinates. In order for this difference to decline systematically, given the error of prediction, the yield curve must conform to a particular pattern. Not surprisingly, this pattern turns out to be a relatively smooth yield curve.
>
> [(57), p. 54]

Recall that the Durand data were as Buse reiterates 'specifically smoothed to ensure uniform changes in the first and second differences' along the yield-to-maturity curves. Buse's contention is then self-evident. Even if we ignore the fact that the Durand data are yields-to-maturity etc., this specific way in which he derived his yield curves themselves biases the results in favour of the Meiselman Hypothesis.

However, although as it happens the impression is formed from Durand's own work that his smoothing technique produces only rough-and-ready yield curves, designed to give an overview of the structure of bond yields, two things must be brought to our attention. The one is that, as already acknowledged, the Durand data were never meant to be the foundation for the kind of rigorous, systematic testing executed by Meiselman and his followers. The other is that it might well have been the case that the smoothing technique adopted produced yield-to-maturity curves that would have been observed if yields *had been available* on bonds of all lives-to-maturity. This last point, trivial as it is, should always be borne in mind, though our own results in section 3.4 provide *prima facie* evidence in support of Buse's thesis.

Buse produced some data of his own for yields on British government securities for the period 1933—63. The data are averages for January of each year: but they are not published by Buse so no details of what the data are, how reliable they might be, how relevant they are for an inquiry into the *term* structure, can be given. However, from what Buse has said the data are yield-to-maturity data; and he does also state explicitly that:

> . . . in the present study the term structure was taken from a smooth freehand 'best fit' curve drawn through the observed yields.
>
> [(57), p. 53]

Anyway, leaving aside the question of data, Buse's results on the Meiselman Hypothesis are catalogued in table 3.5.2. These results differ from those originally published by Buse in 1967 (57) and they are derived from Buse's 1970 paper (10). The later results are identical with the earlier results, apart from rounding effects, save in one respect. Buse indicates that the standard errors of the *a*s were incorrectly calculated in the 1967 paper: the correct standard errors of the *a*s and *b*s appear in parentheses in table 3.5.2. In the 1967 paper all the *a*s were significantly different from zero at the 1% level or better. It will be seen from the table that for $n = 1$ to 6 inclusive the correlation coefficients obtained by Buse are (marginally) better than those obtained by Meiselman. r (or R^2) is again a declining function of n (up to $n = 8$); the values of b decline as n increases up to that limit. All *b*s are again positive (and, of course, significantly different from zero). *But* all the *a*s differ numerically, and some statistically, from zero. In effect, for $n = 10$, 12 and 14, a is significantly different from zero at the 1% level or better; whilst the *a*s for $n = 3$, 5, 6 and 8 are significant at the 5% level or better. Recall that for $n = 1$ to 8 inclusive Meiselman found that a was effectively zero. Now Buse's (1970) finding is that for half of the range of n considered by Meiselman a can be regarded as being different from zero. So, even if there is no error in forecasting the present period's one-year rate, the market will adjust its vector of one-year expected

Table 3.5.2 The results of Buse's (1967 revised) test of the Meiselman hypothesis: U.K. annual data (1933—63)

n	a	b	R^2	d
1	0.117 (0.056)	0.919 (0.06)	0.892	1.78
2	0.183 (0.071)	0.755 (0.076)	0.778	2.34
3	0.140 (0.078)	0.592 (0.083)	0.642	2.19
4	0.177 (0.079)	0.548 (0.085)	0.6	2.2
5	0.173 (0.091)	0.486 (0.098)	0.469	2.04
6	0.143 (0.088)	0.419 (0.094)	0.415	2.15
7	0.184 (0.088)	0.359 (0.094)	0.342	1.99
8	0.134 (0.091)	0.31 (0.098)	0.263	2.04
9	0.21 (0.095)	0.384 (0.102)	0.334	2.13
10	0.258 (0.082)	0.352 (0.089)	0.362	1.97
11	0.216 (0.08)	0.298 (0.086)	0.299	2.04
12	0.23 (0.08)	0.368 (0.086)	0.394	1.97
13	0.232 (0.086)	0.29 (0.092)	0.262	1.75
14	0.262 (0.089)	0.313 (0.096)	0.277	1.86

Source: (10), p. 404.

rates by some constant (for $n = 1$, 5, 6 and 8) at each point in time. Numerically the *a*s do not even follow the Telser pattern.

Buse's 1967 paper was partly a critique of the first test of the Meiselman ideas applied to U.K. data, namely that by Grant (39). Grant's aim was to test the hypothesis on 'more reliable' data, compiled by himself from yield curves constructed for the U.K. over the period 1924—62. Grant's results for the Meiselman Hypothesis using Hicksian forward rates are given in table 3.5.3. They cover the *whole* of his data period. Grant does not indicate whether the *a*s are significantly different from zero or not. Again, for the *whole* of the period 1924—62 Grant tested the inertia version of the Meiselman Hypothesis. His findings are reported in table 3.5.4.

Table 3.5.3 The results of Grant's test (1924—62) of the pure Meiselman hypothesis

n	*a*	*b*	*r*
1	0.86	1.49	0.64
2	1.23	1.93	0.44
3	0.57	1.35	0.62
4	1.17	2.2	0.43

Source: (39), p. 62.

Table 3.5.4 The results of Grant's test (1924—62) of the inertia variant of the Meiselman hypothesis

n	*a*	*b*	*r*
1	1.14	0.82	0.894
2	1.56	0.7	0.812
3	1.31	0.81	0.827
4	1.91	0.7	0.795
5	2.68	0.52	0.638
6	2.73	0.52	0.638
7	2.49	0.58	0.704
8	2.23	0.7	0.809
9	2.18	0.7	0.827

Source: (39), p. 65.

Comparing the equation for a given n, we perceive that the inertia hypothesis is of significantly more value than is the pure Meiselman Hypothesis. For either version of the hypothesis there is no systematic relationship between r and n, there being no such relationship between b and n. The as also fluctuate wildly in value, and are numerically quite large (save for $n = 1$ and 3 for the pure variant of the hypothesis).

In toto the Grant results provide no worthwhile evidence in favour of the pure Meiselman Hypothesis. But Grant's data too came in for some criticism from Buse and from Fisher, as already pointed out in section 3.4. Grant, remember, constructed his yield-to-maturity curves by linear interpolation (between the observed yields); and some of the objections to the reliability of his data on this count, and on others, for the *whole* of his period do seem to have some weight. However from 1952 onwards his data are reasonably free from criticism; and this is why, as indicated in section 3.4, we have used Grant's U.K. data for 1952—62. The results we have presented in section 3.4, for either Hicksian or Lutzian forward rates, bear out the kind of results Grant obtained for the whole of the period 1924—62: but our results, on hopefully more reliable data, lend even less support to the Meiselman Hypothesis.

The apparent deficiencies in the Grant data prompted Fisher (56) to construct *his* own set of data for government bonds in the U.K., on a quarterly basis for the period 1951—63. One advantage of Fisher's method of constructing his yield-to-maturity curves is that it allows us to indicate the effect of the coupon rate on yields. For in looking at the *term* structure, it will be remembered, we should be comparing the yields or returns from a group of bonds which differ

Table 3.5.5 The results of Fisher's test of the pure Meiselman hypothesis

n	a	b	R^2
2	0.003 (0.036)	0.834	0.931
3	0.007 (0.033)	0.735	0.880
4	0.011 (0.050)	0.647	0.810
5	0.018 (0.058)	0.566	0.706
6	0.028 (0.067)	0.49	0.576
7	0.041 (0.075)	0.44	0.44
8	0.057 (0.084)	0.358	0.313
9	0.076 (0.095)	0.304	0.206

Note: Fisher's results all run from $n = 2$. He stated that this was the 'first non-trivial' case of the Meiselman hypothesis. But this is incorrect.
Source: (56), p. 324.

only in that they have differing terms-to-maturity, their coupons, for example, being identical. For a coupon of 2.5%, namely that on British government Consols, the statistical findings of Fisher are set out in tables 3.5.5 and 3.5.6, the latter being based on the inertia equivalent of the Meiselman Hypothesis. Again, as with Buse's annual results for the U.K. *prima facie*, Fisher's results provide substantial support for the hypothesis, and the pure Meiselman Hypothesis outdoes the inertia version of the hypothesis.

If we consider table 3.5.5 first of all we may note that: the *a*s are effectively zero (but numerically they support Telser's contention); the *b*s are positive and decline systematically as n increases; and the values of R^2 follow an identical pattern. The same kind of pattern emerges when we examine table 3.5.6, except that there, two of the *a*s (for $n = 2$ and 3) are significantly different from zero and are *negative.* For any given n the pure Meiselman Hypothesis scores marginally over the inertia hypothesis.

The tests reported on so far in this section: (i) are based on Hicksian forward rates; and (ii) where they apply to the U.S.A. are dependent upon the Durand data. Other results have been obtained:

Table 3.5.6 The results of Fisher's test of the inertia variant of the Meiselman hypothesis

n	a	b	R^2
2	-0.14 (0.05)	0.808	0.869
3	-0.117 (0.055)	0.707	0.808
4	-0.098 (0.061)	0.615	0.726
5	-0.076 (0.067)	0.530	0.615
6	-0.053 (0.074)	0.452	0.487
7	-0.027 (0.082)	0.381	0.360
8	0.0 (0.089)	0.320	0.249
9	0.028 (0.1)	0.269	0.160

Source: (56), p. 325.

(a) by utilisation of Lutzian forward rates, as already noted, by Buse for the U.K. on his own data and for the U.S.A. on Durand's data; and (b) on data taken from U.S. Treasury yield curves, using the Hicksian forward rates, by for example, J. Van Horne (59), and R. Kessel (30).[7]

If we take the Buse results first, those for the U.K. are presented in table 3.5.7 which is the companion table to 3.5.2. The pattern that emerges from the substitution of Lutzian for Hicksian forward rates is very similar to that which emerges from the use of the Hicksian rates themselves. However, all fourteen equations are significant at the 1% level or better when the Hicksian forward rates are used, whereas with Lutzian rates the equations for $n = 8$, 11, 13 and 14 are not significant at that level. In addition those for $n = 13$ and 14 are not significant at the 5% levels. Only four of the *a*s, for $n = 2$, 10, 12 and 14, are significant at the 5% level or better; no single a is significant at the 1% level or better. Over all, the Lutzian results compare closely to those Meiselman obtained himself: but they are not as good as those derived from use of Hicksian forward rates.

Table 3.5.8 contains the results obtained by Buse on Durand's corporate bond data by utilising Lutzian forward rates. The counterparts to these findings can be located in table 3.5.1. As with

Table 3.5.7 The results of Buse's test of the Meiselman hypothesis (Lutzian forward rates), U.K. annual data (1933–63)

n	a	b	R^2	d
1	0.113 (0.058)	0.923 (0.062)	0.887	1.75
2	0.175 (0.074)	0.754 (0.079)	0.766	2.36
3	0.124 (0.081)	0.582 (0.087)	0.616	2.2
4	0.158 (0.084)	0.536 (0.089)	0.563	2.21
5	0.152 (0.098)	0.468 (0.105)	0.416	2.04
6	0.113 (0.095)	0.39 (0.101)	0.345	2.18
7	0.156 (0.097)	0.319 (0.103)	0.254	2.04
8	0.093 (0.103)	0.259 (0.11)	0.166	2.11
9	0.184 (0.11)	0.347 (0.118)	0.237	2.2
10	0.243 (0.097)	0.303 (0.104)	0.234	2.09
11	0.185 (0.096)	0.231 (0.103)	0.152	2.19
12	0.211 (0.098)	0.323 (0.105)	0.252	2.10
13	0.21 (0.107)	0.217 (0.115)	0.113	1.77
14	0.253 (0.113)	0.242 (0.121)	0.126	1.84

Source: (10), p. 404.

the latter all *a*s are statistically speaking zero. The pattern of the *b*s is the same in both tables. However, equation by equation, the choice of Lutzian forward rates improves the Hicksian results, contrary to Buse's U.K. government bond findings.

Van Horne's (59) results, based on yield-curve data that appear every month in the U.S. Treasury *Bulletin*, cover the period January 1954 to September 1963. They are given in table 3.5.9. Again these results follow the pattern produced by the findings of Meiselman, Fisher and Buse. But, on the whole, these equations produce correlation coefficients (statistically speaking) higher than those discovered by Meiselman, and values of *a* that are all significantly

Table 3.5.8 The results of Buse's test of the Meiselman hypothesis (Lutzian forward rates), Durand's data (1900–54)

n	*a*	*b*	R^2	*d*
1	0.0 (0.024)	0.702	0.902	1.66
2	-0.004 (0.033)	0.521	0.733	1.71
3	-0.01 (0.037)	0.393	0.555	1.79
4	-0.036 (0.039)	0.311	0.416	1.77
5	-0.021 (0.037)	0.257	0.350	2.16
6	-0.013 (0.032)	0.208	0.312	2.26
7	-0.023 (0.033)	0.213	0.314	2.13
8	0.001 (0.032)	0.176	0.244	2.41

Source: (10), p. 403.

different from zero at the 1% level or better (and do not follow the Telser pattern). The attempt by Van Horne to develop an hypothesis to account for the size and quality of the constant term has, quite rightly, come in for heavy attack by R. Roll (61). But the results detailed in table 3.5.9 remain unaffected — given that one accepts the data that have been used.

The data used by R. A. Kessel (30) were in fact data on U.S. Treasury bills with less than six months to maturity, and they were for the period 1958–61. The results quoted by Kessel are not given in any detail and they arise *en passant* in his researches on the Liquidity Premium Theory of the term structure, which we shall discuss in depth in chapter 5. There we note that the forward rates calculated by Kessel with which to test the Meiselman Hypothesis are derived from the arithmetic average rather than the geometric average version of Hicks's formula. Kessel ran five regressions on the Meiselman Hypothesis; only one of the correlations, however, was positively high (of the order of 0.85), and the support for the hypothesis was not as strong as Kessel felt it was. The five correlation coefficients were: 0.37, 0.36, 0.21, 0.59 and 0.85. The slope coefficients were: 0.40, 0.26, 0.27, 0.62, and 0.59, respectively. This is all the statistical information provided by Kessel. Such as it is, we

Table 3.5.9 The results of Van Horne's test of the Meiselman hypothesis, U.S.A. Treasury Bulletin data (1954—63)

n	*a*	*b*	*r*
January 1954—September 1963			
1	0.228 (0.02)	0.798 (0.019)	0.973
2	0.276 (0.02)	0.591 (0.022)	0.934
3	0.243 (0.023)	0.434 (0.022)	0.889
4	0.227 (0.023)	0.32 (0.022)	0.819
January 1958—September 1963			
1	0.22 (0.03)	0.829 (0.027)	0.973
2	0.264 (0.033)	0.615 (0.03)	0.941
3	0.261 (0.028)	0.461 (0.025)	0.927
4	0.26 (0.028)	0.349 (0.025)	0.885
5	0.238 (0.029)	0.293 (0.026)	0.838
6	0.218 (0.024)	0.231 (0.022)	0.821
7	0.209 (0.022)	0.206 (0.02)	0.814
8	0.189 (0.019	0.174 (0.017)	0.811
9	0.166 (0.018)	0.175 (0.016)	0.828
10	0.142 (0.02)	0.154 (0.018)	0.758
11	0.135 (0.02)	0.149 (0.077)	0.757

Source: (59), p. 346.

can see that it does not offer much hope for the supporters of the Meiselman Hypothesis.[8]

This completes our appraisal of the existing studies of the Meiselman Hypothesis. We shall endeavour to draw some conclusions from our discussions in the next section and in the concluding section (3.8) of this chapter.

3.6

In the previous sections we have continually raised the question of the significance that might attain to a particular numerical value of the *a*s being realised from the Meiselman-type regressions. We must now discuss this matter, which inexorably brings us into contact with the Liquidity Premium Theory, which we shall examine in detail in chapter 5.

For present purposes it will suffice to state that one of the major features of the Liquidity, or Risk, Premium Theory is the hypothesis that forward rates of interest are *biased* estimates of the market's expected rates. The bias to expected rates is imparted by the risk premium which has to be paid by borrowers on long-term loans to induce lenders to part with their money and offer such loans to them.

The bare essentials of the arguments in favour of the notion of risk premiums can be crystallised in the words of J. R. Hicks (1), the chief protagonist of the risk-theory:

> . . . . Other things being equal, a person engaging in a long-term loan contract puts himself into a more risky situation than he would be in if he refrained from making it. . . . [Borrowers] will have a strong propensity to borrow long.
>
> [(1), p. 146]

But since on the supply side of the capital market 'most people . . . would prefer to lend short':

> . . . . Borrowers would thus tend to offer better terms in order to persuade lenders to switch over into the long market (that is to say, to enter the forward market). A lender . . . would only come into the long market because he expected to gain by so doing; and to gain sufficiently to offset the risk incurred.
>
> The forward rate of interest for any particular future week . . . is thus determined . . . at that level which just tempts a sufficient number of 'speculators' to undertake the forward contract. It will have to be higher than the short rate expected by these speculators to rule in that week . . .; it will, indeed, have to exceed it by a sufficient amount to induce the marginal speculator to undertake the risk.
>
> [(1), p. 147]

In terms of the algebra of the Hicksian 'equalisation theorem formula', the posited existence of risk premiums means that, for an n-year loan (or bond), there are $n-1$ such premiums; such $(n-1)$ forward one-year rates, together with the current one-year spot rate, constitute the spot rate on the n-year loan, and it means in addition that in Hicksian notation:

$$\phi_j = r_j + L_j, \quad j = 2, 3, \ldots, n \tag{3.6.1}$$

or, in Meiselman notation:

$$_{t+j}\phi_t = {}_{t+j}r_t + {}_{t+j}L_t, \quad j = 1, 2, \ldots, n. \tag{3.6.2}$$

where, as usual, ϕ is a forward rate, r is an expected rate, and L is the liquidity premium with $L_j > 0$.

In Meiselman's opinion the connection between liquidity premiums and his empirical inquiries into the Traditional Theory lay in the constant terms, the *a*s in the equation presented in previous sections:

> . . . [The *a*s] may be regarded as a reflection of the Hicksian liquidity premium. Consider $\Delta\, _{t+n}r_t$ when $n = 8$ [see table 3.5.1]. The regression equation $\Delta_{t+8}r_t = 0.01 + .208E_t$ predicts that the forward rate will rise by .01 percentage points if E_t equals zero, that is, the actual one-year rate at time t is equal to the forward rate observed at time $t-1$. Or, alternatively, the regression equation predicts no change in the forward rate applicable to period $t + 8$ when E_t equals approximately —.05. This suggests that (1) the forward one-year rate is typically greater than the expected one-year rate, (2) expectations are revised upward whenever spot one-year rates fall short of forward rates by less than .05 percentage points, and (3) expectations are revised downward when spot one-year rates fall short of forward rates by more than .05 percentage points.
>
> For example, suppose the forward rate for a one-year loan beginning at year t measured at the beginning of year $t-1$ is 2.00 per cent. The regression equation predicts that the forward rate applicable to year $t + 8$ will rise if the actual one-year rate is higher than 1.95 per cent, and will fall if the actual one-year rate is lower than 1.95 per cent. Thus the .05 per cent difference may be a measure of the elusive risk or liquidity premium. However, the standard error of the constant term is .03 or triple its value of .01. Hence the constant term does not differ from zero. Similarly, the standard errors of the constant terms of the forward rates of other maturities are also larger than their respective constant terms . . . This test does not, therefore, contradict the assumption of the expectations hypothesis that the risk premium . . . is zero.
>
> [(8), pp. 45–6]

Thus, Meiselman's argument is that if $a_j = 0$ then $L_j = 0$, for all j; therefore, $\phi_j = r_j$. It has been discovered by J. H. Wood (62) and independently by R. Kessel (30) that it is, in effect, not necessary, or sufficient, for a_j to equal zero for L_j to be also zero. To show this we may substitute equation (3.6.2) into the Meiselman equation where we are referring to changes in *forward* rates. Thus that equation is:

$$_{t+n}\phi_t - _{t+n}\phi_{t-1} = a + b(R_{1t} - _t\phi_{t-1}) \tag{3.6.3}$$

which, with $L = 0$, can be written with $\phi = r$ as in previous versions of the Meiselman equation. Upon substituting (3.6.2) into (3.6.3) we find that:

$$(_{t+n}r_t + _{t+n}L_t) - (_{t+n}r_{t-1} + _{t+n}L_{t-1}) = a + b(R_{1t} - _tr_{t-1} - _tL_{t-1}). \tag{3.6.4}$$

Therefore,

$$(_{t+n}r_t - _{t+n}r_{t-1}) + (_{t+n}L_t - _{t+n}L_{t-1}) = a + bE_t - b(_tL_{t-1}). \tag{3.6.5}$$

Assume now that expectations are fulfilled so that $E_t = 0$: then Meiselman asserts that $(_{t+n}r_t - _{t+n}r_{t-1})$ will also equal zero. Then we may rewrite equation (3.6.5) in this fashion:

$$_{t+n}L_t - _{t+n}L_{t-1} = a - b\ (_tL_{t-1}). \tag{3.6.6}$$

For $E_t = 0$ to imply $\Delta_{t+n}r_t = 0$ we know that $a \equiv 0$. From equation (3.6.6) we observe that:

$$_{t+n}L_t - _{t+n}L_{t-1} = -b(_tL_{t-1}). \tag{3.6.7}$$

Here the liquidity terms reading from left to right are for n, $n + 1$ and 1 periods ahead of point t. As is implied in the quotation from Sir John Hicks given earlier in this section, he assumes implicitly that the liquidity premiums increase the further away from the point t is a given point of time in the future. Though whether they do is a matter for theoretical conjecture and for empirical inquiry, as we shall see from chapter 5 below. Be that as it may, let us assume that the liquidity premiums are ordered in the way suggested by Hicks. It then follows that:

$$L_1 < L_2 < \ldots < L_n < L_{n+1}, \quad \text{all } L > 0 \tag{3.6.8}$$

where the time subscripts refer to 'periods ahead of t'. Substitution of this information into equation (3.6.7) means that the left-hand side of it *should* be negative; and it *is* so with b and $_tL_{t-1}$ being positive. So that equation (3.6.7) is a feasible equation — it is consistent with liquidity premiums of the form given in (3.6.8). So liquidity premiums can exist, whilst $a = 0$ in the Meiselman equation.

In general, when both E_t and $\Delta_{t+n}r_t = 0$, we have, from equation (3.6.6):

$$a = \Delta_{t+n}L_t + b\,(_tL_{t-1}). \tag{3.6.9}$$

Given equation (3.6.8), and $b > 0$ the first expression on the right-hand side of equation (3.6.9) is negative, the second expression being positive. This relationship informs us that, if it is regarded as likely that liquidity premiums, should they exist, are of the Hicksian kind, a *negative* value of a implies that *those premiums must exist.* However, we can also appreciate from equation (3.6.9) that liquidity premiums of the Hicksian kind are also consistent, with a positive value of a. It is not possible, using the Meiselman equation, to say that a given sign of a rules out the existence of liquidity premiums.

These conclusions relating the qualitative nature of a to the question of the existence of liquidity premiums have been derived from the pure Meiselman Hypothesis. If for the latter we substitute the inertia hypothesis, then the relationship between a and liquidity premiums changes, as we shall see shortly. For the present let us confine our attention to the Meiselman error-learning equation.

A cursory glance at the tables in sections 3.4 and 3.5 can give the impression that the results analysed therein provide no coherent, 'universal' evidence on the existence (or possible existence) of liquidity premiums. However, this impression is misleading if one attempts to process the results in some kind of systematic way.

The difficulty about processing such results, founded as they are on a bewildering variety of data, data periods, forward rates, etc., is that there are many ways in which it might usefully be done. One means of sifting out the results is simply to group them in terms of the length of data period on which they were based, and to evaluate the signs of the as (i.e. +, 0 or −) by examination of their statistical significance. This is the method we have chosen to consider here.

The results we shall refer to are those we have reported on for Grant's and Masera's data in the text of section 3.4 together with the findings from our own data catalogued in tables 3.4.1 to 3.4.4. The evidence on the Meiselman Hypothesis that we shall use from section 3.5 is contained in the tables given in that section; we cannot include Kessel's results because he quotes no values for a. Also we cannot refer to Grant's own results, presented in section 3.5, because he does not quote the standard errors of his constant terms.

Let us divide the data sets into: (i) annual observations; (ii) quarterly observations; and (iii) monthly observations. We shall consider these *seriatim.* On an annual basis the relevant tables are: 3.4.1; 3.4.3; 3.5.1; 3.5.2; 3.5.7; and 3.5.8. Tables 3.5.1 and 3.5.8 reveal a fair number of negative values of a. However, if we accept the standard errors as being correct, all such intercepts become zero, statistically speaking. The majority of the remaining as are, statistically speaking, positive. So for all values of n, *statistically speaking,* the Meiselman regressions reported on in this chapter cannot rule out the existence of liquidity premiums. Even if we were to ignore the statistical significance of the negative intercepts they will not enable us to say with much force that such premiums must exist. The evidence as it stands is perfectly compatible with the presence of those premiums.

On a quarterly basis the evidence is similar and quite conclusive. The quarterly results are contained in the main body of the text in section 3.4 and in table 3.5.5. The constant terms are all statistically speaking zero, with two exceptions — there is one that is positive and one (which has a suspect standard error) that happens to be negative. The evidence on a monthly basis, which is in the text of section 3.4 and in table 3.5.9, does not deny the existence of liquidity premiums.

These very definite conclusions will not be affected, however the empirical results are processed, provided that we have regard to the statistical significance of the intercepts. We pass on to see if such a positive conclusion can be supported on the basis of the regressions on the inertia hypothesis.

As indicated earlier the signs of a now have different implications than they had hitherto for the existence or otherwise of liquidity premiums. Now the companion equation to (3.6.4) is:

$$({}_{t+n}r_t + {}_{t+n}L_t) = ({}_{t+n}r_{t-1} + {}_{t+n}L_{t-1}) = a + b\,(R_{1t}R_{1t-1}). \quad (3.6.10)$$

Let it be supposed that $R_{1t} = R_{1t-1}$, then $\Delta_{t+n}r_t$ should be zero. So we can rewrite equation (3.6.10) as:

$$ {}_{t+n}L_t - {}_{t+n}L_{t-1} = a. \quad (3.6.11)$$

Should a be zero, we may draw the conclusion that all liquidity premiums must be the same, if they exist; which means, if we accept the Hicksian pattern on those premiums, that they cannot exist when a is zero. ${}_{t+n}L_t$ is the liquidity premium for n periods ahead of t, while ${}_{t+n}L_{t-1}$ is that for $n + 1$ periods ahead of t. If we accept the Hicksian pattern on liquidity premiums, as given by equation (3.6.8), then the left-hand side of equation (3.6.11) should be negative. Therefore, if $a < 0$ we may accept the contention that Hicksian liquidity premiums exist. If $a > 0$ those kinds of premiums cannot exist.[9]

The relevant evidence appears in the text of section 3.4 where we discuss the results we obtained on Grant's data and on Masera's data, in tables 3.4.2 and 3.4.4 in that section, and in table 3.5.6. So it is very limited, and for this reason we have decided to take it *in toto*; also, since the values of a assume different roles now, we have decided to tabulate the evidence on those values for the inertia hypothesis. In table 3.6.1 the denominator indicates the number of equations for the appropriate value of n. Thus for $n = 1$ we have four equations from the Grant plus Masera results (Hicksian and Lutzian forward rates), one each from tables 3.4.2 and 3.4.4. The *a*s are given a sign according to their statistical significance.

Table 3.6.1 Collective evidence on a: *inertia hypothesis, all data periods*

	Proportion of total		
n	0	+	−
1	4/6	1/6	1/6
2	4/7	2/7	1/7
3	4/7	1/7	2/7
4	6/7	1/7	0
5	3/3	0	0
6	3/3	0	0
7	3/3	0	0
8	3/3	0	0
9	3/3	0	0

This table is compiled from rather diverse results, when we think of the type of data used (with regard to both the time period of the data and their construction), the forward rates derived from them, etc., but the picture is not changed so much if the values of a are classified in other ways. For $n = 1$ especially, and for $n = 2$ and 3, the evidence is unclear; though it is saying for the most part (though there is not a great deal of evidence there) that liquidity premiums *cannot* exist. Though there is very little evidence to go on for $n \geqslant 5$, it is also saying that those premiums cannot exist.

The results on the Meiselman Hypothesis lead us to a very strong agnostic conclusion; liquidity premiums might or might not exist. The inertia hypothesis provides us with a better mechanism for seeing if those premiums — of the Hicksian kind — can exist. We have only a small sample of results on that hypothesis, but they do suggest that, *ceteris paribus*, they do not always exist. If Meiselman had been right in his deductions that, if in his equation $a = 0$, liquidity premiums cannot exist, a clearer (but by no means clear) statement could have been made on the likely presence of liquidity premiums.

3.7

The discussion so far in this chapter has centred round what we have labelled the basic Meiselman Hypothesis, either the pure or the inertia specification of it. This did not, though, constitute the only idea advanced and subjected to empirical verification by Meiselman.

The other major hypothesis tested by him was derived however from his basic hypothesis, and it followed, therefore, from the Hicksian expression of the equalisation theorem:

> Because a long-term rate is an average of current and forward short-term rates we also have the substantive hypothesis that unanticipated changes in the long-term rate are also based on errors made in forecasting short-term rates,
>
> $$ {}_{t+n}R_{jt} - {}_{t+n}R_{jt-1} = h\,({}_tR_{1t} - {}_tr_{1t-1}) \qquad [a] $$
>
> or,
>
> $$ \Delta\, {}_{t+n}R_{jt} = k\,(E_t) \qquad [b] $$
>
> where $n = 0, 1, 2, 3, \ldots$ years and $j = 1, 2, \ldots$ years.
>
> [(8), p. 20]

It is necessary to pause for a while to consider the full import of this statement by Meiselman, for it is not as explicitly expressed as it might have been, and Meiselman only proffered some rather disjointed remarks on its interpretation.

The variable E_t is, of course, the error-variable as we have defined it — the only difference between our writing of it and Meiselman's is that he has explicitly denoted the fact that the error term is concerned with *one*-year rates. It is the dependent variable that requires some comment.

Let us suppose that we are examining that variable for $j = 3$. In effect, we are looking at one type of stock, which has three years-to-maturity at all points in time. Now no matter what value we give to n the variable ${}_{t+n}R_{jt-1}$ must refer to 'the future' at the period in time at which it is 'formulated', namely, $t-1$. Furthermore if $n \geqslant 1$ then the variable ${}_{t+n}R_{jt}$ must also apply to some future period, that is $t + n$, at the relevant point in time, namely t. Therefore, although the left-hand side of both equations [a] and [b] above have been written with capital Rs, which ordinarily denote *actual* rates of interest in Meiselman's notation, only one of the variables that constitute the dependent variables of those equations, namely for $n = 0$, can ever be an actual rate of interest. All others are, basically, expected (or forward) 'long-term' rates of interest.

Thus consider the dependent variable, of [a] or [b] above, for $n = 1$ (and $j = 3$). Then ${}_{t+n}R_{jt}$ is the rate expected at t to rule the market on a three-year bond at $t + 1$; while ${}_{t+n}R_{jt-1}$ is the rate expected at $t - 1$ to obtain in $t + 1$ on a three-year bond. The variable $({}_{t+n}R_{jt} - {}_{t+n}R_{jt-1})$ then represents the change that occurs between $t - 1$ and t in the market's expectations of the three-year bond rate in $t + 1$.

The rationale for postulating equations such as [b] above then follows immediately if we return to the Hicksian formula. For, from the latter, we may write (letting $j = 3$ still), as we know from our discussion in chapter 2 of the work of Hickman,

$$ {}_{t+n}R_{3t} = [(1 + {}_{t+n}r_t)(1 + {}_{t+n+1}r_t)(1 + {}_{t+n+2}r_t)]^{1/3} - 1 \tag{3.7.1}$$

and

$$ {}_{t+n}R_{3t-1} = [(1 + {}_{t+n}r_{t-1})(1 + {}_{t+n+1}r_{t-1})(1 + {}_{t+n+2}r_{t-1})^{1/3} - 1. \tag{3.7.2}$$

Therefore, $\Delta_{t+n}R_{3t}$ depends upon changes made at the *outset* of t to the given forward rates formulated at the outset of $t - 1$. Thus if, at the beginning of t, E should be positive, the basic Meiselman Hypothesis indicates that ${}_{t+n}r_t > {}_{t+n}r_{t-1}$, etc., so that ${}_{t+n}R_{3t} > {}_{t+n}R_{3t-1}$. Thus, as with the Meiselman Hypothesis on changes in forward one-year rates, we would expect the coefficient on E_t to be positive.

The dependent variable in the long-rate hypothesis is the *unanticipated* change in the rate on a given j-year bond. 'To measure the unanticipated change requires taking the difference between the actual change and the anticipated change.' ((8), p. 23). We may carry out such a computation for $n = 0$ in equation [a] or [b] above; and the algebra of the situation shows that $\Delta_{t+n}R_{jt}$ or $\Delta_t R_{jt}$, which we have just elaborated on, is the correct specification of the dependent variable. Thus, for a j-year stock:

$$ {}_tR_{jt} - {}_{t-1}R_{jt-1} \tag{3.7.3}$$

is the actual change on it, or the change in the actual return on it, between $t - 1$ and t; while

$$ {}_tR_{jt-1} - {}_{t-1}R_{jt-1} \tag{3.7.4}$$

is the *anticipated* change in R_j. For ${}_tR_{jt-1}$ is the rate expected at $t-1$ to rule on a j-year bond at the outset of t; and ${}_{t-1}R_{jt-1}$ is the actual rate on such a bond at $t-1$. Subtracting equation (3.7.4) from

3.7.3) produces the *unanticipated* change in R_j which is:

$$ {}_tR_{jt} - {}_tR_{jt-1} \tag{3.7.5} $$

as in [a] with $n = 0$.

In testing equation [a], as with the short-rate version of it, there are $n \times j$ possible equations that can be run. One obvious method by which to reduce the computational and econometric work involved in testing the equation is to select a particular value for j, say, a value that denotes that j is a long-term stock. Such a value is normally taken to be around thirty years or over. But, having decided to select such a stock, it may not be possible to test the hypothesis because of insufficient data. Thus, suppose further that $n = 0$ has been chosen to test the long-rate hypothesis initially. Then with $j = 30$ it is necessary to have data on the thirty-one-year bond rate in order to compile ${}_tR_{jt-1} = {}_tR_{30t-1}$. In general (assuming that $n < j$), data are required on *actual* j + 1 year bonds if the long-rate hypothesis is being evaluated for a j-year bond; for any 'long-term' forward (expected) rate can be expressed in terms of two actual long-term rates. Thus, in general terms:

$$ (1 + {}_{t+n}R_{jt}) = \left[\frac{(1 + R_{j+1,t})^{j+1}}{(1 + R_{nt})^n} \right]^{1/j}. \tag{3.7.6} $$

Thus, at t from the Hicksian formula, the $j + 1$th power of unity plus the *actual* $j + 1$ rate can be written as:

$$ (1 + R_{j+1,t})^{j+1} = (1 + R_{1t})\,(1 + {}_{t+1}r_t)\,(1 + {}_{t+2}r_t) \ldots \\ (1 + {}_{t+n-1}r_t)\,(1 + {}_{t+n}r_t) \ldots (1 + {}_{t+j}r_t). \tag{3.7.7} $$

Similarly:

$$ (1 + R_{nt})^n = (1 + R_{1t})\,(1 + {}_{t+1}r_t)\,(1 + {}_{t+2}r_t) \ldots (1 + {}_{t+n-1}r_t). \tag{3.7.8} $$

Dividing equation (3.7.7) by (3.7.8) produces expression (3.7.6). Then, for given n, and j, information is required at each t on the actual $j + 1$-year rate and on the actual n-year rate. Also if we are assuming that $n = 0$ in Meiselman's equation [b] and we wanted to calculate a series for ${}_tR_{30t-1}$ over a given sample period, n in equation (3.7.6) would be one, of course.

Although he gave greatest attention to the equation for $j = 30$, Meiselman did run his regression also for values of j of 5, 10, 15, 20 and 25. However, because the Durand data are such that it is not possible to calculate the appropriate forward long-term rates, Meiselman decided to approximate the relevant unanticipated interest rate changes by *actual* changes. In the equations to be tested, to recapitulate:

$$ {}_{t+n}R_{jt} - {}_{t+n}R_{jt-1} = F(E_t) \tag{3.7.9} $$

he chose a value for n of zero, but additionally he assumed that:

$$ {}_{t}R_{jt-1} = {}_{t-1}R_{jt-1}. $$

In the light of the fact that, using Durand's data, Meiselman produces generally good results on his own short-rate hypothesis, it must be expected that any test of the long-rate hypothesis, even on the basis of a few j values and one n value, would also produce results lending some support to the hypothesis. Although his main test of equation (3.7.9) relied upon utilisation of the actual change in the j-year rates between consecutive points in time, and is therefore not one hundred per cent a test of the hypothesis, Meiselman's regression produced a fairly satisfactory outcome.

The results for Durand's annual data (1900—54) for certain selected securities based on

$$ \Delta_{t}R_{jt} = {}_{t}R_{jt} - {}_{t-1}R_{jt-1} \tag{3.7.10} $$

are catalogued in table 3.7.1. All the slope coefficients are positive, and they decline systematically as j increases — which is a result that must follow given the earlier results of Meiselman summarised in table 3.5.1 ((8), p. 28). Therefore, the correlation coefficient r declines as j increases, though not quite as systematically as with the short-rate hypothesis. Only for $j = 30$ does Meiselman indicate whether or not a and b are significantly different from zero. In fact, these coefficients in that equation have standard errors of (0.07) and (0.02), respectively, so a effectively becomes zero. Save for $j = 30$, Meiselman again provides no information on the Durbin—Watson statistic for his equations; by implication, he indicates that serial correlation in the residuals is absent when $j = 30$.

Table 3.7.1 The results of Meiselman's test of the long-rate hypothesis

j	a	b	r
5	0.05	0.48	0.87
10	0.04	0.36	0.84
15	0.03	0.30	0.84
20	0.03	0.26	0.83
25	0.03	0.26	0.83
30	0.03	0.25	0.82

Source: (8), p. 28.

Probably because he was concerned with establishing a good equation to account for revisions to what we might regard as a true *long*-term rate, Meiselman analysed the value of the equation for $j = 30$ in some depth and attempted to improve on its specification. On the whole, ignoring the data employed and the additional fact that the equation was estimated for actual changes in the thirty-year bond rate, the equation produced quite a good result and one which is supported throughout the period 1901—54 when that period is examined in detail in the light of the hypothesis being tested (just, in fact, as did this period when Meiselman examined it in terms of the short-rate hypothesis). For in such circumstances:

> The high degree of synchronization of the measured change in the long-term rate and the change in the long-term rate predicted from the regression equation can be seen in . . . table 5 [table 3.7.2]. In the small number of cases in which the long-term rate did not move in the direction predicted from the regression equation, the amount of predicted change was small. For example, in the upper middle cell are four cases in which a rise in rates was predicted but rates remained unchanged. The predicted revisions were 0.02, 0.02, 0.09, and 0.01 of one per cent. . . . *In no case did bond yields rise when a decline was predicted, nor did they fall when a rise was predicted.*
>
> [(8), p. 29: italics in original]

Table 3.7.2 Signs of predicted and actual $\Delta_t R_{30t}$

Predicted	Actual			
	+	0	—	Total
+	21	4	0	25
0	1	1	3	5
—	0	0	24	24
Total	22	5	27	54

Source: (8), p. 29.

In the hope that the thirty-year equation would improve if it were amended, Meiselman put forward the suggestion, which could apply equally well to the short-rate hypothesis where he did not suggest it, that not only might E_t influence $\Delta_t R_{30t}$, but so might E_{t-1} and/or E_{t-2}. The results were not at all satisfactory and we may refrain from analysing them.[10]

There has been very little discussion in the literature of this long-rate Meiselman Hypothesis, probably because, given the nature of yield-to-maturity curve data and so on, if the short-rate hypothesis is 'successful', so too will be the long-rate hypothesis and vice-versa. However, D. Fisher ((55), (56)) has tested the long-rate equation for U.K. Consols and for the U.S.A.; and Buse (107) has also performed some limited testing of the hypothesis.

In his critique of Grant, Fisher (55) tested the long-rate equation against Grant's data for the period 1924 extended to December 1963, with actual changes in 'the' long-rate, namely that on 2½% Consols (c) as the dependent variable. The result, quoted without standard errors or the value of the Durbin—Watson statistic by Fisher, was:

$$\Delta_t R_{ct} = 0.17 + 0.22 E_t \quad (R^2 = 0.397). \qquad (3.7.11)$$

The nearest equivalent equation in Meiselman's own work is that for $j = 30$, which, as we can perceive from table 3.7.1, produced an R^2 of 0.6724. In his later paper Fisher (56), having substituted his own 'better' data for those of Grant, improved the fit of the Consol equation. For quarterly data 1951—63 the result was:

$$\underset{}{\Delta_t R_{ct}} = \underset{(0.05)}{0.161} + \underset{(0.046)}{0.400}\, E_t \; (R^2 = 0.616). \qquad (3.7.12)$$

We have tested this same hypothesis against Grant's data for 1952—62 and Buse has done so for Grant's data beginning with 1951, and the overall results are slightly worse than that given in equation (3.7.11), as would be expected given our earlier findings on the short-rate hypothesis *vis-à-vis* those of Grant himself for the whole of his data period (1924—62).

The dependent variables in all the regression results referred to so far in this section are actual changes in long-term rates of interest. Data difficulties precluded Meiselman from estimating with complete accuracy the unanticipated changes in those rates because, as pointed out previously, it was not possible to calculate correctly the relevant *expected* long-term rates. The fact that Meiselman then decided, rather than not test the long-rate hypothesis at all, to proxy the unanticipated changes by actual changes has met with some criticism from Fisher (56).

From what we have said earlier in this section, and in particular from equations (3.7.4) and (3.7.5), it is apparent that in such circumstances the anticipated or expected change in the given long-term rate is zero. For in such conditions the rate expected at $t-1$ to apply at t is the rate that actually holds at $t-1$: so the expectation is of no change in the long-term rate. Fisher then draws from this the obvious implication that:

> ... then the elasticity of expectation [μ] between long and short rates is zero. . . . Since the Expectations Hypothesis is built on the view that μ lies between zero and one, it is clear that Meiselman would not wish to make the assumption explicitly that $\mu = 0$. The observation that it is well known that movements in long and short rates are closely synchronized provides another reason for dispensing with the same assumption.
>
> [(56), p. 328]

This point, that the Expectations Theory relies on $0 < \mu < 1$, we have illustrated throughout chapters 1 and 2: its statement in this explicit form is due to J. H. Wood (63).

It would be naive to assume, however, that Meiselman was not aware of these considerations and possible 'technical stones' that could be hurled at his assumption about the choice of actual long-term rate changes instead of unanticipated ones. Ultimately, leaving aside the purely semantic or technical arguments, the effect of such a choice from the empirical point of view is that we are confronted with a situation in which, as Meiselman himself says, 'some unavoidable errors are introduced into the calculations'.

Meiselman's contention, which has been strongly supported by Grant (64) in reply to Fisher (55), is that the errors will be small, and they will be smaller the higher is the value of *j*, the length of life of the bond being considered. Thus, to take the example of the thirty-year bond with which Meiselman was so concerned, the rate at $t-1$ expected to rule at t is found from:

$$(1 + {}_tR_{30t-1})^{30} = (1 + {}_tr_{t-1})(1 + {}_{t+1}r_{t-1}) \ldots (1 + {}_{t+29}r_{t-1}). \tag{3.7.13}$$

While the actual thirty-year rate at $t-1$ is derived from:

$$(1 + {}_{t-1}R_{30t-1})^{30} = (1 + R_{1t-1})(1 + {}_tr_{t-1})(1 + {}_{t+1}r_{t-1}) \ldots (1 + {}_{t+28}r_{t-1}). \tag{3.7.14}$$

Thus, if R_{1t-1} should equal ${}_{t+29}r_{t-1}$ the two rates — that expected to hold in t and that actually holding at $t-1$ — will be equivalent. The difference that replacing R_{1t-1} by ${}_{t+29}r_{t-1}$ makes *could* conceivably be small, so that the rate ${}_tR_{30t-1}$ could be proxied by ${}_{t-1}R_{30t-1}$.

However, we cannot judge, *a priori*, whether such an approximation will be justified. Indeed, in order that the estimates of *a* and *b* in the equation actually run should be unbiased and consistent estimates of those parameters in the 'true' relationship, we must, of course, make the assumption that the 'errors' in the dependent variable are temporarily uncorrelated and independent of E_t. But, in any case, the regressions run on $\Delta_t R_{30t}$ will probably slightly over-state the value of that relationship itself; for, as Meiselman himself has duly noted ((8), p. 24), one element of E_t, namely ${}_t r_{t-1}$, will appear as a factor in ${}_{t-1}R_{30t-1}$.

There are objections, therefore, that can plainly be levelled at Meiselman's testing of the long-rate counterpart of his error-learning model. Although they may not be too important, and could be dismissed, for almost aesthetic reasons, and to dispel any unease about the methodology of the tests, it would be more satisfactory if adequate data could be compiled to enable proper testing to be undertaken.

Fisher (55) is in fact the only researcher to have endeavoured to establish a proper test of the long-rate hypothesis. However, he too was faced by inadequate data so that what the Traditional Theory would regard as 'true' expected long-term rates could not be calculated. Therefore, he was forced to invent a method for measuring the anticipated changes in the long rate. He used the Durand data employed by Meiselman and concentrated on the changes in the thirty-year bond rate. Leaving on one side for the moment the method Fisher adopted by which to calculate the unanticipated changes in the thirty-year rate, we may note his results. They were as follows for the period 1911—54:

$$\Delta_t R_{30t} = \underset{(0.03)}{0.05} + \underset{(0.04)}{0.28}\, E_t \quad (R^2 = 0.706). \qquad (3.7.15)$$

This is the Meiselman-type equation for actual changes;

$$\Delta_t R^{u}_{30t} = \underset{(0.02)}{0.00} + \underset{(0.03)}{0.33}\, E_t \quad (R^2 = 0.706) \qquad (3.7.16)$$

where u denotes 'unanticipated'. Equation (3.7.16) is the proper specification of the long-rate hypothesis. Analysing these results at their face value, equation (3.7.15) states that some 70.6% of the actual changes in the thirty-year rate can be accounted for by E_t, while equation (3.7.16) states that 70.6% of the unanticipated changes in the thirty-year rate can be accounted for by the error-learning variable. However, in collating his data on unanticipated changes Fisher found that 52% of the actual changes in the thirty-year rate were accounted for by expectations. Therefore, equation (3.7.16) can be re-interpreted as saying that some 70.6% of 48% of the actual changes in the thirty-year rate can be explained by E_t. Thus, in total, some 85.6% of actual thirty-year bond rate changes have now been accounted for; hitherto only 70.6% could be (by equation 3.7.15).

So, *prima facie*, the choice of the actual rate changes which proxy the unanticipated rate changes does provide less satisfactory empirical evidence on the long-rate hypothesis than that hypothesis is worthy of. But Fisher's comparative results hinge upon the scheme by which he has estimated the expected interest changes from whence, with data on actual changes, the unanticipated changes can be manufactured. That scheme can be described by the following remarks from Fisher himself:

> A proxy for the anticipated change in thirty-year rates can be obtained simply by adjusting the expected change in one-year rates between periods $t-1$ and t, expected at $t-1$ by the known historical relation between one-year rates and thirty-year rates[1]. What might be called an 'anticipated change' in the thirty-year rate is obtained by substituting the 'expected change in one-year rates' for the independent variable in the moving regression. If this 'anticipated' change is then subtracted from the total actual change in the long-term rate in question, a measure of the 'unanticipated' change in the long-term rate is obtained.
>
> [(56), pp. 417–18]

Footnote [1] to this quote might also be given in full in Fisher's own words:

> [1] There are an infinity of such relations possible; a ten-year moving regression of R_{30} on R_1, using data up to $t-1$, to apply to forecasts for time t has been selected.

This is why Fisher's tests for the U.S.A. begin in 1911 and not 1900.

In some senses Fisher deserves some credit for having devised a possible means of estimating (or proxying, we would say) the unanticipated changes in the thirty-year bond rate. But as Grant (64) said in his retort to Fisher, as ingenious as Fisher's method might be it is still based upon an assumption — an assumption that the anticipated changes in the thirty-year rate are a straightforward function of the anticipated changes in the one-year rate — and this is just as difficult, if not more difficult, to accept as Meiselman's own assumption, despite the logical difficulties involved in accepting Meiselman's proxy variable.

We have performed several tests of the Meiselman long-rate hypothesis using *expected* long-term rates of interest. These tests were on our own data, since those already published are inadequate for extensive testing of the hypothesis. We ran the Meiselman long-rate regressions for $j = 5$, 10, 15, 20 and 25 for $n = 0$ and 1 (see equation [b] above); and we did so on our three kinds of data, unweighted, weighted and smoothed. As was only to be expected, the unweighted and weighted data produced almost identical results, and the smoothed data results were by far the best. This does not mean to say that those smoothed data results were good; at times they were very poor. The results are, relatively speaking, consistent with the short-rate Meiselman regressions for our data sets, but on no account are they as good as they were for the short-rate equations.

Let us now examine our findings in more detail. Remember these are true tests of the long-rate hypothesis, since they rely on the calculation of expected long-term rates. For $n = 1$ we found *no* support on any set of data for the long-rate hypothesis; neither was there any support for the inertia hypothesis (where E_t was replaced by $E'_t = R_{1t} - {}_tR_{1t-1}$). For $n = 0$, which is the value of n used by both Meiselman and Fisher, the results were more encouraging. By analogy with our comments on the short-rate Meiselman Hypothesis, we would expect intuitively that as n increases the value of the long-rate hypothesis declines. But we would not expect this to be so dramatic a decline such that, as we make the transition from $n = 0$ to $n = 1$, the hypothesis is reduced to having no explanatory value at all. The data have all been rechecked, and this is what transpired. It would lead us to cast serious doubt on the hypothesis: but this doubt is only a reflection of doubts about the overall usefulness of the short-rate hypothesis itself. For given the findings on that hypothesis on our smoothed data even, we would expect that, since its explanatory power does decline with n, and it is not very great, when we try to explain unanticipated changes in *long* rates which incorporate the changes in short rates, by the error variables, we are likely to get less success than with the short-rate hypothesis.

The regression results for the unweighted data for $n = 0$, for both E_t and E'_t, are not worth quoting. They show no support of any kind for the hypothesis, which again, to repeat the point, is not surprising given tables 3.4.1 and 3.4.3. The results for the smoothed data are catalogued in table 3.7.3 where the error term is E_t: the results for E'_t consistently, in terms of $\bar{R}^2$, were lower than the Meiselman error-variable results, as would be expected given our earlier results on the short-rate hypothesis.

The equations quoted in table 3.7.3 provide the kind of reasonable support the short-term hypothesis commanded on our smoothed data. All the *b*s are positive and significantly different from zero (though for $j = 5$ and 10 there is evidence of strong positive serial correlation in the residuals); they fluctuate quite widely however. The *a*s do follow a pattern: they increase as *j* increases.

The nearest equivalent set of results to those presented in table 3.7.3 are those obtained by Meiselman himself, which were given in table 3.7.1. Our results are less favourable than Meiselman's, for his all have $\bar{R}^2$s over 60%, and they do not exhibit a stable pattern for the *b*s.

There are no results equivalent to table 3.7.3 for the U.K. The only available results are for actual changes in the Consol rate that we have referred to earlier. Those results derived from Grant's and Fisher's data are slightly superior to those quoted in table 3.7.3 for $j = 25$, but, strictly speaking, they should not be compared with the equations in table 3.7.3.

Table 3.7.3 Meiselman long-rate hypothesis: annual smoothed U.K. data

Value of j	Intercept	Slope coefficient	$\bar{R}^2$	d	ρ
5	−0.00175* (0.0002)	0.095* (0.02)	0.523	1.306	0.342
10	−0.00111* (0.0001)	0.0698* (0.013)	0.626	1.091	0.440
15	−0.00074* (0.0001)	0.053* (0.011)	0.575	1.619	0.073
20	0.00287* (0.001)	0.405* (0.10)	0.482	1.8	−0.012
25	0.00313* (0.001)	0.340* (0.11)	0.346	1.8	−0.057

These U.K. findings are the only ones that have been obtained from using data on expected long-term rates and that have also considered values of n in the long-rate equation that are in excess of zero. They allow us to draw these kinds of conclusions:

(a) For $n = 0$ the success of the long-rate hypothesis is limited by the method that has been employed to produce the basic yield-to-maturity data. Smoothing the data increases the empirical support for the hypothesis.

(b) For $n = 1$, and probably for $n > 1$, there is no support of any kind for the long-rate hypothesis, no matter what kind of data are used, and no matter whether the pure Meiselman hypothesis or the inertia variant of it is being tested.

(c) For $n = 0$ the empirical findings all indicate that the inertia hypothesis loses out to the Meiselman hypothesis.

(d) The results (for $n = 0$) do not indicate any pattern in the *b*s though they are positive, but do indicate that the *a*s increase as j increases.

(e) Though it is difficult to compare empirical findings here, it seems that an evaluation of Meiselman's results (table 3.7.1) and our U.K. results (table 3.7.3) show that, in examining the empirical value of the hypothesis, it is important to employ the correct data, that is the expected and not the actual long-term interest rates. Such a comparison of results is perhaps not so inappropriate when we recall that the data from which they were attained are annual, smoothed data, though it is true that Durand's data are for a longer time span than are ours, and they are for corporate bonds.

3.8

We have now arrived at a point where we should summarise the findings of our discussion in this chapter, especially since we have sifted through a good deal of empirical evidence. We begin by considering the Meiselman short-rate hypothesis.

Though it will be possible to find exceptions in the previous text to the conclusions we shall now advance, it does seem that these conclusions are supported in the large by what we have said, and are therefore worth making.

(1) The value of the hypothesis does not seem to depend in any coherent fashion on the length of data period used, i.e. whether annual, quarterly or monthly data are used.

(2) However, its value does seem to depend, on occasions quite crucially, on the means by which yield-to-maturity data have been assembled. One difficulty in making such a judgement is that we are not always comparing like with like, and here our own results for the U.K., 1953—71, are particularly apposite. For they describe the results of processing a given set of raw yield data in different ways, and the end-product is that these results suggest somewhat forcefully that the data-processing method can be very important, and that smoothing the data can improve the value of the hypothesis under scrutiny.[11]

(3) Even where the data have been smoothed, the overall results do not provide evidence that the hypothesis is universally a valid or a powerful one.

(4) For the most part, however, the indication is that the error-learning mechanism of Meiselman's is superior to an inertia version of it.

(5) The results on whatever data, data-period, etc. also do not give us a firm conclusion on whether Hicksian or Lutzian forward rates are better indicators of forward rates. Given the nature of the exercise it is difficult to judge their relative merits since we are testing the hypothesis and the means of measuring forward rates simultaneously. If we bypass that problem there is some evidence that, on balance, the Hicksian rates 'perform better' than the Lutzian rates.

To turn to the long-rate hypothesis now we must make the following conclusions.

(6) How it performs in practice depends upon the nature of the yield-to-maturity data being used.

(7) In testing it as originally specified, in terms of *expected* long-term rates, it is found to perform better than the inertia hypothesis.

(8) Proper testing of it reveals that it has no explanatory power at all for $n = 1$.

(9) For $n = 0$ it performs satisfactorily on smoothed data, but on the whole it still leaves about a half or more of unanticipated changes in long rates unexplained.

In these observations we have mentioned the data problem. One additional general point is that the forward rates, leaving on one side the question of how they are calculated, may not represent expected one-year rates.

If they do not this will be — assuming that the calculated forward rates are the forward rates — because liquidity premiums exist on the market. On this issue the conclusion from the very diverse evidence assembled in this chapter must be on the whole an agnostic one. Liquidity premiums can exist, but it is not possible from the hypotheses tested to conclude, even on a *ceteris paribus* assumption, that those premiums must exist.

Notes to Chapter 3

1. For equation (3.2.6) we constrain λ to have a value between 0 and 1 so that the weights will all be *positive* and *converge*. The weights automatically sum to unity in equation (3.2.6), irrespective of the value of λ. For a general treatment of these and other issues concerned with distributed lag functions see, for example, P. J. Dhrymes (108).
2. In their work on the term structure, G. O. Bierwag and M. A. Grove (58) develop a model to explain the term structure which is based on the Expectations Theory and the Meiselman error-learning thesis (though it is claimed to be more general than the Meiselman analysis). In that model one of the concerns of Bierwag and Grove is to find a formulation by means of which they can estimate *expected* one-year interest rates. They do so by using the distributed lag specification, in which the current expected one-year rate becomes a weighted average of previous spot one-year rates.

Although this is jumping ahead of our story, we should perhaps note here that the Bierwag–Grove model focuses mainly on a Meiselman-type equation for the variable ${}_{t+1}r_t$, the latter being the one-year-ahead *forward* rate. Their model is such that equilibrium is attained when that forward rate equals the *expected* one-year rate, which has been derived as a weighted average of the expected rates of the individuals in the market, those rates having been generated by the distributed lag formulation. Though there are some differences between the Bierwag–Grove equation (of which they run three variants) and that of Meiselman, so that their results cannot be compared directly with his, the results, for Durand's U.S. data, do not provide better explanations of revisions in the one-year-ahead forward rate than Meiselman's results. Also, the regression for Grant's U.K. data performs badly compared with Grant's own results on the Meiselman Hypothesis.
3. One way to describe this would be to say that there is 'uncertainty about uncertainty' (see, for example, C. F. Carter (49)), though we would not wish to suggest here that anything like risk premiums are involved, so we have not chosen to interpret the kind of situation we had in mind in that fashion. What we say could be interpreted to mean that 'risk premiums' are present on the market, but we do not want to suggest that here; and we have no need to do so.
4. Telser has suggested that we can manipulate the Meiselman Hypothesis to indicate that its internal logic forces the *a*s and the *b*s to have these relationships with *n* and with each other. We may present his proof of those relationships, with the help of one piece of interpolation, largely in terms of his own analysis.

We begin with the basic hypothesis:

$$ {}_{t+j}r_t - {}_{t+j}r_{t-1} = a_j + b_j E_t + {}_{t+j}u_t, \quad j = 1, 2, \ldots, n. \tag{1}$$

From (1) for $j = 1$ we have:

$$ {}_{t+1}r_t - {}_{t+1}r_{t-1} = a_1 + b_1 E_t + {}_{t+1}u_t $$

or:

$$ {}_{t+1}r_t - {}_{t+1}r_{t-1} = a_1 + b_1 (R_{1t} - {}_t r_{t-1}) + {}_{t+1}u_t. \tag{2}$$

Since we can write R_{1t} as ${}_t r_t$, this becomes:

$$ {}_{t+1}r_t - {}_{t+1}r_{t-1} = a_1 + b_1 ({}_t r_t - {}_t r_{t-1}) + {}_{t+1}u_t. \tag{3}$$

But we can upgrade the *forecast period* in equation (3) by, for example, one period, so that it is $t+2$ rather than $t+1$. Doing so produces this expression:

$$_{t+2}r_t - {}_{t+2}r_{t-1} = a_1 + b_1({}_{t+1}r_t - {}_{t+1}r_{t-1}) + {}_{t+2}u_t. \tag{4}$$

We may now substitute equation (3) for $({}_{t+1}r_t - {}_{t+1}r_{t-1})$ in equation (4) to produce:

$$_{t+2}r_t - {}_{t+2}r_{t-1} = a_1 + b_1[a_1 + b_1({}_t r_t - {}_t r_{t-1}) + {}_{t+1}u_t] + {}_{t+2}u_t \tag{5}$$

$$\therefore \quad {}_{t+2}r_t - {}_{t+2}r_{t-1} = a_1(1 + b_1) + b_1^2({}_t r_t - {}_t r_{t-1}) + {}_{t+2}u_t + b_{t+1}u_t \tag{6}$$

However, from equation (1) we may *directly* write down an alternative expression for $({}_{t+2}r_t - {}_{t+2}r_{t-1})$, namely:

$$_{t+2}r_t - {}_{t+2}r_{t-1} = a_2 + b_2(R_{1t} - {}_t r_{t-1}) + {}_{t+2}u_t. \tag{7}$$

Equations (6) and (7) are the equations from which Telser draws his conclusions on the requirements concerning a and b as n increases in order that the Meiselman Hypothesis be internally consistent. This is done by equating (6) and (7), from which the conclusions can be generalised. But in writing equation (5) Telser has introduced another error term, the reason for which, be it obvious or not, escapes our notice. He writes ${}_{t+1}\epsilon_t$ for ${}_{t+1}u_t$; and in equation (7), which, we recall, follows *directly* from the basic equation which he has written as (1) above, he has the term ${}_{t+2}\epsilon_t$ rather than ${}_{t+2}u_t$. Yet in equation (4), which is the second equation in Telser's proof, an equation that immediately follows equation (1), he has the error term ${}_{t+2}u_t$ as we have it in the above.

From equations (6) and (7) he draws three conclusions on the conditions that will make them equal, as they must of course be; one of these conditions does, in fact, concern the nature of the relationship between the error terms in equations (6) and (7), which are erroneous if the error terms are written as above, which it seems they should be. These three conditions Telser states in this way:

> Equations [6] and [7] are mutually consistent provided
>
> $$a_2 = a_1(1 + b_1),$$
> $$b_2 = b_1^2,$$
> $$_{t+2}\epsilon_t = {}_{t+2}u_t + b_1 {}_{t+1}\epsilon_t$$
>
> The algebra for the general case is similar and straightforward. It gives
>
> $$a_n = a_1(1 - b_1^n)/(1 - b_1), \tag{i}$$
> $$b_n = b_1^n, \tag{ii}$$
> $$_{t+n}\epsilon_t = {}_{t+n}u_t + b_1 {}_{t+n-1}u_t + \ldots + b_1^n {}_{t+1}\epsilon_t$$
>
> [(46) p. 554]

Acceptance of these findings would have implications for a and b. First, they show that the bs should decline systematically as n increases. Secondly, they reveal that there is a relationship between the as and the bs, given by [i]. From [ii] with $b_1 < 1$, we observe that as $n \to \infty$, $b_n \to 0$. Therefore from [i], as $n \to \infty$, $a_n \to a_1/(1 - b_1)$. That is, as n increases the as should increase in value until, in the limit, they reach a value of $a_1/(1 - b_1)$.

Following the kind of procedure outlined above for $n = 2$ for other values of n it is a simple matter to show that [i] and [ii] are correct; but the last coefficient in the error term equation should be b_1^{n-1}. If we keep to the formulation of the random error term as given in (1) the Telser conditions regarding the relationship between the error term in ${}_{t+n}\epsilon_t$ reduce to the condition that they are all zero.

Let us ignore the interpretation of the error terms and look at the case where $n = 2$, by means of equations (6) and (7). The conditions relating the constant terms to each other and those relating the slope coefficients to each other are *sufficient* conditions for the two equations to be consistent with each other. If we fix values for a_1 and b_1, given the dependent and independent variables — ignoring the random disturbance terms for simplicity — we basically have *one* equation to solve for *two* unknowns, a_2 and b_2.

5. The means by which Lutzian forward rates can be derived has been given by A. Buse ((10) p. 397—8). The starting point is naturally the Lutzian formula for the long-term rate at t, which has been presented in chapter 2 above. This enables us to write:

$$R_{n-1} = \frac{(1+r_1)\ldots(1+r_{n-1})-1}{(1+r_2)\ldots(1+r_{n-1})+(1+r_3)\ldots(1+r_{n-1})+\ldots+(1+r_{n-1})+1} \tag{i}$$

Following Buse's notation we may set the numerator of (i) equal to a_{n-1} and the denominator equal to b_{n-1}. It then follows from (i) that:

$$R_n = \frac{(a_{n-1}+1)(1+r_n)-1}{b_{n-1}(1+r_n)+1}. \tag{ii}$$

Hence:

$$1+r_n = \frac{1+R_n}{a_{n-1}-R_n b_{n-1}+1}. \tag{iii}$$

This can be rewritten in two computationally more acceptable forms as:

$$1+r_n = \frac{1+R_n}{b_{n-1}(R_{n-1}-R_n)+1} = \frac{(1+R_n)R_{n-1}}{a_{n-1}(R_{n-1}-R_n)+R_{n-1}}. \tag{iv}$$

6. For a counter-argument to Buse's view that the Meiselman Hypothesis has no substantive content where the yield data have been smoothed see Telser (46), p. 555.

7. Another small study also exists for three- and six-month U.S.A. Treasury bills: see T. E. Holland (60).

8. The five equations that Kessel ran are not for $n = 1$ to 5 in the hypothesis $\Delta_{t+n}r_t = F(E_t)$. They are as follows: changes in expected two-week rates two weeks hence, and eleven weeks hence, regressed on the forecast error of two-week rates; changes in expected four-week rates twelve weeks hence regressed on the four-week error variable; changes in expected six-week rates eighteen weeks hence regressed on the six-week error variable; and changes in expected eight-week rates sixteen weeks hence regressed on the eight-week error variable. Full details of these equations are given in Kessel (30), Table 3, p. 38.

9. In equation (3.6.1.) we are saying that R_{1t-1} is the one-year rate *expected* at $t-1$ to rule at t. Remember that the Meiselman Hypothesis is about revisions of *expected* interest rates, though it is formulated in terms of forward rates because these latter are regarded as being proxies for the expected rates. On

these grounds we can have the possible existence of liquidity premiums on the left-hand side of equation (3.6.10), but on the right-hand side there should be no premiums. Fisher (56) has even gone so far as to include a liquidity premium in R_{1t} (footnote 3, p. 325), a point that has quite rightly been disputed by Buse ((107) footnote 3, p. 303).

10. The Bierwag and Grove (58) model of the term structure employs independent variables that are similar to lagged Meiselman error terms; and the lagged term improves the empirical value of their error-learning equation.

11. Buse's (107) experiments on Grant's U.K. data also support this contention.

4 The Malkiel Theory, its Hypothesis and their Empirical Value

4.1

In the two preceding chapters we have focused attention, either directly or indirectly, on the Traditional, or Expectations, Theory. The analysis and discussion in this chapter is on Malkiel's contribution (11), which adopts the spirit but not the letter of the Traditional Theory. The theoretical arguments that we shall develop in the following pages, which serve as a backcloth for Malkiel's hypothesis on the term structure, were developed by Malkiel in a chapter which, significantly enough, he entitled 'An Alternative Formulation of the Expectations Theory' ((11), chapter 2, p. 50). The remarks with which Malkiel opened that chapter are particularly appropriate here:

> We begin our construction of an over-all theory of the term structure with a reformulation of the expectations theory. This study takes the position that the traditional expectational approach is, in principle, correct and of substantial importance in understanding the actual behaviour of market interest rates of securities with different terms to maturity.

To this comment Malkiel appends some remarks which give an indication of the ways by which he hopes to accomplish the reformulation:

> Nevertheless, the yield-to-maturity relationship may be more convincingly described and more clearly perceived when *explicit* recognition is given to bond prices. [Here] the nexus between market interest rates and bond prices is examined rigorously. Then the traditional theory will be recast in terms consistent with the practices of bond investors and traders. Even the nature of the motivation of bond investors seems better described by the mechanism delineated here . . . than by the traditional view. Expectations will be introduced through explicit expected price changes rather than expected future short rates. Moreover, a short

planning period will be substituted for the long-run implicit in the received analysis.

In section 4.2 we shall describe the relationships of prices and yields of bonds of different maturities and make a preliminary attempt to assess what implications these relationships might have for the evolution of the term structure. We shall then be in a position where we can set out and critically evaluate Malkiel's hypothesis on the term structure: this will occupy us in section 4.3. It will then become necessary (in section 4.4) to spend some time considering just how some of the variables in that hypothesis can best be measured, so making it amenable to econometric testing. That discussion is followed in section 4.5 by a presentation of Malkiel's own results from such testing of his hypothesis. Section 4.6 then gives details of results on that hypothesis we have obtained from our own data for the U.K., from the Grant 1952—62 data for the U.K. and from the Italian data of Masera, and compares them with those obtained by Malkiel himself. Section 4.7 is a short summary of the chapter.

4.2

In re-specifying the Traditional Theory Malkiel was concerned with emphasising three main things:

(1) Some 'investors' have a short planning period, usually about one year, contrary to the long-run period implicit in the Traditional Theory;

(2) In choosing their optimum investment strategy these 'investors' are more vitally concerned, indeed preoccupied, with the *expected capital gains or losses* that might ensue from following one particular course rather than another, than they are with rates of interest *per se*. This means that these 'investors' pay strict attention to bond *prices* and their likely movements in deciding whether to go 'short' or 'long', with consequent effects upon the term structure;

(3) In forming some opinion as to what those movements in bond prices will be, 'investors' have in mind what Malkiel calls a 'normal' range of interest rates, or 'the' interest rate, which as they see it, provides a backcloth against which they may judge the likely changes in specific current interest rates. In this manner they can

form an opinion of *expected* specific interest rate changes. So reference is still made to expected interest rates, but it is done so because such reference indicates to investors the capital gains or losses likely to arise from their investing in different types of bonds; i.e., it provides, in the market's view, information on relative movements in the prices of specific bonds of different maturities.

Malkiel felt it necessary to include all of these factors as the foundation for his particular theory because his inquiries into the actual behaviour of investors on the bond market showed them to be important. Malkiel's investors are sparked by the same objectives as are those of the Expectations Theory: they are concerned with the maximisation of their expected holding-period return, which means that over the holding period, the (equilibrium) expected returns on all assets must be the same, as in the Expectations Theory: *but* the holding period is a short one, say a year, rather than a long one.

We must now look into factors 2 and 3 above so that we can illustrate how, given a short planning period and the above motive, the term structure might evolve in the Malkiel Theory. We may begin with factor 3 because it will enable us directly to see its relationship to factor 2, and thence to the term structure *per se*.

Technically, Malkiel refers to the normal range as 'the expected normal range of interest rates' ((11), p. 59). The basic idea is that the market, just as in the confines of the Traditional Theory, has a view on a band or range within which interest rates will move, or are *expected* to move. We shall defer comment about the formation of such a band or range until section 4.3. We simply assume for now that it exists. It will be noted that we have referred to a normal range of interest rates. In setting out the essentials of his theory Malkiel obviated the need to consider the whole spectrum of rates or yields in the formation of that range by supposing:

> . . . that interest rates for securities of all maturities are fixed at 4½ per cent by the arbitrary decree of a *deus ex machina*.
>
> [(11)], p. 60]

Additionally:

> For simplicity, we shall consider that all bonds carry coupons of 4½ per cent and, therefore, the prices of all securities are fixed at par.
>
> [ibid.]

Malkiel's arguments are easier to follow if all securities carry identical coupons, if all securities bear the same rate of interest, and if we consider only one range — for the long-term rate.

Given the aim, or *motivation*, of investors in the circumstances Malkiel has contrived, their sole concern will be to assess how far *the* interest rate (or 'interest rates', we may say) could move within the range, so as to estimate the likely *capital gains* and *losses* that could ensue from 'going long' relative to 'going short'. Malkiel supposes, in addition to the information already given, that 'the normal range of interest rates' is 2 to 5%. The market, it is assumed, then opens with 'the' *actual* rate of interest at 4.5 per cent, which is almost at the upper limit of that range.

Malkiel initially rules out what he calls 'expectations proper', in that he assumes that the market does not have in mind any expectations as to which way bond prices will move, such that, say, a movement upward is expected more than is a movement downward. Malkiel observes that:

> . . . investors must be aware of the fact that, in terms of potential bond-price movements, this level of rates leaves less to be feared than hoped. The worst situation that could confront an investor is for him to suffer capital losses corresponding to a rise in interest rates to 5 per cent. On the other hand, rates could fall to 2 per cent. . . . The resulting capital gains would be substantial, especially on longer-term securities.
>
> [(11), p. 60]

Malkiel would contend that this statement does depend upon the market having no explicit view at all of how the actual rate will change, though it might equally well be argued that it implicitly contains some view of the 'bracket' in which 'the' rate of interest is likely to move.

Malkiel's observation suggests that investors may follow *a kind* of Shacklean [(52), (53)] approach to the evaluation of the alternative outcomes likely to arise from a particular investment of funds. That is to say, they will look at two focus-outcomes or, in more general language (which does not, therefore, faithfully conform to Shackle's usage of these terms and the development of his 'theory of expectation'), we may say they will focus attention on only two outcomes, namely the *best* and the *worst*; Malkiel's view is then clearly that, in the given conditions, the investors' opinion of what the market holds in store for them depends upon a comparison of these two outcomes. Given the numerical values assumed in Malkiel's example, it is suggested that the balance lies with 'more to hope than to fear'. Yet in a way such an evaluation of the situation confronting investors in the given model implicitly supposes that they feel it is possible for the rate of interest to reach either the upper or lower bound of the range, *and* that 'the chances' of either event occurring are equal. Malkiel comes near to conceding this point, as we shall see shortly when he assigns an equal probability to the occurrence of both the worst outcome and the best outcome in order to see the implications for the term structure of his theory.

One aspect of 'the mathematics of bond-price movements' covered by Malkiel concerns the relative effect on long- and short-term bond prices of changes in interest rates, or yields, when initially bonds were selling at par. In such circumstances Malkiel has shown that,[1] as in the present illustration, when the interest rate rises, the fall in the price of a short bond is less than that in a long bond; so the view that interest rates are going to rise to the upper extremity of the range will mean to rational investors that, as the market opens, short bonds become relatively more attractive to hold than long bonds. This aspect of bond-price movements is illustrated in figure 4.2.1 where we have mapped out on a more comprehensive basis than Malkiel ((11) figure 3-1, p. 58) the movements in bond prices as interest rates change.

So, at the time when active trading can begin on the market if investors reckon that the rate of interest is definitely going to rise towards the upper limit of the range, the market's preference should turn strongly towards shorts: there will consequently be selling of longs to enable investors to take up the more preferred short position. The effect will be that the actual (equilibrium) rates of interest on short and long bonds now differ — the rate (or yield-to-maturity, we should say) on shorts will fall, while that on longs will rise. The yield-gap will be positive, and will be reflected in an upward sloping yield-to-maturity curve.

It now becomes a simple matter to see what kind of new term structure will emerge on the market if investors should feel that the rate of interest is going to fall to the lower extremity of the normal range. Capital gains must, of course, follow such an event: but (again, in the confines of the assumed environment) the advantage now lies with long bonds. The maximum 'achieved yields' over the (one-unit) holding period can be obtained only by investors who attempt to divest themselves of short bonds in an endeavour to increase their holdings of long bonds which promise to produce the greater capital gains. Such a switching of investments will naturally modify the term structure, so that, instead of a horizontal yield curve that had been imposed on the market prior to the outset of trading, there will emerge a downward sloping yield curve, since a yield-gap will materialise that is negative. The degree of shifting between the two ends of the market, and hence the profile of the yield curve, will depend upon the amount of switching required to bring the expected

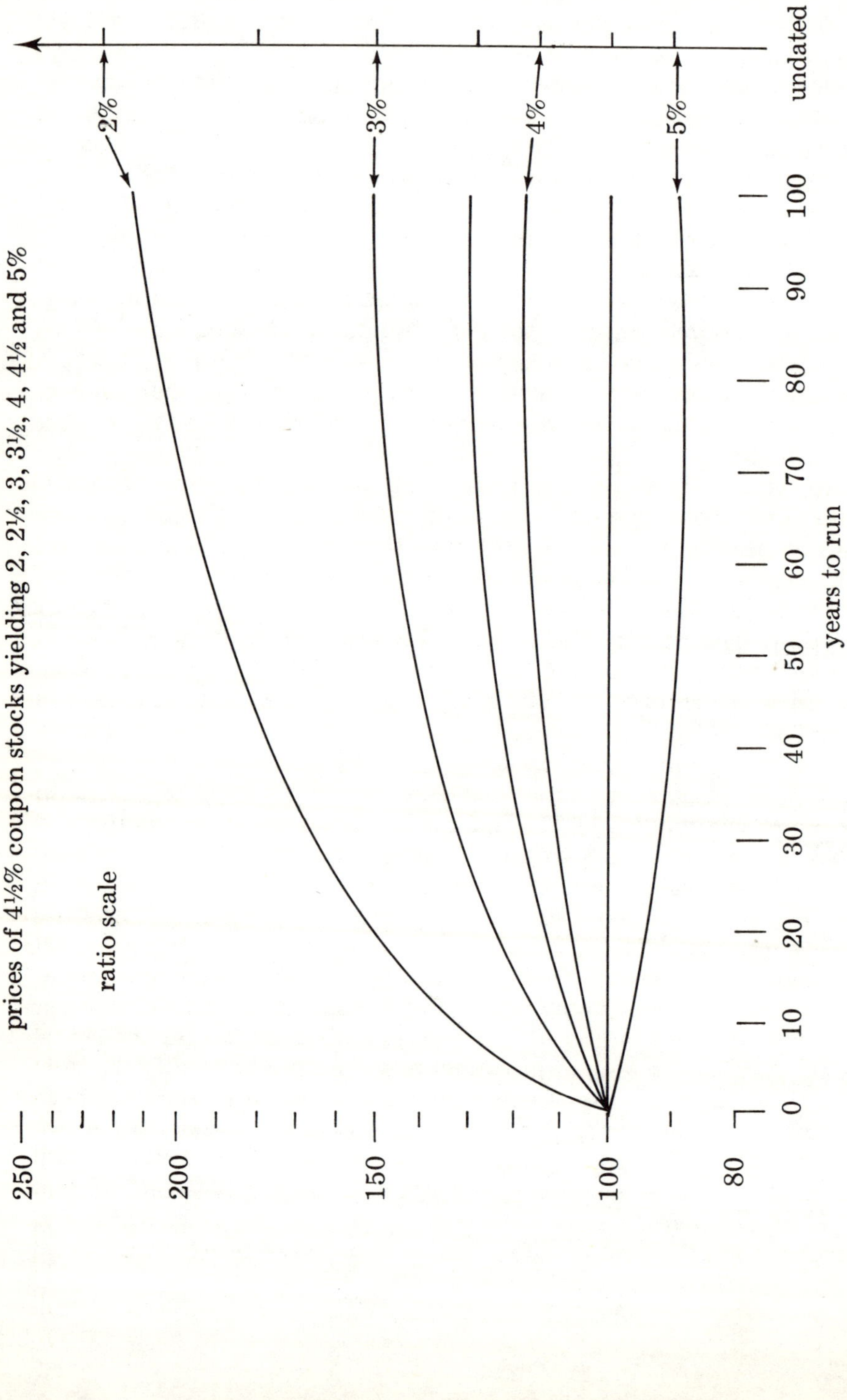
prices of 4½% coupon stocks yielding 2, 2½, 3, 3½, 4, 4½ and 5%
ratio scale
250
200
150
100
80
0
10
20
30
40
50
60
70
80
90
100
years to run
undated
2%
3%
4%
5%

Figure 4.2.1

returns, or yields, from the two kinds of bonds back into line so that a new *equilibrium* is attained.

One crucial factor, however, as to what kind of yield curve will materialise when trading is allowed to restart depends upon the market having some idea in its mind as to which way the interest rate is going to change. So far we have considered merely what would happen if either of the extreme outcomes were relevant. For the market to determine which end of the maturity spectrum to move into (indeed, for it to make a decision whether or not to change its prior-to-opening holdings of bonds), it must form some opinion as to whether the rate is going to increase or decrease: for the best and worst outcomes have to be 'netted out'. To this extent expectations have to be brought within the scope of the analysis. Although, to repeat the point, Malkiel's own method of handling this matter is one which he feels he can sensibly describe as where 'expectations proper' do not enter into the market's calculation of its appropriate investment policy. His suggestion is to let the market focus on the two extreme outcomes, and to do so *equally*, since the market is supposed to hold indifferent expectations concerning which outcome will be realised; that is to say, it is supposed to regard either outcome as *equally likely*. A measure of such equivalence is assumed to be the probabilities of the best outcome and of the worst outcome, or of the events or state of nature that will bring about the given outcome, the probability, naturally, for either outcome being 0.5.

This means that the Bayesian insufficient-reason, or, more expressively, equal-ignorance, criterion has been adopted. In respect of this concept Malkiel writes:

> Unfortunately, from an empirical point of view, this principle encounters serious difficulties. There is really an infinite number of states of nature which could be regarded as 'equally likely'. For example yields might remain unchanged, rise 0.5 per cent, fall 0.5 per cent, etc. Why should the extremes of our normal range be singled out as the natural parametrization of the states for which this criterion is appropriate? . . . . By selecting the extremes of the possible range of price movements we achieve the same result as would be obtained by use of the uniform distribution over the entire range. The narrower the expected range of fluctuations, the smaller will be the derived yield differentials. But the differences in results will be only differences in degree. If however, investors believe that there will be no range of fluctuation during the coming year, then the derived yield curve will be horizontal, which is precisely what we would expect.
>
> [(11), pp. 63–4]

In demonstrating the effect, in the present example, of the normal range of interest rates on the yield curve *per se*, we have so far assumed that *either* the worst *or* the best outcome is realised. On Malkiel's assumptions it now becomes necessary to see what kind of yield-to-maturity curve materialises when *both* outcomes are possible and are equally likely to occur.

The example has the initial rate of interest above the middle of the normal range and indeed quite close to the latter's upper bound. In such a situation there will be a change of portfolio by some investors, who will switch into longer-term bonds out of shorter-term bonds. Since the initial rate of interest is nearer the upper bound than the lower bound, the difference between the worst and the best outcomes is positive for any kind of bond, but the overall balance of advantage lies with long bonds.[2]

Suppose we have one long-term and one short-term bond. The formal mathematical approach to determining the balance would be to evaluate the capital gain and loss on the long-term bond in the two eventualities and multiply both quantities by 0.5, the probability of occurrence of either event. The result would be 'the mathematical expectation' of *gain* from investing in the long bond. This expectation would have to be compared with that for the short bond. But, given that the two probabilities of occurrence of the worst and best outcomes are equal, we can (as we have done in the preceding paragraph) ignore the probabilities in evaluating the *relative* advantage, or gain, from going long rather than going short or vice-versa. Let us adopt this notation:

(i) G_s and G_l represent the capital gain from *s*hort and *l*ong bonds respectively;

(ii) L_s and L_l represent the losses; and

(iii) μ_G and μ_L are the probabilities of the gain and loss events. Then the *mathematical expectation* of 'gain' from investing in the long bond (E_l) is:

$$E_l = \mu_G G_l - \mu_L L_l. \tag{4.2.1}$$

Likewise E_s is

$$E_s = \mu_G G_s - \mu_L L_s. \tag{4.2.2}$$

Given that E_l is positive, whether to go short or long depends upon the ratio E_l/E_s. But since $\mu_G = \mu_L$, this simplifies from (4.2.1) and (4.2.2) to:

$$\frac{E_l}{E_s} = \frac{G_l - L_l}{G_s - L_s}. \tag{4.2.3}$$

In the assumed conditions, (a) the denominator and the numerator of equation (4.2.3) are positive; (b) $G_l > G_s$; (c) $L_l > L_s$;

(d) $G_l/L_l > G_s/L_s$. Given (d), $E_l/E_s > 1$, therefore making long bonds attractive relative to short bonds.[3] So with the rate of interest at the outset near to the upper limit of the normal range, at the start of trading there will be a positive attempt by the participants in the financial market to alter their portfolio; they will sell short bonds for long bonds. The consequence of this will be that a new yield curve will emerge that is descending; a new structure of yields will be established that, *ceteris paribus*, causes trading to cease when and where equilibrium has been restored with the mathematical expectation of gain from long and shorts being forced into equality by the arbitrage that has occurred as a result of E_l/E_s exceeding unity at the opening of the market.

It will be recalled that, in previously discussing the yield curve, where the rate of interest was near the upper limit of the range and where it was implicitly expected that the worst would happen, an ascending yield curve resulted. It was only when it was assumed that the best would happen that a descending yield curve obtained. Now that it is felt that it is equally likely that either outcome will occur, with the interest rate lying above the mid-point of the range, the nature of bond price movements is such that the resultant effect on the yield structure is the same, in general, as when only the best is imagined to be possible, for the advantage is very much with holding long bonds. In the assumed conditions there is more 'to hope than to fear', so it is not very surprising that the term structure which emerges is similar in form to that which results from belief that only the best outcome will materialise.

In similar fashion it can be shown that, should the rate of interest fixed prior to the start of active trading be *below* the mid-point of the normal range, say near its lower limit, investors will have more 'to fear than to hope', so causing an ascending yield curve to be realised, if it is still believed that $\mu_G = \mu_L = 0.5$. This is the type of yield-to-maturity curve that is produced when the market believes completely and unanimously that the worst outcome, that is a rate of interest equal to the upper limit of the normal range, will be in evidence at the end of the one-year period now about to be embarked upon.

This discussion has shown that a simple construct such as the expected normal range of interest rates, aided by some assumptions about investors' behaviour and some technical details on the relationship between bond prices and their yields, can go a good way towards explaining the term structure. Malkiel, remember, would contend that the kind of arguments advanced so far have been able to explain that structure without explicit reference to expectations, a factor so central to the Traditional Theory, though it has relied on other assumptions of the Traditional Theory, for example on the existence of no transaction costs, or of transaction costs of such forms that they do not prevent arbitrage taking place because it is no longer profitable.

We turn now then to look at 'expectations'. Malkiel's view is that:

> By expectations proper . . . we simply mean that investors may believe that a certain course of interest-rate movements is more likely than any other, or they may make specific forecasts of future interest rates.
>
> [(11), p. 65]

Malkiel, as we have already pointed out, concedes that expectations form part of the discussion in that the market has an expected normal range, a range that it expects to obtain throughout the holding period; but also, the market regards it as perfectly possible for rates of interest to change, and to change in either an upward or downward direction, their 'expectation' of either change being equal. True, the market does not say that movement in one direction of the normal range limits is more likely than in the other. But short of making some judgement on expected changes in rates of interest, the normal range, and all the surrounding apparatus, can tell us nothing about how the term structure is determined and how, therefore, it might change period by period.

If we do take cognisance of the existence of such expectations we can have instances where the results on the term structure derived hitherto are strengthened. However, there will be times when those previous results are weakened or even completely overturned, giving way to the view that true expectations can be powerful individual influences in determining the term structure.

Thus, suppose that in the model outlined earlier, with the rate of interest set at 4.5%, we know that the market believes that the probability of occurrence of the best outcome is 0.75, and that of the worst outcome 0.25. Here we have a situation wherein the market expects, again, that rates will either move to one extreme or the other of the normal range, but that now there is more evidence that they will move to the lower limit. Such a situation, it is immediately apparent, lies between one where $\mu_G = \mu_L = 0.5$, and where $\mu_G = 1.0$, $\mu_L = 0.0$. Consequently, as trading opens the market will wish to engage in trading, and it will wish to sell shorts for longs. The effect will be to produce a new equilibrium position where the expectations of gains from shorts and from longs are equivalent, there being a *descending* yield curve, a curve which must have a steeper slope than that where $\mu_G = \mu_L = 0.5$, but a less steep slope than where $\mu_G = 1.0$.

Similarly, if it should happen that at the outset of trading the rate of interest is below the mid-point, then if μ_L should exceed 0.5 the yield curve will be more steeply *ascending* than when $\mu_L = 0.5$.

In these two instances the earlier conclusion on 'equally likely' 'expectations' has been strengthened, so expectations are a reinforcing agent, as it were, on the term structure rather than a determining factor — if we accept Malkiel's interpretation of the presence of expectations.

But it is not very difficult to see intuitively that there will be many examples where expectations *shape* the term structure. Thus, let us imagine that the rate of interest is near the upper bound of the normal range, say 4.5% as in Malkiel's model. Instead of supposing that $\mu_G = \mu_L = 0.5$, we may let $\mu_G = 0.1$ and $\mu_L = 0.9$. This situation is clearly approaching that where $\mu_G = 0.0$, namely where the market believes, with certainty, that rates will rise to the upper limit. With a probability ratio (μ_L/μ_G) now in excess of unity, events are *weighted* in favour of the kind of bond producing the smaller loss and away from the type producing the greater gain, for losses are (very much) more expected than are gains. In such circumstances the choice of the market may well turn out to be to purchase shorts rather than to purchase longs (as when $\mu_G = \mu_L = 0.5$). Such a choice will produce an *ascending* yield curve, the reverse of what happened with gains and losses having equal probabilities.

Some simple algebra will enable us to see these points and to summarise our discussion so far on the Malkiel approach. We retain all the assumptions Malkiel has made concerning the size of the normal range and so on, so that the relative advantage of going long rather than short, or vice-versa, can be found by use of the formulae presented earlier in equations (4.2.1) and (4.2.2), now reproduced below for convenience:

$$E_l = \mu_G G_l - \mu_L L_l \tag{4.2.4}$$

$$E_s = \mu_G G_s - \mu_L L_s . \tag{4.2.5}$$

It will be recalled that E_l is the mathematical expectation of 'gain' from investing in long bonds and that G_l and L_l represent the gain and the loss from investing in long bonds which will ensue with rates at the extremities of the normal range.

Rearranging the terms in these equations slightly and dividing the one equation by the other we find that:

$$\frac{E_l}{E_s} = \frac{G_l - WL_l}{G_s - WL_s} \tag{4.2.6}$$

where $W = \mu_L/\mu_G$. Should $W = 1$ then we are back to equation (4.2.3). For an initial rate of interest that is within the normal range, before the market opens, there naturally will be unique values for G_l, L_l, G_s and L_s in equation (4.2.6). Therefore we have a unique single valued function $(E_l/E_s) = f(W)$. However, it is easier to cope with negative L_l, E_s and to see the effect of W on the relative profitability of going long by subtracting equation (4.2.5) from equation (4.2.4). If we perform this operation we have:

$$E_l - E_s = \phi = \mu_G(G_l - G_s) - \mu_L\,(L_l - L_s). \tag{4.2.7}$$

But:

$$\mu_L = 1 - \mu_G. \tag{4.2.8}$$

Therefore:

$$\phi = -(L_l - L_s) + [(G_l - G_s) + (L_l - L_s)]\,\mu_G. \tag{4.2.9}$$

Or, in general terms for an initial rate of interest i:

$$\phi_i = \alpha_i + [\beta_i - \alpha_i]\,\mu_{G,i}. \tag{4.2.10}$$

Here α_i is negative, being equal to $-(L_l - L_s)$, because the signs of gains and losses have already been taken account of in the basic equations, (4.2.4) and (4.2.5). From 'the mathematics of bond price movements' noted earlier, $(\beta_i - \alpha_i)$ is positive. There is a simple linear relationship between ϕ and μ_G, and therefore between ϕ and W since $W = f(\mu_G)$. For each i there will be a 'curve' connecting ϕ and μ_G, and in terms of figure 4.2.2, which illustrates equation (4.2.10), the lowest line (LR) is for an initial i at the *lower* bound of the normal range, while the highest positioned line (UR) is for an initial value of i at the *upper* end of the range.

Let us say just a few words about these lines. On UR, at a probability of gain of zero (i.e. at the origin), ϕ must be zero, for even though the expectation of capital loss is unity the amount of the capital loss expected will be nil since i = upper value of the normal range. This is an extreme case; the other such case occurs at one end of LR where, when the probability of gain is unity, the amount of the gain expected is nil; therefore again $\phi = 0$, so that the yield curve would remain horizontal, there being no incentive for asset-switching.

The *maximum maximorum* value of ϕ will occur when $\mu_G = 1.0$, obviously, but when, simultaneously, i is at the upper bound of the

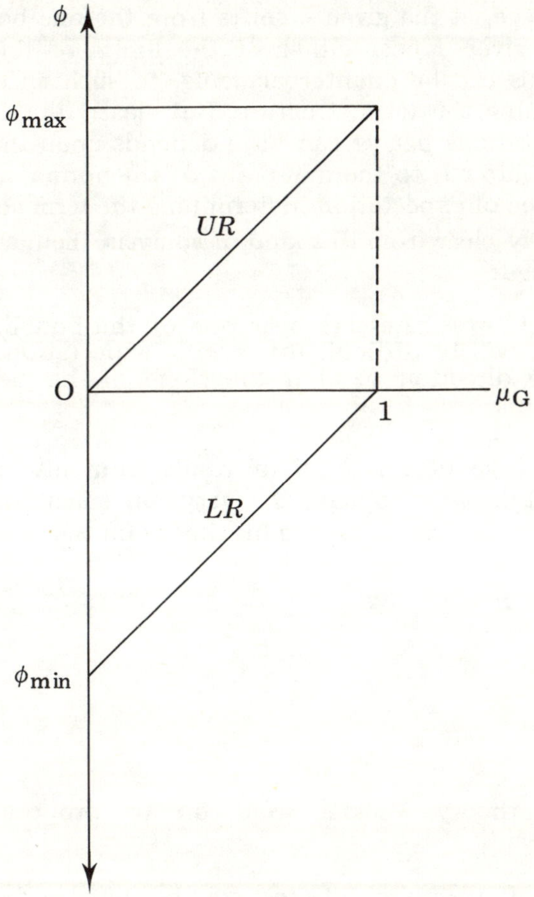

Figure 4.2.2

normal range, so that the value lies at the right-hand limit of *UR*. Likewise, the minimum value of ϕ occurs when $\mu_G = 0.0$ and i is at the lower end of the normal range; so it is located at the left-hand limit of *LR*.

For curves *UR* and *LR*, of course, the advantage lies with one type of bond or the other for all μ_G. What are important are those curves that are based on interest rates that lie within the normal range. For an initial rate of interest near the upper bound of the normal range, the curve will lie below that of *UR*; similarly, for an interest rate near the lower bond of the range, the curve will lie above *LR*. Such curves show that there will be some value of μ_G (and hence of μ_L) at which the advantage, at the given i, shifts from the one bond to the other. So, for a given i near either of the limits of the normal range, expectations can be counterbalancing, to such an extent that they *can* determine the term structure. But clearly the degree of success that expectations *per se* can have depends upon the level of i. The nearer the latter is to the mid-point of the normal range, the greater is the chance of expectations determining the term structure.

It is fairly clear from this kind of analysis, then, as Malkiel himself has remarked:

> . . . if interest rates are near one of the bounds of the normal range, it will be difficult for specific expectations working in the opposite direction to alter the slope of the yield curve.
>
> [(11), p. 82]

It was because of this kind of result from his basic model that Malkiel felt disposed to make the, very convenient, decision to ignore 'expectations proper' in testing his theory on the term structure.

4.3

From his theory Malkiel went on to propose the following hypothesis:[4]

> The hypothesis we wish to test may be stated as follows: When the level of interest rates is near the upper bound of the normal range of interest rates, the spread between long and short rates should be relatively small (algebraically), perhaps negative. When the level of rates is near the lower bound of the normal range, the long—short yield spread should be relatively large. Taking the long rate as representative of the general level of rates, we may write this postulated relationship as
>
> $$L - S = h\left(\frac{L - L_{\mathrm{LN}}}{L_{\mathrm{UN}} - L_{\mathrm{N}}}\right) \qquad \text{[i]}$$
>
> [(11), p. 82]

Malkiel has adopted this notation for defining the variables in equation [i]: L and S are the long and short rate, respectively, L_{LN} is the lower bound of the normal (long) rate range, and L_{UN} is the upper bound of that range. There are three assumptions implicit in equation [i] related to the ideas we have so far discussed. The first assumption, which we have already noted, concerns the absence of any *direct* representation of expectations of interest rates. The second assumption is that the long rate is 'a surrogate for the level of interest rates' ((11), p. 83) and the third assumption is that the appropriate yardstick for estimating normal expected interest rates is the (recent historical) normal range for the long-term rate of interest.

In the Malkiel model described and developed hitherto we did not differentiate between the short rate and the long rate when the market opened. Yet, even if we were to imagine that there were only two types of bonds on the market, a short bond and a long bond, it would be irrational of investors to look only at the likely movement of *either* the short rate *or* the long rate, even if it is supposed that there is a belief in the market that there is a particular band within which *both* interest rates will move. The market will look at likely changes within that band for *both* rates of interest, even if they are equivalent at the opening of the market. But what Malkiel has done in the model outlined earlier is to suppose that the normal range applies to both rates of interest, and that, whichever way the two kinds of interest rates are expected to move within the normal range, they will both be expected to move *together* and by the same amount.

The crucial question is this: do Malkiel's conclusions and hence his hypothesis, given by equation [i], depend upon the existence of only *a* normal band for interest rates and upon situations where, before trading, the yield-gap is zero? Or, to put the issue in an alternative form: is Malkiel entitled to generalise his conclusions in the way he has, suggesting that a knowledge of the long rate, and its propinquity to the extremities of the normal band, is sufficient for us to deduce the kind of yield structure that will emerge on the market?

There are evidently two types of situations that are germane here, namely: (a) where at the outset of trading the long rate differs from the short rate; and, (b) where two expected normal ranges exist in the minds of investors. As we shall see, it is perfectly possible to amend Malkiel's basic model to accommodate these situations while, contrary to what we might think *prima facie*, leaving his conclusions, and hence equation [i], quite unaffected. In considering the situation envisaged in (a) let us continue to suppose for simplicity that there is only one normal range for interest rates. Our interest lies solely in those instances where the long rate lies near to the upper or the lower bound of the range. We may begin by considering the former position, doing so under 'the equally likely' assumption.

It will be remembered that under such assumptions, when the two rates of interest were equivalent prior to trading, the resulting (new) yield curve was a descending one, since on balance long bonds were judged to be (prospectively) more lucrative than short bonds. In the present conditions it will almost certainly be *possible* for this conclusion to be reversed only if the short rate stands above the long rate; for then there is a possibility that the gain on shorts will be greater than on longs while the loss will be less. But such a situation is only likely to be a possibility: since a *very* high rate for a short time produces less advantage than a moderately high rate for a long time; no material advantage, in effect, will rest with the short bond. Should the short rate stand below the long rate at the outset then the advantage possessed by the long bond is likely to be higher than hitherto, and as the short rate approaches the lower extremity of the normal range the long bond's advantage will be increasingly enhanced.

These intuitions follow from our previous discussions and the mathematics of bond-price movements upon which they were largely based. It is not possible to prove rigorously and generally that, where the short rate stands above the long rate, the previous findings on the term structure are unlikely to be reversed when the long rate is approaching the upper bound of the range. Remembering that investors have only a short holding period, for example one year, and given that the coupons on long and short are identical although their initial prices are now different, the differential in the expected returns from investing in the two bonds will still depend overwhelmingly upon the 'capital change effects'; and it is unlikely that, if the short rate stands initially above the long rate for a similarly dimensioned normal range, the 'capital change effects' (netted, of course) will favour shorts. This supposes, however, that the short and the long bonds are truly short and long bonds, e.g. one—five years and around twenty years, respectively.

It may be contested that, in drawing these observations on the effects of extending Malkiel's basic framework, we have applied the 'equally likely' assumption and have done so to both rates of interest. But the justification for doing so is that we have assumed that there is only one normal interest rate band, plus the fact that short- and long-term interest rates frequently move somewhat similarly in reality. If we were to introduce 'expectations proper' into the analysis, given this last fact they would only affect our conclusions in the same manner as they did those of Malkiel's deduced from his basic model.

Enough has been said on this matter. We may merely offer the general statement that, provided that there is *a* normal range for interest-rate movements, the relationship of the initial, before-trading, long rate to the normal range will be an indicator, *ceteris paribus*, of the new rate structure that will emerge, even where the long and the short rates differ at the opening of trading.

Let us make some remarks about the effect on the determination of the term structure (as Malkiel has seen it) of the possible existence of a normal range for short rates along with the range for long rates. If it is supposed that the short-rate band lies *within* the long-rate band, and that the 'equally likely' assumption means that it is as likely that *both* rates will go to the top of their respective bands as it is that they will *both* proceed to fall to the bottom of their respective bands, then the previous conclusions relating the location of the long rate in its range to the type of yield curve that will be in evidence on the market when trading has begun will hold. However, should the long-rate band be subsumed in the short-rate band, then it could be *possible* on occasion for the previous conclusions to be weakened or reversed.

Since interest rates move together it is defensible to interpret the 'equally likely' assumption to mean that both short and long rates will move simultaneously to the probable limits of their ranges. If we do then posit that the short rate's normal range is contained within the long rate's normal range, Malkiel's conclusion follows even if we ignore the short rate's normal range. Thus, if we discount the existence of 'expectations proper', Malkiel's views on the term structure, of the kind epitomised in equation [i] above, hold even if we amend two of the assumptions of his 'model'. Although the introduction of expectations proper complicates matters, given the movement of interest rates, a realistic representation of those expectations would for the most part leave this conclusion untarnished. Consequently, in looking at the determination of the yield-gap, our attention can be concentrated on a *representative* interest rate and its normal range (be it a long or a short rate).

There is one major issue relating to equation [i] that we have so far omitted from our discussions. The variables in equation [i] do not have any time-dimension factors attached to them. That equation is a deduction from a model where an explicit reference to time was of crucial importance. We had basically a situation where there was an initial period, t_0, and an immediately ensuing period t_1. At t_0 the term structure was presented to the market as a *fait accompli*. This was a period in which active trading was made unnecessary by decree. But during such an interval we must suppose the market was forming its expectations of the normal long-term interest-rate range that was to hold for the next and, as it saw things at the time, immediately subsequent time periods. So at t_0 the market had expectations about the normal range for t_1. But then the term structure that emerged during t_1 on the market, as active trading was initiated, depended upon the relationships between the *actual* long-term rate at t_0 and the normal range for t_1. It was the relationship between the *inherited* long rate and the expected normal range for t_1 that, in the confines of the model, determined the term structure that materialised in t_1.

In putting a time dimension to the variables in equation [i] Malkiel gave them all the same time period instead of lagging the argument L. Consequently, the dependent and the independent variables in the equation contain a common variable, which has its own econometric implications as we shall note in section 4.4. But such a procedure embodies an economic paradox, in that 'today's' yield-gap depends upon half of itself: we almost have a tautology here.

Yet there are grounds for ignoring this fact and for deciding not to lag L on the right-hand side of equation [i], and to support the contention that it does so little injustice to the proper specification of the hypothesis concerned that it can be ignored. In testing an equation of the kind specified in equation [i] we have quite obviously got to select a time span for each period for the years over which we intend to assess its value. This may be a week, a month, a quarter or a whole year.

Suppose we take a year as the unit of measurement by which we select our observations on interest rates in order to test an equation developed from hypothesis [i]. Although it is supposed that the holding period of all investors who engage in financial investment is typically of short duration, such as one year, this selection of one-year data does not mean that it is being imagined that the market acts as one such that it only trades at one-yearly intervals. Such a situation would be blatantly quite a ludicrous one. Of course we have to assume that all investors have the same length of holding period on average, but not that they coincide in calendar time: there is continuous trading between the data observation points.[5] Therefore, if we have observations on an annual basis it would be quite wrong to use the observations on L at $t-1$ to determine the yield-gap, $L-S$, at t. We would want to take something like the inherited long rate that applied to the day before the beginning of period t. It could still be argued, however, that we should extend this line of reasoning to taking the inherited long rate as the rate that obtained on the market at the beginning of trading at time t, which might be 31 March 1970, and regarding it and the normal long-rate range as determining the yield-gap at the close of trading on that date. The supposition being that asset-switching can occur, and will occur, because investors are rational and have no costs of investment and dis-investment, within a short time span, such as the day upon which we observe the market. As a proxy for the inherited, beginning-of-period long rate, Malkiel is suggesting that we can take the actual long-term rate.

4.4

In this section it is necessary for us to inquire into the empirical testing of an hypothesis such as that contained within equation [i] in section 4.3. For convenience we reproduce that equation now:

$$L - S = h\left(\frac{L - L_{LN}}{L_{NR}}\right) \tag{4.4.1}$$

where L_{NR} denotes the expected normal long-term interest-rate range.

To render this equation amenable to econometric analysis it becomes necessary, *inter alia*, to specify the means by which the normal range is to be calculated. Malkiel himself summarises his own method of assessing the range as follows:

> We suggest further that investors form their expectations of the limits of the normal range as if they took the average of rates over some period in the immediate past and added a specific number of standard deviations to either side of the average. The standard deviations would be calculated over a very long period of bond-market history and be considered constant from year to year. . . . The number of standard deviations to be added would be determined by the confidence limits set by investors and their typical horizon period.
>
> [(11) p. 84]

Thus, for Malkiel, since, for example, the lower bound of the range is equal to 'the average' minus a constant (k) times σ (the standard deviation), equation (4.4.1) becomes:

$$L - S = f\left(\frac{L - L^{N} + k\sigma}{2k\sigma}\right) \tag{4.4.2}$$

where L^N is the 'average' long-term rate, hereafter labelled the *normal* long-term rate. We have now replaced 'the expected normal long-term rate' by 'the normal long-term rate'.

It follows at once that a straightforward approximation to hypothesis (4.4.2) is given by:

$$L - S = F(L - L^N). \tag{4.4.3}$$

If we then make the further assumption that this relationship can be linearised, at point t, we find that we have arrived at Malkiel's *basic testable equation:*

$$(L - S)_t = a + b(L - L^N)_t \tag{4.4.4}$$

to which, for econometric purposes, we suppose we can legitimately add u_t, a random error term. We would expect, *a priori*, in subjecting equation (4.4.4) to a test against a given set of data from our discussion in section 4.2, that b should be less than zero, if the Malkiel hypothesis is *prima facie* to have any empirical relevance.

Having reduced the hypothesis to equation (4.4.4), by assuming σ to be constant over time and so on, there remains, on the surface at least, only one problem to be resolved before the equation can be tested. This naturally relates to the estimation of L_t^N, the normal long-term rate. As can be gathered from the preceding quote from Malkiel, his methods of estimation were similar to those of the distributed lag schemes, which we have said a little about in chapter 3 in connection with error-learning models. We shall briefly review his methods before commenting on our own, which are a simple extension of his.

Malkiel argued that:

> . . . . We suggest, as an initial hypothesis, that investors at any point in time examine only actual interest rate fluctuations over, say, the past 15 years in forming their expectation of the normal interest rate fluctuations.
>
> [(11), p. 84]

Therefore, L^N, or L_A, the *average* long-term rate in Malkiel's notation, is formed as an average of the previous fifteen years' bond rates.

Thus on Durand's annual data Malkiel calculated estimates for L^N at t based upon the fifteen previous actual values of L beginning with L in $t - 1$. This arithmetic average method naturally supposes that each of the past fifteen interest rates have equal weights (1/15) in the mind of the investor: no one rate of interest in his view has prior claim on his thoughts.

A variant of this kind of average is provided by the 'geometric average', based upon a form of distributed lag scheme, wherein the weights attached to each past interest rate decline systematically the further back the time at which it ruled on the market. In fact, for Malkiel in using this kind of average;

> The mid-point of the normal range for period t was computed by
>
> $$L_{A,t} = \sum_{i=1}^{15} {}_{t-i}R_{30}\,\lambda^i \Big/ \sum_{i=1}^{15} \lambda^i \qquad [1]$$
>
> λ was allowed to vary from 0.9 to 0.1.
>
> [(11), p. 90]

Here R_{30} $(= L_{30})$ is the actual rate on a thirty-year corporate bond based on Durand's data. The results Malkiel quotes from testing his hypothesis against Durand's data are, in fact, for letting $\lambda = 0.9$ in equation [1] and from the arithmetic average method of calculating $L_{A,t}$ $(= L_t^N)$, though [1] does, of course, embrace that average if $\lambda = 1.0$.

Scheme [1], with λ taking values of 0.1 to 0.9, was used by Malkiel as an alternative to the arithmetic average; he also put forward two other alternatives to take account of the 'historic' interest-rate range. Thus:

> The choice of the second and third alternatives was motivated by the supposition that the (mid-point of the) long-run historic range of interest-rate fluctuations also plays a part in determining the normal range. In measuring the historic range, we went back 20 years prior to the beginning of the Durand series and found the high and low yields from 1880 until period $t-1$, the year preceding each observation. This historic range was then adjusted whenever a rate was observed to fall outside of the previous range. . . . The mid-point of the historic range and the moving average over the past 15 years were then consolidated by simply taking the weighted sum of the two, where we arbitrarily selected weights of 0.5.
>
> [(11), p. 92]

This method was adopted for both the $\lambda = 1.0$ and the $\lambda = 0.9$ estimates.

Malkiel did also change these estimation procedures by basing them on data over a ten-year rather than a fifteen-year period. So in effect he used eight means by which to estimate L_t^N: the two averages over fifteen and ten years, and those averages accompanied by information on the 'historic' range of interest rates.

We turn now to elaborate on our own choice of methods for

quantifying 'the' normal long-term rate of interest. In testing the Malkiel hypothesis we are not, of course, immune from the problems that occur in testing the Meiselman Hypothesis. Our tests of the theory may depend upon the particular proxy which we choose to adopt for 'the normal range', as proxy for 'the expected normal range'. The 'guessing game' that we are playing in regard to the normal rate or range should be kept obviously to a minimum and should be played with as much relevance to reality as we can impart to it. In our opinion the use of the 'historic' range, as Malkiel has delineated it and used it, seems inappropriate in the light of that kind of observation.

Although we did, in fact, experiment with variables of that kind, our testing of the Malkiel hypothesis was undertaken for the most part without reference to them. Our approach, despite some of the disadvantages implicit in it, was to employ various distributed lag schemes to represent 'the' normal rate, so that the sum to infinity of weights in each scheme as it stood was unity. Because of this characteristic they facilitated experiments wherein σ varied (or could vary) over time; so that a *direct* test of Malkiel's hypothesis given in equation [i], section 4.3, could be effected. Our approach in subjecting his hypothesis to empirical evaluation differed from Malkiel's in another fundamental respect: it additionally offered us the chance of *estimating* the average lag in the adaptive expectations process and the value of the respective λs. But more about measuring σ and estimating λ later in this section.

There are now, of course, many types of distributed lag schemes (see, for example, Griliches (31)). But we employed only three kinds: (i) the Koyck (or what is sometimes referred to, slightly incorrectly, as the Koyck—Nerlove) lag ((32), (33)); (ii) the Pascal lag developed by Solow (34);[6] and (iii) the Almon lag (35). Some of the results from using only the Koyck and Pascal lags are reported on here, and most of them are based on the Koyck lag.

The particular form of the Koyck lag used was this:

$$L_t^{\mathrm{N}} = \sum_{i=0}^{n} \lambda^{i+1} L_{t-(i+1)} \quad 0 < \lambda < 1. \tag{4.4.5}$$

Apart from the obvious common-sense difficulties that arise from including L_t in L_t^{N} without making the explicit distinction between beginning-of-period and end-of-period variables, we cannot include L_t in L_t^{N}, if we are to construct a series for L_t^{N}, in view of the dependent variable in the Malkiel hypothesis.

In equation (4.4.5) then the normal rate is a geometrically declining weighted average of past, actual values of the long-term rate of interest, as far back in time as period $t - n + 1$. If we let n approach infinity then we can see from equation (4.4.5) that the sum of the weights, that is the sum of the λ^{i+1}, will not be unity unless the value of λ happens to be one-half.[7] If we alter (4.4.5) so that it reads as follows:

$$L_t^{\mathrm{N}} = \sum_{i=0}^{n} (1-\lambda)\lambda^i L_{t-(i+1)}, \quad 0 < \lambda < 1 \qquad (4.4.6)$$

we find that the weights will sum to unity irrespective of the value of λ. But clearly, should $\lambda = 0.5$, equation (4.4.6) would become equivalent to equation (4.4.5).

Although the distributed lag scheme represented by equation (4.4.6) has frequently been employed in recent econometric research as a means of representing the notion of 'adaptive expectations',[8] the idea that is central to it is, as one would expect, also implicit in equation (4.4.5). They both represent possible specifications of the idea of 'adaptive expectations', and are 'error-learning' hypotheses.

We have adopted scheme (4.4.5) *inter alia*, because we wanted to construct a series for L_t^{N}, a series that would, under certain conditions to be discussed later, enable us to attempt to quantify σ — and not to leave it as a constant. Since such a step requires that the weights sum to unity, as they are to be regarded as 'probabilities', use of scheme (4.4.5) means that $\lambda \equiv 0.5$. However, in principle it is possible to test econometrically if such an assumption is realistic.

We turn now to make a few brief remarks about the Pascal lag. That lag can be represented by this scheme for the appropriate set of weights:

$$w_i = \frac{(r+i-1)!}{(r-1)!i!}(1-\lambda)^r\lambda^i; \quad i = 0, 1, 2, \ldots; \quad 0 < \lambda < 1. \qquad (4.4.7)$$

It can easily be appreciated that the Pascal lag subsumes the Koyck lag in that if $r = 1$ the weights are identical, one-for-one, with those embodied in scheme (4.4.6). In most econometric work, including Solow's own work on the Pascal lag, a value of 2 has usually been assigned to r. Then we can express equation (4.4.7) in a much simplified manner, since it can now be written as:

$$w_i = (1-\lambda)^2 (i+1)\lambda^i. \qquad (4.4.8)$$

The weights in the Pascal distribution from equation (4.4.8) do in fact sum to unity irrespective of the value of λ (provided, of course, that λ lies between zero and unity).[9]

As already intimated, and this much is clear from what we have said on Malkiel's assessment of L_t^N, when using either lag structure it is possible to compute a series for the normal long-term rate of interest, so providing ourselves with a kind of 'observed' series on that rate. To do so it is necessary to decide upon a value for the parameter λ in either distribution. In using scheme (4.4.5) $\lambda \equiv 0.5$. So we calculated series for L_t^N with $\lambda = 0.5$. To do so we have also to fix the value of n; we chose 14 for the latter. This too was something of an arbitrary decision. But when $n = 14$ scheme (4.4.5) provides us with a sum of all the weights of all the discarded terms to infinity that amounts to a negligible 0.0000305, and it means that in going back fifteen periods and with λ at 0.5 we are not far away from the kind of values used by Friedman (38) in his study on the consumption function. Furthermore, we have chosen to use the same number of past interest rates as has Malkiel. For the Pascal distribution we chose a range of values for λ from which we constructed normal interest rate series.

But we must not forget that we have put forward and utilised these distributed lag schemes to provide us with a *proxy* for the *market's* view about what kind of long term rate of interest is 'normal' or 'appropriate' or 'right' for a given period. So the lag schemes have to be applied to past rates of interest in an appropriate manner to provide normal rates. This means that, if we consider scheme (4.4.5), which has in it both the Koyck weights and the relevant past rates of interest, and substitute this method of assessing 'the' normal rate into the Malkiel hypothesis, or equation (4.4.4), we have no need to compute a normal series *per se*. This is familiar enough from the use of the Koyck transformation — which has been used implicitly in some of our previous remarks on distributed lag functions.

Thus, if we substitute (4.4.5) into (4.4.4) we find that:

$$(L - S)_t = a + bL_t - b \sum_{i=0}^{n} \lambda^{i+1} L_{t-(i+1)} + u_t. \qquad (4.4.9)$$

If we multiply equation (4.4.9) through by λ and lag it one period we have:

$$\lambda(L - S)_{t-1} = \lambda a + \lambda b L_{t-1} - b \sum_{i=0}^{n} \lambda^{i+2} L_{t-(i+2)} + \lambda u_{t-1}. \qquad (4.4.10)$$

Upon subtracting (4.4.10) from (4.4.9) and simplifying we find that:

$$(L - S)_t = a_0 + a_1 L_t + a_2 L_{t-1} + b\,\lambda^{n+2} L_{t-(n+2)} + a_3 (L - S)_{t-1} + w_t \,. \tag{4.4.10a}$$

With λ lying within the range 0 to 1, as *n* approaches infinity the fourth term on the right-hand side of equation (4.4.10a) disappears, so we are left with this equation:

$$(L - S)_t = a_0 + a_1 L_t + a_2 L_{t-1} + a_3 (L - S)_{t-1} + w_t \tag{4.4.11}$$

where:

$$a_0 = a(1 - \lambda); \quad a_1 = b; \quad a_2 = -2b\lambda; \quad a_3 = \lambda \tag{4.4.12}$$

and:

$$w_t = u_t - \lambda u_{t-1}. \tag{4.4.13}$$

If we consider equation (4.4.11), however, it is apparent that, if we estimate it by ordinary least squares (O.L.S.) we shall meet some difficulties. We shall refer to these again in the ensuing sections of this chapter, but they arise from the fact that L_t is an explanatory variable while also being part of the dependent variable and that the explanatory variables include a lagged dependent variable. But even if we ignore these matters or circumvent them, equation (4.4.11), as now or in a more suitable form, if estimated, does not enable us to discover what the value of λ 'should' be in the assumed circumstances and for the given set of empirical data. If we take the O.L.S. estimates of the coefficients in equation (4.4.11) we cannot obtain a unique, consistent, estimate of λ by unscrambling them. The reason for this is not hard to find: the equation is over-identified — we have *four* coefficients by which to estimate the *three* structural parameters, *a*, *b* and λ. To obviate this difficulty it is necessary to attempt to estimate equation (4.4.11) subject to the *non-linear restrictions* on the coefficients in it given by equation (4.4.12). Where appropriate we endeavoured to do this; and the methods of non-linear estimation we utilised are the Taylor's linearisation method and the Gauss—Newton method.[10]

Given the econometric results from testing the Malkiel equation by using these kinds of distributed lags, it could be possible to judge the relative value of the lag structure, and to make some estimate of the 'appropriate' value of λ. Having done the latter it would then be a straightforward task to calculate the 'average lag', or the average length of time it takes for expectations to be revised if they are in error, or the average length of time it takes for the normal rate to adjust to the actual rate of interest.

The average or mean lag, α, for scheme (4.4.5) is:

$$\alpha = \left(\frac{\lambda}{1-\lambda}\right)^2. \tag{4.4.14}$$

With $\lambda = 0.5$, so that the weights sum to unity and a stationary solution to (4.4.5) is possible (thus the actual rate of interest can be stable *and* be equal to the normal rate), equation (4.4.14) indicates that the average lag will be one period. For schemes (4.4.6) the average lag is $\lambda/(1-\lambda)$, which is, as it must be, the same as that implied in a first-order Pascal distribution. The average lag in such distributions, α_p, can be represented generally as:

$$\alpha_p = \frac{r\lambda}{1-\lambda} \tag{4.4.15}$$

where r is the order of the distribution. Thus, if λ should equal 0.5 in any Pascal distribution, the average lag must be identical with the order of that distribution.[11]

The measures suggested for the assessment of the normal rate of interest enable us to undertake direct and indirect testing of the Malkiel hypothesis, as we shall see, and though it is not in the event as easy to choose between one distributed lag scheme and another, and between one selected value of λ and another, they further allow us to place some quantitative value on the value of σ at any moment in time. So the original Malkiel hypothesis re-presented in equation (4.4.1) above can be linearised and tested as it stands. For, if we take scheme (4.4.5), for example, a value of $\lambda = 0.5$ with $n = 14$ will produce a set of weights that totals unity nearly enough for our present purposes. Then we may argue that the weight applicable to each past rate of interest that is incorporated in the formation of the normal rate is akin to a probability of occurrence of that rate of interest, and that the value of L_t^N we have arrived at as a 'geometrically declining weighted average' is a *mathematical expectation* of the rate of interest on the given long bond. Such a procedure is tantamount to premising that: (i) the rates of interest that feature in the probability distribution when investors are forming the mathematical expectation of return are the interest rates that actually ruled on the market in the previous fifteen periods; (ii) *no other rates of interest are regarded as possibilities by the market*; (iii) each relevant interest rate is supposed to be relevant in only one state of nature, as it were. This does raise difficulties of interpretation where a past value of the long-term rate of interest appears more than once in the construction of a particular normal rate. There are problems in giving this kind of meaning to the formation of the normal rate by a distributed lag scheme such as equation (4.4.5) where the weights are rigidly fixed. But this is one possible interpretation of such a scheme, and one which at least will provide information (even if tentative and subject to the same kinds of reservations as are implicit in a scheme such as (4.4.5) *per se*) on the value of σ, which one suspects intuitively should be allowed, if possible, to vary over time. Again, although we are still faced with the fact that this involves more than a joint test of the hypothesis and the specification of the variables that constitute the hypothesis, it is theoretically feasible from the econometric results to pass some kind of judgement on the efficacy of allowing σ to vary.

Given the adoption of distributed lag schemes, sometimes with predetermined weights to enable values of σ to be approximated, there will be many forms in which the Malkiel hypothesis can be tested. We have seen this explicitly only partly from our discussion in this section, but we shall perceive it more fully in sections 4.5 and 4.6. But it must not be forgotten that our concern is in finding some kind of surrogate for the normal long-term rate of interest.

4.5

In this section we shall present a very cursory report on the empirical results Malkiel obtained for his hypothesis; and we shall do so partly by reproducing some of the tables in which he himself so conveniently summarised his findings.

The basic hypothesis, with constant σ (and so, in linearised form, based on equation (4.4.4)) Malkiel tested only against Durand's (40) annual data beginning in 1900. For, as we have pointed out previously, if we estimate the equation, namely:

$$(L - S)_t = a + b\,(L - L^{\mathrm{N}})_t \qquad (4.5.1)$$

by ordinary least squares as it stands the results mean very little. Since L_t appears as both a dependent and an independent variable, there will be bias in the estimates of a and b; and the overall fit of equation (4.5.1) will mean nothing unless the bias can be quantified and the goodness-of-fit appropriately adjusted. Malkiel's approach was to run the regression (4.5.1) for Durand's data and then abandon it. The statistical results of doing so for the period 1900—42 in the U.S.A. were:

$$(L - S)_t = \underset{(0.095)}{0.335} - \underset{(0.125)}{1.585}\,(L - L^{\mathrm{N}})_t \qquad (4.5.1a)$$

where L_t^{N} was a fifteen-year arithmetic average of the thirty-year rate.

The obvious way to remove the bias in the regression coefficients is to transpose L_t from the left-hand side of equation (4.5.1), so producing an hypothesis that explains the short rate when the new equation is multiplied through by minus unity. This naturally produces this equation:

$$S_t = -a + (1 - b)\,L_t + bL_t^{\mathrm{N}}\,. \qquad (4.5.2)$$

As can be seen at a glance from equation (4.5.2), the coefficients on L_t and L_t^{N} should sum to unity if the hypothesis is to be verified empirically, for otherwise the basic equation does not hold. Initially Malkiel estimated equation (4.5.2) by ordinary least squares and this produced the following result on Durand's data for 1900—42.

$$S_t = \underset{(1.294)}{-1.894} + \underset{(0.125)}{2.606}\,L_t - \underset{(0.317)}{1.233}\,L_t^{\mathrm{N}} \qquad (4.5.2a)$$

$$R^2 = 0.972.$$

(We should perhaps note that, since Malkiel was using a fifteen-year data set to calculate L^{N}, equations (4.5.1a) and (4.5.2a) are based on twenty-seven observations.)

Prima facie, it might be thought that equation (4.5.2a) does not support the Malkiel hypothesis despite the apparently highly significant coefficients and high goodness-of-fit, for the coefficients on L_t and L_t^{N} actually sum to a number in excess of unity. However, that excess is not significantly different from zero at the 1% level (of significance), according to Malkiel's calculations.

We can judge whether it is or not by re-estimating equation (4.5.2) by restricted least squares (R.L.S.). That is to say, we can minimise the error sum of squares from applying equation (4.5.2) to the data *subject to* the fact that the two slope coefficients sum to unity. It is then possible to invoke an F-test to decide whether or not the restriction works, or, to put the matter alternatively and more openly, to tell if the empirical data can support the hypothesis that the slope coefficients be constrained to sum to unity. The F-test is based, therefore, on a comparison of the error sum of squares from the O.L.S. estimate and the R.L.S. estimate of equation (4.5.2). If the data can support the constraint, then we would expect that the coefficients from the O.L.S. estimates would not differ significantly from those based on R.L.S. and that, accordingly, the error sums of squares from the two estimators are virtually identical.[12]

As we have already indicated in section 4.4, Malkiel varied the means by which he estimated the value of L_t^N. The results he obtained for Durand's data (1900–42) where $\lambda = 0.9$, as well as $\lambda = 1.0$, and where a weighted average of a moving average and the historic range of the long rate was employed, are detailed in table 4.5.1. We see from the values of the Durbin–Watson statistic (d) that there is considerable serial correlation in the residuals. Malkiel assumed that this autocorrelation could be accounted for by a first-order auto-regressive scheme (of the actual residuals), of the form we mentioned in chapter 3 in introducing our ρ statistic. That is, it is assumed that the pattern of movement in the hypothetical errors can be represented by that in the actual errors (residuals), and that the pattern is of this form: $\rho_t = \rho u_{t-1} + \epsilon_t$, ϵ_t is a random error term, and $|\rho| < 1$. On the supposition that this is a correct specification of the serial correlation in a given equation, we can naturally remove that correlation by transforming the data upon which the equation is tested by means of ρ. This then means that the dependent variable in each equation becomes $(S_t - \rho S_{t-1})$, while the independent variables likewise become $(L_t - \rho L_{t-1})$ and $(L_t^N - \rho L_{t-1}^N)$.[13] The statistical outcome of the adoption of such a method of transforming the data to remove the auto-correlation in the disturbances in equations (4.5.3)–(4.5.6) in table 4.5.1 is reported on in table 4.5.2, which reproduces Malkiel's results.

We should now say a word or two about the results presented in tables 4.5.1 and 4.5.2. The first thing to be said is that the goodness-of-fit of every equation is extremely high, and that it is impossible to choose between the equations on this basis. However, as would be expected, the 'transformed equations' on an equation-by-equation basis produced lower, numerically if not statistically speaking, R^2s. But it appears that the choice of a first-order auto-regressive scheme to represent the serial correlation in the residuals was reasonable enough, and that the F-statistic is more favourable for the satisfying of the summational condition in the transformed equations. Malkiel judged the relative value of these equations by reference to the F-statistic. But even on that criterion it is difficult to support his contention that

Table 4.5.1 Malkiel's results, Durand data, fifteen-year averages, $S_t = a_0 + a_1 L_t + a_2 L_t^N$

Equation number	Calculation of L_t^N	a_0	a_1	a_2	F^*	R^2	d	ρ
4.5.3	λ=1	−1.876 (1.319)	2.606 (0.128)	−1.238 (0.323)	1.6	0.969	0.888	0.573
4.5.4	λ=0.9	−2.863 (1.226)	2.812 (0.164)	−1.201 (0.360)	5.157	0.966	0.846	0.595
4.5.5	0.5 (average, λ=1) + 0.5 H**	0.504 (1.973)	2.611 (0.130)	−1.843 (0.498)	0.272	0.968	0.858	0.589
4.5.6	0.5 (average, λ=0.9) + 0.5 H**	−0.266 (1.954)	2.767 (0.156)	−1.809 (0.541)	0.009	0.966	0.823	0.606

Source: Malkiel (11), table 4—1, p. 91.
*F-test to judge whether $a_1 + a_2 = 1$: all values of F satisfactory at the 1% level of significance.
**H is the mid-point of the 'historic range'.

Table 4.5.2 Malkiel's results, transformed Durand data

Equation Number	a_1	a_2	F	R^2	d
4.5.3a	2.544 (0.209)	−1.310 (0.636)	0.185	0.924	1.852
4.5.4a	2.631 (0.250)	−1.029 (0.599)	1.719	0.917	1.843
4.5.5a	2.563 (0.218)	−2.042 (1.023)	0.296	0.921	1.799
4.5.6a	2.634 (0.252)	−1.724 (0.981)	0.013	0.915	1.807

Source: Malkiel (11), table 4—1, p. 91.

> The alternatives that seem to work best . . . are those where both a moving average and the long-run historical range are used in calculating the mid-point of the normal range.
>
> [(11), p. 93]

There is, in fact, little if anything to choose between use of one value of λ and another or use of one method for given λ than another. But on the whole the results reveal quite outstanding results for the Malkiel hypothesis, even when one takes full account of t-statistics and the F-values, as well as the magnitudes of the R^2 s.

Besides using fifteen-year averages, as we have already pointed out in the previous section, Malkiel ran his basic regression with S_t, the dependent variable, against Durand's annual data by relying on ten-year averages on which to form estimates of a series for L_t^N. He used the data for 1900—42 and then pooled those data with the data for 1951—65. Again, for both sets of data he transformed the observations by using estimates of ρ. The overall results were very similar to those reported in tables 4.5.1 and 4.5.2 above, though they were marginally inferior to them.

In order to test how sensitive his hypothesis might turn out to be with respect to the type of data used, i.e. annual data and data for the U.S.A., Malkiel ran regressions against data of differing lengths and for the U.K. (Grant's for 1924—62, omitting 1939—51). To allow him also to test his hypothesis against other data for the U.S.A., in fact against Treasury yields data (1951—65), Malkiel had to opt for seven-year moving averages by which to calculate L_t^N.

His results reveal that, at least as far as the Durand annual data are concerned, lowering the number of observations built into L_t^N does lessen the value of the Malkiel hypothesis, giving some tentative support to the view that investors might not be exclusively concerned with recent events. They also indicate that, contrary to Malkiel's views of things, there are some differences between the choice of data and the empirical relevance of the hypothesis. But there is no systematic relationship between, for example, the choice of length of observation points and the value of the hypothesis. The only conclusion that we might feel tempted to offer on choice of data is that the hypothesis appears to perform better against the U.K. data. But even this conclusion can at best be only highly tentative because the sample size upon which it would be based is exceedingly small here and because of the method of derivation of the data themselves.

On this last point it is probably useful to recall some of the questions raised about Durand's data and Grant's data in chapters 1 and 2. We could then suggest that: (i) the Durand and the Grant data sets are not strictly comparable because (aside from the fact that the one is for corporate bond yields and the other for yields on government stock) they have been formed in ways that are (potentially) very different; (ii) it would probably have been better to restrict the use of Grant's data to the period 1952–62. We have done this in utilising Grant's data to test variants of the Malkiel hypothesis.

In summary of his results Malkiel writes as follows:

> The regression coefficients of the alternative formulation [i.e., using S_t as the dependent variable rather than $(L-S)_t$] were consistent with the theory. The average coefficient of the long rate was approximately 2.5. This says that, *ceteris paribus*, a change in the long rate of 10 basis points will be associated with a 25 basis point change in the short rate. (One of the principal results of the theoretical analysis was that short rates would be more volatile.) Moreover, the theory also suggested that the higher the (mid-point of the) normal range (L_t^N) the more likely it was for the short rate to be low relative to the long rate. Hence, the negative coefficient of (L_t^N) (which averaged approximately −1.5) also supports our reformulation of the expectations theory. We conclude that the data do not contradict our hypothesis.
>
> [(11), p. 101]

The sentence in round brackets in this quotation is not in parentheses in the original. We have chosen to bracket it in this way since it facilitates reference to it to do so. In fact, we have not explicitly touched upon the question of whether short rates would be more volatile given the Malkiel theory than long rates. As it happens we have implicitly covered this point in sections 4.2 and 4.3, and the Malkiel Theory, if acted upon, will bring about a situation on the financial market wherein short rates have higher volatility than long rates. This was also a contention of the Traditional Theory examined in chapter 2; if a theory of the term structure is to have any claim to our attention as a useful empirical device, it must be able to explain away the fact that, on average over time, financial markets do display evidence that short rates are subject to wider fluctuations than are long rates. The Malkiel Theory indicates that, *ceteris paribus*, this will be a characteristic of investment markets, just as the Traditional Theory does.

Malkiel continues on this traditional tack:

> These tests, utilizing three different sets of interest-rate time series and several alternative time periods, offer independent evidence corroborating the findings of Meiselman that expectations play a major role in determining the rate structure.
>
> [(11), *ibid.*]

To take up this statement on Malkiel's own ground, we may say that this is definitely true only if, by highlighting expectations, we are either excluding 'expectations proper' or assuming that expectations are formed on an 'equally likely' basis; and we have to ignore several things, of course, in making even this kind of proposition, as we now know full well. These things encompass the means by which L_t^N is estimated, the assumption that σ is not a function of time, the type of data used.

Yet we can make a not-too-conditional statement on the worth of Malkiel's own results by saying that they seem to support his hypothesis extremely well over the period tested on the supposition that L_t^N is calculated as a series with a high value of λ, with σ being constant.[14]

4.6

We come at this juncture to consider the results we have generated from empirical testing of various forms of the Malkiel hypothesis. This testing was carried out against Grant's data for the U.K., our own data for the U.K. and the data produced by Masera for Italy. A good many of the regressions run will receive only summary mention here because for various reasons they produced poor or inconclusive results.

Before we attempt to tabulate some of the more important findings for the Malkiel hypothesis that we have uncovered from our inquiries, it seems sensible to set out briefly the nature of the main equations we developed and tested, even if this means emphasising points made in earlier sections of this chapter.

If we let σ be constant over time and 'measure' L_t^{N}, 'the' Malkiel equation is, with a random disturbance term added:

$$(L - S)_t = a + b\,(L - L^{\mathrm{N}})_t + u_t. \qquad (4.6.1)$$

Because of the technical difficulties involved in analysing any results obtained from this equation, we tried it out for only one set of data, namely the quarterly data for Grant (39) for 1952–62. Taking account of those difficulties we may instead estimate this equation:

$$S_t = - a + (1 - b)\,L_t + b\,L_t^{\mathrm{N}} - u_t \qquad (4.6.2)$$

or, alternatively:

$$L_t = \frac{a}{1 - b} + \frac{1}{1 - b}\,S_t - \frac{b}{1 - b}\,L_t^{\mathrm{N}} + v_t \qquad (4.6.3)$$

where,

$$v_t = \frac{1}{1 - b}\,u_t \qquad (4.6.4)$$

which will be a random error term also, provided that u_t in the 'structural equation' is also a random error term. In estimating these two 'reduced form' equations we should impose the restriction that the slope coefficients sum to unity, otherwise they are not a direct translation of the original (linearised) hypothesis expressed in the equation (4.6.1), the 'structural equation'.

In subjecting these equations to empirical evaluation, apart from relying on (i) the fact that the Malkiel hypothesis can be expressed in linear form and (ii) the over-time constancy of σ, we are, naturally, also relying on whatever estimators we have used to obtain L_t^{N}. Seen as a series *per se*, we believe that if some kind of average is to be employed as an estimator it should be of the distributed lag form, giving predominant influence to recent values of interest rates; and that in doing so we should go back in time no more than about four years. Therefore, as stated in previous sections of this chapter, we report results obtained from letting the normal rate be formed over fifteen *periods* by either a Koyck or a Pascal distributed lag scheme. However, to make comparisons with Malkiel's own work somewhat easier, we also include results based on his methods of evaluating the normal rate.

For the given distributed lag used to calculate L_t^N, and hence for the particular value of λ chosen, we can (in line with what we have said in section 4.4) calculate a further series, namely that for σ_t. We did this for the Koyck lag scheme with $\lambda = 0.5$ and for the second-order Pascal lag with various values of λ. Utilising the values of σ arrived at enables us to test the 'normal range' version, the full version, as it were, of the Malkiel hypothesis.

Recall from section 4.4 that that hypothesis is:

$$(L - S)_t = f\left(\frac{L - L^N + k\sigma}{2k\sigma}\right)_t \qquad (4.6.5)$$

which it is further supposed is a linear relationship. We may let $k = 1$, and then, *ceteris paribus*, 2σ will be reasonably proportioned to the normal range. It could be argued that it might be more appropriate to let $k = 2$. But, of course, if we were to split the independent variable in equation (4.6.5) into $[(L - L^N)/2k\sigma]$ and $(k\sigma/2k\sigma)$, this would affect the values of the parameters attached to these variables only in that they too will be scaled appropriately. Also, if equation (4.6.5) is estimated as it stands, the parameter on the 'compound' independent variable with $k = 2$ will be one-half of what it will be with $k = 1$; and, naturally, the explanatory value of the hypothesis is unaffected by this particular scaling of the data.[15]

Given that σ is measured, we can test equation (4.6.5) as it stands and then, more appropriately, in its reduced form specification. Thus we have:

$$(L - S)_t = a + b\left(\frac{L - L^N + \sigma}{2\sigma}\right)_t; \qquad (4.6.6)$$

$$L_t = \frac{a}{1 - \dfrac{b}{2\sigma_t}} + \frac{b}{1 - \dfrac{b}{2\sigma_t}}\left(\frac{\sigma - L^N}{2\sigma}\right)_t + \frac{S_t}{1 - \dfrac{b}{2\sigma_t}} \qquad (4.6.7)$$

$$S_t = -a + \left(1 - \frac{b}{2\sigma_t}\right) L_t + b\left(\frac{L^N - \sigma}{2\sigma}\right)_t. \qquad (4.6.8)$$

But we have to estimate equation (4.6.7) as:

$$L_t = a + b\left(\frac{L - L^N + \sigma}{2\sigma}\right)_t + S_t \qquad (4.6.9)$$

and (4.6.8) as:

$$S_t = -a - b\left(\frac{L - L^N + \sigma}{2\sigma}\right)_t + L_t \qquad (4.6.10)$$

with all the obvious disadvantages such a procedure entails. In estimating these equations, they should satisfy the constraint that the coefficients on S_t and L_t, in equations (4.6.9) and (4.6.10) respectively, are unity.

The equations produced above are for situations where a series on L_t^N has been formed and where, in line with Malkiel's own position, no allowance has been made for 'expectations proper'. At this juncture it seems appropriate to pause and consider some of the empirical results obtained from such a procedure.

Grant's and Masera's data made it possible for us to test these equations by forming a series for L_t^N, and we did so by using the Koyck, Pascal and Almon lag schemes and the methods advanced by Malkiel. The yield-to-maturity data we have assembled on an annual basis for the U.K. from 1953 did not enable us to test the Malkiel Theory using an 'observed' series for L_t^N. We may begin our overview of our results by focusing our attention on those derived from the use of distributed lag schemes.

In general the results from the Italian data, no matter which distributed lag scheme was used for L_t^N, were of no significance whatsoever. This is partly because the nature of Masera's data is such that the longest length-of-life security is one for nine years, so that there is no true long-term stock, neither is there really even a medium-term stock. In most instances the overall fits were statistically speaking zero. If anything the choice of $\lambda = 0.5$ and the Koyck scheme produced the 'best' results.

For the U.K. the best results were obtained by using the Koyck lag scheme with $\lambda = 0.5$, where L_t was interpreted as the yield on 2½% Consols and S_t was the one-year rate, though using the second-order Pascal lag with $\lambda = 0.2$ produced only slightly inferior results — as might be expected, since the pattern of weights produced in these circumstances is similar to that given by the Koyck lag with $\lambda = 0.5$. The U.K. results, for Grant's data 1953—62, are listed in table 4.6.1. We shall now comment on these equations *seriatim.*

Equation (4.6.1)′ is an extremely poor result and the very unsatisfactory value of d, indicating positive serial correlation in the residuals, reflects this fact. The weak overall fit of the equation probably indicates that the regression coefficients in it are not unduly biased after all: a rough check on this, using the variance of the actual errors from equation (4.6.1)′ as a proxy for the hypothetical errors in equation (4.6.1), reveals this to be so. Thus, all in all, the coefficients a and b are likely to be significantly different from zero, so that b has its *a priori* sign. Equation (4.6.1)′ is very much inferior to the only version of it tested by Malkiel, namely

Table 4.6.1 *U.K.: Grant's data—quarterly, 1953—62 (λ = 0.5)*

Equation number	Equation	$\bar{R}^2$	d
(4.6.1)′	$(L-S)_t = 1^{*}.024 - 1^{*}.1465\,(L-L^{N})_t$ $\quad\;(0.107)\quad(0.14)$	0.18	0.77
(4.6.2)′	$S_t = -1.147 + 2^{*}.15\,L_t - 1^{*}.1246\,L_t^{N}$ $\quad(0.64)\quad(0.37)\quad\quad(0.387)$	0.67	0.77
(4.6.3)′	$L_t = 0.3448 + 0^{*}.2131\,S_t + 0^{*}.7705\,L_t^{N}$ $\quad(0.21)\quad(0.037)\quad\quad(0.056)$	0.93	1.0
(4.6.6)′	$(L-S)_t = 1^{*}.55 - 0^{*}.999\left(\dfrac{L-L^{N}+\sigma}{2\sigma}\right)_t$ $\quad(0.233)\quad(0.331)$	0.16	0.78
(4.6.9)′	$L_t = -2^{*}.81 - 0.326\left(\dfrac{L-L^{N}+\sigma}{2\sigma}\right)_t + 0^{*}.573\,S_t$ $\quad(0.276)\quad(0.271)\quad\quad\quad(0.072)$	0.61	0.47
(4.6.10)′	$S_t = -1^{*}.82 + 0^{*}.964\left(\dfrac{L-L^{N}+\sigma}{2\sigma}\right)_t + 1^{*}.059\,L_t$ $\quad(0.55)\quad(0.343)\quad\quad\quad(0.135)$	0.66	0.78

equation (4.5.2), though it should be remembered that, there, Malkiel was using annual data, and data constructed by the smoothing method, in addition to the arithmetic average estimates of L_t^{N} based on fifteen *years'* observations.

Removing the simultaneous bias from equation (4.6.1)′ by letting S_t or L_t be the dependent variable greatly improves the overall value of the hypothesis. For both equations, however, there is still serious auto-correlation in the residuals. Even so, the slope coefficients in equations (4.6.2)′ and (4.6.3)′ are still likely to be significantly different from zero; and the constant terms would, of course, still be effectively zero if we were to take account of the serial correlation in the residuals. In view of the fact that L_t^{N} is derived from a distributed lag scheme, it is not very surprising that equation (4.6.3)′ produces such a good overall fit, and in particular one that is superior to that produced by equation (4.6.2)′.

What, though, do these equations tell us about the two basic parameters, a and b, of the Malkiel Theory and hence about that theory itself? To answer this question we may take another look at equations (4.5.2) and (4.5.3) upon which they are based. To estimate both equations by ordinary least squares it is necessary to suppose that S_t is exogenous in equation (4.6.2) but endogenous for equation (4.6.3), and vice-versa for L_t. But, assuming that u_t is a random error term, we can then estimate these equations and obtain unbiased, consistent, unique estimates of the 'compound' parameters in them. However, because each equation is over-identified, we cannot obtain *unique* estimates of a and b by unscrambling these compound parameters, although, if we estimate the equations by R.L.S. so that the restriction given by the theory is imposed upon them, namely that the slope coefficients in either equation sum to unity, then we can obtain unique estimates of a and b.

We observe from equations (4.6.2)′ and (4.6.3)′ in table 4.6.1 that these restrictions *are* fulfilled; estimating the equations by R.L.S. and using an F-test shows that the data do support the restriction. When the latter is imposed the parameters in equations (4.6.2)′ and (4.6.3)′ naturally do not change very much; so we can use those parameters given in table 4.6.1 from which to deduce the value of a and b. This then provides us with *two* versions of the structural equation, namely:

$$(L-S)_t = 1.147 - 1.246\,(L-L^{\mathrm{N}})_t \qquad (4.6.2)''$$

$$(L-S)_t = 1.59 - 3.616\,(L-L^{\mathrm{N}})_t. \qquad (4.6.3)''$$

The reason for these two totally different equations is that we should use either one *or* the other *or* attempt to estimate them simultaneously. But for various reasons such estimation is not possible.

If we wish to compare these results directly with those of Malkiel we should concentrate on equations (4.6.2)′ and (4.6.2)″. The values of the coefficients in these equations are not far off the *average* values from all of Malkiel's results; but the slope coefficients restriction works better on this particular piece of testing than it does on average for Malkiel, though, as already noted, the overall explanatory power of the hypothesis on this specification of it is far less than the average R^2 in the tables presented in section 4.5.

Equation (4.6.10)′, for example, supposes that σ can be measured in a particular manner and it can change over time. *Prima facie* this result is as good as that given by equation (4.6.2)′; but this means that the question as to whether we should allow σ to be constant or to vary over time is still in the air. Because it is not possible to separate L_t out into a single dependent variable there is some difficulty in giving any judgement on the importance of allowing σ to be a variable. In addition, as always, the success of any attempt to specify the influence of σ depends upon the means by which L_t^N is itself calculated. In equation (4.6.10)′ the restriction that the coefficient on L_t be unity is satisfied; and b comes out as −0.964. These results are reasonably good from the viewpoint of the Malkiel Theory, and for the way we have specified it.

So far we have not made any comments about the constant terms in these equations, nor, for that matter, about the constants in Malkiel's own results. If we look at the two short-rate equations in table 4.6.1 we see that they are negative (though that in (4.6.2)′ is statistically speaking zero at the 5% level): this means that a is positive. Except for equation (4.6.2)′ a is also statistically speaking greater than zero. We shall say something further about the role of the constant term a in Malkiel's theory in the concluding section of this chapter.

To obtain a more direct comparison with the results produced by Malkiel we have run his equation for U.K. and Italian data with L_t^N calculated with $\lambda = 1.0$, 0.95 and 0.9, with $n = 15$, via scheme [1] in section 4.5 above, namely:

$$L_t^N = \sum_{i=1}^{15} {}_{t-i}L_k \lambda^i \Big/ \sum_{i=1}^{15} \lambda^i \qquad [1]$$

where k is the length-of-life of 'the' long bond; for the U.K. Consols are the long stock and nine-year bonds have to be the long stock for Italy. Given that the U.K. data are on a quarterly basis whilst the Italian are on a monthly basis (1957—67) the distributed lag scheme [1] has a slightly different interpretation for the one set of data than for the other.

The U.K. results are reported in table 4.6.2, those for Italy are given in table 4.6.3.

Let us consider these results *per se* before drawing any comparison between them and those of Malkiel.

We consider table 4.6.2 first. The results for $(L - S)$ should not perhaps be discussed, but if we were to take them at their face value they would indicate a positive a (very much significantly different from zero statistically speaking), and a negative b (also very much different from zero). But, of course, the coefficients in these equations will almost certainly be biased, and their standard errors will be understated because of the very serious auto-correlation that exists in the residuals. For what it is worth, the $\bar{R}^2$ increases as λ decreases. As far as the three equations for S_t are concerned they exhibit the same characteristic, although less so; and, statistically, there is basically nothing to choose between one value of λ or another. Here, the constant terms are statistically speaking zero.

Table 4.6.2 U.K.: Grant's data — quarterly, 1953—62

Equation number	λ	Equation	$\bar{R}^{2\,(a)}$	d	ρ
4.6.11	1.0	$(L-S)_t = 1\overset{*}{.}2191 - 0\overset{*}{.}6946\,(L-L^{\mathrm{N}})_t$ (0.149) (0.249)	0.139	0.61	0.69
4.6.12	0.95	$(L-S)_t = 1\overset{*}{.}2216 - 0\overset{*}{.}798\,(L-L^{\mathrm{N}})_t$ (0.140) (0.255)	0.173	0.641	0.671
4.6.13	0.9	$(L-S)_t = 1\overset{*}{.}206 - 0\overset{*}{.}869\,(L-L^{\mathrm{N}})_t$ (0.132) (0.261)	0.194	0.672	0.655
4.6.14	1.0	$S_t = -0.3119 + 1\overset{*}{.}76\,L_t - 0\overset{*}{.}97\,L_t^{\mathrm{N}}$ (0.799) (0.25) (0.34)	0.662	0.636	0.666
4.6.15	0.95	$S_t = -0.2522 + 1\overset{*}{.}87\,L_t - 1\overset{*}{.}09\,L_t^{\mathrm{N}}$ (0.765) (0.26) (0.34)	0.678	0.678	0.643
4.6.16	0.9	$S_t = -0.266 + 1\overset{*}{.}934\,L_t - 1\overset{*}{.}145\,L_t^{\mathrm{N}}$ (0.742) (0.264) (0.336)	0.686	0.711	0.626
4.6.17	1.0	$L_t = -0.029 + 0\overset{*}{.}31\,S_t + 0\overset{*}{.}83\,L_t^{\mathrm{N}}$ (0.34) (0.045) (0.09)	0.873	0.604	0.674
4.6.18	0.95	$L_t = -0.03 + 0\overset{*}{.}303\,S_t + 0\overset{*}{.}824\,L_t^{\mathrm{N}}$ (0.31) (0.042) (0.08)	0.889	0.679	0.636
4.6.19	0.9	$L_t = -0.0125 + 0\overset{*}{.}297\,S_t + 0\overset{*}{.}82\,L_t$ (0.291) (0.04) (0.08)	0.897	0.725	0.615

(a) All values of $\bar{R}^2$ are significantly different from zero at the 5% level or better.

The signs of the L_t and L_t^{N} coefficients indicate that the *b*s are negative. Those coefficients are different from zero at the 1% level, and because of this might remain highly significant even if cognisance is taken of the, once again, very serious positive serial correlation in the residuals. The coefficients on L_t and on L_t^{N} sum to approximately 0.8, which at accepted levels of significance is not different from 1.0. The pattern of the results for L_t is similar to that for S_t, the only difference now is that the slope coefficients sum to 1.1 and *a* could be *negative* if the constant terms had only been significantly different from zero.

Table 4.6.3 Italy: Masera's data — monthly, 1957–67

Equation number	λ	Equation	$\bar{R}^{2\,(a)}$	d	ρ
4.6.20	1.0	$(L-S)_t = 0\overset{*}{.}436 - 0.548\ (L-L^N)_t$ $(0.098)\quad(0.328)$	—	0.465	0.766
4.6.21	0.95	$(L-S)_t = 0\overset{*}{.}448 - 0.454\ (L-L^N)_t$ $(0.098)\quad(0.347)$	—	0.436	0.781
4.6.22	0.9	$(L-S)_t = 0\overset{*}{.}46 - 0.333\ (L-L^N)_t$ $(0.097)\quad(0.364)$	—	0.404	0.797
4.6.23	1.0	$S_t = 4\overset{*}{.}055 + 0\overset{*}{.}957\ L_t - 0\overset{*}{.}7811\ L_t^N$ $(1.5)\quad(0.373)\quad(0.326)$	$0\overset{**}{.}044$	0.356	0.83
4.6.24	0.95	$S_t = 4\overset{*}{.}0 + 0\overset{*}{.}906\ L_t - 0\overset{*}{.}73\ L_t^N$ $(1.5)\quad(0.384)\quad(0.35)$	$0\overset{**}{.}033$	0.343	0.83
4.6.25	0.9	$S_t = 3.99 + 0\overset{*}{.}84\ L_t - 0.65\ L_t^N$ $(1.546)\quad(0.39)\quad(0.37)$	—	0.33	0.84
4.6.26	1.0	$L_t = 1\overset{*}{.}72 + 0\overset{*}{.}057\ S_t + 0\overset{*}{.}622\ L_t^N$ $(0.34)\quad(0.022)\quad(0.057)$	0.507	1.3	0.35
4.6.27	0.95	$L_t = 1\overset{*}{.}563 + 0\overset{*}{.}052\ S_t + 0\overset{*}{.}656\ L_t^N$ $(0.344)\quad(0.022)\quad(0.06)$	0.524	1.34	0.33
4.6.28	0.9	$L_t = 1\overset{*}{.}423 + 0\overset{*}{.}046\ S_t + 0\overset{*}{.}688\ L_t^N$ $(0.35)\quad(0.022)\quad(0.06)$	0.538	1.4	0.3

[(a)] a dash (—) indicates that $\bar{R}^2$ is not significantly different from zero at any acceptable confidence level; two asterisks indicate that it is significant only at the 1% level; an unasterisked $\bar{R}^2$ is significantly different from zero at the 5% level and better.

We turn now to reflect on the results for Italy detailed in table 4.6.3. These results differ considerably from those for the U.K., except that they all indicate auto-correlation in the error terms and that the L_t equations are better than those for S_t. Let us take the equations, as before, *seriatim*.

Those for $(L-S)$ indicate that: as λ increases $\bar{R}^2$ decreases but is always statistically speaking zero; a is positive; b is negative, but effectively zero. The hypothesis is valueless on this set of data, on this method of estimating L_t^N. This is also the conclusion when we examine the S_t results: the overall goodness-of-fit of each equation is really zero, and the hypothesis that the slope coefficients sum to unity is *not* satisfied by the data. Matters improve somewhat when we pass on to the L_t equations. $\bar{R}^2$ is a decreasing function of λ; and the slope coefficients do not sum to unity, arithmetically or statistically speaking. Here a comes out positive and b negative. For these equations the auto-correlation of the residuals is less of a problem than for the other Italian equations and for the U.K. equations.

In comparing these results with those of Malkiel it is clear at the outset, therefore, that *in toto* the results for Italy are very much inferior to those he has produced for the U.S.A. and the U.K. In fact, the results, because we should look solely at the S_t equations, are inferior to any of those that Malkiel has produced, whether we base our judgement on table 4.6.2 or on table 4.6.3. Though we may be being too hard on the hypothesis in the light of its performance against the Italian data: for the latter are data on a rather special set of bonds, and additionally the longest life bond is one of nine years, which is perhaps not long enough to estimate the 'normal long-term rate'.

The results we have just quoted for Italy and the U.K. however seem to suggest that, *interalia*, the question of the choice of data period and possibly the cyclical/trend structure of the data themselves might be important in influencing the outcome of testing the Malkiel hypothesis. Of even more potential importance in this direction is the use of distributed lag schemes by which we proxy the 'normal' long-term rate of interest. Their effects on the results are linked to the structure of the data to which they are being applied. The distributed lag schemes (implicitly) reflect an attempt to extrapolate the scalar quality of the variable concerned: in this case, that is to say, they are used for projecting the series of, or future developments in, 'the' long-term rate of interest as foreseen by an individual. But this extrapolation, because of the nature of the problem we are dealing with (that is, we need a macro-view of the 'normal' rate, and we have only observed data to go on), has to be performed on past, actual, values of the long-term rate of interest. Depending on the structure of the data this can mean that trends in the actual observations are being calculated or accentuated. After all, such lag schemes are often used to 'smooth' time series data.

Having made these observations, let us move on to make a brief comparison between our own results and those of Malkiel. When we do compare the empirical findings obtained by Malkiel from his *specification* of his hypothesis for the U.K. (as in table 4.6.2) with those from our own specifications of it, on balance, save for the $\bar{R}^2$ of the S_t equation (table 4.6.1), our specification is marginally better than that of Malkiel, although the lowish values of the $\bar{R}^2$ means that the hypothesis *per se* leaves a good proportion of the variation in S_t unexplained. Remember that one difference though between our empirical testing of the Malkiel hypothesis and that of Malkiel himself, for the U.K., concerns the method of evaluating L^N, for we have eschewed the utilisation of the 'historic range' concept.

In all results referred to, quoted and discussed at this stage, whether they concern Malkiel's own results or our own, λ is a *predetermined* variable. We have noted in section 4.4 that it is possible to estimate any of the Malkiel equations in a 'reduced form' specification by letting λ be any value, a value to be determined by the econometrics itself if at all possible. This can be a useful procedure since, in principle at least, it means that the degrees of freedom, as it were, in testing the hypothesis are increased by one: now what is being tested is the hypothesis *per se*, its form (e.g. linear), and the scheme by which L_t^N is assessed — a formidable list in this context even so.

For our present purposes we may concentrate our energies solely on the S_t equation since this becomes 'the' equation in the Malkiel hypothesis. This is:

$$S_t = -a + b\,L_t^N + (1 - b)\,L_t - u_t. \tag{4.6.29}$$

Into this equation we may substitute whichever (proper) distributed lag scheme we wish to adopt. Here we may just look at the effects of using the Koyck scheme (4.4.5) and the second-order Pascal lag (4.4.8).

Substituting (4.4.5) into equation (4.6.29) and simplifying produces this equation:

$$S_t = a_0 + a_1\,L_t + a_2\,L_{t-1} + a_3\,S_{t-1} + w_t \tag{4.6.30}$$

where:

$$a_0 = -a\,(1 - \lambda); \quad a_1 = (1 - b); \quad a_2 = \lambda(2b - 1); \quad a_3 = \lambda; \tag{4.6.31}$$

and:

$$w_t = \lambda u_{t-1} - u_t. \tag{4.6.32}$$

Utilising the Pascal lag provides us with this equation:

$$S_t = b_0 + b_1\,S_{t-1} + b_2\,S_{t-2} + b_3\,L_t + b_4\,L_{t-1} + b_5\,L_{t-2} + z_t. \tag{4.6.33}$$

Here:

$$b_0 = -a(1-\lambda)^2; \quad b_1 = 2\lambda; \quad b_2 = -\lambda^2; \quad b_3 = (1-b);$$
$$b_4 = (b + b\lambda^2 - 2\lambda); \quad b_5 = \lambda^2(1-b)$$

and:

$$z_t = -u_t + 2\lambda u_{t-1} - \lambda^2 u_{t-2}. \tag{4.6.35}$$

Technically it is possible to estimate both of these equations by O.L.S. But such a step, of course, is fraught with difficulties. The presence of lagged dependent variables is going to produce biased estimates of the parameters in the equations. To complicate matters, should u_t be a random variable, then w_t and z_t will be auto-correlated; and anyway the error terms in the equations will not be independent of the lagged dependent variables. It is highly likely therefore, that O.L.S. estimation of equations (4.6.30) and (4.6.33) will merely provide us with biased and inconsistent parameter estimates. If we assume that u_t is auto-correlated in a particular way it is possible to obviate some of these difficulties, though that of biasedness will still remain.

Thus, for equation (4.6.30) we could assume that:

$$u_t = \mu u_{t-1} - w_t \tag{4.6.36}$$

where $\mu = \lambda$, and w_t is a random error term. Likewise for equation (4.6.35) we might assume that:

$$u_t = 2\beta u_{t-1} - \beta^2 u_{t-2} - z_t \tag{4.6.37}$$

where, $\beta = \lambda$, and z_t is a random error term.

Without having to make any detailed assumptions about the error terms (save that they are auto-correlated in the reduced form equations), the Liviatan (74) technique, which in some senses appears to be superior to that of Koyck (32) or of Klein (75), can be used on equations such as (4.6.30) and (4.6.33) to obtain consistent estimates of the 'compound' parameters in them. We did, in fact, use that technique to estimate both equations for the U.K. and for Italy; and we did so in two different forms, the second of which was to add an extra 'instrumental variable' at the first stage. But on the whole the results were not too good, especially for Italy. As far as we could tell we were paying a high price for the (dubious?) attainment of consistent estimates.

Even after one has gone to the trouble of obtaining 'two-stage' consistent estimates of the parameters on the variables in equations (4.6.30) and (4.6.33), it is not possible to unscramble those estimates to obtain the values of the 'structural' parameters. As far as the latter are concerned, the 'reduced-form' equations are over-identified. To enable us to estimate the structural parameters, a, b and λ, we must estimate equation (4.6.30), for example, subject to the conditions given in (4.6.31) and the *non-linear* constraints which they imply exist on the parameters in equation (4.6.30).

But before saying something about such estimations it might be worth while just to present the O.L.S. estimates of equations (4.6.30) and (4.6.33) for the U.K. (Grant's data) and for Italy. Although these could be inconsistent estimates the results, so far as it is possible to judge this, are better than the Liviatan-type results we obtained, which as we noted earlier were quite poor. Table 4.6.4 catalogues the O.L.S. results for equations (4.6.30) and (4.6.33) for the two countries.

In terms of overall performance, judged by reference to $\bar{R}^2$, the equations for the U.K. and for Italy are superior to any of the results for S_t we have specified hitherto, though they still fall far short of those from Malkiel's own testing against U.K. data — and, of course, of that against Durand's data. As might be expected, when the long-rate versions of the equation reported on in table 4.6.4 are evaluated they produce $\bar{R}^2$s of almost one. Also, it is not surprising that these results are superior to those that have been found by using L_t^N as 'a' variable. The lagged variables make a great deal of difference to the kind of outcome that does materialise. As would be imagined, there is a fair degree of multicollinearity present in these equations, so that some variables are apparently insignificant where perhaps they really are significant. But to judge from a comparison of the two forms of the equation (for either country separately) by reference to $\bar{R}^2$ it is probably likely that the extra lagged variables in the Pascal form of the equation do not add very much to the value of the overall relationship. The $\bar{R}^2$s tend to indicate that there is nothing to choose between either 'reduced-form' equation of the Malkiel Theory or, significantly now and contrary to previous conclusions on this count, between the one set of data or the other. The value of the Durbin—Watson statistic, though superficially pointing to the absence now of auto-correlation in the residuals, must be judged with caution, since we have lagged dependent variables in the vector of explanatory variables and our sample sizes are rather small (though that for Italy is 117). Not one of the equations in table 4.6.4 has parameter estimates which meet *a priori* expectations, assuming that we expect $b < 0$ and $\lambda > 0$, as can be seen from equations (4.6.31) and (4.6.34). This might make us wonder whether or not some of the hypotheses embodied in

Table 4.6.4 Malkiel hypothesis: Koyck and Pascal lag 'reduced-form' results; U.K. quarterly data and Italian monthly data

Equation number	Equation	$\bar{R}^2$	d	ρ
4.6.38 (U.K.)	$S_t = -0.048 + \overset{*}{1.414}\, L_t - \overset{*}{1.184}\, L_{t-1} + \overset{*}{0.725}\, S_{t-1}$ (0.53) (0.36) (0.35) (0.11)	0.82	2.35	−0.18
4.6.39 (U.K.)	$S_t = 0.34 + \overset{*}{1.17}\, L_t + 0.19\, L_{t-1} - \overset{*}{1.232}\, L_{t-2} + \overset{*}{0.56}\, S_{t-1} + 0.189\, S_{t-2}$ (0.52) (0.35) (0.6) (0.44) (0.15) (0.15)	0.84	2.2	−0.1
4.6.40 (Italy)	$S_t = -0.15 - \overset{*}{0.44}\, L_t + \overset{*}{0.56}\, L_{t-1} + \overset{*}{0.9}\, S_{t-1}$ (0.67) (0.17) (0.16) (0.04)	0.82	1.5	0.25
4.6.41 (Italy)	$S_t = -0.0096 - \overset{*}{0.378}\, L_t + \overset{*}{0.815}\, L_{t-1} - 0.33\, L_{t-2} + \overset{*}{1.135}\, S_{t-1} - \overset{*}{0.252}\, S_{t-2}$ (0.66) (0.17) (0.19) (0.17) (0.09) (0.09)	0.83	1.96	0.02

equations (4.6.30) and (4.6.33) have any value or are correctly specified.

But there are, as we have already intimated, many problems involved in an attempt to evaluate the worth of equations such as (4.6.30) and (4.6.33) and of the ideas which underlie them. So, *en passant*, perhaps we may draw attention to one major and general problem with the estimation of equations involving distributed lag formulations that was made and developed by Griliches (31), namely, that it is not always a simple matter to say what kind of formulation (e.g. Koyck, or *n*th order Pascal) is implied in the reduced-form equation written as in (4.6.30) or (4.6.33) by means of 'compound parameters'. This means, naturally, that even apart from the other considerations that must be borne in mind when evaluating the Malkiel Theory via these equations, it is difficult to judge within that theory whether the one distributed lag function is superior to the other. So what we have managed to say on this score in the previous paragraph — little though it be — must be taken with caution.

To give a simple illustration as to why this is so we may consider equation (4.6.30) and the following hypothesis, which states that it is believed that the error term in the reduced-form equation itself, w_t, is auto-correlated:

$$w_t = \gamma w_{t-1} + \epsilon_t, \quad 0 < \gamma < 1 \qquad (4.6.42)$$

where ϵ_t is a random disturbance term. So, if we want to obtain O.L.S. estimates of the reduced form of equation (4.6.29), where those estimates are (hopefully) to be consistent ones, we could obviate the need to use any technique such as that of Liviatan of course, but we would have to lag equation (4.6.30) and multiply it by γ. Taking the resulting expression from (4.6.30) would produce an equation in which the error term appeared as ϵ_t (i.e., $w_t - \gamma w_{t-1}$). But this equation would leave us with S_t being a function of the variables S_{t-1}, S_{t-2}, L_t, L_{t-1} and L_{t-2}, that is the same variables as appear in the first reduced-form Pascal equation, (4.6.33). Therefore we could regard the estimation of equation (4.6.33) *at least* as *either* a test of the Pascal-type distribution, with, say, an error term z_t, which is random on the assumption that u_t follows scheme (4.6.37) and β there equals λ in scheme (4.6.35), *or* of the Koyck-type distribution, also with a random error term, which has however been derived by assuming that w_t is *non*-random.

But, suppose that in using the Koyck lag it has been assumed, for example, that equation (4.6.42) holds. Whether γ should equal λ or not, the makeup of the compound parameters in the new reduced-form Koyck equation will differ from those given in equation (4.6.33) for the Pascal lag, under the assumed conditions. In effect, using (4.6.42) and for simplicity letting $\gamma = \lambda$, equation (4.6.30) becomes:

$$S_t = -a(1-\lambda)^2 + \lambda S_{t-1} - \lambda^2 S_{t-2} + (1-b)L_t + (3b\lambda - 2\lambda)L_{t-1} - \lambda^2(2b-1)L_{t-2} + \epsilon_t. \quad (4.6.43)$$

Therefore, if equations (4.6.43) and (4.6.33) are being estimated, one means of helping to differentiate between them and their properties is to impose upon them the non-linear restrictions that exist on their parameters, so as to get separate estimates of λ, a and b, which estimates, for each equation, will be unique. In this way it is possible for the computer to differentiate between the two types of equations.

Even so, it must not be forgotten that, if we can apply the non-linear restrictions successfully in whatever set of 'reduced-form' equations we do decide to run, any evaluation of the alternative distributed lag schemes will be implicitly based on assumptions made about the error terms, apart from the specific form the lag distribution is to take (e.g., in this instance it is assumed that the 'appropriate' Pascal lag is a second-order distribution). Of course, it is possible to enter so many caveats in qualification of the results being obtained that the issues become somewhat blurred and it is difficult to make any clear-cut judgements at all.

We made numerous experiments with the distributed lag formulations in an attempt both to see which formulation seemed the 'correct' one for the data on hand, and to evaluate the values of the basic parameters. The experiments involved the direct application of non-linear estimating techniques to the 'reduced-form' equations and the use of the 'gridding method' suggested by Theil (72). The latter method circumvents the need to use non-linear techniques. If we look at equations (4.6.30) and (4.6.33) they only pose difficulties because of λ. If we give a value to the latter it is possible to rewrite the equations in such a way that they contain the same number of independent variables as they do parameters to be estimated (now, just a and b). But this method is very time-consuming and is somewhat inefficient. The idea is to select that value of λ which produces the best overall fit, though the estimation of the basic parameters via non-linear techniques is also very time-consuming and inefficient, because those techniques rely on iterative methods. It is difficult both to obtain a solution for each equation and to judge if that solution is the optimum one.

In the event it proved impossible to differentiate between the Koyck-lag and Pascal-lag forms of the equations. It was also difficult to quantify the basic parameters in each specification of the Malkiel hypothesis. However, a came out as positive and b as negative and generally less than one in absolute value. From some of the non-linear estimates there were sensible values of a and b with good overall relationships but with negative values of λ. On the occasions when λ was positive it lay below 0.70. In the Koyck-lag equations the gridding method seemed to support a value of λ that was not far off the value of 0.5 we had arbitrarily assigned to it earlier in our investigations.

These conclusions are not perhaps after all that negative, but they are nowhere near as positive as we would have liked them to be. They do leave the question of the appropriate lag scheme and its structure rather in abeyance, though not totally.

So far we have considered the practical merits of the Malkiel hypothesis in the light of data compiled by commentators other than ourselves. To round off the discussion in this part of the chapter we may now take a cursory look at the outcome of testing the theory against a new set of data, the set we have collated for the U.K. on an annual basis for the period 1953—71. The methods by which we have constructed that set of data we have discussed in chapter 1 above. It will be recalled that we have used three variants of the data, namely: (i) a set derived from a partial sifting out of the observed, market-given, data on bond yields and their terms-to-maturity, which is not far removed from the raw data therefore, and for which we have constructed yield-to-maturity curves by the 'unweighted linear interpolation' method; (ii) a set derived by transforming the data by 'weighted linear interpolation'; and (iii) a set obtained by 'smoothing' the data. These sets we refer to as unW, W and S, respectively, in the econometric results which follow.

The time span we have chosen for our data period makes it impossible for us to test anything other than the 'reduced-form' versions of the hypothesis, as given by equations (4.6.30) and (4.6.33). When run against the three kinds of data sets these equations came out as portrayed in table 4.6.5. These estimates are O.L.S. estimates, so they are directly comparable to those catalogued in table 4.6.4 above for the U.K. We have not attempted to estimate these equations in any other way.

Let us say a few words about the equations in table 4.6.5. Both sets, as would be expected, exhibit the characteristic that the best overall results (judged solely by reference to $\bar{R}^2$, though) are provided by the unweighted data, the next best are provided by the

Table 4.6.5 Malkiel hypothesis: Koyck and Pascal lag 'reduced-form' results; U.K. annual data, 1953—71

Equation number	Equation	$\bar{R}^2$	d	ρ
4.6.44	$S_t^w = \underset{(0.445)}{0.8209} + \underset{(0.118)}{0.3642^*} L_t - \underset{(0.135)}{0.0587} L_{t-1} + \underset{(0.143)}{0.6408^*} S_{t-1}^w$	0.906	1.530	0.088
4.6.45	$S_t^{unW} = \underset{(0.005)}{0.0087} + \underset{(0.001)}{0.9998^*} L_t - \underset{(0.003)}{0.0026} L_{t-1} + \underset{(0.003)}{0.0009} S_{t-1}^{unW}$	0.999	2.436	−0.332
4.6.46	$S_t^s = \underset{(0.627)}{0.2941} + \underset{(0.180)}{0.8728^*} L_t - \underset{(0.256)}{0.0140} L_{t-1} + \underset{(0.284)}{0.0702} S_{t-1}^s$	0.852	2.032	−0.091
4.6.47	$S_t^w = \underset{(0.426)}{0.4660} + \underset{(0.109)}{0.4351^*} L_t - \underset{(0.132)}{0.1646} L_{t-1} + \underset{(0.125)}{0.2013} L_{t-2} + \underset{(0.228)}{0.4267} S_{t-1}^w + \underset{(0.203)}{0.1401} S_{t-2}^w$	0.927	1.405	0.228
4.6.48	$S_t^{unW} = \underset{(0.005)}{0.0062} + \underset{(0.001)}{1.0000^*} L_t - \underset{(0.004)}{0.0027} L_{t-1} + \underset{(0.003)}{0.00002} L_{t-2} - \underset{(0.004)}{0.0006} S_{t-1}^{unW} + \underset{(0.003)}{0.0019} S_{t-2}^{unW}$	0.999	2.049	−0.045
4.6.49	$S_t^s = \underset{(0.818)}{0.1207} + \underset{(0.197)}{0.9192^*} L_t - \underset{(0.274)}{0.0372} L_{t-1} + \underset{(0.263)}{0.0272} L_{t-2} - \underset{(0.329)}{0.0636} S_{t-1}^s + \underset{(0.288)}{0.1535} S_{t-2}^s$	0.839	2.116	−0.214

weighted data, while the smoothed data produce the worst results — although, in view of the high $\bar{R}^2$s, it would be more appropriate if worst were to be inserted in inverted commas. But if we examine each equation in more detail the results are not that impressive. For very few of the parameters are significantly different from zero, almost certainly because of the presence of excessive multicollinearity in most of the equations. Nevertheless, from equations (4.6.31) and (4.6.34) we can appreciate from a glance at equations (4.6.44)–(4.6.46) that they contain the correct *a priori* signs on the slope coefficients. This is also true for equation (4.6.47), with the sole exception of the coefficient on S_{t-2}: for equations (4.6.48) and (4.6.49) the signs on that variable's coefficient and on S_{t-1} are not as expected. This itself could have arisen because the separate influences of the explanatory variables have not been assessed by these equations, though a contributing factor will be the small number of degrees of freedom we have.

These equations give some support to the reduced-form equations for the data period we have used, and also leave us with the possibility that the parameter values (of b and λ) fall within the ranges required for an acceptance of the hypothesis. However, to repeat what we have noted in connection with table 4.6.4, it is not surprising that these reduced-form results outstrip those from the other forms the hypothesis can assume. Even if we take the worst of the results from table 4.6.5, they compare favourably with those of table 4.6.4, and they begin to produce overall results of the kind of order Malkiel managed to achieve for his data sets and data periods.

4.7

The Malkiel Theory provides a systematic framework in which Keynes's notion of the normal rate of interest can be developed more fully. It has the advantage that it is a market-view theory, which therefore enables us to look at the term structure at any moment by means of just one equation. Some of this advantage is dissipated however by the fact that the key variables such as the (expected) normal rate of interest have to be calculated if the hypothesis on the term structure is to be of operational value.

The Malkiel hypothesis does have considerable empirical worth.

But its degree of success in explaining real-world phenomena on the term structure does seem to depend upon certain features such as:

(a) The data upon which the hypothesis is tested. The characteristics of the data involve their country of origin, the length between the observation points, the securities upon which they are based, and the method by which the (yield) data are calculated.

(b) The way that the normal rate is proxied.

(c) The assumption made about the width of the (expected) normal range from observation point to observation point over the sample period.

It is difficult to make any concrete statement on the importance of any one of these items *per se* and even on their relative importance for the statistical testing of the Malkiel hypothesis. As far as the data go it is also not possible to differentiate between one characteristic of them and any other; for the quarterly data, such as Grant's, are calculated on a different basis from the annual data of Durand. But our own testing of the hypothesis on U.K. data does suggest that the derivation of the data is of considerable importance.

Despite these difficulties, the Malkiel hypothesis does stand up rather well to empirical testing. The explanatory power of the hypothesis is at times very high and the values of b are negative as the hypothesis requires. The values of a are for the most part positive. This can perhaps give us some indication about the likely existence of influences on the term structure other than the 'expectational' influences incorporated in Malkiel's hypothesis. Malkiel himself suggests that the constant term in his original hypothesis (that is, a) can be regarded as indicating that liquidity premiums exist if it is positive, because a positive a would mean that the yield-gap was positive when the long rate was at the mid-point of the normal range. So on this line of argument the evidence presented in this chapter is overwhelmingly in support of the (likely) existence of liquidity/risk premiums,[16] though a could be positive for other reasons also — hence the use of the caveat 'likely'. For example, a could be positive because the various methods of estimating L_t^N from the historical market yields have systematically understated the 'true' expected normal long-term rate.

Before we bring this chapter to a conclusion there is one issue that we have left untouched in our analysis thus far. We have been discussing the determination of market prices and yields for bonds — corporate or government — yet we have explicitly dealt with only one side of the market. In his original presentation of his theory

Malkiel omitted the *borrowers*' side of the market.[17] On the investor's side the view is expressed that all investors behave in the same way, and have the same expected normal interest rate ranges, and so on. In short, investors can be considered as one.

Now, suppose we do explicitly introduce the borrowers into the picture. If we assume that they too plan their borrowing according to the normal interest rate range, that they all have the same knowledge of that range and all view the movement of 'the' interest rate in that range in the same way as investors do, then it should follow that the Malkiel hypothesis on the term structure holds firm, and all that happens is that the difference between the long rate and the short rate is accentuated at each point in time.

Thus, suppose that the long rate is near the lower bound of the normal range. Just looking at the investors' side of the market would produce the conclusion, according to the Malkiel hypothesis, that the current long rate should stand above the current short rate. Investors will move into the short end of the market and out of the long end. But now let us take account of supply. Borrowers 'ought' to borrow long-term, in which case the supply of long bonds will increase and the supply of shorts may fall. These supply changes will aggravate the decline in the price of long bonds and the decrease in short yields. The yield-gap will be larger than it would have been if supply had been passive; but it will be of the same sign. However, it may look cheaper to borrow short-term. If there are 'inexperienced' borrowers in the market the yield (positive) difference between the long rate and the short rate will be much smaller than if supply changes were ignored.

Consider now the situation where 'the' rate of interest is near the upper bound of the normal range. *Ceteris paribus*, analysis of the demand side of the market produces a situation in which the long rate stands below the short rate. What will be the effect of a (long) rate of interest near the upper bound of the normal range on the supply side of the market? Regular short-term borrowers 'ought' still to borrow short, but regular long-term borrowers might decide to (perhaps 'ought' to decide to) borrow short-term for a while, with a view to returning to their normal practice of borrowing long-term when the level of the interest rate is more centrally located in the normal range. These supply changes reinforce the demand shifts of investors.

These points only scratch the surface of the effects of the actions of borrowers in the Malkiel model. But they show that, on rigorous assumptions, akin to those postulated regarding the behaviour of investors, borrowers' activity should support the Malkiel hypothesis.[18] However, it is not always possible to be dogmatic about what will happen to the supply of bonds, for the model should contain at least two types of borrowers, 'short-term' and 'long-term' borrowers.

Notes to Chapter 4

1. A proof of this proposition, which Malkiel calls 'Theorem 2' on the mathematics of bond-price movements, can be found in Malkiel (11), pp. 54–5.
2. These arguments rest on Malkiel's 'Theorem 4' on bond-price movements. That theorem he states as follows:

> Price movements resulting from equal absolute (or what is the same, from equal percentage) increases and decreases in yield are asymmetric; that is, a decrease in yields raises bond prices more than the same increase in yields lowers prices.
>
> [(11), p. 55: in italics in the original]

To prove this theorem we have to begin with the yield-to-maturity equation for a bond, which we can write as:

$$P = C\left[\frac{1}{1+i} + \frac{1}{(1+i)^2} + \ldots + \frac{1}{(1+i)^n}\right] + \frac{F}{(1+i)^n} \tag{1}$$

where the symbols are as we have used them hitherto, so that i is the yield-to-maturity. If we solve the geometric expression in parentheses in equation (1) we can manipulate the equation so that it becomes:

$$P = \frac{C}{i} + \frac{(F - C/i)}{(1+i)^n}. \tag{2}$$

From equation (2) we derive a familar result — which happens to be Malkiel's 'Theorem 1' — that bond prices move inversely to yields. For we have from (2), that:

$$\frac{\partial P}{\partial i} < 0. \tag{3}$$

Malkiel then argues that 'Theorem 4' is proven if this condition holds:

$$\frac{\partial^2 P}{\partial i^2} > 0. \tag{4}$$

This condition does hold. The curve relating P to i is downward sloping to the right and is convex to the origin (with P on the y-axis and i on the x-axis of a Cartesian diagram). From which we can deduce the theorem.

3. These conditions follow from the theorems ('Theorems' 2 and 4) on bond-price movements.
4. *Prima facie*, it might seem somewhat odd that we have decided to start a new section at this point. We have done this because Mr John F. Richards convinced us that we ought to make the distinction between Malkiel's 'theory' and his 'hypothesis'. Though the distinction has been made largely on analytical grounds, we feel that it helps us in setting out the material in the main text, and hope that it will help the reader, for it seems to us that it is valid to suggest that there is a theory in Malkiel's work from which there emerges his hypothesis on how the term structure is to be explained. Now there are methodological considerations involved here, and this is not the appropriate place to argue out the question of whether or not it is possible to differentiate between a theory and an hypothesis. Often, of course, in economics we take the two things as synonymous; just as we regularly treat 'theory' and 'model' as synonymous when they should not be so treated. Here Malkiel has built up a framework of analysis, an approach to the term structure. From this Keynes-type portrayal of the activity of investors on the financial market he has built a theory; therefrom an hypothesis, a crystallisation of the main ideas in his theory, emerges. That hypothesis obviously depends upon the analytical framework adopted to look at the financial market. But it can be evaluated to discover if it will hold when the assumptions of the analytical framework are altered in ways that seem desirable — to see, in other words, if the assumption of the original framework, which is what we have called Malkiel's 'pilot model', have been appropriately and well chosen, and are as simple and as few as possible, so that with minimum fuss a simple, potentially powerful, testable hypothesis has been developed on the term structure. Though we carry out this kind of analytical exercise in part in section 4.3, we can still keep this section separate from section 4.2.
5. The volume of trading is not uniformly spread over time. There might be a case therefore for taking observations on a volume basis rather than on the basis of units of time. The problem here is that some measure of volume is required. Such a measure is not readily at hand; for the number of markings is only a proxy as it gives no information on the size of transactions.
6. Though it would seem that Dale Jorgenson (111) was the first to introduce this kind of distributed lag function.
7. Proof: The sum of the weights, S, is:

$$S = \lambda + \lambda^2 + \lambda^3 + \ldots + \lambda^{n+1}.$$

Then:

$$\lambda S = \lambda^2 + \lambda^3 + \ldots \lambda^n$$

$$\therefore \quad S(1 - \lambda) = \lambda \text{ as } n \rightarrow \infty$$

$$\therefore \quad S = \frac{\lambda}{1 - \lambda}; \quad \text{which can only be unity if } \lambda = 0.5.$$

8. See, as an example, Feige (36).
9. Proof: The sum of the weights, S, is:

$$S = (1 - \lambda)^2 (1 + 2\lambda + 3\lambda^2 + 4\lambda^3 + \ldots). \tag{1}$$

Then, multiplying equation (1) by λ and subtracting the resulting expression from the equation, we have:

$$S = (1 - \lambda)(1 + \lambda + \lambda^2 + \lambda^3 + \ldots). \tag{2}$$

Having multiplied equation (2) by λ and subtracted the result from (2) we find that, as $n \to \infty$:

$$S(1 - \lambda) = (1 - \lambda) \tag{3}$$

$$\therefore \quad S = 1.$$

10. On these techniques see, for example, E. Malinvaud (43) and especially N. R. Draper and H. Smith (44).
11. The average lag can be located in the way suggested by Griliches (31). Thus, for example, if we consider equation (4.4.5), the Koyck weights in this scheme are:

$$W_i = \lambda + \lambda^2 + \lambda^3 + \ldots + \lambda^{n+1}, \quad i = 0, 1, 2, \ldots, n \tag{1}$$

or

$$W_i = \lambda(1 + \lambda + \lambda^2 + \lambda^3 + \ldots). \tag{2}$$

Then, using Griliches's notation, letting $|z| \leqslant 1$, we can write this expression for the generating function of this sequence of weights:

$$W(z) = \lambda(1 + \lambda z + \lambda^2 z^2 + \lambda^3 z^3 + \ldots) \tag{3}$$

$$\therefore \; W(z) = \frac{\lambda}{1 - \lambda z}. \tag{4}$$

The average lag is given by the first derivative of $W(z)$ evaluated at $z = 1$ (See Griliches (31), p. 19):

$$\frac{d}{dz}\left(\frac{\lambda}{1 - \lambda z}\right) = W'(z) = \frac{\lambda}{(1 - \lambda z)^2} \tag{5}$$

$$\therefore \; W'(1) = \alpha = \left(\frac{\lambda}{1 - \lambda}\right)^2 \tag{6}$$

where, to quote Griliches:

> Using a dummy variable, z, we define a polynomial function:
>
> $$A(z) = a_0 + a_1 z + a_2 z^2 + a_3 z^3 + \ldots$$
>
> If this function converges in some interval $-z_0 < z < z_0$, then $A(z)$ is called the generating function of the sequence (a_i). In addition, if all the a_is are non-negative and $A(1) = 1$, i.e. they sum to unity, then $A(z)$ is a probability generating function.
>
> [(31), p. 19]

12. The precise form of the F-test is:

$$F = \frac{(S^* - S)/g}{S/(n - k - 1)}. \tag{i}$$

where S^* is the error sum of squares for the restricted equation; S is that magnitude for the unrestricted equation; g is the number of restrictions imposed;

n is the number of observations in the data set; and k is the number of independent variables in the equation. Thus F has g, $n-k-1$ degrees of freedom. On this test statistic for linear constraints see, for example, H. Theil (72), chapter 3 and Stewart and Rayner (73).

13. On this see, for example, H. Theil (72), pp. 250–4. To be strictly accurate in running say equation (4.5.2) by transforming the data using the estimate of ρ, we should ignore the first observation. The rationale of applying a transformation matrix to data on the dependent and independent variables can be seen by supposing we have this basic equation:

$$y_t = \alpha x_t + u_t \tag{1}$$

but where:

$$u_t = \rho u_{t-1} + \epsilon_t \tag{2}$$

If we multiply (1) by ρ and lag it one period we find that:

$$y_t - \rho y_{t-1} = \alpha(x_t - \rho x_{t-1}) + (u_t - \rho u_{t-1}) \tag{3}$$

But by equation (2) this transformed equation contains a *random* error term.

14. Malkiel did not attempt to let λ be determined by the econometrics. Though he did try to obtain consistent estimates of the equation

$$S_t = F(S_{t-1}, L_t, L_{t-1})$$

on Durand's data by using Liviatan's method (74) of finding those kind of estimates.

15. We have perhaps stated this in rather a bold and cavalier fashion. Our prime consideration had been the econometric properties of the results. However, this should not be allowed to overshadow the economics of the situation; and it could be that, in allowing σ to vary over time, we have not gone far enough. What we have implied here is that the range can be defined in the same way each period — even though it will vary, naturally, if σ changes period by period. But σ is only a proxy for the spread of yields around 'the mean'; therefore some multiple of σ is only an approximation to the range. Thus, it might be appropriate to vary the scalar by which σ is multiplied for some periods in the sample. This is not something that can easily be accomplished with the information at our disposal.

16. In fact, it is not possible to show rigorously that the mid-point of the normal range will always be a 'break-even' point, that is the point where the long rate equals the short rate (with the actual rate equal to the normal rate). So a positive value for a is consistent with the Malkiel hypothesis. However, in a general sense it is likely that the greater part of a can be attributed to influences other than those contained within the hypothesis itself.

17. We are informed by Mr J. F. Richards that Malkiel has attempted to rectify his omission of borrowers from his theory in a paper published in 1967. However, we have not been able to track down the reference and neither has he.

18. It would not be doing justice to the outstanding work that Malkiel has done in this field to close this chapter without making some acknowledgement to the fact that the hypothesis we have discussed in this chapter crystallises just some of the ideas he has developed in his book (11). There he tried to introduce transaction costs into the analysis of the term structure, and he investigated many aspects of the term structure. Nevertheless, the hypothesis we have discussed here is central to his work and it represents his major contribution to the formation of ideas on the term structure.

5 Liquidity or Risk Premiums and the Term Structure of Interest Rates

5.1

In chapters 2 and 3 we have referred to the Liquidity or Risk Premium Theory of the term structure. We now devote our attention to that theory, though in the process of our analysis we shall have occasion to make reference to some of our earlier observations on it. This is particularly true of section 5.2, where we give a brief description of the fundamental tenet of the liquidity approach, while simultaneously inquiring into the concept of risk premiums, and of the appropriateness of sometimes calling them liquidity premiums. We shall find ourselves looking forwards as well as backwards because, in marshalling our arguments on the 'premiums theory', we shall be drawn towards discussion of the Hedging Pressure Theory, since the former theory may be envisaged as a weak form of the latter.

The Expectations Theory assumed that the market for bonds exhibits complete shiftability — that is between 'a' bond and any other bond. The Liquidity/Risk Premium Theory, as we shall see, argues that such perfect substitutability does not exist, but that substitutability can be attained at a price, a price which is 'the' liquidity/risk premium. The payment of premiums is envisaged as counterbalancing the reluctance of lenders to make longer-term commitments, so that the market can still be viewed as in the Expectations Theory as a single market. In contrast, the Hedging Pressure Theory takes the view that such counterbalancing of lenders' reluctance is not possible in some instances and that in consequence the market for bonds is segmented, and that factors such as 'expectations' play no inter-segment role in determining the term structure of interest rates. Section 5.3 takes us through some of the implications for the term structure, and for the Expectations Theory from which it is developed, of the Liquidity Preference Theory. Some empirical evidence on the existence and size of liquidity premiums is set out and analysed critically in section 5.4, mainly on Kessel's (30) researches, and section 5.5, and its importance for the Expectations Theory is noted. To round off the chapter a summary of its empirical conclusions is provided in section 5.6, which includes a comment on the empirical evidence on liquidity/risk premiums provided in chapters 3 and 4.

5.2

As we have already witnessed in chapter 3, the so-called Liquidity Premium or Risk Premium Theory of the term structure really first found explicit and formal statement in the work of Sir John Hicks (1). Remember that Hicks derives his theory of the term structure (which, of course, in the extreme where liquidity premiums are zero, subsumes the Traditional Theory) by following Keynes's ideas on commodity futures markets (Keynes (7); again see also B. A. Goss (77)), arguing that loans in the money market can be envisaged as being made up of a spot transaction and an appropriate number of forward transactions. He then argues that the demand and supply functions for long and short loans will embody certain peculiarities and that, therefore, *ceteris paribus*, long and short loans will be imperfect substitutes for each other. However, the structure of rates can be made to be such that the imperfections are removed, so that investors do move from one end of the market to the other. The means by which this can be achieved is by the payment of 'liquidity premiums'.

Thus, to substantiate and develop these points we may begin by following Hicks again:

> It is not normal to think of the market for long-term loans in terms of hedgers and speculators; but that distinction does in fact continue to be relevant here. Other things being equal, a person engaging in a long-term loan contract puts himself into a more risky position than he would be in if he refrained from making it; but there are some persons (and concerns) for whom this will not be true, because they are already committed to needing loan capital over extensive periods. . . . These persons will want to hedge their future supplies of loan capital, just as they will want to hedge their future supplies of raw materials. They will have a strong propensity to borrow long.

> On the other side of the market there does not seem to be any similar propensity . . . .
> Taking these things together, . . . *the forward market for loans* (like the forward market for commodities) *may be expected to have a constitutional weakness on one side, a weakness which offers an opportunity for speculation.*
>
> [Hicks (1), p. 146, italics added]

Therefore the argument is that lenders will have a *preference* for lending short-term but borrowers would *prefer* to borrow on a long-term basis; in order to bring about equilibrium some special inducement, as it were, has to be offered to lenders to coax them into lending long, namely to committing themselves forward. As Hicks has argued:

> A lender who did this would be in a position exactly analogous to that of a speculator in a commodity market. He would only come into the long market because he expected to gain by so doing, and to gain sufficiently to offset the risk incurred.
>
> [Hicks (1), p. 147]

Hicks continues:

> The forward rate . . . for any particular future week . . . is thus determined, like the futures price of a commodity, at that level which just tempts a sufficient number of 'speculators' to undertake the forward contract. It will have to be higher than the short rate expected by these speculators to rule in that week, since otherwise they would get no compensation for the risk they are incurring . . . .

This would mean that the expected rates on longs would stand *above* the expected rates, or returns, on shorts. Thus, the return expected from investing consecutively in n one-year loans, or bonds, would be lower than the return expected (equals actual return) from investing in an n-year loan, or bond.

When it is not necessary to pay liquidity premiums to produce equilibrium in the long and short markets, naturally we have the conditions pertaining in the Traditional model wherein the expected n-year bond return is equivalent to that expected from investing in n one-year bonds. The Hicksian situation for an n-year holding period can then be expressed in the usual way:

$$(1 + R_{nt})^n = (1 + R_{1t})\,(1 + {}_{t+1}\phi_t) \ldots (1 + {}_{t+n-1}\phi_t) \tag{5.2.1}$$

but where *now*, in a world of liquidity premiums:

$${}_{t+j}\phi_t = {}_{t+j}r_t + LP_{jt}, \quad j = 1, 2, \ldots n-1. \tag{5.2.2}$$

In equation (5.2.2), for $j = 1$, ${}_{t+1}r_t$ is the one-year rate expected at t to hold at $t + 1$, whilst LP_{1t} is the liquidity premium required by the market to induce it, in effect, to undertake what is here a two-year commitment. Similarly, only liquidity premiums of LP_{1t} to $LP_{n-1,t}$ will induce the market to purchase an n-year bond.

Hicks's own view was that:

$$LP_{1t} < LP_{2t} < \ldots < LP_{n-1,t}. \qquad (5.2.3)$$

That is, liquidity premiums are an increasing function of the length of the loan undertaken, or of the maturity of the bond being purchased. The reason for this is the alleged increasing 'riskiness' of the investor's committing himself to longer and longer investment periods. This is a point that we shall return to later in this section.

There are three issues in this theory and the 'pure' Hicksian conception of it that we must now discuss:

(i) Is it valid to argue that the market does have a *constitutional weakness* and, furthermore, a weakness on the long side?

(ii) What kind of factors might induce investors to demand 'risk premiums' for going long? In what circumstances, and to what extent, are we entitled to say, as we have done hitherto and others have done: for risk premiums read liquidity premiums?

(iii) Will the risk premiums or liquidity premiums, whatever they turn out to be, follow the pattern laid down in equation (5.2.3) above?

In examining these queries we shall not take them *seriatim*. Rather we shall begin with (ii), assuming, for the sake of convenience, that the answers to the two parts of (i) are in the affirmative. If we were looking at the whole of the market for 'loans' — corporate bonds, private loans as well as government and municipal issues — then one possible source of *risk* for lenders is that the borrower would default on the loan. (Hicks does look at such a market and he ascribes the payment of a risk premium largely to the existence of default risk.) But in discussing the term structure in terms of government bonds only and restricting our studies to markets in politically and economically stable countries, we may ignore default risk and argue that a *pure risk* premium does not exist. Then what kind of risk does the investor face if, in the assumed conditions, he invests in a 'long' rather than a 'short' bond? For it must be remembered that if he decides now, say, to purchase a ten-year bond rather than a combination of bonds, assuming that at this moment he has a ten-year investment or holding period, he will know with *certainty* what the return on the ten-year bond will be. The only means by which there can be an element of *risk* in the investor's buying a ten-year bond arises from the possibility that once the investment has been undertaken he will need to *shorten* or *lengthen* his holding period. Uncertainty about his future cash requirements, and hence about his investment period, will impart some degree of risk into the purchase of a 'long' bond. So, for example, to compensate the investor for the possibility of capital loss should he be forced to sell out prior to the elapse of his original holding period, it will become necessary to pay him a premium, which may truly be regarded as a risk premium. This will mean that for him the (expected) return from 'going long' will have to exceed the expected return from 'going short' (which will be the actual return from 'going short' if we are thinking of a short bond as a one-year bond), the differential between the expected outcomes of two strategies being some function of the risk premiums. So, on this line of argument, an investor's preference is an expression of the feeling that he is uncertain as to the time span for which he can allow his given wealth to be invested.

In the case of his holding period extending beyond that originally envisaged, the risk is not of capital loss but of possible income loss because on the maturity of the bond the funds must be recommitted and the return to be obtained for the extended period will be uncertain. This uncertainty about his expectations concerning future one-year rates is still crucial if the investor is absolutely certain about his holding period. To a given expectation of a one-year rate expected to hold at a stated date in the future, he can then be imagined, or be supposed, to add a risk factor. He will want to have in mind the kind of '*maximum*' return that is going to obtain on any future holding of a one-year bond. The return he wants from any given long bond will have to reflect these maximum anticipated returns on short bonds. This seems a perfectly straightforward and feasible way of rationalising the risk factor. (This possible interpretation of it is supported by, for example, J. W. Conard (78) p. 74.)

This so-called risk factor, however, would appear to be fundamentally a *liquidity premium.*[1] For we might argue that, if the investor is uncertain about future rates of interest, he will not want to commit himself on a 'long basis'; he will desire to keep his position liquid so as to allow himself room for manoeuvre in the future. He will not want to sacrifice the chance of future speculative gains. The investor will have a *preference for liquidity* and will therefore tend to shorten the term of his investments, possibly even taking up a fully liquid position with respect to a portion of his wealth by holding it in the form of money. This behaviour could be changed if the would-be short lender is offered an inducement to overcome his innate preference for liquidity, namely a return for going long that is in excess of the return he could expect from remaining liquid.

This kind of argument finds support in several distinguished sources. For example, Sir Dennis Robertson argued at the same time quoting another illustrious source, Irving Fisher (6):

> There is a gap between the *normal* long and the *normal* short rate, the latter standing below the former on the average by an amount which can be regarded partly as a measure of the extra trouble and inconvenience to the borrower of continually renewing short loans, and partly of the greater freedom of manoeuvre, or ease of disentangling himself without loss, which the short loan confers on the lender. If we regard the long rate as the rate *par excellence*, then in the case of short loans, as Fisher put it long ago, 'the readiness or convenience takes the place of some of the interest'.
>
> [(76), p. 393: italics added]

We shall have occasion to refer to this passage later in this chapter, though it is of interest to note now that Robertson is *implicitly* sympathising with the market constitutional weakness hypothesis of Hicks.

We are here expressing views about what is, after all, no matter how this is interpreted or manifests itself, a preference for liquidity in the Keynesian sense, and it is not surprising that some of them, either explicitly or implicitly, find support in the *General Theory* (81), or in *A Treatise on Money* (82), where, of course, Keynes was attempting to demonstrate the possibility of investors taking up a fully liquid position (e.g. holding cash) with respect to part of their portfolio; though his arguments apply in degrees to the *desire* of investors to invest in 'more liquid' bonds rather than in 'less liquid' bonds.[2] Thus we find this proposition, which is argued out in the *General Theory*.

> . . . . There is, however, a necessary condition failing which the existence of a liquidity-preference for money as a means of holding wealth could not exist.
>
> This . . . is the existence of *uncertainty* as to the future of the rate of interest, *i.e.* as to the complex of rates of interest for varying maturities which will rule at future dates. For if the rates of interest ruling at all future times could be foreseen with certainty, all future rates of interest could be inferred from the *present* rates of interest for debts of different maturities, which would be adjusted to the knowledge of the future rates.
>
> [(81), p. 168: italics in original]

To which Keynes appends his 'two views' or 'bull—bear' arguments advanced originally in the *Treatise* ((82) pp. 151—2, 256—7):

> There is, moreover, a further ground for liquidity-preference which results from . . . uncertainty as to the future of the rate of interest . . . . For different people will estimate the prospects differently and anyone who differs from the predominant opinion as expressed in market quotations may have a good reason for keeping liquid resources in order to profit, if he is right. . . .
> [(81), p. 169]

This famous bull—bear view of the market, is founded naturally upon the existence of two divergent overall views of the future of bond prices/interest rates. The Expectations Theory, and (apparently) the Hicksian Risk Premium Theory, built upon the market having a uniform view of expected rates. Diverse expectations, of no matter what degree, are ruled out *ex hypothesi*.

However, the kind of argument contained in Keynes's 'two views' situation is applicable in the present context. It is perfectly legitimate to argue that there is a consensus in the market as to the future one-year rates of interest but that, invoking the *ceteris paribus* caveat to rule out the other factors that may plausibly cause risk premiums to arise, simultaneously, the market feels uncertain about these rates. Accordingly it may only be persuaded from taking up the extreme Keynesian position in regard to the composition of 'its portfolio' by extra *compensatory*, monetary rewards, via the payment of liquidity premiums. On Keynesian principles, it is sensible to see these payments having to increase, *ceteris paribus*, in the way Hicks suggested they would.

Let us now turn to point (i) that was raised in connection with the Hicksian analysis of the Risk Premium Theory. To repeat it the question was:

(i) Is it valid to argue that the market does have a *constitutional weakness* and, furthermore, a weakness on the long side?

The difficulty with answering this question is that it is one that has to be answered, in effect, with an eye on *truth* rather than on *validity*. In other words, it is very much an empirical rather than a theoretical/logical matter whether or not the query can be answered in the affirmative. Though we might venture to suggest that a mixture of casual empiricism and intuition would lead us to feel that there was something in what Hicks said, especially in the confines of the kind of financial market he had in mind, or better still in one that was predominantly concerned with 'private' loan transactions.

But our field of inquiry is limited to the market for government debt and, on occasions, that for prime-quality corporate bonds, and, although it is difficult to find a means of uniquely testing Hicks's hypothesis, we have managed to assemble some evidence on this question. This is presented and commented on in chapter 6 when we discuss the Hedging Pressure Theory of the term structure, but we now mention one or two points that have emerged from our review of empirical work on this question. It would appear that the major holders of government bonds do have 'preferred habitats' among the maturity composition of available debt; *but* those preferred habitats do not coincide completely, there being a degree of overlap, and they do not fall solely at the lower end of the maturity spectrum. They tend to occur over very short-term, short-term, or medium-/long-term debt. As far as the market as a whole goes, dominated by the various institutional investors, there does not appear to be much constitutional weakness on the side indicated by Hicks; indeed the evidence suggests a possible weakness on the short side.

Supposing, however, that we continue to assume that the financial market does have a constitutional weakness on the long side, and that that weakness has to be corrected by the payment of risk premiums or liquidity premiums or whatever we wish to label them: will those premiums be ordered in the same way that Sir John Hicks has suggested that they will? This brings us on to query (iii) raised earlier in this section, on which we need only make a comment.

If a 'risk factor' is payable for any of the reasons we have discussed earlier (ii), then it would seem that there should be a risk factor for every unit of time ahead of the present, and that, furthermore, as Hicks has stated, the risk factor should be an increasing function of maturity.

We can say in summary of our discussion that:

(a) If the market — whether for all loans, or just for government debt — does have the constitutional weakness imputed to it by J. R. Hicks, then it must follow that some 'compensation', namely a return in excess of the one-year expected return, must be paid to investors to encourage them to move out of their safe, preferred, short-term habitat into the more 'uncertain' long market.

(b) As a generality, such compensatory payments for 'the market' will exist for each year of a loan contract in excess of one year; and they will have to increase as the market is being cajoled into longer and longer commitments.

(c) These special, compensatory, payments will have arisen because of 'uncertainty' in the widest sense.

All these conclusions taken in conjunction will hold in reverse, that is if under (a) we hypothesise that the market has a constitutional weakness on the other side.

The Risk/Liquidity Premium Theory can be put into perspective by looking at it in the light of the Expectations Theory. One of the difficulties with the former theory, unlike to some extent the latter theory, is that there exists no formal definitive statement of the assumptions upon which it is founded. Though we have suggested in this section that the Risk Premium Theory is founded on the assumptions of the Traditional Theory, it is probably more in order to say that the theory appears to accept most of the major ingredients of the Expectations Theory,[3] such as the premise that investors hold universal expectations about future interest rates.

What the theory abandons is the assumption that, for all investors, all securities are perfect substitutes the one for the other. Once we try to take steps to account for the imperfect substitutability then, accepting the overall preference of lenders for shorter-term maturities, we can do so in effect, by dropping certain aspects of the Traditional model, by rescinding either one or the other of its two certain assumptions upon which it is founded. Though we have suggested in In this respect we may suppose that expectations are held with uncertainty rather than with complete certainty. If we call this allowance for uncertainty a risk factor, or measure it as a risk variable in the statistical sense and assume that all relevant risk factors are universally held, then we have a means of rationalising lenders' willingness to override their natural tendency to go to the short end of the maturity spectrum, and a reason for their willingness to *diversify* their portfolios, with an outcome that leaves the *expected* holding-period returns on longs greater than the *expected* returns on shorts (see chapter 2).

5.3

Following this preamble on the liquidity premiums approach we may now sketch out the implications it has for the term structure of interest rates, and especially for the Expectations Theory on to which it was grafted. In our previous discussion we have reached the conclusion that, if there is a Hicksian-type market in existence, 'liquidity premiums' will have to be paid, and that these premiums will have to be of such a nature that they increase monotonically with *n*, the number of 'years' ahead for which the market is persuaded to commit its financial resources. We have said nothing explicit in the preceding paragraphs to enable us to measure those premiums in a *quantitative* way. We shall not attempt to fill in that lacuna in our portrayal of the Liquidity Premium Theory until we proceed to empirical matters in the following sections of this chapter.

With the information at our disposal let us then consider figure 5.3.1. For 'a' point in time this diagram epitomises the Hicksian viewpoint on liquidity premiums. Beyond, say, approximately a fifteen-year commitment, it seems more than possible that the liquidity premium (*LP*) curve will flatten out and have a slope approaching zero: this intuitive expectation can be substantiated more rigorously by application of the observations we have made on 'the mathematics of bond-price movements' in chapter 4, taken in league with the qualitative observations we have made regarding 'liquidity premiums' earlier in this chapter. This curve is envisaged as denoting the *full* element of liquidity premiums required by the market

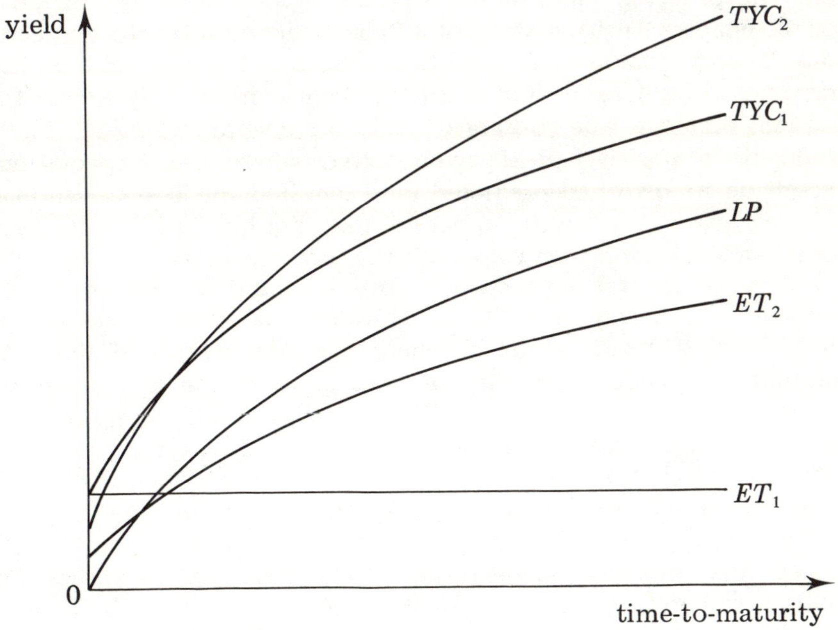

Figure 5.3.1

to persuade it to purchase a j-year bond ($j = 2, \ldots n$). Thus 'the' liquidity premium embodied in the rate of interest on an n-year bond will be a function of the liquidity premiums, $LP_1, LP_2, \ldots LP_n$.

If the arithmetic version of the Hicksian equalisation formula is used:

$$R_{nt} = \frac{R_1 + r_1 + \ldots + r_{n-1}}{n} \tag{5.3.1}$$

where $r_1 = {}_{t+1}\phi_t = {}_{t+1}r_t + LP_{1t}$ etc., then it is possible to express 'the' liquidity premium for any length-of-life bond depicted on the curve LP on figure 5.3.1 by a straightforward formula:

$$LP_n = \frac{\sum_{i=1}^{n-1} LP_i}{n}. \tag{5.3.2}$$

When the geometric Hicksian formula is used expression (5.3.2) naturally becomes more cumbersome, but equally naturally it embodies the same principle.

Let us now suppose that *the market* expects all future *one*-year rates to be equal to the present, spot, one-year rate. Then we should find, according to the Expectations Theory, that at the given point in time, the observed yield-to-maturity curve was horizontal (proposition 3, chapter 2). This state of affairs is denoted by the Expectations Theory 'curve' ET_1 on figure 5.3.1. However, if liquidity premiums should exist and be of the form exhibited by LP on the diagram, then the true (observed) yield curve would be TYC_1. There would be a positive yield-gap observed where the Expectations Theory on its own had predicted (and required for its own validity) no such gap. It is quite apparent that liquidity premiums have played an active role with respect to the term structure.

Indeed, in an instance such as this it would be appropriate to describe its role by use of the language we adopted in chapter 4. Thus, in this example the payment (or demanding) of liquidity premiums has been a *determining* agent as far as the term structure of interest rates is concerned. But, equally clearly, there will be other situations where it is conceivable that these premiums are strengthening factors accentuating the Expectations Theory's predictions. Again we may refer to figure 5.3.1, and imagine that the market holds the expectation that all future one-year rates will exceed the present one-year rate. The result is an ascending yield curve (proposition 1b in chapter 2) represented here by ET_2. If we add the curve LP to ET_2, then the actual yield curve becomes TYC_2. Similarly, we may note a situation where the Liquidity

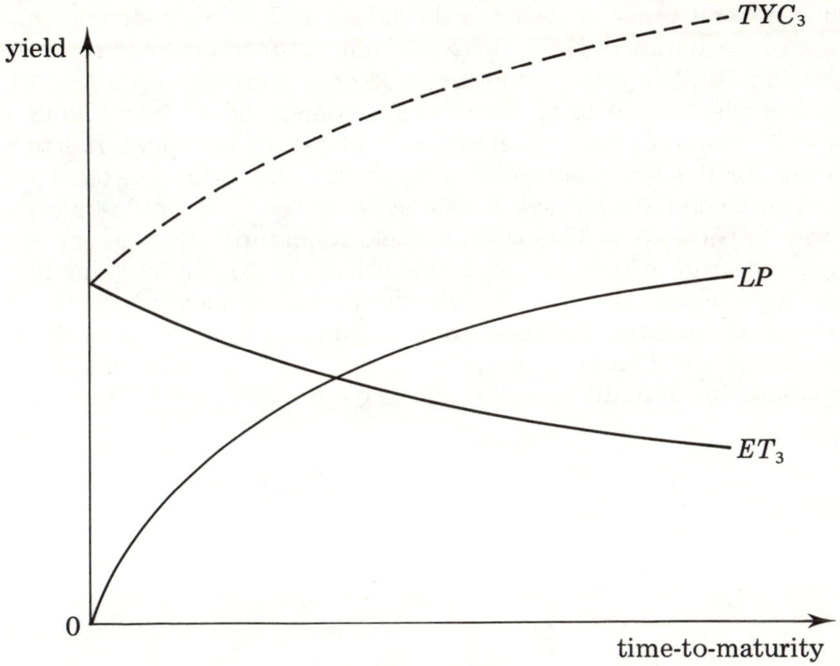

Figure 5.3.2

Preference Theory can weaken, or even reverse, the predictions that are derived solely from the Traditional Theory. To do so we turn to figure 5.3.2. ET_3 represents the forecast of the market following the philosophy of the Traditional Theory, being based on the universal assumption that one-year rates are going to decline monotonically in the future (proposition 2a in chapter 2), making the additional supposition that, at the time being considered, liquidity premiums are paid which follow the pattern laid down by the curve *LP*. The observed yield curve would then be TYC_3, a yield curve that exhibits characteristics completely the opposite of those embodied in ET_3.

These implications for the Traditional Theory of the preference by the market for relatively liquid assets are only a pictorial representation of equation (5.2.1), evaluated with and without liquidity premiums forming part of each and every forward one-year rate. For that formula applies in the Hicksian Risk/Liquidity Premium Theory, since this theory is based implicitly on the behaviouristic assumption of the Expectations Theory: though for Hicks, all available financial assets are imperfect substitutes for each other and can be made market substitutes only by the introduction of risk/liquidity premiums.

One general point is well worth making before we conclude this section. The humped yield curve has not figured very much in our discussions of the term structure, but quite often the plotting of empirical yield-to-maturity data reveals some kind of hump, sometimes of a pronounced nature, at the short part of the curve. It is not possible for the Expectations Theory to rationalise the existence of such a curve on a simple, systematic basis. In tests and would-be tests of the Expectations Theory the yield-to-maturity curves, as we know, are more often than not smoothed out to diminish humps. Since such humps do occur in observed data we should have some means of accounting for them, rather than merely explaining them away as statistical freaks and special cases. The Expectations Theory supported by liquidity premiums may produce, and hence by

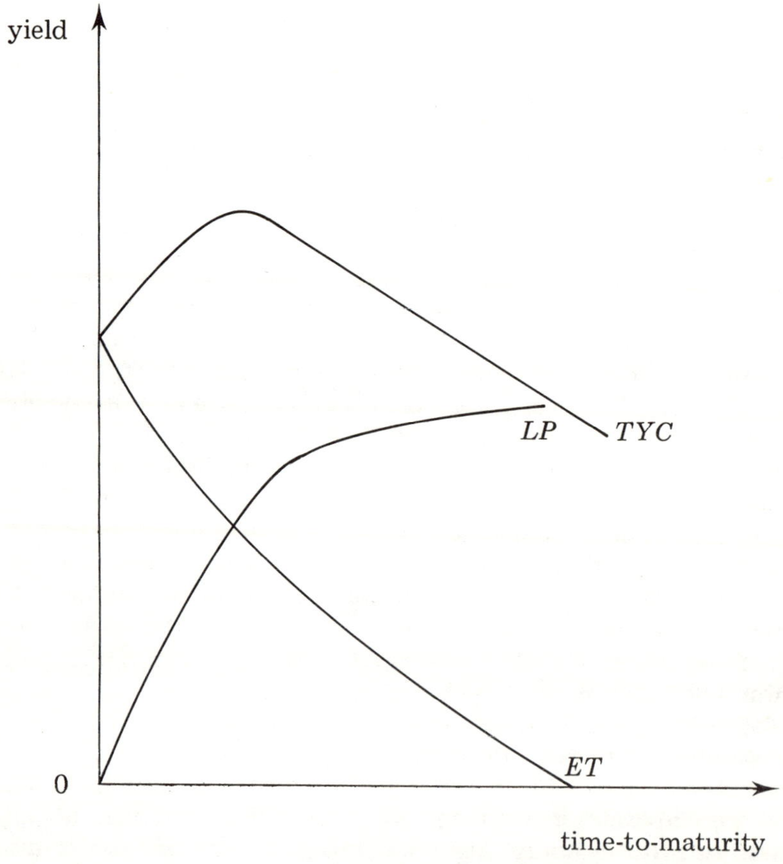

Figure 5.3.3

implication offer some kind of 'mongrel' explanation for the occurrence of yield curves that are humped at the short maturity end. An example of this appears in figure 5.3.3 (see Conard (78), chapter 7).

5.4

At this juncture we start to turn away from the analytical side of the theory to examine it in the confines of the real world. We do so by considering some of the empirical evidence that already exists in the literature. For the most part this will mean that we shall be concentrating our energies on the very substantial work of R. A. Kessel (30). It is with his study and its findings that we shall begin this section.

Somewhat paradoxically perhaps, Kessel's researches arose out of an attempt to substantiate and extend the findings of Meiselman (8), in would-be support for the Expectations Theory. Kessel was motivated by a desire to subject the Expectations Theory to empirical scrutiny, but to do so in a way which to him we can say perhaps seemed a 'fairer' way than that employed by, say, Meiselman. His aim was to try to allow for the presence of liquidity premiums in the market's forward rates, where those forward rates were derived from yield-to-maturity data and to make such allowance, almost invariably, to the one-period ahead forward rate, so as to obtain a 'truer' estimate of the rate the market *expected* to obtain on, say, a twenty-eight-day Treasury bill twenty-eight days from 'now', or on a one-year bond one year ahead. These 'proper' expected rates were then used in the main test procedure adopted by Kessel which was to: (i) assess the accuracy of these rates, 'the market's expectations', in predicting subsequently observed rates; (ii) see how these predictions compared with predictions made on the basis of forward rates *per se*, and with the inertia hypothesis. Besides the numerous tests of prediction, Kessel also performed a few tests on the pure Meiselman short-rate hypothesis.

Kessel's view was that, as far as his results on liquidity premiums and on predictive accuracy were concerned, they indicated that: (a) liquidity premiums do exist; (b) when the market's forward rates are cleaned of those premiums, the Expectations Theory has much to commend it. In his own words:

> The evidence presented supports the Hicksian theory of the term structure of interest rates; it supports the view that both expectations and liquidity preference determine the term structure of interest rates. These results show that forward rates should be interpreted as expected rates plus a liquidity premium. If forward rates are so interpreted, then the expectations of the market seem to forecast subsequently observed short-maturity spot rates; the relationship between expected and subsequently observed spot rates cannot be rationalised as the workings of chance.
> [(30) p. 42]

The evidence was compiled mainly from U.S. Treasury bills of very short duration — all, in fact, with lives under one year. Kessel did some testing using one- and two-year government bond data, and using Durand's data. For one-year-ahead liquidity premiums, which he was concerned with, the latter data provided no support for his hypotheses. The support for them that Kessel alleges at best comes only from his own data, and fundamentally from those on Treasury bills.

His tests of the Meiselman Hypothesis, as we have reported in chapter 3, were however reasonably successful; and indeed more so than his inquiries into liquidity premiums.

We must now follow up this rather sparse statement of Kessel's results with a detailed appraisal of his empirical findings and of the methods by which they were obtained.

As a platform for his study Kessel begins his excursions into the Expectations Theory and the Liquidity Preference Theory by adducing certain facts which he regards as evidence establishing the existence of liquidity premiums on the financial market. We might usefully review his evidence on this count; for it turns out to be not quite as strong as or as incontrovertible as he would like us to believe.

The evidence can be summed up, without over-simplifying it, as follows:

(a) In examining the weekly data he collated on U.S. Treasury bill yields for 1959 to March 1962, he discovered that on occasion the *forward rates* on one-week money in September 1959 and September 1960 were *negative*.

(b) If the Expectations Theory is to provide an appropriate explanation of the term structure, Kessel argues that the predictions based on expectations should correspond closely with the actual rates that the market was attempting to forecast. He then tests the ability of *forward* 14-, 28-, 42-, 56-, 63- and 91-day Treasury bill rates to predict spot rates for those bills observed 14, 28, 42, 56, 63 and 91 days, respectively, after the forward rates were inferred for the period, beginning of 1959 to March 1962. The outcome of those tests is that, on average, there is for all length-of-life bills a positive error between the forward rates and the actual rates, leading to the conclusion, according to Kessel, that:

> These results . . . strongly support the belief that forward rates are biased and high estimates of future short-term rates.
> [(30), pp. 24—5]

We must now make a closer inspection of the evidence under (a) and (b) and assess its importance and relevance. Let us then consider (a).

If it is found that forward rates are negative then it follows from equation (5.2.2) for $j = 1$, namely:

$$_{t+1}\phi_t = {}_{t+1}r_t + LP_{1t} \tag{5.4.1}$$

that only if LP_{1t} existed, and additionally only if it were negative, could $_{t+1}r_t$ be positive whilst simultaneously $_{t+1}\phi_t$ was negative. So unless we accept the fact that the market really can conceive of periods when one-year rates, one year ahead, are going to be negative, which is contrary to what we would naturally suppose on commonsense grounds, then the appearance of negative forward rates would imply the existence of some kind of adjustment factor that the market applies to 'expected rates'.

Where that factor is negative, as it must be if (5.4.1) is negative, and $_{t+1}r_t$, the expected one-year rate one year ahead, is positive, this implies *negative* liquidity premiums, if we so interpret the adjustment factor. This itself is contrary to the qualitative nature of such premiums as suggested, indeed necessitated, by the Hicksian analysis.

However, there is clearly a crucial calculation involved in the assessment of the existence of liquidity premiums via the employment of forward rates, and that calculation concerns the unearthing of those forward rates themselves. The two methods that we have employed up to this point, and which other researchers have utilised, are based on (especially) the Hicksian formula for the 'equalisation of holding-period yields' and (to a much lesser extent) on the Lutzian analogue to the Hicksian formula. Kessel, in fact, uses neither of these methods, at least not completely faithfully. To be precise, he adopts the *arithmetic average* of the Hicksian formula, given in equation (5.3.1). To repeat it, this states, using the Hicksian notation for simplicity, that r_2 is the one-year rate 'expected' at t to rule in t+1 (forward rate), and $r_1 = R_1$:

$$(n)R_{nt} = r_1 + r_2 + r_3 + \ldots + r_n. \tag{5.4.2}$$

Therefore:

$$(n+1)R_{n+1,t} = r_1 + r_2 + r_3 + \ldots + r_{n+1} \tag{5.4.3}$$

from which it follows that:

$$(n+1)R_{n+1,t} - (n)R_{nt} = r_{n+1}. \tag{5.4.4}$$

Thus, for the calculation of, say, all relevant *one-year-ahead* one-year forward rates the formula is:

$$2R_{2t} - R_{1t} = r_2. \tag{5.4.5}$$

For one-year rates one year ahead, however, equation (5.4.5) produces results that are close to those derived from applications of the Lutzian formula and are almost indistinguishable from those obtained using Hicks's formula. So evidence of negative forward one-year rates might lead us to suspect the Expectations Theory. In other words, they are unlikely to have arisen because of a statistical artefact — though it should be pointed out that the figures of forward rates arrived at by application of equations (5.4.2)–(5.4.5) will be *biased downwards* compared to forward rates calculated from using Hicks's geometric average formula. As far as one-year-ahead forward rates go this bias will be imperceptible. However, it will increase the further ahead in time the forward rates apply. The 'bias' that is in the Hicksian and the Lutzian formulae, of course, will also become evident and will increase the further into the future we are estimating forward rates. It is indeed perfectly possible to discover negative forward rates for several periods into the future from the Lutzian formula while the Hicksian formula shows those rates to be positive. Since the arithmetic average version of the Hicksian formula has an inherent bias in it that exceeds that in the Hicksian formula *per se*, it could happen that negative forward rates appear as with the Lutzian formula. So once we move away from very short-term, one-year rate 'predictions', we must be on our guard about making wholesale and general deductions from the signs of forward rates.

Though there is, in the event, very little of substance that one can raise in objection to point (a) of Kessel's evidence in support of his contention that some kind of premium does exist on the market, since the evidence is based on forward rates for very short periods ahead. Yet the evidence is limited, and it does suggest that such a premium is negative rather than positive.

We may turn now to point (b) concerning Kessel's arguments in favour of the thesis that premiums are paid on the market. In doing so, as we have already done, either explicitly or implicitly, we shall be recapitulating, and drawing on, our earlier statements on and arguments concerning the Traditional Theory and the Meiselman Hypothesis (chapters 2 and 3). Kessel supports the view that it is correct to propound the idea that expectations can determine the term structure even if they are not correct, or we should say, if they turn out to be incorrect, expectations. Having conceded this much, however, Kessel then maintains that in some sense there should be some evidence of 'accurate predictions' by the market if it acts according to the tenets of the Expectations Theory:

> . . . given free entry and competition in securities markets, should not one expect to find a relationship between expectations as inferred from the term structure of interest rates and subsequently observed actual rates? It is of course unreasonable to expect expectations or predictions of future short-term rates to be absolutely accurate . . . [but] the average difference between predicted and actual rates ought to be insignificantly different from zero. The absence or presence of a mean bias in the relationship constitutes a test of whether or not forward rates are expected rates.
>
> [(30), p. 23]

The point Kessel is making here is that, if on the average forward rates do not match up to subsequently observed spot rates, those forward rates cannot merely depict expected rates: they must embody some other variable, namely, liquidity premiums. Remember that for testing point (b) Kessel used data he had compiled on U.S. Treasury bills for the period beginning 1959 to March 1962. His weekly data observations varied from 113 to 146. From the data observations on 14-, 28-, 42-, 56-, 63- and 91-day bills he calculated the arithmetic average of the errors of $({}_{t+1}\phi_t - {}_{t+1}R_{t+1})$, that is of minus the Meiselman error term. These average errors turned out to be positive, being in the range 0.199 to 0.669.

Straightaway, one elementary point can be made and this is that the average value is going to change as the data period is lengthened or shortened. It is more than doubtful whether the average prediction error has any meaning whatsoever. This is so, of course, even if one believes, or accepts, the kind of swings-and-roundabouts argument that figures at the heart of this 'on the average' generalisation. For there is a great deal of difference, as we have come to see only too frequently in what we have portrayed in these pages, between the conceptualisation of a problem and the analysis and evaluation of it in the real world.

We may for our purposes, however, ignore the empirical issues on this score and look at the conceptual ones. Even so it is difficult to attach much meaning, let alone to accept, the notion that 'on balance' the market should get its predictions right. But the issue would be quite categorically settled in favour of that view if we could demonstrate that we expect *a priori*, that is from the Expectations Theory *per se*, that the market will or must always make accurate forecasts of future interest rates.

This question may be reformulated as: 'If the market holds an expectation for all future one-year rates, and acts upon those expectations, will it follow *inevitably* that those expectations are *fulfilled*?' Consider then the Expectations Theory — in its 'weaker' form, rather than in its 'stronger', Lutzian, perfect-foresight form — as set out according to the Hicksian formula in the way we have presented it in chapter 2. Let the market be of the opinion that all one-year rates in the future will be higher than the one-year rate is now (the spot rate). This implies that the long rate stands above the short rate (proposition 1a, chapter 2). But what has caused this yield-gap to materialise? How have the expectations of the market influenced 'today's' term structure? It is of course the activity of arbitrageurs, the only type of market participant that can exist in the world of the Traditional Theory, which has been responsible for the new structure of rates. When the market opens to trade at the start of today there will be a yield-gap based on previous expectations, all kinds of length-of-life bonds being held by those active in the market. So those bonds will include long bonds and short bonds, on which equilibrium prices and interest rates will have been fixed at the end of yesterday's trading. The market today opens then with, say, a given ten-year rate and a one-year rate. If the market's expectations are of the kind postulated previously, investors *en bloc*, as it were, will be selling their previous holdings of long bonds and buying one-year bonds. This will mean that, *ceteris paribus*, by the end of today's trading the one-year rate will have fallen from what it was at the outset of trading, whilst simultaneously the long-term rate will have risen, as the price of long stock falls with the reduction in demand. (*Given* supply: we have seen in chapter 2 that we can ignore supplies of bonds for given expectations, but if, and only if, changes in stocks of bonds do not affect expectations.)

Under the assumptions made we have a new term structure that reflects the relatively more lucrative nature of short bonds. The term structure has been determined by individual investors acting rationally in a world described by the suppositions of the Traditional Theory. *But* all that has happened on today's market is that a new *present* equilibrium structure of rates has been arrived at. All that has happened with regard to future points in time is that a series of expected one-year (and as we have also seen, particularly in chapter 3, of *n*-year) rates have been *formulated* by the market. A simple observation may be: but there is nothing in the term structure today, when it is determined by the Traditional Theory, to indicate that the expectations of the market need be, or will be, self-fulfilling. For the market only determines, as it were, future (or estimated future) interest rates, not actual future rates, when it is fixing actual present market yields.

The Expectations Theory does not leave us with an ineluctable situation wherein expectations simply have to be fulfilled, and to be so to establish its worth. It then becomes necessary to ask the question: if the market finds its predictions out of line with subsequent events, will it bother to continue to form expectations, and to act upon them? Kessel's view, which is supported by others, as we have pointed out in earlier and later chapters of this book, is that it will not. We take rather the opposite viewpoint.

It seems in principle to be stretching the imagination too far to ask us to accept the view that if the market gets its predictions wrong — even consistently — it will abstain altogether from forming expectations of future interest rates. For, in the confines of the kind of financial world we are envisaging, the only spur to action is the market's view of likely movements in one-year, and hence in all, yields. To act at all the market must form some expectations. One alternative that the market might follow, if consistent over- or under-predictions of one-year rates make it feel that it is just wasting its time and effort on forecasting those rates, is for it to take the view that the *status quo* will remain. But even this myopic, inertia hypothesis à la Hickman is an *expectations*-ridden one. Also, the market is as likely to land itself into situations of loss by following this line of defence against the uncertain future as it is by more elaborate kinds of expectations-forming schemes, of the kind that possibly lie behind the Traditional Theory. It is of course perfectly feasible that the outcome of a conscious, deliberate attempt by the market to forecast future interest rates may be that the market adopts an hypothesis which in the event becomes indistinguishable from the inertia hypothesis. The limit of any expectation concerning the one-year-ahead one-year rate can be regarded basically as that hypothesis. Thus, *reductio ad absurdum*, we could perfectly legitimately, and sensibly, regard the inertia hypothesis as being an *expectations* hypothesis.

At times the feeling is generated that the view is being propounded that the inertia hypothesis, rather than a more sophisticated, deliberate, expectations-forming hypothesis, is accepted and followed by the market because it holds the philosophy, derived from getting its forecasts wrong, that 'anything can happen' to future rates of interest. So an air of indifference is created. But in suggesting that it then says: we shall do as well by assuming that future one-year rates will not be different from the present spot rate as by making any other presumptions; we cannot rule out the possibility that the market has in mind a band within which the future one-year rates are liable to lie, and that it judges the situation to be such that it is more likely, or just as likely, that the spot one-year rate now will also hold in the future. In one way or another it is possible to rationalise, and we would argue hard to deny, the view that expectations enter into the selection of even the inertia strategy.

Indeed, this discussion must be put within a general context in this way. Unless it is believed that the Hedging Pressure Theory is correct, that is that individuals and institutions are complete risk-averters and take up a *fully* hedged position,[4] then it will follow that expectations are one of the ingredients in the asset-choice decision for investors and that they *act* upon those expectations. The market will not be prepared to act in a vacuum. However, if it believes that there is no value at all in making any predictions of future yields (implying uncertainty, complete uncertainty about expectations or even complete ignorance concerning the future), the market would, *ceteris paribus*, end up as being a segmented one, investors investing in that length-of-life bond which makes their assets and 'liabilities' fully matched.

But if, for whatever reason, they are not prepared to take up such positions, then it will be in their interests to form some ideas, no matter how precise, of what future yields are likely to be. It would seem possible with regard to the 'anything can happen' thesis that they will limit the range within which future rates can move. This is increasingly likely to be so the less distant the time for which the one-year projections are being made. This simple intuitive observation, incidentally, gives us a clue as to why distant predictions are liable, 'on the average', to prove more in error than less-distant ones.

However, it is extremely difficult to see how the kind of evidence Kessel has cited can be used to substantiate the view that liquidity premiums do exist in theory, and in practice, particularly when it is remembered that Kessel's data are also *implied* data, being based on yield-to-maturity curves. This carries with it the by now all-too-familiar difficulty. It is also important to make a more general observation on the kind of data that Kessel has utilised. His data are for the very short end of the yield curve, in fact mainly for securities having less than one year to run to maturity, and partly for bonds having lives of one to two years. The yield curve is always suspect at the short end, and it is at its most suspect for the life span used by Kessel. But given that these sort of data form the basis of the empirical investigations, it can be argued that it is not appropriate to extend any findings to other, 'longer', segments of the yield curve. It is highly likely that Treasury bill data will reveal the existence of liquidity premiums since that particular market will be dominated in the real world (from which, to state a platitude, of course, 'the evidence' itself comes) by special kinds of investors, for example institutions such as banks (in the U.K. we may add the discount houses) and commercial enterprises, with idle, spare funds they wish to invest for a short while rather than leave in cash. The market is likely to be overwhelmingly one which, for one reason or another, is liquidity-conscious.[5]

We cannot reach any definitive conclusion on these matters; yet it is valuable, and appropriate, to bring to the fore the fact that it is feasible to register dissension with Kessel's standpoint by advancing arguments and ideas that are equally as plausible as are those that can be put forward by advocates of that standpoint. Additionally we should not forget that certain caveats can always be made about the data that have been collated. But it is now time that we passed on to empirical matters and considered the measurement of liquidity premiums, accepting, for the sake of procedure, that Kessel has established a *prima facie* case that they exist.

In sections 5.2 and 5.3 we discussed the qualitative properties of liquidity premiums; and, given the Hicksian assumption, it was held to be apposite to suggest that $L_{1t} < L_{2t} < \ldots < L_{nt}$. Kessel in his quantitative investigations of liquidity premiums concentrates for the most part on LP_1, or in general on what we may call one-period-ahead liquidity premiums. So he draws no conclusions on the appropriateness of Hicks's suggested pattern for liquidity premiums.

In investigating LP_1 Kessel takes as his fundamental premise the notion often suggested in the literature that it will depend upon the present spot one-period or one-year rate. Though Kessel's method of measurement is beset with difficulties when the required statistical analysis of it is undertaken, the conceptualisation of the measurement of liquidity premiums is rigorous and inventive, even though quite simple. We start with the identity (5.4.1) that is familiar to us from our previous discussions:

$$_{t+1}\phi_t = {}_{t+1}r_t + LP_{1t}. \qquad (5.4.6)$$

The hypothesis is then introduced to account for LP_{1t}, there being, as usual, no hypothesis advanced to explain ${}_{t+1}r_t$ (the appropriate one-period rate expected at t to hold at the start of $t + 1$):

$$LP_{1t} = F(R_{1t}). \quad (5.4.7)$$

From (5.4.6) and (5.4.7) it follows that:

$${}_{t+1}r_t = {}_{t+1}\phi_t - F(R_{1t}). \quad (5.4.8)$$

The following identity is then introduced:

$${}_{t+1}r_t = {}_{t+1}R_{1t+1} + Z. \quad (5.4.9)$$

Here Z is an *error of prediction.*[6] This identity, taken in conjunction with equation (5.4.8), produces Kessel's testable hypothesis, namely:

$${}_{t+1}\phi_t - F(R_{1t}) = {}_{t+1}R_{1t+1} + Z \quad (5.4.10)$$

or:

$${}_{t+1}\phi_t - {}_{t+1}R_{1t+1} = F(R_{1t}) + Z. \quad (5.4.11)$$

That is:

$$LP_{1t} = F(R_{1t}) + Z. \quad (5.4.12)$$

It is from equation (5.4.12) that Kessel has measured one-period, including one-year, liquidity premiums. But for estimating purposes it is necessary to add a random error term (ϵ_t) to equation (5.4.12) and to specify the nature of $F(R_{1t})$. For Kessel that relationship is linear, and it therefore becomes (it is not clear whether he supposes a_0 to exist, though it could be argued that it should not):

$$LP_{1t} = a_0 + a_1 R_{1t} + (Z_{t+1} + \epsilon_t). \quad (5.4.13)$$

There are several difficulties that immediately come to mind with the measurement of liquidity premiums via equation (5.4.13). Some of these are: (i) that measurement includes a *test* of the *hypothesis* contained in equation (5.4.7); (ii) even granted the correctness of such an hypothesis, what is also being tested is the view that it is a linear relationship; (iii) the fact that the compound error term contains the prediction error.

There are two issues that arise out of (iii). The one concerns the compound error term *per se* and whether, in effect, we can consider it to have the usual properties supposed when ordinary least squares is being applied to an equation such as (5.4.13). If we accept Kessel's view that on balance, on the average that is, no matter what the time period for which the observed data are relevant happens to be, the *expectation* is that term Z will be zero, then we are beginning to put the error term on to the required footing. But even if we accept the hypothesis that $E(Z) = 0$, there is no *a priori* justification for our stating that Z is a random variable. One suspects that, if anything, the reverse is more likely: the feeling would be that the values of Z are related to each other and could well exhibit a kind of cyclical pattern around a trend value of zero. (Additionally we have no means of knowing, *a priori*, how Z is likely to affect the variance of the error term.)

The second issue connected with (iii) is that, irrespective of the points we have just made, errors can be made in relying on equation (5.4.13) to measure and to predict liquidity premiums because the error term in that equation is likely to be correlated with LP_{1t} itself. This can be verified from equations (5.4.9) to (5.4.11). This then means, since the hypothesis is that $LP_{1t} = F(R_{1t})$, that the compound error term in equation (5.4.13) is correlated with R_{1t}, with the usual implications for the estimates of a_0 and a_1.[7]

So conceptually and statistically, there are difficulties that arise in regard to Kessel's scheme for estimating liquidity premiums. Despite these difficulties Kessel proceeded to quantify one-year liquidity premiums by equation (5.4.13) and to apply the premiums so calculated to test the 'true' predictive power of the Expectations Theory and to assess the importance of the Liquidity Preference Theory. His results, using that equation, were based on various sub-periods of data on U.S. Treasury bills for the period October 1949 to March 1962, selected partly on a cyclical basis, and on data on U.S. one- and two-year government stock for April 1954 to February 1961.

The main points in his empirical testing may be detailed (and commented upon) briefly as follows, taking the matter on from where Kessel had 'shown' that 'liquidity premiums' did exist:

(1) He ran his liquidity premium equation over the three business cycles October 1949—February 1961 (total of 137 monthly observations) for 28-day Treasury bills; and for 138 weekly observations on 28-day Treasury bills and 91-day bills for January 1959—February 1961. The only explicit statistical information we are given about these regressions is that for the latter period the regression coefficient on the spot rate is 0.43 (standard error of 0.05) and for the former period it is 0.22 (standard error of 0.03). These are clearly coefficients that are significantly different from zero at the 1% level or better. However, no Durbin—Watson statistic is quoted, neither is there any indication of the size of the overall relationships exhibited by the liquidity premium equation. It is also

clear from the information Kessel gives, based on the regression coefficients, that he has restricted the constant term in the equations to be zero. Again, no test on the appropriateness of this procedure is included. On the evidence given it might be contended that there is a *prima facie* case in support of the view that Kessel draws from these results, namely, that liquidity premiums are a (increasing) function of spot rates. But how strong the evidence is cannot be ascertained.

(2) Accepting that under (1) he had proved his hypothesis relating liquidity premiums to spot rates, he then attempted to answer the question: are those premiums related rather to the business cycle than to the level of spot interest rates? On this question his position was that, for the three latest business cycles in his data, there was an upward trend in the data on interest rates; so, he argued, if we take the data on 28-day bills, the liquidity premium variable should be related to *time*. He confirmed that this was the case; so he accepted the view that premiums *were* a function of spot rates. This is the test carried out in (1), save that for spot 28-day rates the independent variable in the liquidity equation was time. But, if there is a strong time trend in interest rates, then what else would we expect to find other than that substituting time for spot 28-day rates makes no difference to the overall view about liquidity premiums? To test for liquidity premiums with respect to cyclical behaviour requires something like a change-in-structure test procedure to be carried out for the three cycles.[8]

(3) Up to this point the tests we have summarised were designed to prove the existence of liquidity premiums, and of liquidity premiums that are determined quantitatively by spot rates of interest. The natural sequence to these tests are those that represent the objective of Kessel's study, tests designed to exclude liquidity premiums from the market's estimates of forward rates so that the 'true' expectations of the market can be used to test the predictive power of the market, or of expectations so formed. A number of tests were designed and performed to show that expectations, based on forward rates cleaned of all influence of liquidity premiums, do provide better predictions of subsequently observed rates of interest than do other variables purported to measure expectations. The evidence on this issue is that 'true expectations' are not always 'good' predictors of interest rates, but that they are better than inertia hypotheses. However, on the basis of the only test of this nature reported on by Kessel, for the three cycles 1949–61, the 'true expectations' are not very much better predictors than forward rates *per se*.

(4) One important factor for assessing 'the predictive attributes' of 'true expectations' is that — given that we accept the validity and accuracy of the method by which liquidity premiums are quantified — the liquidity premium equation should be stable over time. But, again, the test procedure used by Kessel on this count is inadequate and misplaced. Using the liquidity premium equation fitted for the two cycles 1949—58, he estimated liquidity premiums for the 1958—61 cycle. His test of the stability of the liquidity preference function was to judge the relative accuracy of forward rates less the liquidity premiums and of the inertia hypothesis in predicting spot rates for the 1958—61 cycle. What is required here again is at least a test for change in structure, one cycle from another: even then we would not be sure of the stability of the liquidity preference function since we are also testing the way that it can be represented or manifests itself.

(5) It will be quite clear from our preceding commentary that Kessel is vitally preoccupied with assessing the ability of expectations, 'true expectations', to forecast future rates of interest. This is, as we have seen, the *raison d'être* of his approach. In this regard it seems that as far as he is concerned the *pièce de résistance* is an experiment he made on the basis of the implicit acceptance of all the previously noted tests, and which is identical with (4) in spirit. This experiment uses data on one- and two-year government stock (so moving away from the very short end of the market) to predict the one-year-ahead liquidity premium for the 1958—61 cycle, by means of the liquidity premium equation estimated for the 1954—58 cycle. From this information 'true expected' rates were calculated and the power of those expectations *vis-à-vis* inertia hypotheses to predict subsequently observed one-year rates was assessed. 'Expectations' perform better than unadjusted forward rates which, in turn, perform better than inertia. However, as Kessel concedes, the explanatory power of none of these variables is high.

The data for this exercise, including the estimated liquidity premiums, are provided by Kessel. We attempted to replicate his findings on those premiums by running the liquidity premium equation against data for the 1954—58 cycle. However, possibly because Kessel had rounded up his observed yield data for one- and two-year government stocks, we were unable to reproduce the equation he must have obtained. Another reason for this could have been that Kessel restricted the constant term to be zero. But our findings indicate that, while the coefficient on R_{1t} should be approximately what Kessel must have estimated it to be (slightly in excess of 0.5), the constant term might be very significantly different from zero (and is approximately —1.5). One factor that motivated us to estimate the liquidity premium equation was to discover the size of the goodness-to-fit of the equation. But its $\bar{R}^2$ was only of the order of 32%: the zero-order correlation coefficient between the dependent and the independent variable was 0.58. The Durbin–Watson statistic was 0.19 and Orcutts coefficient was 1.0: *prima facie*, therefore, first differences of the variables should have been taken rather than their levels. So it is difficult to say whether the equation should have a constant in it, or how much faith we can place in the significance of the slope coefficient. Though Kessel did not rely on correlations to assess the predictive accuracy of the alternative 'expectations' variables, it is instructive to note that the simple correlation coefficients between R_{1t+1} and R_{1t}, ${}_{t+1}\phi_t$ and ${}_{t+1}r_t$ are, respectively, —0.40; —0.41; and —0.31: poor relationships indeed; and on a correlation basis at least showing that better results could be obtained by taking forward rates or present spot rates as the market's expectations.[9]

This is not the full extent of the testing of theories of the term structure that are recorded in Kessel's monograph, however. In addition, for example, he tested the Meiselman short-rate hypothesis for Treasury bill data for the period 1958—61, which we have noted in chapter 3; also, he attempted a simple test of the Hedging Pressure (Market Segmentation) Theory. That test also is somewhat deficient and does not allow us to draw from it the conclusion that Kessel did, namely that this theory loses out to the Expectations and/or Liquidity Preference Theory.

Despite the criticisms that we have levelled at Kessel's tests of expectations and of liquidity preference, there is much that lies behind his work and his empirical researches on the cyclical nature of interest rates and of the term structure that is extremely deep and thorough and which we cannot touch on in this book.

Nevertheless, the empirical inquiries into liquidity premiums, although founded on a simple yet clever interpretation of how they can be represented, suffer from a number of points of view, as we have endeavoured to illustrate, even if necessarily briefly, in the foregoing remarks. It would seem fair to conclude, therefore, that these empirical inquiries have not produced the results that Kessel claims for them, and that they have:

(1) only shown that there would seem to be *prima facie* evidence that liquidity premiums exist;

(2) not been able to substantiate the view that one-year-ahead (or

one-period-ahead, to put the matter in general terms) liquidity premiums are a function, and a strong function, of one-year, or one-period, spot rates of interest;

(3) not provided reliable estimates of liquidity premiums *per se*;

(4) provided only limited, and not very substantial, evidence in support of the view that the market does predict 'one-period'-ahead 'one-period' rates quite adequately, which is required if Kessel's basic premises are correct;[10]

(5) not provided any evidence about the stability of the liquidity premium equation, even granted the correctness of the premises which lie behind that equation;

(6) for the most part dealt with a very small and difficult-to-handle part of the yield curve.

To reiterate a more general final point on the empirical evidence: it is really for *one-period-ahead* liquidity premiums, although it is the case that those premiums are based on the use of 28-day bill rates in conjunction with 56-day bill rates, backed up simultaneously with evidence on those premiums drawn from 91-day with 182-day bill rates. But often either pair of rates is used separately, and where they are used together there is no *continuity* of the evidence they can provide on liquidity premiums, that is for, one, two, . . . periods ahead of the present, even if Kessel had made available in depth the evidence he had assembled. One of the major elements of the Hicksian view of the Liquidity/Risk Premium Theory, we recall, is that there is a systematic relationship at a point in time between the liquidity premiums required by the market to persuade it to hold bonds with dates of maturity stretching further and further into the future. It is naturally true to state that it is the quantification of liquidity premiums that is the paramount requirement: but it follows from such quantification, of course, that it should allow us to see if the premiums are consistent with the Hicksian view of the market and hence are really liquidity premiums, expressing the market's preference for liquidity.

We shall have occasion to refer to Kessel's suggestions for measuring liquidity premiums in the next section of this chapter where we report on some of the tests we ran in the spirit of his work on U.K. data.

But before we proceed to look at some U.K. evidence, we must say a word about Kessel-type evidence on U.S. data other than that which he himself compiled for Treasury bills and one-/two-year government securities. Kessel attempted to test one of his own ideas against Durand's data. He found, however, that the liquidity premium equation for one-year rates was useless, having given an overall fit of 4%! Though there are many deficiencies in Durand's data, as we know already, this kind of finding — even though it is for corporate data, where default risk (as Conard ((78), p. 78) has also noted) adds a new dimension to premiums — must cast further doubt on some if not all of the hypotheses contained in the liquidity equation, or it must suggest that liquidity premiums *are zero*; and therefore, although on average the market does not predict accurately for one year ahead, on the basis of the Durand data expectations are the spur to action and are well proxied by forward rates.

In an extensive study, J. W. Conard and J. Freudenthal (reported in Conard (78), chapter 7) also replicated Kessel's tests for the existence and the measurement of liquidity premiums on short-term government securities. Their conclusion was as follows:

> . . . . We found consistent support for Kessel's view that there is a substantial and persistent liquidity premium on short-term governments. This includes bills of various length, as shown in Kessel's studies, and one-year governments. However, we do not find consistent evidence of liquidity premiums on longer government securities (e.g., five-year securities), and our study makes us hesitate to conclude that liquidity premiums were persistently positive even at the short end of the Durand yield curve for corporates.
>
> [(78), pp. 79–80]

Their tests on the measurement of liquidity premiums, despite the opening comment in this quote, also cast serious doubt on Kessel's conclusions and indicated that for longer-term government stock the liquidity premium equation provides no worthwhile results. In short, Conard states:

> . . . our studies raise some questions about the generality of the view that risk premiums are positive functions of the level of rates, though they do not contradict Kessel's finds with respect to Treasury bills . . . .
>
> [(78), p. 84]

In their tests Conard and Freudenthal attempted to measure Z, the prediction error, which causes some but not all of the difficulties, as we have seen, in interpreting the results obtained from the liquidity premium equation.

Having proxied Z,[11] Conard argues that (using our notation):

> The results suggest that Z is positively correlated with R for all securities studied by Kessel and by us. It appears that $LP + Z$ is probably more closely correlated with R than is the error term Z in the case of twenty-eight-day bills and ninety-one-day bills, giving mild support for Kessel's conclusions with respect to these securities. None of the correlations is high enough to give much confidence in the results, but some further support is provided by Kessel's second test, whereby a positive correlation is found between $LP + Z$ on twenty-eight-day bills and the rising trend of rates between 1949 and 1961. It should be added that our indication of a positive correlation between Z and the level of rates, while not contradicting Kessel's conclusions, does suggest a much smaller influence of R on LP than he inferred from his procedures, which abstracted from any effects of Z.
>
> The test Freudenthal and I employed gave exactly the opposite results in the case of longer term securities, where the time span of forecasts was a year. . . . We do not take the numbers that literally but they do seem to us to leave 'unproven' the existence of a positive relation between risk premiums and the level of interest rates.
>
> [(78), pp. 84–5]

So the strongest support, on U.S. data, for Kessel's procedure for testing the existence of liquidity premiums and for measuring them comes from his own, Treasury bill, data. Moving away from *very* short-term government securities produces no measurable support for his hypothesis. But even his own data provide support of really only a weak and unsystematic kind for the liquidity premium equation and what is implied in it.

5.5

In this section we shall examine what emerges from attempts to look at liquidity premiums in the context of the market for British government stock. These attempts embrace tests we performed both on Grant's data (39) and on our own data, and the attempt made very recently by J. P. Burman and W. R. White (80) to measure liquidity premiums in an entirely different way from that followed by Kessel and by us.

It seems logical to begin by making some observations on our endeavours at measuring liquidity premiums. Remember that the data we are using are yield-to-maturity data and that there are the usual errors (possible errors) involved in the calculations of forward rates based on such data. For the study of liquidity premiums we relied mainly on the Hicksian formula to quantify those forward rates. The basic data are for securities of one and more years to maturity, and not for Treasury bills. We found no evidence of negative forward rates in these data though such forward rates would lead us to anticipate, if anything, the existence of *negative* liquidity premiums.

Nevertheless we did employ Kessel's liquidity premium equation, despite all the reservations we have expressed about using it for any statistical work and for consequently putting universal values to liquidity premiums. It is only necessary to give our findings in summary form, and we may start with those for *one-year* liquidity premiums (LP_1), which are derived from the direct application of equation (5.4.13). For our own data for 1953 to 1971, no matter which of the data we used — unweighted, weighted or smoothed — the overall results were exactly identical: the overall relationship was statistically speaking zero (very much the same as was found for Durand's data); the constant terms were statistically speaking zero; so too, of course, were the coefficients for R_{1t}; but the signs of the latter coefficients were all positive. For Grant's data the result was more respectable and perhaps we may quote it in full:

$$_{t+1}\phi_t - {}_{t+1}R_{1t+1} = -\underset{(0.56)}{1\overset{*}{.}326} + \underset{(0.137)}{0\overset{*}{.}3774}\, R_{1t} \qquad (5.5.1)$$

$$\bar{R}^2 = 0.15,\ d = 0.64,\ \rho = 0.68.$$

The Durbin—Watson statistic exhibits strong positive serial correlation in the residuals — which is not so surprising, given the relative smallness of the overall fit. Still notwithstanding, the coefficients will probably be significantly different from zero at respectable confidence levels. The R^2 is significantly different from zero at the 5% level. Here the constant term is negative, as we believed it should have been in Kessel's equation for the 1954—58 cycle for one-year rates; and imposing the restriction that it is zero, as would be expected, is rejected by the data.[12] The R_{1t} coefficient has its *a priori* sign, given Kessel's view — the generally accepted view — that the higher are spot rates the higher are liquidity premiums.

Not much investigation along the present or any other lines has been undertaken to evaluate other than 'one-period-ahead' liquidity premiums. (Conard and Freudenthal did some testing following Kessel's procedure for what effectively amounts to LP_3.) We made some efforts, therefore, to examine liquidity premiums for other than LP_1, and to make a comparison of them at each point of observation over our data period. We may now take a look at the procedures we followed on that count and at the kind of empirical results we uncovered.

Suppose the data are on an annual basis, as ours are for the U.K.; then we may calculate a series of two-years-ahead forward one-year rates (${}_{t+2}\phi_t$), which, using the identity expressed in (5.4.6), gives:

$$_{t+2}\phi_t = {}_{t+2}r_{t+1} + LP_{2t}. \tag{5.5.2}$$

If we invoke the hypotheses contained in equations (5.4.7) to (5.4.11) we end up with an equation similar to (5.4.13):

$$_{t+2}\phi_t - {}_{t+2}R_{1t+2} = b_0 + b_1R_{1t} + (Z_{t+2} + v_t) \tag{5.5.3}$$

where Z_{t+2} is the error of prediction. However, it is likely, or we might suggest that it is more than likely, that if $LP_{1t} = F(R_{1t})$, then $LP_{2t} = F(R_{2t})$ — though to the extent that R_{1t} and R_{2t} are more or less correlated, the choice of R_{2t} will give similar or less similar results to R_{1t}. Equation (5.5.3), or that equation with R_{2t} as the independent variable, will suffer from some of the conceptual and statistical drawbacks, of course, that we have raised in connection with equation (5.4.13). But having said this the current investigation is not entirely without use. Subject to all these limitations, it will at least give us some idea, accepting the earlier one-period-ahead liquidity premium results (despite the conclusions they forced us to draw from them), as to whether or not the hypotheses indicate that liquidity premiums might be present, and be higher, two (and more) periods ahead in time. In view of our critical approach to the question of liquidity premiums we shall attempt to specify, with the necessary caveats, what the present inquiries have revealed.

For our three kinds of data on U.K. government bonds we did, in effect, estimate these equations:

$$_{t+n}\phi_t - {}_{t+n}R_{1t+n} = a_{0n} + a_{1n}R_{1t} + A_t \tag{5.5.4}$$

$$_{t+n}\phi_t - {}_{t+n}R_{1t+n} = b_{0n} + b_{1n}R_{nt} + B_t \tag{5.5.5}$$

where $n = 2$ to 6 ($n = 1$ we have already reported on), and A_t and B_t are compound error terms. We also assessed the predictive accuracy of forward rates (i.e. the market predictions unadjusted for liquidity premiums) and of inertia for $n = 2$ to 6.

The main findings can be summarised as follows, beginning first of all with the liquidity premium equations:

(I) *Unweighted data*
For $n \geqslant 3$ both equations (5.5.4) and (5.5.5) produced results showing that no overall relationship was present and that, for

example, liquidity premiums were zero or that they did not depend upon R_{1t} or R_{nt}, or that they were constant, equal to LP_{1t}. But for $n = 2$ the results were better:

$$_{t+2}\phi_t - R_{1t+2} = -\underset{(0.87)}{2\overset{*}{.}054} + \underset{(0.173)}{0\overset{*}{.}416}\, R_{1t} \tag{5.5.6}$$

$$\bar{R}^2 = 0.229,\ d = 1.36,\ \rho = 0.32$$

$$_{t+2}\phi_t - R_{1t+2} = -\underset{(0.93)}{1.75} + \underset{(0.17)}{0.334}\, R_{2t} \tag{5.5.7}$$

$$\bar{R}^2 = 0.14,\ d = 1.50,\ \rho = 0.35.$$

In equation (5.5.7) the overall relationship just fails to be significantly different from zero at the 5% level. In both equations there is evidence of positive auto-correlation in the residuals, although the t-values of the coefficients in (5.5.6) are fairly high, and taking account of the serial correlation in the residuals might still leave those coefficients statistically speaking significantly different from zero.

These results reveal very much the same things as did that for $_{t+1}\phi_t - R_{1t+1}$. Yet if we were to interpret the complete failure of the latter equation as implying that LP_{1t} is zero, then, with LP_2 positive for all rates of interest in excess of 0.5% and $LP_3 - LP_6$ being zero, liquidity preference barely exists and it cannot follow the Hicksian pattern.

(II) *Weighted data*
Exactly the same qualitative and almost the same quantitative results as for the unweighted data.

(III) *Smoothed data*
No support at all for either liquidity premiums equation for $n = 2$ to 6 (and for $n = 1$, as noted previously).

But what about the other issues mentioned earlier concerning the 'predictive accuracy' of the various expectations hypotheses? It will be apparent from what we have just said that forward rates less 'liquidity premiums' are liable to be very poor forecasters for R_{1t+n}, $n = 1$ to 6. This turns out to be the case, although intrinsically, because of the poor fits of the liquidity equation, the results are valueless anyway. No matter which way one chooses to measure this, the predictive power of unadjusted forward rates and of spot rates is very much superior to that of 'true expected' rates, and on occasion is reasonably high. On balance, the use of forward rates produced better forecasts, and the subsequently observed spot rates were more highly correlated with them, than inertia. But there was no pattern in the predictions such that, for example, the market's power to predict nearer-term spot rates was higher than its ability to predict further-term rates. In terms of correlation, the $\bar{R}^2$ s varied between 25 and 60%, some of the highest correlations being for four-years-ahead one-year rates.

These findings, if anything, confirm the doubts we had about the quantitative assessment of liquidity premiums from the kind of hypotheses and operational equation advanced by Kessel. They also lead us to conclude that, until we have more accurate, market-opinion data, it is not likely that we can get very far statistically with this kind of approach; and that for predicting future one-year rates, for example, we are likely to produce forecasts less subject to error if we ignore liquidity premiums measured in this way and rely solely on implied expected rates via forward rates as our predicted values.

One of the other attempts we made to measure liquidity premiums was by following up the idea put forward by Sir Dennis Robertson in the passage quoted from him in section 5.2. Intuitively speaking, there seems a great deal to be said in favour of this idea, *prima facie*. Yet having conceded this much we again find ourselves in the kind of impasse with which we are familiar. For from somewhere it is necessary to manufacture normal long and short rates: the difficulty with such an exercise is it is not always easy to make it look as if things have not been 'pulled out of a hat'. Also, in Robertson's proposition the implication is that there is 'a' liquidity premium, or something akin to a representative liquidity premium. To test for the existence of liquidity premiums to evaluate the Hicksian theory in depth would involve the calculation of numerous normal 'long' and 'short' rates. Ultimately, with this conception of liquidity premiums, because 'guesstimates' have to be made of the normal rates, the problem is that the empirical findings are the outcome of combined tests of various hypotheses as well as of the main hypothesis itself.

Because our own data for the U.K. were not over a sufficiently long time span to enable us to calculate normal rates, we attempted to use Robertson's method on Grant's data. We undertook several experiments to measure the normal rates, and in the process using several distributed lag specifications. But given the reasonable success of the simple Koyck distributed lag process in forming normal rates, with a λ of about 0.5, we finally settled on that method; though the limitations, and implications, of the distributed lag approach, which we constantly stressed in earlier chapters, must be borne very much in mind when evaluating the results on liquidity premiums. Again, it was decided to limit the assessment of normal rates to representative rates: the results quoted here were based on the yield on 2½% Consols and on the one-year rate. The liquidity premiums as calculated varied quite considerably over the period. Taking the thirty-year rate as the long rate made no appreciable difference to the measurement of liquidity premiums or to the equations that were estimated on the basis of these premiums.

Even accepting the efficacy of the present approach in helping us to untangle the complex issues that are at hand, there is the additional question of what a liquidity premium calculated by the present method actually represents. Technically speaking, we would have to say that it is a kind of amalgam of all the relevant liquidity premiums, that is for periods 1 to n ahead of the present point in time, t. To use it as an estimate of liquidity premiums we shall have to make the *assumption* that it approximates the one-year-ahead liquidity premium, or that, contrary to what Hicks said, liquidity premiums are constant.

Using Grant's quarterly data for the U.K. over the period 1952—62, these results then emerge:

$$ {}_{t+1}R_{1t+1} = \underset{(0.34)}{2.793^{*}} + \underset{(0.094)}{0.391^{*}}\ {}_{t+1}r_t \qquad (5.5.8) $$

$$ \bar{R}^2 = 0.30,\ d = 0.49,\ \rho = 0.76 $$

$$ {}_{t+1}R_{1t+1} = \underset{(0.57)}{1.725^{*}} + \underset{(0.131)}{0.557^{*}}\ {}_{t+1}\phi_t \qquad (5.5.9) $$

$$ \bar{R}^2 = 0.31,\ d = 0.52,\ \rho = 0.74 $$

$$ {}_{t+1}R_{1t+1} = \underset{(0.56)}{2.13^{*}} + \underset{(0.14)}{0.499^{*}}\ R_{1t} \qquad (5.5.10) $$

$$ \bar{R}^2 = 0.24,\ d = 0.45,\ \rho = 0.78 $$

All of these equations exhibit strong positive serial correlation in the residuals. But the pattern that emerges here in terms of correlation is also repeated in terms of the predictive capacity of the three 'expected' rates. There is nothing to choose between the 'true' expected rates and the forward rates; both, though not being such good predictors, are better predictors than inertia. Also, in terms of both correlations and predictive power, the 'true' expected rate calculated from the present method of assessing liquidity premiums performed better than those based on equation (5.5.1) above.

An entirely different approach to the measurement of liquidity premiums has been taken by Burman and White (80). They report very little success for their method; and, apart from the conventional difficulties that surround any method of measurement, such an outcome is not particularly surprising, for as appealing as their method is *prima facie*, it too has many deficiencies. Their measure is defined as follows:

> . . . . It is the percentage change in the price of a stock caused by a 1% change in the yield. It is applied to the expected price, and is formally defined as the ratio of a very small percentage change in price to the corresponding change in yield. It is proportional to the measure of volatility of a stock as calculated by brokers; and is familiar to economists as the interest—elasticity of the price. The volatility is zero when a stock matures at the horizon and normally reaches a maximum for an irredeemable stock; but, since it varies inversely with the coupon, the volatility can actually exceed this 'maximum' for a very long-dated low-coupon stock standing well below par. [(80), p. 473]

We have referred to the stockbrokers' index of volatility in chapter 1. The Burman—White liquidity premium similarly provides an index which measures, or proxies, the degree of 'risk' in a given stock, should expectations of interest rates prove to be incorrect. So the way to envisage investors utilising that index of volatility is to think of them as making some allowance for *uncertain expectations*, and as doing so by topping up their expected short-term rates of interest by premiums that reflect the likely worst possible upward movement in the appropriate long rates. The allowance, reflecting the proportionate capital loss that would entail from such a movement, is provided by the Burman—White index.

The Burman—White index is devised for situations in which investors are to be induced to move outside their preferred habitats. Assuming the supply side as given, then we may suppose for the sake of argument that the market on the demand side is broken up into three segments (though Burman and White feel their results indicate that empirically it should be broken up into only two segments) — those who prefer one-to five-year bonds, those who prefer five- to ten-year bonds and those who prefer bonds with more than ten years to run before they mature. To encourage, say, the short-term investors to become medium-term investors, it is necessary to offer them some inducement — or they will ask for this inducement as it were, it being reflected in actual bond yields — which will be a payment made to provide short-term investors with some insurance against the possibility that their expected rates of interest in the future, as envisaged at their investment-decision point, will turn out to be in error, so possibly providing them with a holding-period return *ex post* that is less than that which would have been obtained from the holding of a bond that exactly met their liabilities, on which, naturally, at the decision point the return is certain. Here we are talking about the payment of a premium that we could label a risk premium. Though arguing as we have done hitherto on a kind of *reductio ad absurdum* basis, this could still be viewed alternatively as a liquidity premium, a premium demanded because of the risk of being illiquid, to put the two ideas together, at an already-determined date in the future. For in this conception of the financial market investors have preferred habitats, largely because they have *known* future liabilities of a short-, medium- and long-term character. But in that it is explicitly contended that lenders have preferences that *in aggregate* can span the maturity continuum, and implicitly supposed that they have known liabilities, here we are moving outside the Hicksian framework. Because of uncertainty of future returns outside a certain preferred holding period, investors will demand risk premiums to make them move, at the margin, from one segment of the yield curve to another. Indeed, at the margin they will be prepared to move so long as there is in their view enough inducement to do so to compensate for the loss of certainty over the returns they would have made at a known date in the future.

Thus, in such circumstances, perhaps we can avoid splitting hairs and legitimately talk about the payment as 'risk premiums'. Also, in that regard the Burman—White index would seem to have much to be said for it as a rough indicator of potential loss from investment in given kinds of bonds. However, the difficulty with the index is to make it operational, certainly where the only data available are *ex post*, and *aggregate*, data. For example: (1) some assumption has to be made as to how the market is segmented; (2) the conditions for consistent aggregation in each segment must be assumed to exist, so that all the crucial variables, e.g. expected bond prices, can be supposed to be identical for all investors in a given segment; (3) the investment period for each segment has to be quantified. But then even if, say, the market has been split on the basis of casual empiricism or whatever, into its constituent parts, and an assumption has been made about investment periods, there remains the further major difficulty: (4) somehow or other, expected bond prices and yields have to be arrived at.

It becomes apparent once again that, if attempts are being made to measure risk premiums by this method and to test the existence of the risk premium theory *per se*, many parameters are involved, and it is therefore not likely to be clear what results do emerge. To apply this kind of measure to the whole of the yield curve, in order to see for example how accurate any particular view might be of how the market is or is not segmented, would be an herculean task, likely to produce very little meaningful return.

Therefore, it is no surprise to discover that Burman and White had little success with their method in their attempts to estimate U.K. yield curves that allowed for segmentation and for risk premiums. Their task was made all the more complicated, though, by their desire to make allowance in the yield curve for taxation and for coupons (see chapter 1 above). As a summing up of the problems faced in measuring risk premiums this way, we might let Burman and White speak for themselves:

> A rather more serious problem which was encountered in the process of estimation was the virtual impossibility of assigning a value to the risk premium. This difficulty stems from the fact that the data used record the results of decisions to buy or sell stocks and so embody indistinguishably the many factors such as expected returns and risk premiums which may have led to the decisions being taken.
>
> [(80), p. 477]

And:

> In conclusion, it must be admitted that the theoretical model which has been developed to estimate the yield-to-maturity curve has not been fully tested and so its validity still remains open to some doubt. This is particularly so with regard to the risk premium. Different values were assigned to the risk premium but the effect of these on the final curve was negligible, which implies that the estimates of the expected yields and returns over the decision period cannot be considered as wholly reliable.
>
> [(80), p. 479]

5.6

In section 3.6, we collated the various bits and pieces of possible evidence that seemed to emerge from application of Meiselman-type hypotheses on the possible *existence* of liquidity premiums. Our general conclusion, summarised in the earlier tables presented in that section, indicated that the majority view seemed to be that it was *possible* that such premiums, risk or liquidity or whatever we choose to call them, did exist, though the evidence, such as it was, from the tests of the pure Meiselman Hypothesis and of the inertia hypothesis conflicted somewhat. The empirical evidence in chapter 4, especially in section 4.5, also suggested that premiums may exist, or that, to put the matter in truer perpective, the available evidence was not inconsistent with the payment of premiums.

None of the evidence was strong; neither did it point to the definite existence of risk/liquidity premiums; nor did it, or does it, enable quantitative measurement of such premiums to be undertaken. The empirical inquiries reported on in this chapter, for data similar in time span and by country to that used in chapters 3 and 4, also do not enable us to make any definitive statements to the effect that, say, such premiums do exist, follow a certain pattern, and can be measured in a certain way.

They do demonstrate the difficulty of producing evidence that risk/liquidity premiums are paid and especially of measuring those premiums. In particular they make us cast doubt on the appropriateness (especially) of Kessel's suggestions, and, at least, they indicate that they are not ideas that find universal acceptance; for even if they perform not too badly against U.S.A. Treasury bill data, they perform very poorly indeed against bond data, and especially those on the U.K. A lot of the difficulties that we are faced with when investigating the worth of the Liquidity Premium Theory arise out of the fact that all the data that are being used are *derived* data — they are not independently given data — and so the yields data reflect in some measure the liquidity premiums, if they do actually exist, that we are endeavouring to identify and measure.

If anything, the empirical findings indicate that if we are attempting to predict, say, future one-year rates we shall do as well, if not better, by employing *forward* rates data. This is certainly true for the U.S.A. bond data, and for the U.K. bond data; it even applies to a great deal of the U.S.A. Treasury bill data utilised by Kessel. 'True expected' rates only appear to predict as well as forward rates for the U.K. data where they have been calculated by the Robertsonian method, a method that is not free of difficulties of interpretation and application.

Notes to Chapter 5

1. For a model that can be used to support the view that 'risk factors' are liquidity premiums, and which discusses in a wider context than that of financial markets the conditions necessary for such premiums to exist (and hence for long rates to stand above short rates), see J. Hirshleifer (102). See also H. A. J. Green (103).
2. Though to be sure, to follow Keynes's own views strictly, it is *uncertainty*, and technically uncertainty about future capital values, that Keynes invoked as the *major* factor in shaping liquidity preference, as we have indicated in the following part of the text (see J. Robinson (65)). But the other considerations can be incorporated within the Keynesian scheme.
3. We should at this point say that, since the analysis of the Risk Premium Theory has been undertaken on that kind of assumption, it has ignored *transaction costs*, and *tax considerations*. Both of these could be important factors in determining the degree of liquidity possessed by a particular bond; for they could affect the costs involved in its *marketability*. The implied assumption has been made, however, that these kinds of factors affect all bonds alike, or that they are zero, or that they might affect different bonds differently but not by enough to account for a significant proportion of any 'premium' that exists.
4. See chapter 6 below on the Hedging-Pressure Theory.
5. In footnote 3 to this chapter we referred to transaction costs and 'liquidity'. The kind of data used by Kessel are likely to have little in the way of transaction costs attached to them, and hence the return on them is likely to be lower than that on short and long bonds since those lower returns will reflect their marketability at low cost. But Kessel has done some preliminary investigations of transaction costs — always a difficult, indeed virtually impossible, undertaking — which seems to indicate that those costs cannot account wholly for interest rate differentials on bills and on bonds (See (30), pp. 45—9).
6. Perhaps we should note that we have not followed Kessel's choice of notation for the prediction error in these equations. He used U, which we have replaced by Z to avoid confusion with u, the conventional symbol for the disturbance in statistical equations.
7. It should be conceded that Kessel is aware of this point, even though, despite its potential importance, he relegates it to a footnote ((30) n. 27, p. 26).
8. Of, for example, the Chow (79) or similar kind (see J. Stewart (73)).
9. Kessel used the three 'forecast rates', that is forward rates, 'expected' rates and rates given via the inertia hypothesis, to predict actual one-year-ahead one-year rates; and from the differences between those predictions and the actual rates that emerged in the market he calculated mean square errors for the three forecast rates. These came out as: 2.09; 1.91; and 0.91, for inertia, forward rates and 'expected' rates, respectively. On this basis 'expectations' win: but their predictive power is not very substantial.
10. His two premises, it will be recalled, are: (1) the *a fortiori* one that liquidity premiums exist; (2) the *a priori* one that those premiums, especially for one period ahead, are functions of the relevant spot rate.
11. Intrinsically the method put forward by Conard and Freudenthal to measure the influence of Z in the liquidity premium equation is as full of ingenuity and simplicity as is Kessel's procedure. They examine the influence of Z in the liquidity premium equation by transferring Z back to the left-hand side

of the equation so that it is the error in the dependent variable. Their argument then runs as follows.

The data used by Durand, and that used by Kessel on Treasury bills, exhibit a strong relationship between forward rates and spot rates (where the time span of the forecast equals the length of life of the given bill, or in the case of bonds of one or more years of life, where the time span of the forecast is one year). From this fact they are able to draw this implication:

> This means that if changes in rates (ΔR) are large, as they often are over a year or more, the difference between forward rates and realised rates will be roughly equal to (but opposite in sign from) the change in rates. But this difference is . . . $LP + Z$ . . . . The problem is to determine how far these derived values of $LP + Z$ represent error, and how far they represent risk premiums.
>
> It is our judgement that insofar as $LP + Z$ fluctuates with ΔR its movement may be attributed chiefly to error. Our logic is as follows: (1) The relationship could hardly reflect *LP*, because the subsequent change in rates is not known when the forward rate is established with its *LP* component. (2) . . . [it] could plausibly reflect error, since the large amount of inertia in the model must . . . imply a large component of error whenever rates change substantially.
>
> [(78), p. 100]

From the regression they ran over the period 1958–61 they were able to conclude that 81% of R_t was explained by ΔR, and this latter itself explains 99% of the changes in Z: thus, 80% of the changes in Z (81% of 99%) can be explained by R_t ((78), p. 103). So:

> . . . the part of the movement of $LP + Z$ attributable to R can be wholly explained by movement of Z, and there is no basis for inferring that risk-premiums are correlated with the level of rates on forecasts of a year.
>
> [ibid.]

They indicate that similar results were formed for the period 1951–63 and for one-year-ahead forecasts derived from four- and five-year bonds (that is, of LP_4).

The point that they make to the effect that if

$$ {}_{t+1}\phi_t \simeq R_{1t} \qquad \text{(a)} $$

then

$$ {}_{t+1}\phi_t - {}_{t+1}R_{1t+1} \simeq -\Delta R_{1t} \qquad \text{(b)} $$

makes a useful starting point. But there are some conceptual and statistical difficulties associated with its use, though, to be fair, Conard concedes that spurious correlations may emerge from the application of (b) to empirical data. Yet the problems encountered by use of equation (b) are not that much greater than those encountered in the estimation of Kessel's equation.

12. If we take the mathematical interpretation of the constant term, that is as the value of the liquidity premium when the spot rate of interest is zero, then some would argue that it should be zero if the Kessel hypothesis is correct; that there is a relationship between liquidity premiums and spot rates. There is always difficulty in rationalising the value of a constant term for a given hypothesis. But in the present example it is probably better to argue, in effect, that the constant term should be negative rather than zero if the hypothesis relating liquidity premiums to spot rates is to be substantiated, and if the constant term is to be subjected to interpretation and evaluation.

6 On the Hedging Pressure Theory of the Term Structure

6.1

As we have proceeded throughout this book we have gradually progressed further and further away from the Traditional Theory. We have now reached the limit of that progression. The Hedging Pressure Theory is at the other end of the pole from the Traditional Theory on all relevant counts. It places itself in that position at the outset by taking the stance that, in contradistinction to Lutz's assumption (3) (see chapter 1) in the Traditional model, lenders (and maybe borrowers) do not shift about between the various parts of the maturity continuum, though investors are not debarred from holding bonds of differing lengths of life.

But investors are regarded as having *preferred habitats* over the available maturity range of bonds. They might indeed have just one preferred habitat, which itself can be a range (e.g., five- to ten-year bonds or simply a range embracing 'medium' bonds). These preferred habitats are held to be determined solely by the structure of the *liabilities* of the particular investors. The view is that investors will attempt to match their assets (and hence their holdings of government debt) and their liabilities. If, for example, the latter are predominantly long-term, the argument is that the investor's assets will, *ceteris paribus*, be also predominantly of a long-term character. We insert 'other things being equal' here in case there are external constraints, such as the lack of an adequate supply of long-term bonds, which prevent the investor from undertaking this matching strategy. Should particular investors be fully matched then they have taken up a fully hedged position. If they match by-and-large, then they are taking up a weak or partially hedged position.

The main contention of the full Hedging Pressure Theory is that investors will not be influenced by expectations at all. Even if they form expectations of future returns on alternative assets, they do not act upon those expectations. Speculative activity, in other words, is something they do not indulge in. Thus, *ceteris paribus*, this extreme version of the theory puts forth the view that, given their liabilities, investors' financial behaviour will be governed solely by their desire of being certain that they can at least meet those obligations. Investors will go for a completely certain return from their particular wealth position over their (what will be for many of the major investors on the market — the institutional investors) known holding period: they will match the life spans of their assets and their liabilities.[1]

When the Hedging Pressure Theory is looked at in this light it is perhaps instructive to see it as an extreme variant of the 'Risk Premium' Theory. If investors will only ever take up a fully hedged position, then they are not prepared at any price to accept any 'risk'. The view could then be expressed that their utility functions are such that they reflect the fact that they prefer the certainty of making a given minimum return, plus the certainty of receipt of capital sum, to the uncertain prospect of making a return in excess of the minimum with at least the capital sum recovered in full. In a way, their behaviour could be described as 'safety-first'.

The weaker, or as some would perhaps put it, the more realistic, form of the Hedging Pressure Theory does allow some switching out of preferred habitats when interest rates move far enough to counterbalance the innate preference for matching. It is also possible for a particular structure of liabilities to be accompanied by switching between bonds in a preferred habitat range. This view of the behaviour of investors says that they do have preferred habitats, or a preferred habitat, to which they will on balance adhere but which, as suitable opportunities arise, they are not adverse to move out of. The notion of risk premiums is relevant here also.

Suppose it should happen that we have only three types of investor on the government debt market. We might for the sake of illustration call these: the discount houses; the banks; and the life insurance companies. Suppose further that each of these institutions take up fully hedged positions. Then, if they all have different liabilities such that for the three institutions respectively they can be classified as 'short-term', 'medium-term' and 'long-term', we find that the market is *segmented*. Each part of the maturity spectrum is distinct from the other. So the Hedging Pressure Theory has implications at the market level, where yields are determined. There is a direct link between that theory and the way the market is constituted. This has led to the use by researchers in this field of the term Market Segmentation Theory, with this term often being taken as synonymous with Hedging Pressure Theory. This term itself is often replaced by that of 'Institutional Theory'. It is easy to see how these terms have arisen and indeed have grown out of each other.

How segmented the market is will depend upon the degree of hedging pressure that is present in the behaviour of the separate investors on the market and the nature of the liabilities of those investors. But for the market to be *definitely* segmented, in the sense that activity in one part of the market (e.g. the short end) does not influence activity in any other part (e.g. the long end), the Hedging Pressure Theory must hold for all investors. It will not matter in those circumstances if several investors have the same kinds of liabilities and operate in the same parts of the bond market. The appearance of several investors in a part of the market will merely affect the trading that goes on there. *Ex definitione*, the purchases of bonds by each of the investors is determined wholly by his (or its) liabilities in the given conditions: expectations play no part in influencing behaviour. There will be no economic link between the various sub-markets, although in the present context the market will not be segmented by class of investor. Yet it still might be possible to say that it is segmented just by looking at those parts of the market in which investors operate, without having to resort to an analysis of their investment behaviour, if we should find that, say, on a continuing basis, parts of the maturity spectrum are actually deserted.

Should we examine data on the bond market as a market, then, if we find that it can be divided into segments such that certain kinds of institutions deal solely (or predominantly), continually, in one part of the total market, and that there are certain distinct classes of investor (e.g. short-term, long-term), then this market-segmentation will provide *prima facie* evidence that the Hedging Pressure Theory does apply to investors' behaviour. But there may not be any apparent division of the market into segments such as embrace separately, say, short, medium or long bonds. The Hedging Pressure Theory can still be valid because the various investors on the market may have preferred habitats, and preferred habitats that are ranges, and which themselves overlap with the ranges of one or more investors in the market.

In the immediately following section of this chapter we shall recapitulate, and develop a little, these analytical points on the Hedging Pressure Theory, noting to what forces it ascribes the determination of the term structure. It will be of some assistance to our discussion, however, if we make reference to empirical observations in that section; observations that are centred round the early pioneering work of J. M. Culbertson (28a), and that are concerned with the features that identify the theory and the means by which it might be subjected to empirical testing. Section 6.3, proceeding naturally from the previous discussion, is devoted to a critical appraisal of the existing evidence on the Hedging Pressure Theory. Thereafter section 6.4 gives details, with supporting critical evaluation, of empirical evidence on that theory that we have managed to assemble for the U.K. by means of an analysis of statistical data of the activity of the major institutions investing in U.K. government stock, and by some econometric analysis of the assumptions underlying the theory and the predictions contained within it. As we shall argue below when we are, in fact, developing the theory and its predictions, if anything approaching a successful attempt is to be made to subject the theory to empirical inquiry, indeed to test any of the theories, or to discover if any particular variable can explain, or be a contributory factor in explaining, the term structure (a *market* phenomenon) in the real world, then it must be carried out in the context of a general equilibrium model of, at least, the whole of the financial sector. In section 6.5 we briefly summarise some of the work we have been, and are, doing on such a model for the U.K., and we present and discuss the results we have obtained from it so far that throw some light on the Hedging Pressure and other theories of the term structure. The work on this kind of model is not complete, and perhaps will not be in one individual's lifetime, neither has this kind of model been used for the present purpose before; indeed, the model referred to in section 6.5, together with our earlier (very much) first run of a static model (84), provide the first material published on such a model for the U.K.

After this abundance of empirical evidence — evidence of a diverse nature at that — on the Hedging Pressure Theory *per se*, and occasionally by implication at times for other theories of the term structure, the final section of this chapter endeavours to draw together the main findings of that evidence.

6.2

The Liquidity/Risk Premium Theory is founded on the view that the market is 'lopsided'. Investors taken as a whole prefer to lend short and in consequence need special inducements to make them shift from their preferred habitat into the longer end of the market. The reasons for the market having a preference for short-term financial assets can be many, as we have suggested in chapter 5, although they might all conceivably be reduced to an expression of preference for 'liquidity'. Now the Hedging Pressure Theory puts forward the idea that investors do have preferences for certain kinds of financial assets but it explicitly suggests a reason why they have preferred habitats.

Fundamentally, if it is conceded that all investors are not alike on the market, the Hedging Pressure Theory, by its very name, means that there is segmentation of the market. The total market is effectively split into smaller sub-markets. There is for the most part no economic overlap between markets, and indeed none whatsoever in the full-hedging-pressure version of the theory. It is demand and supply *solely within these markets* that determine the price of the given bonds, thus their yields, and thence the structure of yields. Expectations of interest rates in one market are not supposed to influence interest rates in any other market; so in equilibrium this means that the actual interest rate in any one market is determined independently of that in any other market. That is, the demand for a given bond in one investor's segment of the market will not depend upon any rate or rates other than the own-rate and the rates on any bonds that should appear in his segment.

The first substantial attempt to advance the hedging-pressure view of the determination of the term structure was that of J. M. Culbertson ((28a), (28b)). Though he has become associated with the formulation of the theory and with its development, it is interesting to note that in his seminal article (28a) on the theory he did not go completely for a full-hedging-pressure conception of the organisation of the financial market; neither did he advocate the view that the evidence he had compiled on that theory gave unqualified support to it, despite the impression often given in the literature.

If any role could be denied to expectations, to the effect that they are not formed, or if they are not acted upon, by the participants in the financial market, then the cornerstone of the Traditional Theory would have been removed; furthermore, even in a world that is slightly different from that envisaged in the Traditional Theory, so that if expectations were to be formulated we would suppose them to be shrouded in a mist of uncertainty, the ultimate outcome would be to rule out the existence of any kind of *speculative* activity. The *sine qua non* of such activity in the financial market is the existence of uncertainty concerning the future yields on the assets traded on that market. It was Culbertson's considered opinion that no effective role could be assigned to expectations.

While some critics of the Traditional Theory might rest their case against it on theoretical or 'intuitive' grounds, for example by denying that the market will form expectations of market yields for more than short periods ahead in time, Culbertson, although he supports that kind of attack on the theory, is concerned to challenge the basic philosophy of the Traditional approach by empirical inquiry. *Effectively*, Culbertson builds up his case against the theory by following the thesis that figured so prominently in the later work of R. A. Kessel, namely that, if the Traditional approach is to be seen to be a sound one, expectations must be fulfilled.

Though he does adduce empirical evidence which leads him to reject the Traditional Theory, Culbertson makes it clear at the outset that he can see very little role for expectations:

> . . . expectations of lenders and borrowers regarding future changes in interest rates, where these exist, evidently must affect inducements to hold and to issue debt of different maturities. However, the behavior of most borrowers and lenders is not ordinarily governed by such expectations. The effect upon the rate structure of those patterns of speculative (i.e., expectationally governed) behavior that do exist depends upon the nature of their planning periods, . . . , and other such details . . . . Thus, both the relative importance as a price-determining factor and the characteristic effect of speculative activity are matters that finally must be settled by reference to the facts regarding the particular market during the particular period. In general, however, in debt markets such behavior is more prominent in the market for debt that is more unstable in price, that is, long-term debt, and it is predominantly based upon near-term expectations, rather than upon those related to the more distant future. These considerations do not support the view that long-term rates should tend to equal the average of short-term rates expected over the period to maturity of the long-term debt . . . .
>
> [(28a), p. 490]

Culbertson believes that expectations can at the most influence behaviour only in the very short term and then that influence will be transitory and determine the behaviour of only a relatively small number of 'active traders' among investors.

If we take the Traditional model and make the assumption that expectations are held with some uncertainty, we can have speculative behaviour as opposed solely to arbitrage. Should we remain within the confines of that model we know that, *ex ante*, if investors act upon their expectations the holding-period return from purchasing one length-of-life bond will equal that return from buying any other length-of-life bond. For Culbertson the Traditional Theory, and the role of expectations in affecting the term structure, is to be evaluated by an examination of such returns. If, as he sees it, those holding-period returns are not equal, the theory is invalid. It must be conceded that the role of sole determinant of the term structure that is assigned to expectations would disappear — though expectations might have some influence on the structure — if *ex ante* holding-period returns were not identical. But Culbertson used *ex post* holding-period returns as a basis of his test of the theory. To deduce anything about the importance of expectations in this manner requires the presupposition to be made that *expectations are fulfilled*. We have already argued out a viewpoint on that requirement.

Culbertson was led to inquire into the Expectations Theory by a scrutiny of holding-period returns from an overview of his data. The latter were for the U.S.A. for the period 1920—57 and they covered short-term bonds (proxied mainly by Treasury bills) and long-term bonds (in the range, 10—20 years). The yields on these bonds were yields-to-maturity put on an annual from a monthly basis. For the time span of his data Culbertson traced out the broad relationship that existed between 'short' and 'long' rates; and he found, perhaps not surprisingly, that the long rate usually stood above the short rate. He does, in effect, note only two occasions when the short rate stood above the long rate, both instances occurring at *peak* levels of both rates. The conclusion is also drawn from his data that the movements in the two rates of interest have tended to occur simultaneously, without any evidence, therefore, that the one rate leads the other.

The existence of this positive yield-gap then led Culbertson to maintain that speculative activity is absent from the financial market. If expectations are to play any part in the determination of the yield structure, then a positive yield-gap should not persist, since it reflects a situation of continuing lost opportunities for gain by investors. Advantage would have been taken of such possibilities if expectations had any worthwhile influence on activity in the market.

There are several difficulties with accepting Culbertson's interpretation of his evidence. For example, there is the evidence itself: it is based on yield-to-maturity data, which have the normal drawbacks, although this point is countervailed by Culbertson's later use of holding-period data. Then we might make the remark that this kind of evidence is founded on 'the swings and the roundabouts' kind of 'on the average' accuracy of expectations.

To confirm the impression created by the time series evidence, Culbertson performed a detailed test on holding-period returns for one year in his data period, 1953, which was chosen because in that year there were considerable fluctuations in short and long rates. In calculating holding-period returns an attempt was made to measure them properly, though no account could be taken of transaction costs — which it was felt would not affect the yield-*gap* materially. The holding period was posited to be of short duration, and two such periods, one of one week and one of three months, were selected. For those holding periods, annual rates of return were calculated on Treasury bills and on Treasury stock (12/67—72) for the fifty-two weeks of the year. These were *ex post* returns, from which Culbertson concluded:

> . . . holding-period yields fluctuated over a much wider range than maturity yields, . . . holding-period yields on long-term debt fluctuated over a much wider range than those on short-term debt, . . . the shorter the period of time over which the holding-periods are computed the wider was the range of fluctuation . . . .
> Thus, it appears that during periods in which the level of interest rates is changing . . . yields for short holding periods on long-term debt characteristically differ greatly from those on short-term debt; *evidence of anything approaching perfect speculation is absent.*
>
> [(28a), italics added]

Expectations were then to be pushed into the background as a force determining the term structure, at least outside the short run. This evidence produced by Culbertson to deny any significant role to 'speculative behaviour', and hence to expectations, suffers from the drawbacks mentioned hitherto, not the least of which is that the data employed are on an *ex post* basis. J. B. Michaelsen (85) made this same point in his critique of Culbertson's position. Once this objection is allowed, then all that remains of Culbertson's empirical evidence against the existence of speculative activity is material that we could loosely describe, at best, as suggestive: there is no hard core to it, although Culbertson endeavours to justify his standpoint by more detailed investigation of the behaviour of yields and the maturity structure of debt in the U.S.A. for the years 1916—55.

Looking at the findings of Culbertson on holding-period returns, Michaelsen has even gone so far as to contend that, notwithstanding the problems of interpreting those returns, they *support* the Traditional Theory that expectations play a major part in the determination of the term structure. However, his justification for advocating this interpretation of the evidence is itself open to serious doubt, and met with a strong rebuff from Culbertson himself (86).

The substance of Michaelsen's hypothesis can best be expressed in his own words:

> We can posit a simple and plausible relationship between *ex ante* and *ex post* yields such that Culbertson's findings will be

> consistent with the implication of the expectational theory that anticipated yields over short holding periods will be the same for default-free securities.
>
> . . . . The relationship I propose is that the realised yields on different default-free securities over any short period are (behave as if they were) the sum of a single anticipated vield common to all such securities and a random disturbance specific to each. This is equivalent to assuming that speculative activity by investors indifferent to the maturity of these securities will cause their anticipated yields to be the same, and that the estimates on which these investors base their activity are not subject to systematic bias.
>
> [(85), p. 170]

Michaelsen is of the opinion that Culbertson's data can be used to test his thesis, though they do not make it possible to undertake a 'rigorous' test of it. In a later contribution Michaelsen sets out in more detail the nature of his thesis and does attempt more thoroughgoing tests of it based upon his own data (87).

The first test of his hypothesis that he performed on Culbertson's data was developed from the argument that, *ceteris paribus*, the expectation would be that the disturbances in the relationship advocated (by himself) would be negligible. Michaelsen's hypothesis — which is basically an identity, of the kind employed by Kessel — would then lead to the further expectation that:

> . . . . We would expect the average difference in realised yields between pairs of . . . securities . . . in a sample of successive short holding periods to tend toward zero.
>
> [(85), p. 170]

For all that follows from the use of his identity is that, given the *assumption* about the error terms, 'on average' (which creeps into the discussion yet again), realised yields will equal expected yields. It is not possible to dispute the existence of the identity, quite naturally, though it is possible to challenge the assumption about the error term. We have previously discussed this issue in connection with Kessel's researches. To assume that the 'error term' is of the form posited by Michaelsen is implicitly to accept the view that the market should, on balance, make accurate forecasts. Even if one concedes that in some general sense intuition suggests that the criteria of accurate forecasting is an appropriate one to apply, we again are confronted, once we attempt to subject it to empirical scrutiny, by the vexed question of what 'on the average', or 'on balance' actually means, and of how any sample of data can be selected that is devoid of any ambiguities on this count.

Yet Michaelsen proceeds to utilise Culbertson's data in a way that will make it amenable to his test. What he does, in effect, is to take the data Culbertson has provided on one-week holding-period rates for the year 1953, and to process those 52 returns merely by counting the number of times the bill yield exceeds the bond yield. This exercise produces a total of 26 pluses and 22 minuses: in four cases Michaelsen cannot interpret Culbertson's data sufficiently clearly so an indifferent result, of zero, is assumed. Statistical tests convince Michaelsen that the difference between 26 and 22 is not significantly different from zero.

To assess the pluses and minuses that he has arrived at Michaelsen arranges them according to the number of consecutive runs that occur for them. Thus out of the 52 pluses, minuses and zeros he finds that: on 20 occasions one of them held for only one week; on 7 occasions there were two successive pluses or minuses; on 2 occasions there were three consecutive pluses or minuses; on 1 occasion only did one or the other signs hold for four and eight consecutive weeks, the total number of runs, as he called them, being equal to 31. It is to the latter total that he applies his statistical test of his hypothesis:

> If 26 +'s, 22 —'s and 4 zeroes are arranged at random, say as in 52 consecutive spins of a roulette wheel . . . the expected number of runs is 30. The observed number . . . is 31; the probability of a deviation from the expected value this large, or larger, if the process is random, exceeds 0.56. Further . . . 22 and 26 are not significantly different, so that this sample provides no evidence for rejecting the hypothesis that the average difference in actual outcomes is other than zero.
>
> [(85), p. 172]

His conclusion is then that this evidence is enough to prove his hypotheses relating realised yields to anticipated yields, that 'on average' this equality would materialise, so destroying Culbertson's claim to have shown that speculative activity does not exist on the market.

This method of testing his hypothesis is suspect on a number of counts, and it is not surprising that Culbertson was quick to point out its deficiencies in his rebuttal of Michaelsen's claim to have destroyed Culbertson's conclusions (86). We need not concern ourselves with full discussion of these matters, though we may note one or two of the more important of the points made. The test is not based on a *numerical* netting out of the differences between the two types of holding-period returns, as Michaelsen concedes it should be. He would claim here that he could not undertake such a test because the data in Culbertson are not given in tabulated form but have to be read off his charts. Culbertson dismissed that argument, and proceeded to show that, using the data solely provided in his chart, the differences in three-month holding-period returns for bills and bonds did not average to zero over the year. Another point is that to look at the pattern of the pluses and minuses in the way that Michaelsen has done can tell us very little. The pluses and minuses need to be plotted as they occur, but then the true nature of the pattern, e.g., random or non-random, cannot be ascertained without some benchmark (zero here) being used: but there is no quantification in Michaelsen's analysis, for the zero values are suspect. Knowledge of the values of the pluses and minuses taken in time sequence would provide us with *more* useful information, enabling us to apply a more reliable guide to the pattern in the 'residuals' between the bill and bond yields.

On closer inspection we must be forced into the conclusion that Michaelsen's hypothesis, as he applied it, is not able to reverse the findings of Culbertson as he, Culbertson, saw them.[2] However, despite the impossibility of turning Culbertson's data on their head so that they support the Traditional Theory and allow speculative activity to predominate in the financial market, we may still argue that Michaelsen *was* right in stating that Culbertson's test of the role of expectations was invalid — despite Culbertson's own protestations to the contrary (86) — because it was based on *ex post* and not on *ex ante* data. Furthermore it was founded on the view that expectations should be fulfilled on, once more, a kind of average basis.

It would be possible, as with all studies of this nature, to level critical remarks at the data used by Culbertson, with regard to such things as length of holding period; but that is a fruitless exercise, and one that is largely redundant, to our mind, given the points we have made so far. We thus find ourselves in a position where we are sceptical about the possibility of ruling out expectations and speculative activity; by reference to Culbertson's findings, or at best from his point of view, we find ourselves in an agnostic position. But Culbertson himself was in no doubt about the value of the data he had compiled; and this led him to put forward a theory which we now call the Market Segmentation Theory, which he did by reference to the preference lenders may have for liquidity and to empirical observation of the U.S. bond market and of the behaviour of some of the institutions in that market.

These considerations led him to take the view that expectations are likely to affect market behaviour in the short run, but that a great deal of activity in the market, particularly at the long end, is based on *non-speculative* behaviour, as he put it.

> Non-speculative behaviour . . . is probably the predominant type of debt market behaviour . . . .
> . . . . It involves making choices on some basis that is independent of any particular expectation. . . . This can be done in a number of possible ways. A common one is to select a portfolio maturity structure suited to the liquidity needs of the investor . . . and then hold to this portfolio structure through whatever short-run shifts may occur in expectations or interest rates. The behaviour of most financial institutions is of this general character, with investment concentrated in long-term debt except in so far as liquidity needs require the holding of short-term debt.
>
> [(28a), pp. 498–9]

But Culbertson's empirical analysis of the maturity structure of the debt and of the state of interest rates does not provide any rigorous testing of this kind of hypothesis, either at the market level or at the institution level, by, for example, looking in detail at the portfolio behaviour of major financial institutions, although the evidence does offer some sort of *prima facie* support for the idea that the maturity structure of the debt is a major factor in the determination of the structure of interest rates.

At this point, even if this seems an abrupt procedure, we must terminate our comments specifically related to Culbertson and widen our observations somewhat in an endeavour to recapitulate in summary fashion on the main points in the Hedging Pressure (Market Segmentation) approach, the prediction it contains, and the means by which it would seem that we should choose to subject it to empirical test.

The extreme version, as we may put the matter, of the theory believes that speculative activity, or expectations-based activity, is not present on the financial market in any form. Though individual or institutional investors may formulate expectations of future interest rates and bond prices, they will not, for one reason or another, act upon those expectations. To use Culbertson's phrase, investment is non-speculative. In order that it be non-speculative investors must hold bonds until they mature, and the length of life of the bond(s) they buy must accordingly match their holding period, this matching, or the choosing and the maintaining of a preferred habitat, being based largely on liquidity needs, or of risk, where risk relates to the chance of not being 'fully liquid' at a known stated date in the future. Given the existence of such a date, the easiest (as measured by the saving in time and convenience of not having to review the given portfolio) and, *ceteris paribus*, surest choice for an investor is to match his assets to his liabilities.

A more realistic form of the theory would be that investors have a preferred habitat range; that there is movement between bonds within a relevant maturity range possibly owing to expectational factors of a short-run nature.

Whichever way we choose to view the Hedging Pressure Theory, or the notion which figures in Culbertson's seminal contribution that we should be thinking along market-segmentation lines, it is founded on the premise that speculative activity — expectations-induced activity — is not very prevalent on the financial market. This means that the demand of given investors for given bonds is for the most part independent of expected interest rates on other bonds, and that where the demand functions do contain expected interest rates on other bonds as arguments those rates are *ceteris paribus* on bonds within the given investors preferred habitat range. Given the demand functions of all investors for all bonds on the market, a change in the supply of any bond will change the term structure of interest rates.

The predictions of the Hedging Pressure (Market Segmentation) Theory reduce to one: *ceteris paribus*, the maturity structure of the outstanding debt determines the term structure of interest rates; changes in that maturity structure will change the term structure. *Supply* is 'the' factor in this theory.

Behind this empirical prediction lie those concerning the demand functions of investors for financial debt. We might allow ourselves to call these *pronouncements* on the nature of those functions, though in a formal sense it would seem more appropriate to call them premises or hypotheses. They are testable hypotheses and, depending upon the fulness with which they are tested, they provide us with a preliminary empirical assessment of the 'supply prediction' of the theory.

The theory's prediction differs from that of the Traditional Theory in that the latter, on the *ceteris paribus* assumption, denies (or excludes) any role for supply. The Liquidity/Risk Premium Theory enables supply to have *some* influence on the term structure, whereas the Hedging Pressure Theory, as portrayed in its extreme form, places the whole onus of the determination of the term structure on supply and in its more realistic form appears to give supply a major role. It is the different premises about demand for financial assets, and hence the assumption about the continuity of assets in the maturity spectrum, which these theories make that produce these differing emphases on supply.

How might we go about the task of subjecting the Hedging Pressure Theory to empirical investigation? One way would be to begin not with the prediction of the theory, as we have called it, but with the hypotheses that underlie that prediction. This would necessitate the splitting up of the investors in the market into specified sub-groups, e.g. the personal sector, the commercial banks, the discount houses (for the U.K.), the pension funds, the insurance companies, and other non-bank financial institutions. Then a detailed theoretical and econometric study would have to be made of the portfolio and debt management behaviour of these categories of investors. We would have to start such an inquiry with some guess, or to put it more euphemistically with some conjecture, as to the motives of investors which fitted in with the theory under review, e.g. the development of a Royian Safety-First postulate (83). From this would be developed, under various assumptions about length of holding period and the like (on the same kind of procedure as was introduced into chapter 2), the demand of the investors for a possible range of financial assets. Though those demand functions *per se* would have to be tested by econometric analysis on a time series basis over a run of observation points, it would be necessary to reformulate the portfolio selection problem of the given investor on a motivational hypothesis which produces asset demand functions that contain independent variables to which the Hedging Pressure Theory attaches no significance, that is the expected returns on a range of assets.

By such a procedure it would be possible to form some idea as to the relevance of expectational factors for individual investors and thence by implication for the market as a whole. Such a procedure is not as simple and as straightforward as it sounds, hence the deliberate choice of the words 'some idea'. Let us list some of the problems that would be encountered if such a procedure were to be followed:

(1) Short of undertaking the impossible task of looking at the forces that determine the way that any and every single investor chooses his portfolio at any one point in time, it is inevitable that some aggregation of investors into groups, delineated probably as we have suggested previously, will be necessary. This produces familiar problems, such as: how to decide that the aggregation is appropriate; that, if it is, it can have meaning only if it is supposed that the institutional factors operating on all investors in a group are the same, and if they have the same view about expectations (either as to what they expect future interest rates to be if they have some part to play in the choice of their optimum portfolio, or that they should be ignored).

(2) There is an additional aggregation problem. Though it might be true that under (1) the correct groupings had been made, there could

still exist *overlap* between the groupings. This is because some investors will, owing to the nature of their liabilities, desire to hold short as well as medium or long bonds. Other investors will be holding, or demanding, short-term assets as part of their portfolio to satisfy their liquidity needs. So the demand for a given bond is likely to be an amalgam of the demands of several different types of investor.

(3) To evaluate fully the role of expectations it would obviously be necessary when reformulating the bond demand equations to *measure* expected returns on short, medium, and long bonds. Here an ancillary difficulty, that of how to assess the appropriate length of the holding periods, becomes germane. But even when that is sorted out the fundamental problem of quantifying *expected* capital gains/losses remains as large as ever.

(4) These two issues, even when we have overcome the other problems or assumed them away, make it almost impossible to compare the results obtained from market-segmentation hypotheses and those obtained from an expected stance, and hence to pronounce definitive judgement on the relative merits of these two ways of approaching the question as to what factors determine the term structure of interest rates.

Nothing has been said in the above about the technical, theoretical and econometric problems that are inevitably going to arise. Additionally, there are the difficulties of data collection. Let us first take up the issue of econometric analysis. Bearing in mind point (4) above, we should build a 'general equilibrium' model of the bond market, indeed of the whole financial and monetary sectors, or an even wider-based model, to take account of the possible interdependence between the various parts of the market. Such a model ideally should be estimated using an estimator that is truly a simultaneous one. A suggestion such as this, however, will bring with it further critical, indeed from some observers we might say sceptical, comments: it is not immune from criticism. It too is fraught with difficulties.

Though it is true that the theoretical and econometric problems that arise in the single-equation or partial approach are very much magnified when a model is developed and estimated, we would still argue that, at least conceptually, we should attack issues such as the present ones by following such a step, albeit an adventuresome one. In that way we are setting the demand for the various kinds of bonds in the context of the demand for other financial, and possibly real assets, and of the *supply* of all assets. We shall say something further about model-building and its problems in section 6.5.

A kind of compromise exists between these two approaches. Ignoring some of the complexities of the problem, a 'macro-view' can be adopted and equations developed which look at the difference between certain interest rates, such as the 'long' and the 'short' rate, as functions of expected rates of interest on long and short bonds and of variables that reflect the maturity structure of marketable government debt. The latter variables may be the number of long bonds outstanding, or the 'average maturity' of the existing debt. There are difficulties, however, over the interpretation of such results — and for the sake of argument we may assume away the questions of measuring expected returns on the relevant bonds and of quantifying the maturity of the relevant debt. For they do lack a satisfactory theoretical base, and they are mixtures of elements in from both the partial and the general equilibrium approaches. They are not reduced from equations from a full-scale model, because they will have omitted some, and if the model is even of only modest size, several, explanatory variables, and they will not be equilibrium equations.

It will therefore be only with some difficulty that these kinds of results can be untangled to throw light on the questions at issue concerning the relative values of the Hedging Pressure (Market Segmentation), Risk/Liquidity Premium and Expectations Theory. *Prima facie* one might be tempted into saying something like this:

(i) If the coefficients on the expected interest rates (or expected returns) are not significantly different from zero, while at the same time those on the maturity of the debt are statistically speaking other than zero, the Traditional Theory can be forgotten about *and* so can the Risk/Liquidity Premium Theory.

(ii) If the coefficients on all variables are statistically speaking different from zero, the Expectations Theory must be rescinded *but* so too must the *extreme* version of the Hedging Pressure (Market Segmentation) Theory.

(iii) If the coefficients on the maturity structure of the debt variables are the only ones that are statistically different from zero, the Expectations Theory can be disregarded *and* so too can the Risk/Liquidity Premium Theory. The Hedging Pressure (Market Segmentation) Theory, in its extreme form, stands alone.

(iv) If the coefficients on the expected return variables are the only ones that are significantly different from zero, the Expectations Theory is validated, and the other theories can be discarded.

Indeed, there would be very little point in subjecting equations of the present type to statistical testing if we felt that they would tell us nothing at all and if we had no *a priori* expectations about the signs and significance of the coefficients in the equations when they had been estimated, in order that this or that theory might emerge unscathed, or even with something positive to its credit. We would not only be tempted to make the above deductions [(i)—(iv)]; we would be forced into making them. But even if the results of testing equations of this nature indicate that multicollinearity is not present, the coefficients have what are regarded as correct *a priori* signs, and so on, we cannot make deductions (i)—(iv) with much confidence.

So much will not be explicitly specified in these equations. For one thing, even though our interest focuses on the structure of rates in the bond market, it is wrong to ignore the equity, and nowadays the property market. Some institutions can invest, will and do invest, in all three markets; others are prevented by law and custom (cf. Culbertson's comments quoted earlier in this section) from doing so. But just as a simple illustration, let us suppose that in an equation of the kind we are talking about our reference point is the long—short yield-gap on government bonds. Let the maturity structure of the debt be represented by the outstanding stock of long bonds and of short bonds: then let the coefficients on those stocks turn out to have positive and negative signs, respectively. *Ceteris paribus* (an assumption very much needed here and one that contains many '*ceteris's*'), this in view of our earlier observations would perhaps make us feel that we could allow ourselves the liberty of suggesting that the Hedging Pressure Theory and/or the Risk Premium Theory had some empirical value after all.

But suppose in the *ceteris paribus* we hold the stock of short bonds constant and, while also keeping the expected yields on long and short bonds constant, we imagine that there is a small increase in the stock of long bonds. We could be bound to trace through this effect in a straightforward manner: the quantity of long bonds demanded being given, there must be a fall in their price, hence the yield on them must rise. Nothing has happened in the bond market to change the return on shorts: hence, the yield-gap rises. This ignores completely the possible substitution between 'long'/'shorts' and other financial and/or real assets. If, as we know happens in the U.K., those institutions that invest in the medium/long end of the bond market are also heavy investors in the equity market (we think here of life insurance companies and the growth of equity-linked policies: see (115)), then it is *possible* that, as they divest themselves of new funds, for example, they might not be concerned with matching their assets and liabilities all of the time, because, since they have a continual inflow of funds, they can invest those funds so that on *average* (we meet this slipping phrase yet again!), perhaps by the end of each financial year, they have their desired 'matching portfolios'. They may be prepared to move into different markets because of, rather than despite, their different commitments. This might be because they can match their portfolio over a run of months, *or* it may be because they are, to some degree, prepared to be *speculators*.

The point is that any of the equations we are now discussing should enable us to discriminate between theories. However they can be formulated, unintentionally, in such a way that to one extent or another they are *a priori* denying the relevance of a theory. If at all possible it would seem, therefore, that if the bond market is being looked at as a whole, the assets, even if we only keep to financial assets, which the investors on the bond market also hold should be brought into the analysis somewhere. In the present example we might easily make entirely the wrong deduction about the effect of an increase in the supply of long bonds on the long—short yield-gap and so, in effect, have attributed the rise in that gap to the said increase in long bonds. Other factors directly concerned with the equity market could have brought about this result: for example, if long bonds and equities *are* substitutes, at the margin, it could have been that there was a rise in the market's expectation of return on equities, which, *ceteris paribus*, would reduce the demand for longs unless their yields rose pro rata and hence led to a rise in their yield. An increase in the supply of longs at the same time would leave the cause of the ensuing rise in yields indeterminate.

None of this would matter that much if there happened to be a perfect positive correlation between the supply of long bonds and the expected return from investing in equities. But the example seems to indicate the kind of interpretative difficulties that exist with these kind of 'aggregate view' equations, and to point to the need to avoid jumping to conclusions.

However, it is precisely because these sorts of equations give the impression that they will provide answers for us on the term structure just at a glance, and because they do not require the production and testing of detailed explicit statements and hypotheses about this and that investor's portfolio behaviour, or the time-consuming and frustrating effort that has to go into the construction of a comprehensive model, that they have frequently been used in the literature, even though they are in a kind of no-man's land between the partial and the general equilibrium studies. In the research studies that we shall refer to in the rest of this chapter these 'aggregate view' equations have been used; and in our own researches we have experimented with all three approaches, the partial, the 'aggregate view' and the model approach, in seeking to test the theory first broached in a substantial form by J. M. Culbertson.

6.3

In this section the empirical studies that we shall refer to are those undertaken by others; in the following two sections we take a look at our own efforts at evaluating the Hedging Pressure (Market Segmentation) Theory for U.K. data. Apart from one study, those discussed in this section base their observations on U.S. data. The studies are partial in nature though they do not follow the statistical format mentioned in section 6.2 when examining particular institutions' financial behaviour, and some of them employ 'aggregate view' equations, as we have called them. A natural procedure in considering some of the existing empirical studies is to say something about those that first of all take the partial view and study particular institutions, and then follow this discussion with a look at the kind of results that have been obtained from use of the 'aggregate view' equations.

Those studies that have examined the portfolio behaviour of financial institutions with the object of throwing light on the efficacy of the theory have done so in a way that is near to the spirit of Culbertson's method of drawing attention to the possible part that they might play in affecting the term structure. To be specific, their approach is not of the econometric kind mentioned in section 6.2 in our observations on the partial approach testing of the theory. Rather than executing any actual statistical testing of the theory, they either draw up aggregate data on the main characteristics of the portfolio structure of certain financial institutions over a given time span, or (in some circumstances we should say and/or) make use of interviews with the managers of the relevant institutions to formulate their conclusions on what motivates their behaviour on the financial market.

The first kind of attack on the question at issue is a useful exercise but only as a preliminary to the second kind of attack on it, or to extensive econometric analysis of the reasons for the observed investment in the structure of the portfolio. But before that analysis is begun it could be argued that it should be preceded by both steps. Something of value can emerge from the interview method of approach; but it also has its limitations, which are familiar. It also carries with it the disadvantage that, even supposing all institutions in a given category have been successfully interviewed, the answers it provides, since they are difficult to put into concrete terms, do not *per se* provide information of much value for predictive purposes. It is much more doubtful whether a data analysis of the portfolio structure of financial institutions can *per se* tell us enough about the behaviour behind that structure, and hence about whether this or that theory of the term structure is likely to be the one that counts in the real world.

We may begin our discussion of these tests with those of Malkiel (11) and of Kane and Malkiel (88), which together produced evidence on both counts. Both of these are large and very detailed studies, and it is therefore scarcely possible to do justice to them or to the enormous work, especially the fieldwork, that has obviously gone into them. We can however make an attempt to pick out some of the salient points from their work and to put them into some perspective.

Malkiel himself (11) takes the methodological approach outlined earlier in this section; that is, he begins with an overview of the portfolio structure of the major financial institutions, which is followed by (in his case he would say backed-up by) evidence of a micro-nature on the behaviour of certain institutions drawn from interviews.

His starting point is the monthly survey of ownership of U.S. government securities published in the U.S. Treasury Department's *Treasury Bulletin* on the basis of nominal values. The data he uses are on a semi-annual basis for the years 1954 to 1964, and are for commercial banks, mutual savings banks, fire and casualty companies and life insurance companies. He arbitrarily aggregates holdings of bonds into four maturity segments: under one year; one to five years; five to ten years; and over ten years. The percentage of each institution's portfolio held within each segment is then calculated for the whole period from the information on the total amount of bonds outstanding in each segment. This information, which is portrayed on four charts ((11) pp. 148—9), reveals at a glance that there is considerable fluctuation in all of the percentage figures: there is certainly no evidence of stability for any institution, especially when all four maturity segments are taken into consideration. The most striking fluctuations are for life insurance companies.

To the evidence for financial institutions is added some for non-financial corporations. The data Malkiel used for the latter are for the period 1960 to 1964, again on a semi-annual basis. But they are aggregated across all reporting corporations, providing figures of the proportion of their total portfolio that was placed in the four maturity segments. Again these figures reveal fluctuations for all segments.

These pieces of aggregate data on portfolio structure lead Malkiel to make these deductions:

> All financial institutions tended to increase their relative shares of 1- to 5-year issues during this period. What is remarkable is the extent to which life insurance companies (classically long-term investors) increased their holdings in this maturity sector. Similarly, mutual savings banks and fire and casualty companies bought significant quantities of these issues. This offers *prima facie* evidence that certain classes of financial institution not only can but do make substantial shifts in the maturity composition of their portfolios . . . it appears that corporations (supposedly short investors unwilling to stray from the Treasury-bill market) were at times induced to purchase significant quantities of intermediate issues.
>
> Finally [we may] note . . . the substantial shifts out of and into the long-term market by the [financial] institutions . . . . . These aggregate cross-sectional data appear to be patently inconsistent with the extreme institutional hypothesis. . . . This conclusion would be even more strikingly demonstrated were we to deal with portfolio flows rather than stocks. . . . Only in one respect do these data support the arguments of the institutional school. We do find that certain institutions maintain portfolios that have a relatively short average maturity while other institutions tend to hold portfolios composed primarily of long-term bonds.
>
> [(11), p. 151]

The kind of criticisms that can be levelled at these observations has partly been anticipated by Malkiel himself ((11), pp. 157—8), nevertheless, it appears worth while to point to some of those criticisms as an addendum to our earlier general discussion on the methodological problems that are involved in the empirical testing of the Hedging Pressure (Market Segmentation) Theory, or the Institutional Theory, as we have now seen Malkiel label it.

At the very best, this sort of evidence, on the composition of portfolios, is only *prima facie* evidence. If we take it however at its face value we would be led to say that it lends some support to, or at least does not tend to refute, the weak form of the Hedging Pressure Theory. So the point would have to be put stronger than Malkiel has put it: all that the data do not support, when they are taken at their face value, is the extreme of the theory, that is, *full* hedging.

But in fact, even if we do continue to see the data in that way for the moment, we could question some of Malkiel's observations on the interpretation of the data. For example, what is noteworthy in the data he has processed is that, looking at life insurance companies, from about June 1956 there has been a fall in the percentage of their portfolios held in five- to ten-year bonds (with the occasional reversal), while just about simultaneously the share of their total portfolios held in bonds with over ten years to maturity has increased (with again the occasional reversal). As far as their holding of short bonds goes, only over the period December 1958 to end 1959 was there any increase in their relative holdings that looked anything like a deviation from a 'normal', reasonably stable, holding of such bonds.

Leaving on one side the objections that could be raised against these kind of deductions because the data are only semi-annual, and are aggregate data, let us now make some brief points about the interpretation of the data as they stand. One important point is that they ignore the *liabilities* side of the balance sheet of all institutions. Changes in asset holdings could be held to reflect a change in liabilities (both size and, mainly, structure); equally, they might be adduced to reflect changes in the structure of portfolios owing to a change in (expected) interest rates. Also, despite some attempt by Malkiel to cover the *supply* side of the bond market, the information he provides is in no way comprehensive and cannot be set against the 'demand' data. This is an important point, and mention of the supply side naturally brings us up against the 'identification problem' — hence the insertion of demand in inverted commas. Without specifying the characteristics of the supply side of the market — and of the demand side — it is not possible to tell whether holdings of given bonds have been affected by the available supply. It is indeed unlikely that we shall observe equilibrium values for asset holdings at any time; they will be out of equilibrium because of constraints emanating from the supply side of the market. These can be such that institutions *have* to hold bonds in a maturity range other than the one they would *desire* to hold them in, or that they have to hold a disproportionately large amount of, say, medium bonds because long bonds are not available at the appropriate time.

Now the retort might be made to this suggestion that the data are explicitly stated to be stock and not flow data. But this can be dealt with quite easily. The stock data at the mid- or end-point of any year for the holding of bonds will reflect not only any changes that have been made to the stock of bonds in the portfolio at the beginning of the period, but, most obviously, the distribution of the inflow of funds that will take place continually between data-points. There will be both stock-adjustment and flow-dispensation elements in the composition of the portfolio outstanding at any point in time. But even if there were not a continuing inflow of funds, institutions could still adjust their portfolios period by period, even if they did not act according to expectations if, for example, their portfolio was out of equilibrium or if the liabilities changed. If it is supposed that everything that affects the portfolio behaviour of an institution remains fixed, then the movement in the portfolio will be the consequence of a supply constraint of one form or another causing a stock-adjustment process to be set in motion whereby the disequilibrium will be replaced by equilibrium.

We shall say a few more words in section 6.5 on the nature of stock-adjustment in portfolio behaviour models. Now it will suffice to reiterate that an analysis of data on the portfolio behaviour of financial institutions can tell us very little about how they behave, or did behave, and hence about what motivates them, unless we are prepared to make some strong and sweeping generalisations. For it is possible to stipulate necessary and sufficient conditions upon which it is correct to use the kind of data Malkiel has used to deduce the kind of observations he has deduced. These conditions require us to suppose, *inter alia*, that equilibrium exists in the portfolios of all financial institutions, and that over the time span of the data sample their liabilities did not change in structure.

One of the objectives of an inquiry into the portfolio composition of financial and other major investors on the bond market will be to see if assumptions such as these would have been the correct ones to make. There is a need to move on from this aggregate data allegedly coming from one side of the market to at least a fuller investigation of the behaviour of financial institutions, and if possible to the construction of a framework that will enable the supply side of the market to be incorporated into the analysis. This last step takes us into the realms of model-building; and it is a step that Malkiel does not take.

He has (11) produced detailed reports of his attempts to dig deeper behind the aggregate data he has presented in looking at the behaviour of some financial institutions by interviewing managers of a sample of commercial banks and of 'long-term' investors, as he calls them, namely life insurance companies and mutual savings banks.

The numbers in the samples were ten, three, and three respectively. Malkiel is aware of the difficulties in processing evidence from these kinds of interviews, and in some respects he anticipates the points that we have noted should be borne in mind when evaluating and using this type of evidence.

On the basis of the interviews of the portfolio managers of ten banks, the banks were placed into three categories, depending upon the extent to which their portfolio behaviour was alleged to have been influenced by expectational factors. The outcome of this grouping was as follows: two banks were classified as being primarily influenced by expectational considerations; five banks were held to be significantly affected by expectational factors; whilst three banks were judged as not having expectational influences uppermost in their minds when choosing their portfolio, and these were banks whose behaviour supported the market-segmentation view of the world. So basically, a good proportion of these banks could be 'persuaded' to lengthen the average maturity of the government debt in their portfolios, though there was no consensus of opinion on the 'premiums' that would be necessary to bring about such a situation.

The evidence he marshals for long-term investors was obtained from interviewing managers of three life insurance companies and three mutual savings banks. He was able to increase the sample of these two types of institutional investors by examining their dealings in government securities. To increase the size of the sample still further, and to expand its coverage in terms of the type of investors, a pension fund investment advisor was able to provide details of the portfolio trading of five pension funds. In all, therefore, twenty-one institutions were studied. Again, the institutions were grouped into three — no evidence, limited evidence, and extensive evidence of expectations-induced behaviour; there were five, eleven and five institutions in these groups, respectively.

Taking the evidence for short-term and for long-term investors together, Malkiel suggests that:

> An inescapable conclusion . . . is that, except in isolated circumstances, it is unreasonable to talk of segmentation in any absolute sense. Nevertheless, all the financial institutions interviewed did exhibit clear maturity *preferences*. Commercial bankers do consider themselves to be primarily short-term investors. . . . Similarly, . . . pension funds and life insurance companies view themselves as 'ordinarily long-term investors'. . .
>
> [(11), pp. 165–6, italics in the original]

Further evidence on whether or not institutional factors dominate in the market was provided in the study that Malkiel published with

E. J. Kane (88), which was in mimeographed form at the time of publication of Malkiel's own work and which is based on the same kind of investigation reported on in the latter: but the information collected in the Kane—Malkiel study was obtained from a mail survey, and the sample of institutions it covered was somewhat broader than in Malkiel (11). Their general conclusion is very similar to that noted above: they believe that many investors do formulate, and are influenced by, expectations of future interest rates, though there are some whose behaviour is very much in line with the market-segmentation view. However, they also note that all those investors who are affected by expectations of future interest rates do not hold the same opinion as to what these rates will be ((88), p. 344).

A study similar in approach to that of Malkiel is that of W. T. Terrell and W. J. Frazer (90). They also base their study on data drawn from the 'U.S. Treasury's Survey of Ownership' of government debt; but their sample period is end-March 1960 to end-June 1969, and it is on a quarterly basis. They examine the portfolio composition of a broad range of institutions: pension and retirement funds (of state and local governments); life insurance companies; mutual savings banks; savings and loan associations; fire, casualty and marine insurance companies; general funds of state and local government; commercial banks; and non-financial corporations.

The portfolio compositions of these institutions are looked at from a variety of viewpoints and are described not by reference to one 'statistic', as in a study such as Malkiel's, but in terms of several 'statistics'; and these at least give the appearance of imparting more depth and meaning into the analysis of their portfolio structure. To be specific, rather than just trace out the proportions of debt of various maturities held by a given institution in its total portfolio for all points of the sample period, the Terrell—Frazer approach is to quantify several characteristics of the nature of the distribution of the portfolio at a point in time and to plot these points for the sample period. Thus, for each point in the sample for a given institution, the mean, the quartiles, a coefficient of skewness, and a coefficient of kurtosis (peakedness) are calculated for the maturity aspect of its portfolio (graphed on pp. 17—18 of (90)).

Since we can examine their findings only briefly we may do so by referring particularly to the two ends of the maturity spectrum. The 'shortest' portfolio, which is that of non financial corporations, is also one of the least dispersed; it is the most skewed and the most peaked throughout the sample period (1960—69). The next 'shortest' portfolio is possessed by the commercial banks. Their mean maturity shows very little movement, with an average of 40 months, though the standard deviation or dispersion of the portfolio shows slightly more fluctuation, with an overall decline from 45 to just under 40 months. The coefficient of skewness moves within a band of 3 to 4.5, but the coefficient of kurtosis fluctuates very considerably within a wide band (12 to 34).

Turning to the long end of the market we can consider life insurance and pension and retirement funds together. If we examine these two institutions over the period for which data are available for both (end 1961 to 1969), we find that their mean values are the 'longest'. They are the most dispersed, the least skewed and the least peaked. Their mean values declined from a high of 250 months to approximately 220 months with some fluctuation. The very high standard deviation follows the general path of the mean, falling from 150 months (for life insurance companies and 140 for pension funds) to 115 months. The coefficient of skewness is effectively zero for both and the coefficient of kurtosis is constant at about 2. It is interesting to examine life insurance for the full sample period which includes 1960—61. In this period the mean value increases from an initial value of 150 months to 250 months; the standard deviation follows this upward pattern from an initial value of 100 months; and the coefficients of skewness and kurtosis are clearly out of line with those of the later data period (end 1961 to 1969).

Terrell and Frazer attempt to specify the nature of the liabilities of each of the investor groups in their study, with a view to seeing if these correspond with the data provided on the maturity composition of their portfolios, that we have just commented on. They do this by describing four items for all the institutions: (1) maturity of expected investment realisation; (2) provision for unanticipated outlays; (3) certainty of return and marketability of other assets; (4) homogeneity of liabilities and/or dates of anticipated outlay (see (90), table 1, p. 16). For example, commercial banks are posited to have to make a large provision for unanticipated outlays, while they are also regarded as having a low certainty of return and a low marketability of other assets, whereas pension funds are presumed to have a long expected holding period. Most of the eight investor groups are assumed to have a high homogeneity of liabilities and/or a high knowledge of the dates of anticipated outflows of funds.

Taking the evidence on the portfolio composition of the investor groups in conjunction with the presumptions on the nature and structure of liabilities, Terrell and Frazer concede that:

> The distributions reported . . . for the various groups are shown to be influenced by the liability structures of the institutions in

> question. Apparently funds are being held in store for meeting an anticipated need and for increasing the certainty of the availability of funds on prescribed terms. Thus, there is support for the presence of a liquidity-hedging motive.
>
> Further, during the 1960—69 period for which data are examined the maturity distributions of holdings by the various groups are remarkably stable. Since this stability occurs over a time when the Treasury's yield-curve . . . and the level of interest rates changed markedly, some doubt is cast on the relevance of the received expectations theory of the term structure in two respects: (1) institutions are not indifferent about their maturity profiles; and (2) changes appear in the term structure without concomitant adjustments in the quantities of short-term relative to long-term ones.
>
> [(90), p. 11]

If we consider the evidence presented by Terrell and Frazer we must conclude that the portfolio compositions do on the whole fit the 'selected criteria' scheme outlined earlier. But if we examine the mean *together with* the standard deviation (for the mean on its own tells us less than data that Malkiel has used on the proportion of each asset in the total bond portfolio), then there is some evidence that institutions do not have rigid portfolios and do diversify; and that for some of them even the 'selected criteria' are not fully met. But, taking the observations on the portfolio structure of the institutions at their face value, they do suggest that the *weaker* form of the Hedging Pressure (Market Segmentation) Theory has some validity; namely, that institutions have *preferences* for certain bonds. There also appears to be some movement in the portfolio structure of these institutions; but on the evidence presented by Terrell and Frazer it is not possible to say what caused this, nor can we say that the fluctuation that they note occurred in the structure of rates did *not* cause changes in portfolio structures.

The disadvantages of this type of approach are basically the same as those that apply to a study of the Malkiel kind. There is no *observed* information on the liabilities of each institution: at least Malkiel's interviews provide useful back-up information. Here we cannot say that there is anything stronger than *prima facie* support for an institutional approach to the determination of the term structure. We lack details of the size and of the composition of the liabilities for a given institution, and of whether or not at each point in time the portfolio composition is an *equilibrium* one.

To these remarks Terrell and Frazer would probably retort that they can be discounted by the fact that, although they are wishing to stress the demand side of the bond market, they have brought in the supply side. The considerations which apply, as they see it, to that side of the market indicate that the debt outstanding, and hence in the portfolios of the given institutions, is a direct reflection of demand. They argue that Treasury debt was issued in the U.S. in such a way that it was demand-determined:

> In issuing new debt the Treasury deals directly with lending institutions. Prior to each marketing undertaking, the diverse maturity needs of investors are considered through consultation with institutional representatives. . . . This procedure is referred to as 'tailoring' debt to the market.
>
> [(90), p. 13]

This does not, however, automatically allow us to state that the observed data that Terrell and Frazer have used on the composition of portfolios must reflect the true desires of the appropriate institutions. For it might well be that they demand (the observed) quantities of certain types of bonds from the Treasury because they are out of equilibrium. Also Terrell and Frazer note that over their sample period there were exceptions to the tailoring of the debt, which appear to be of rather more importance than they suppose. On the one hand, over the years 1961—65 a deliberate attempt was made to increase the length of the outstanding debt by early refunding of long-term bonds; on the other hand, there were no new issues of bonds at all after late 1965 when market redemption yields went above the 4.25% coupon limit fixed on bonds in 1917.

This makes it very difficult to pass any judgement on the behaviour of the bond holdings of the financial and non-financial institutions, because the observed data on the structure of their portfolios cannot be presupposed to be *demand-given* data. A relative lack of new medium/long bonds over the earlier part of the sample period, coupled with the absence of any new bonds on the market in the later part, could all too easily have been a true supply constraint, preventing institutions from obtaining their desired holdings. The latter, if they could have been fulfilled on a reasonable yield basis, might well have enhanced the 'findings' of Terrell and Frazer or gone against them.

Their study is more comprehensive and more extensive than we have the space to indicate here. But though it is a more detailed inquiry, ultimately it can offer us no stronger a conclusion than Malkiel's study of the same kind of data for an earlier period. Their study does not provide sufficient data on the demand side of the bond market; and it lacks the follow-up from interviews or from econometric analysis of the behaviour of the institution in relationship to such variables as expected interest rates. There is some econometric analysis in their study which deals with the 'aggregate view' equations, which we shall note shortly.

In marked contrast to the Terrell–Frazer analysis, the paper by L. S. Wehrle (94) provides us with a very detailed micro-study of just one major financial group, that of life insurance companies, for the period 1947–57. Additionally the sample is very small, being confined to four such companies. To explain the portfolio composition of these companies Wehrle utilises a standard portfolio choice model which takes explicit account of the size and nature of the liabilities that life insurance companies undertake.

He recognises that investment managers may have one or more objectives in mind when selecting their portfolio. The first objective could be seen as an attempt to attain capital security. Thus the investment manager meets this objective by purchasing securities that are default-free (in consequence therefore limiting himself to government and municipal issues). In no circumstances will he be enticed into accepting default risk though he does recognise that in the maintenance of such a portfolio yield considerations must have a role, albeit secondary or tertiary. The second objective is to achieve income security, and this can be realised by matching. As we illustrated in chapter 5, matching assets to liabilities in a portfolio reduces income risk to a minimum. The third objective, that of maximising yield, stands rather in contrast to the two previous objectives in that it implies the existence of competition between companies within the industry in order that they might maintain their long-run growth; it also implies a rather more flexible investment policy, which admits the possible opportunity costs of 'keeping long' to reduce income risk or purchasing only default-free securities though at the same time recognising their importance.

Wehrle's study examines flow data of assets for four companies, which have been selected to give a wide coverage of the industry in terms of geographical disposition, size and growth rates and the age of the company. His work reveals an intensive examination of the trading in securities that the companies engaged in; also, from interviews with the investment managers, valuable insights into their respective portfolio objectives are provided. Again we cannot comment here in depth on this painstaking and useful study but we can summarise his findings on the portfolio behaviour of this sample of companies.

The four companies in the sample had rather different portfolio objectives over the reference period, and although they were producing a broadly similar product their assessment of yield-income certainty and default risk varied. There was little evidence of perfect matching but the overall objective of investment managers was to 'keep long', implying a greater emphasis on income certainty, and in consequence a downward sloping yield curve with consequent negative liquidity premiums was noted. In passing we can offer another explanation of the form of this curve in terms of the possible shortages of very long bonds over the time period of the study.

Of course we cannot generalise from a study of this type. Indeed, the time period is too short to cover in any manner the changing liability structure of an industry where liabilities can extend, for instance with whole-life contracts, over fifty years or more. Additionally, techniques of analysis have changed since this study was first written (1959), so that now a similar study would include more econometric estimation and testing and less of a reliance on graphs and tables. However it is 'micro'-studies of this type which examine the actual behaviour of companies within a broad aggregate group, which analyse government bonds in terms of the choice set of assets available, and which resolve some of the difficulties we have noted in this book of reliance on aggregative studies and the isolation of the bond market from the whole market for financial claims.

We come now to consideration of 'aggregate view' equations. The studies of this nature that are most noted are those by A. M. Okun (91), J. H. Wood (89), R. H. Scott (92), N. Wallace (70), F. Modigliani and R. Sutch (93) and de Leeuw (37); and we shall take a look at these studies before returning to the Terrell—Frazer study. Except for the last mentioned work, these contributors reveal that relative debt supplies are not a dominant influence on the term structure. Our reference to the work of Wood and of Wallace is second-hand via Malkiel (11), and consequently we will note only the conclusions they have come to.

The study by Scott is a rather weak one and it makes this 'aggregate view' approach (which has to be *ad hoc*) even more *ad hoc* than it should be. Scott endeavours to estimate the influence of 'liquidity' of the debt in the economy on the term structure. That 'liquidity' reflects the maturity of government debt and is measured as the inverse of the average maturity of the outstanding debt. This is a procedure that is not immune from criticism, but the most dubious elements in Scott's study concern the choice of explanatory variables in his equations, equations that purport to 'explain' the long and the short rate separately and then the differential between those rates. For example, if we consider the differential equation, the explanatory variables are: 'debits to demand deposit accounts — a measure of the level of spending'; 'the change in the net free or borrowed reserve position of member banks of the Federal Reserve System'; 'the money supply — currency plus demand deposits'; 'time deposits'; 'total U.S. Government securities held by the public outside of the Federal Reserve and commercial banks'; 'average length of time to maturity of the marketable federal debt' ((92), p. 136). For the two equations he tests, against monthly data for 1952—59, the one contains all these except the last as explanatory variables, whilst the other contains all these variables.

We can offer a few comments on these explanatory variables. It is difficult to see why two forms of money are included as these are likely to be highly correlated with each other. More appropriate would have been a composite money supply variable or perhaps a net worth variable. The inclusion of one of these would have brought the interest rate differential equation nearer to the kind of influence that will bear on it in the economy. Scott, we noted, includes *total* debt (and this also enters the separate equation for the short and the long rate), which seems a little odd as this too might be partially correlated with the money supply. It might have been more sensible to have separated total debt into short and long supplies or some variables proxying their relationship, though in a superficial way this is what the average maturity-of-the-debt variable does.

The object of the exercise for Scott is to ascertain whether that maturity variable, as an indicator of the structure of the debt, influences the term structure. To see if it does he runs the two regressions noted above, where for the second one the maturity variable has been added to the set of explanatory variables. The first equation yields an R^2 of 0.744 and the second one of 0.7781. Scott does not quote the $\overline{R}^2$ s, which is the relevant statistic to use to see if the maturity variable has made any significant addition to the explanation of the yield-gap; it turns out that the two values of the adjusted coefficient of determination are 0.737 and 0.764 respectively. There is a marginal gain from adding the maturity variable. It is clear from Scott's results that there is multicollinearity between some of the variables in his equation, and that that multicollinearity is increased with the addition of the maturity variable. There will undoubtedly be rounding error in the estimates of the coefficients, so it is not possible to make predictions about the effect of changes in the maturity of the debt on the yield-gap. Nor can we tell how good the overall relationship is between the yield-gap and the dependent variables, because, though technically multicollinearity does not affect the goodness-of-fit with the coefficients having their wrong numbers, even though they are not formally biased estimates, they could, because they are 'wrong', affect the value of R^2. Though Scott finds that the average-maturity-of-the-debt variable has the correct *a priori* sign, namely positive, it can tell us very little, all things considered, in terms of his framework, about the effect of debt supplies on the term structure. The observations we have made about the yield-gap equations apply with equal force to Scott's equation explaining the short rate and the long rate separately (we may note that for the long rate equation the sign on the average-maturity-of-the-debt variable is the opposite of what the expectation would be if the Hedging Pressure Theory were to be valid, i.e. negative instead of positive).

It is not possible to accept the view put forward by Scott that his results indicate that debt supplies help influence the term structure and the level of interest rates. Okun's study for the U.S. Commission on Money and Credit, one of the pioneering studies on this approach, concluded in fact that the maturity structure of the debt had little influence on either the yield-gap or the level of rates. His work concerned the period 1946—59 on a quarterly basis, and he too used an average-maturity-of-the-debt variable; but this was one that covered only bonds over five years, a choice that was criticised by Scott in his own study. He estimated an equation for the short rate and one for the long rate. The explanatory variables for the former rate were the supply of short-term debt, the supply of long-term debt, and a set of macro-variables (including income, and the potential supply of money, a step followed in part by Scott). To explain the long-term rate these variables were also used, but were augmented by the inclusion of the average-maturity-of-the-debt variable. These kinds of equations are getting nearer to the sort of equations that can emerge from a fully developed model of the financial system. The R^2s for the short-rate and the long-rate equations are 0.948 and 0.967, respectively: in both equations the debt-supply variables have positive signs, and so too does the average-maturity variable in the long-rate equation. All coefficients appear to be significantly different from zero. But from these equations Okun deduces that, if the supply of short bonds is reduced by a billion dollars whilst the supply of twenty-year bonds is increased by the same amount, the yield-gap will only rise by three basis points (0.03). Merely changing the supply of long bonds will not materially affect this result; at least it will not affect it enough to lead us to suggest that relative debt supplies exert a powerful influence on the term structure. Wood and Wallace produced conclusions that also must be regarded as tentative, but they showed that not much support could be found for the institutional concept of the structure of the debt market.

The most thorough-going investigation of the term structure via the 'aggregate view' method was that undertaken by Modigliani and Sutch (93), which also came out against the institutional view and in favour of the Hicksian Risk Premium Theory. It may be appropriate to sketch — in the circumstances that led to this particular investigation.

In the late 1950s the vice-president in charge of the research department of the Federal Reserve Bank of New York considered that the United States needed to develop a new balance among instruments of economic policy (see Roosa (114)). The maintenance of the foreign exchange value of the dollar and the balance of payments appeared to militate against an overlong pursuit of an easy money policy to stimulate investment. During the John F. Kennedy administration an attempt was made to achieve this latter objective by reducing taxes and incurring conscious federal budget deficits. The President was opposed to budget deficits that were not properly funded by sales of long-term bonds, and in January 1961 Robert V. Roosa was made under-secretary for monetary affairs in the U.S. Treasury, where he was responsible among other things for the funding of the public debt into longer-term bonds. The Federal Reserve Bank of New York had excluded bonds, dealing only in Treasury bills, for ten years prior to February 1961, when it decided to go along with the administration's new debt-funding policy to the extent of buying some Treasury bonds in place of some Treasury bills. This policy decision of the New York Fed. perhaps ought not to have been looked at merely in isolation from the administration's funding policy decision; but nevertheless it was widely regarded as an attempt by the New York Fed. to 'twist' the yield curve by attempting to raise the short rate relative to the long rate, and was nicknamed 'operation twist'. The *raison d'être* of the study by Modigliani and Sutch was to evaluate whether 'operation twist' had been a prime cause of the subsequent narrowing of the yield-gap.

Over the period of 'operation twist' the observed yield-gap, the differential between the long rate and the short rate, did fall. But Modigliani and Sutch were uneasy about jumping to the conclusion that the yield-gap had narrowed because of the twist operations. In the first place, they argued that in the interest-rate structure over time a cyclical trend could be observed and in the recovery phase short and long rates typically came close together as the short rates increased. Secondly, there was firm evidence that the policy was not pursued with any great vigour and, in fact, the funding policy of the Treasury was acting in directly the opposite way, for they suggest that, by advance refundings, supplies of long securities (over five years) increased. At the same time, the supply of short-term securities also increased, particularly those with under six months to maturity. As Malkiel (11) comments in his review of the 'twist operation', pursuading an investor to exchange a five-year for a forty-year security would require very little in the way of yield differential, but to induce a very short-term investor to switch say from thirty days to one year would require a large compensation. Our discussion in chapter 5 did comment on this very crucial portion of the yield curve for short-term maturities, indicating that 'liquidity premiums', should they exist, are likely to rise monotonically with respect to maturity, but are particularly important at the early stage of the curve.

To test whether it is in order to discount 'operation twist', Modigliani and Sutch's initial approach was to use a simple equation, estimated by O.L.S., wherein the yield-gap, for 1952—61 on a quarterly basis, was regressed solely on the short rate, that of Treasury bills. The values predicted by this equation were then compared with the actual values for the period of 'operation twist'. A close relationship was found to exist between these values. Though this might be taken as indicating that 'operation twist' did not cause a change in structure, as it were, so that those factors that determined the term structure were the same in the period of 'operation twist' as they were before it was initiated, Modigliani and Sutch did not believe that it provided evidence firm enough to support such a contention. Indeed, this is a view that we must share owing to the primitive nature of the equation employed and to the fact that it contains as the only independent variable a part of the dependent variable.

Modigliani and Sutch then tried to turn their regression equation into a well-specified hypothesis. They developed a framework of analysis for looking at the term structure which is similar to that developed by Malkiel which we have discussed in chapter 4. They suggested a 'model' which follows the spirit of Hicks's treatment of the term structure, wherein expectations and risk/liquidity premiums determine the term structure because investors have preferred habitats. Modigliani and Sutch, in fact, call their theory a preferred habitat theory.

What materialises from this is that the simple equation mentioned above was amended by the addition of a variable to account for the market's expectations — of the short rate. Those expectations were represented by a distributed lag formulation which it was hoped captured the notion behind those formulations and the view stressed by Duesenberry (95) that the market may be influenced by the most recent changes in the rate of interest in forming its future expectations of that rate. De Leeuw (37), on his work on the financial sector of the U.S., had been the first to marry these two divergent views. The end result was that, instead of the previously noted equations, Modigliani and Sutch estimated an equation that would, as they saw it, explain the term structure, which contained as a second explanatory variable a weighted average of the sixteen previous quarters' values of the short rate, and the lag structure was found by using the Almon (35) technique. This equation produced an R^2 of 0.975, and a Durbin—Watson statistic of 1.42; the slope coefficients were significant at the 1% level or better; so too was the constant (though the Durbin—Watson statistic does indicate some positive serial correlation). The sign on the spot short rate was negative, that on the expected short rate was positive. To this equation they added a variable which was a measure of the change in the maturity of the debt, and they found that it had no significant effect in explaining the long—short interest differential. Though they found that their amended equation did not predict well for the period 1962 (1) to 1965 (2), its predictive power was enhanced not by the inclusion of the debt variable but by the introduction of a dummy variable to account for the creation and growth of time certificates of deposit on the term structure. Regulation Q (of the Board of Governors of the Federal Reserve System, Washington) imposed a statutory ceiling on the rate paid on time deposits, a ceiling that was allowed to increase successively throughout the period. It was this that led to the growth of time certificates of deposit on the market. These certificates are what we might call 'bank commercial bills'. They were substitutes for government bills and so they helped keep up the short-term rate of interest — at least we should say that helped to raise it above what it would have been if it had only been affected by the increase in the *supply* of short debt issued by the U.S. Treasury.

The view of Modigliani and Sutch was that expectations could account for the term structure both before and during 'operation twist', that the twist in the term structure that did occur was brought about by the time certificates of deposit, and that the change in structure that took place was not attributable to debt-management policy. We note that these conclusions on the role of expectations have been derived by use of a particular specification of expectations and by use of an equation that could produce spurious correlations between the yield-gap and those variables that purport to explain it.

Earlier in this section we considered the Terrell—Frazer institutional data on the Hedging Pressure (Market Segmentation) Theory; now we must say a word or two about their 'aggregate view' equation results. They transpose their data into logarithmic form and regress the log of the ratio of the short to the long rate against the log of the ratio of the supply of short to long debt. The normal view would be that the slope coefficient should be positive. However, because of the Treasury activity in the bond market in the 1960s which we have commented on previously, they argue that at least up to the end of 1964, when Roosa left the U.S. Treasury, the sign should be negative, and that thereafter it could still be negative, though it might be positive. They run their regression for two years at a time throughout the sample period; and their findings on the slope coefficient are very much as they felt they should be. But on this basis the slope coefficients are nearly all zero, statistically speaking; and the R^2s are on the whole very low. Even if we are prepared to accept their observations on the supply side of the market and go along with their views about the coefficients on the debt ratio variable, their results tell us very little — but they are not very much support for the Hedging Pressure (Market Segmentation) Theory. Also, the reservations that apply to the Terrell—Frazer portfolio behaviour analysis of financial and non-financial institutions are still clearly relevant here.

At the outset of this critical overview of the 'aggregate equation' approach to the question of the effect of debt supplies on the term structure, we referred to the work of F. de Leeuw (37). This very substantial piece of research is somewhat different in approach from the studies we have touched on so far in this section. Although the equation de Leeuw estimates on the term structure has certain similarities to the equations we have encountered hitherto, it has been derived as a reduced-form equation and has been estimated as part of a *model* of the financial sector in the U.S. De Leeuw's attempt at explaining the term structure employed a model that was not quite the kind of fully-fledged model of the financial sector (with or without real sector links) argued for previously in this chapter — for example, it is smaller than those that we have subsequently developed — but one of the main differences from the type of model we shall outline in section 6.5 is that we have equations to explain a number of interest rates. In de Leeuw's model only a few interest rates are explained; and only with respect to the U.S. securities market. Instead of splitting it into maturity segments and solving for interest rates in each segment, his model aggregates over all maturities. He then solves for the term structure by the *explicit* introduction of an equation which has as its dependent variable the gap between the yield on U.S. 'long-term' debt and the yield on U.S. Treasury bills; this is a reduced-form equation arrived at under special assumptions which are explained below.

The general approach adopted by de Leeuw of looking at the demand—supply relationships in each selected market, and the means by which he derives these relationships, are similar to the portfolio balance approach — of the Tobin—Brainard kind ((96), (97) and (98)) — that we have utilised. But as far as the term structure is concerned, de Leeuw does take another path from us. Whereas we would let the rates on various maturities of government stock be solved by the system simultaneously, from the demand—supply equations and the appropriate 'balance equations', for which a given yield-gap equation could be derived, de Leeuw relies on his reduced-form equation. This is derived from the demand equations for 'long' and for 'short' government stock, aggregated over all relevant sectors. Those demand equations in de Leeuw's model represent the change in the holdings of either kind of stock, deflated by a measure of wealth. The common independent variables in the equations are the expected (= actual) returns on short stock and the expected returns on long stock; while in either equation there is the lagged ratio of own stocks to wealth, together with a variable in each equation which is a 'weighted combination of all the other influences on holdings' ((37, p. 498). It is by making certain vital assumptions about the inter-relationship of these equations that de Leeuw is able to proceed to his reduced-form specification of the term structure equation.

To see what these are it is simplest if we detail the two demand equations posited by de Leeuw, at time t:

$$\frac{\Delta S}{W} = a_0 \frac{S_{t-1}}{W} + a_1 r_S + a_2 r_L + a_3 D \qquad (6.3.1)$$

$$\frac{\Delta L}{W} = b_0 \frac{L_{t-1}}{W} + b_1 r_S + b_2 r_L + b_3 D' \qquad (6.3.2)$$

De Leeuw hypothesises that: $a_0 < 0$; $a_1 > 0$; $a_2 < 0$; $a_3 > 0$; $b_0 < 0$; $b_1 < 0$; $b_2 > 0$; and $b_3 > 0$. The notation used here is partly our own and is as follows: S is the supply of short-term stock; L is the supply of long-term stock; W is a wealth variable; r_S and r_L are, respectively, the returns expected on short-term and long-term stock; and D and D' represent 'other influences' on the demands for these government securities.

The first presumption de Leeuw makes is that the two types of security are *perfect* substitutes; this enables him to say that the interest-rate coefficients in equations (6.3.1) and (6.3.2) will be numerically equal *and* large (i.e. he puts $a_1 = -a_2 = -b_1 = b_2$). He then makes the further deduction from the substitutability presumption that a_3D should approximate b_3D'; and he makes these two equal. But because short-term and long-term stock are substitutes in the technical sense of that term it does not necessarily follow that the 'other influences' term in the two equations should be the same: for those two terms need not contain the same variables, whether we are thinking of scalar variables (such as income) or of variables denoting expected returns on alternative assets.

He further assumed that if the short stock is taken to be short enough then capital gains/losses can be ignored and therefore r_S becomes the actual short-term rate of interest; while for long-term securities the expected return has to be calculated, and it is assumed that it is equal to the long-term rate of interest adjusted for an expected capital gain/loss.

Letting R_L and R_S be the actual long-term and short-term rates of interest, respectively, these two assumptions mean that equations (6.3.1) and (6.3.2) can be written in this form, taking account of the sign of the various parameters:

$$R_L - R_S = -K - \frac{1}{2a_1}\frac{\Delta S}{W} + \frac{1}{2a_1}\frac{\Delta L}{W} - \frac{a_0}{2a_1}\frac{S_{t-1}}{W} + \frac{b_0}{2a_1}\frac{L_{t-1}}{W} \qquad (6.3.3)$$

where K is the expected capital gain/loss on longs. This equation has the yield-gap dependent upon the size of the long- and short-term debt on the market and changes in those stocks.

But a further assumption has to be made before equation (6.3.3) is operational, and therefore before its empirical possibilities can be assessed. That is, K has to be estimated. It is at this point that de Leeuw makes use of the Keynesian idea — of the kind we have seen that Malkiel employed — that expected capital gains/losses are related to the difference between the actual long-term rate of interest and the normal long-term rate of interest. In other words, capital gains are expected when the spot long rate lies above the normal rate and vice-versa, the normal rate being left undefined but being assumed to possess characteristics that are similar to those embodied in distributed lag or moving average formulations of previous interest rates. Therefore K might be approximated by the difference between the actual long rate and an average of past values of it. The sign on K would be expected to be positive. But de Leeuw also utilised and tested the suggestion put forward by Duesenberry which we have noted elsewhere in this book, namely that it was possible for the Keynesian notion to be reversed; for it could be maintained that, if there have been *recent rises* in the interest rate, investors may expect the rate to *continue* to rise ((95), p. 318). In that case the expectation would be that capital *losses* might ensue in the short run. The Duesenberry hypothesis could then be regarded as one that related expected capital gains/losses to the difference between the actual long-term rate and *immediately* past long-term rates.

De Leeuw combines both of these hypotheses, for it is perfectly possible for them to exist side by side even though the sign expected on the Keynesian K variable is the opposite of that anticipated for the Duesenberry K. The hypotheses were combined by calculating, prior to estimation, values of the normal rate by de Leeuw's own particular (inverted-V) distributed lag function, the weights in the latter being varied such that they produce Keynesian (i.e. with long lags) and Duesenberry (i.e. with short lags) K variables. These were slotted into equation (6.3.3). The estimates of that equation indicated that both the K variables were important in determining the yield-gap, and that both had their expected signs, when run on quarterly U.S. data for the period 1952—60.

With respect to the debt variables in the estimates of equation (6.3.3) it was found that:

> *Changes* in debt proportions . . . also enter the equation with expected negative signs. The proportions themselves either had signs opposite to expectation, were smaller in relation to their standard error or both. . . . The implication . . . is that while changes in debt management operations influence interest rates for a brief period, the average composition of the debt over longer periods does not have a perceptible influence.
>
> [(37), p. 503: italics in original]

This conclusion also applied with roughly the same force to the period 1952—62, so that the final equation used by de Leeuw for the term structure in his model, which was then estimated by 2*SLS*, omitted the variables containing the stocks of short and long U.S. securities; it contained the other variables in equation (6.3.3), with K denoted by both a Keynesian and a Duesenberry variable. The same conclusions hold when the equation is estimated as part of a model rather than as a partial equation: but the goodness-of-fit, which was never very high, falls for the final equation to 55% (and the standard error of the estimate is quite high). The term structure equation is not then a very powerful one.

It would seem to indicate, however, that for the period of the 1950s the supplies of U.S. government debt had very little part to play in influencing the term structure except possibly in the very short run. There are difficulties in placing much weight on such a finding to refute the Market Segmentation Theory. Some of these difficulties are all too familiar to us at this stage of the book: we may list a few.

We can begin with comments that apply specifically to de Leeuw's equation. To some extent the assumptions that were made at the outset could be responsible for the insignificant part that debt structure seems to play on the term structure over de Leeuw's data period. One of the objects of inquiry into the determination of the term structure is to discover *if* certain financial assets *are* substitutes for each other. To assume that they are substitutes prior to empirical investigation of the term structure is tantamount to saying that, *ceteris paribus*, relative debt supplies have fundamentally no influence on that structure. At least we can say that it is likely to bias the results against the Hedging Pressure Theory, and in favour of the rival theories.

Part of the difficulty on this count has arisen because of the endeavour to produce a reduced-form term structure equation rather than to let the term structure equation emerge from a general equilibrium model of all markets in the financial sector. Specification of demand and supply equations for each kind of government stock would help sort out the question of which stocks, if any, were substitutes. The outcome might well support the hypothesis that all stocks are substitutes for each other. But the data must be allowed to determine this kind of question. Also, the influence of debt supplies on the term structure has further been constrained as it were by concentration on the reduced-form equation, specified as it is from the demand side.

Then again there are the customary quibbles. The empirical results, other comments apart, depend upon the way that expected capital gains/losses are estimated. This consideration involves both the hypothesis as to what those capital value changes depend upon, e.g. normal rates, and how those normal rates, or other salient variables, are to be quantified.

We have said enough to make us wary of jumping to too many conclusions from equations such as (6.3.3); for others seem to want to use the evidence gained from it at least to rebut the Hedging Pressure Theory. But having said all this, we must acknowledge the fact that de Leeuw was aware of the limitations of his model and that a more detailed specification of the government bond market could be argued for. We must also remember the constraints under which de Leeuw was working; for example, his model had to be relatively easily assimilated into the Brookings Model, he was working at a period when not that much work had been done on aspects of his model, and indeed no detailed econometric *model* of the financial sector had appeared before his study. He was working very much in uncharted seas — and even to date the situation on the empirical side has not advanced that much.

The empirical studies discussed up to this point have been based on U.S. data. There is at least one study, of very recent vintage, that examines the role of *market* segmentation in the U.K. government bond market. This is the study by Burman and White (80) that we have referred to in chapters 1 and 5 above. Their work was concerned with the variables that should figure in the formation of the yield curve, and so represents a roundabout, and more suspect, method of examining the efficacy of the Market Segmentation Theory than those set out and analysed in this chapter. Inevitably, though, it is endeavouring to find answers to the same question, e.g. on the substitutability of bonds for each other.

We have made some comments on the Burman—White approach in chapters 1 and 5 and we need say nothing further now other than that doubts must be expressed about the conclusions they have drawn from their study, though those conclusions are that we should perhaps regard the U.K. bond market as being segmented into two parts. (Even this conclusion may perhaps be less obvious from the yield curve after the realignment of the Bank of England's minimum lending rate in July 1973.)

We shall attempt to summarise the findings we have discussed in this section at the end of the chapter after we have looked at some of the evidence we have been compiling for the post-Second World War U.K. government bond market.

6.4

In this section we consider some empirical evidence on the Hedging Pressure Theory from *partial* studies of the U.K. This evidence is similar in kind to that discussed in section 6.3 for various institutional investors, and it suffers therefore from all the diffi-

Table 6.4.1 Government marketable debt — non-official maturity holdings as a percentage of the maturity structure of market holdings*

Date	Banking Sector			Other financial institutions			Overseas			Other holdings			Total market holdings**		
31 March	Treasury bills	Stocks 0–5	Stocks over 5	Treasury bills	Stocks 0–5	Stocks over 5	Treasury bills	Stocks 0–5	Stocks over 5	Treasury bills	Stocks 0–5	Stocks over 5	Treasury bills	Stocks 0–5	Stocks over 5
	% of the total			% of the total			% of the total			% of the total			£m.		
1963	40.8	39.7	9.1	0.4	6.2	32.0	43.7	19.2	11.2	15.1	34.9	47.7	2582	3510	10,747
1964	44.5	36.7	9.0	0.8	7.2	33.3	43.9	18.8	11.2	10.8	37.3	46.5	2592	3977	10,256
1965	35.2	35.1	8.4	0.5	8.8	35.6	56.5	20.7	12.3	7.8	35.4	43.7	2091	3906	10,321
1966	49.9	29.3	9.7	0.5	11.9	37.7	43.3	19.0	11.5	6.3	39.8	41.1	2305	4298	9,766
1967	40.7	40.9	8.4	0.5	12.7	37.2	52.4	18.9	10.8	6.4	27.5	43.6	1723	4555	10,725
1968	21.5	35.1	6.9	0.2	14.2	44.1	74.7	16.3	11.7	3.6	34.4	37.3	3077	5665	10,065
1969	19.5	30.1	7.0	0.1	14.8	45.1	78.2	18.7	12.0	2.2	36.4	36.0	3218	4743	10,024
1970	21.5	28.0	6.9	0.3	18.2	43.7	73.8	21.4	11.5	4.4	32.4	37.9	1443	4763	11,302
1971	45.6	25.0	8.3	0.4	20.5	45.6	47.4	21.0	12.7	6.6	33.5	33.4	955	4592	12,383
1972	42.5	40.2†	4.7	0.3	16.9	50.4	53.1	15.9	13.0	4.1	27.0	31.8	1321	5911	13,480

*Nominal holdings. For a full discussion of sources and definitions see the notes accompanying the annual tables published in the Bank of England *Quarterly Bulletin*, March issues, 1964—73.
**Excluding holdings of public bodies.
†For an explanation of this large increase see the Bank of England *Quarterly Bulletin* March 1973, p. 39.

culties and drawbacks to which we drew attention in that section and in section 6.2.

In table 6.4.1 we present some first-step *prima facie* evidence on the theory. Therein we provide details of the holdings of major sectors of marketable British government debt for the period 1963—72. 'The banking sector' incorporates the clearing banks, the Scottish and Northern Ireland banks, the discount houses, the National Giro, the acceptance houses, the overseas banks and other banks. 'Other financial institutions' embraces what are normally called non-bank financial intermediaries (i.e., insurance companies, building societies, national and trustee savings banks, investment and unit trusts, the various pension funds). The 'Overseas holders' group consists of international organisations, central monetary institutions and others. Finally, the 'Other holders' embraces holdings by all other groups such as the personal and company sector.

This kind of grouping clearly involves a great deal of aggregation across institutions and categories of investor. The value of the data provided in table 6.4.1 is further reduced since it is not possible to have observations on the maturity composition of the national debt before 1963 save in the form of a split between Treasury bills and the rest of government stock. As it is, from 1963 it is feasible only to separate out the latter into two classifications by maturity, namely those with up to, and those with more than, five years to maturity.

In the light of the present inquiry the limited division of government debt by maturity is a serious drawback. This is something we can try to circumvent to some degree, however, when we summarise some preliminary findings on the portfolio policy of the life insurance companies in the U.K. later in this section. Bearing in mind these and other limitations, we can make some observations on the contents of table 6.4.1 *per se*. Let us take the various sectors in order. It is very apparent that as far as the banking sector is concerned there have been great fluctuations in its percentage holdings of the three kinds of government debt outstanding, the greatest fluctuations occurring at the short end of the spectrum. As far as the other financial institutions are concerned they have, with minor exceptions, increased their market share of over-five-year bonds, and have done so quite markedly; the same is true of their holdings of short-term bonds with the exception of the year 1972. The main changes that have occurred in the overseas sector's holdings relate to Treasury bills and to short-term bonds; and their market share of Treasury bills has indeed shown a marked fluctuation, being exceptionally large in the years 1968, 1969 and 1970. Though there has been some fluctuation in the market shares of Treasury bills and of over-five-year stock of the 'other holders' group, those shares exhibit a downward trend.

Looking at all four sectors simultaneously we can make these simple deductions: the market for Treasury bills was dominated by the banking sector and overseas sector; the short-term bond market was dominated by the banking sector and the 'other holdings' sector, with these two sectors usually holding 60%-plus of the existing stock of short bonds; the medium/long bond market was dominated by the other financial institutions and the 'other holdings' sector, with the former consistently having the larger share of the market since 1968.

Empirical points such as these can be regarded only as weakly suggestive of the existence of this or that type of financial market. Yet in that vein it seems that the banking sector has a preference for the short end of the market, and the non-bank financial intermediaries a predilection to go into the medium/long end of the market. These sorts of impressions tend to square with the *a priori* expectation about the bond preferences of those institutions, given the *a priori* expectations about the nature of their liabilities — and possibly suggest that some degree of matching of assets and liabilities does occur on the bond market.

But for many reasons we cannot say more than this, and indeed we are really pushing this superficial evidence too hard in going that far. The data in table 6.4.1 are taken from official sources but are not so detailed as the Treasury ownership data produced by the U.S. Treasury which were employed by studies such as that of Terrell and Frazer. They are not processed in any way; and as a consequence many relevant things are missed out. If we are going to ignore such things as the liabilities side of each of the relevant balance sheets and the like, and draw conclusions from maturity composition figures, then the data on the ownership of the national debt can be classified in a better form than it is in table 6.4.1. What can be done is to measure the importance of particular maturities of government stock in terms of the total amount of such stock held by each sector and to disaggregate the sectors somewhat — this produces the maturity composition of debt data which was used in some of the studies of the U.S. that we have discussed in section 6.3 above.

Table 6.4.2 gives the composition of government stocks held in the three maturity ranges available for the four sectors. This gives us a different picture of the preferences of those sectors for this or that maturity of bond. Indeed, if a table such as table 6.4.1 is to be used at all to give us a view of the market in government debt, then it would have to be conceded that the best that it could offer us would be a snapshot view of the organisation and structure of the market.

Table 6.4.2 Government marketable debt — non-official holders' maturity structure** (percentages of total holdings by each sector)*

Date	Banking sector			Other financial institutions			Overseas holders			Other holders		
31 March	Treasury bills	Stocks 0—5	Stocks over 5	Treasury bills	Stocks 0—5	Stocks over 5	Treasury bills	Stocks 0—5	Stocks over 5	Treasury bills	Stocks 0—5	Stocks over 5
1963	30.8	40.7	28.5	0.3	5.9	93.8	37.5	22.4	40.1	5.8	18.2	76.0
1964	32.6	41.3	26.1	0.6	7.6	91.8	37.4	24.7	37.9	4.3	22.7	73.0
1965	24.7	46.1	29.2	0.2	8.5	91.3	36.3	24.8	38.9	2.7	22.8	74.5
1966	34.3	37.5	28.2	0.3	12.2	87.5	34.0	27.8	38.2	2.5	29.1	68.4
1967	20.2	53.6	26.2	0.2	12.7	87.1	30.9	29.5	39.6	1.8	20.8	77.4
1968	19.8	59.5	20.7	0.1	15.4	84.5	52.2	21.0	26.8	1.9	33.5	64.6
1969	22.8	51.8	25.4	0.1	13.4	86.5	54.7	19.2	26.1	1.3	32.0	66.7
1970	12.9	55.0	32.1	0.1	14.9	85.0	31.4	30.1	38.5	1.1	26.2	72.7
1971	16.7	44.0	39.3	0.1	14.3	85.6	15.1	32.2	52.7	1.1	26.8	72.1
1972	15.7	66.4†	17.9	0.1	12.8	87.1	20.7	27.7	51.6	0.9	26.9	72.2

*Nominal holdings. For a full discussion of sources and definitions see the notes accompanying the annual tables published in the *Bank of England Quarterly Bulletin* (March issues, 1964—73).
**Excluding holdings of public bodies.
†For an explanation of this large increase see the *Bank of England Quarterly Bulletin* (March 1973) p. 39.

To begin to make any deductions about bond preferences from maturity composition data, we have to start from a table such as table 6.4.2. We would then want to split up the sectors as much as possible and to increase the maturity split of the debt. It is impossible to accomplish the latter objective for all sectors. What is possible, however, is a wider split by holder, i.e. disaggregation by sector as we have illustrated in part in the case of the financial institutions sector. These data are of course annual, and the difficulty of sector and maturity coverage becomes acute when quarterly data are required. This was a problem we faced in the building of a financial model (section 6.5 of this chapter) and we have to admit that at times 'guesstimates' have had to be made on bond holdings.

In table 6.4.3 the banking sector has been separated out into the deposit banks and the discount houses. The 'other financial institutions' have been divided into four categories of institutions with those such as pension funds being aggregated. We may consider the institutions in the order in which they occur in table 6.4.3. As far as the deposit banks are concerned, the proportions of total holdings of government debt that they hold in the three maturity classes have changed markedly over the period 1963—72. There is a pronounced preference — or there *appears* to be such a preference — for short-dated stock, although it is clear that within that category they have, or appear to have, done some switching between Treasury bills and short bonds. It is also apparent that they have on occasion varied the proportion of stock they hold in the over-five-year category.

For discount houses the overall impression given by the statistics presented in table 6.4.3 is very much akin to that which it provides for deposit banks. In other words, there have been significant changes in the proportions of total stock held in all three classes of debt. There appears however to be a distinct preference — and a stronger preference in fact than that of the deposit banks — for short-term stock; save for the year 1971 they held 90% and above of their total holdings of government debt in short stock. Again, within the latter category there appears to have been a considerable degree of switching between bills and bonds. Also, at times, for whatever reason, it seems that the discount houses are prepared to move proportionately more into medium-/long-term stock.

For building societies the figures also reveal that there have been changes in the proportion of stock held in the three types of debt. But there has been more fluctuation in their holdings of medium-/long-term bonds than in those of the banking sector. Also, the building societies held only a small share of their government debt in

Table 6.4.3 Government marketable debt — holdings by maturity of selected financial institutions (percentages of total holdings of each institution)*

Date	Banking sector						Other financial institutions											
	Deposit banks			Discount houses			Building societies			Savings banks (investment)			Pension funds			Insurance companies		
31 March	Treasury bills	0—5	Over 5	Treasury bills	0—5	Over 5	Treasury bills	0—5	Over 5	Treasury bills	0—5	Over 5	Treasury bills	0—5	Over 5	Treasury bills	0—5	Over 5
1963	29.5	36.6	33.9	46.1	52.1	1.8	1.6	26.7	71.7	—	24.4	75.6	0.3	2.4	97.3	0.1	2.0	97.9
1964	32,6	37.6	29.8	45.4	53.6	1.0	3.5	43.0	53.5	—	25.0	75.0	0.4	2.7	96.9	0.2	2.9	96.9
1965	26.4	38.1	35.5	29.2	68.1	2.7	1.3	54.3	44.4	—	31.5	68.5	0.3	3.4	96.3	0.1	2.3	97.6
1966	34,6	31,5	33,9	47,4	51,8	0.8	1.6	61.4	37.0	—	39.3	60.7	0.3	6.4	93.3	—	2.4	97.6
1967	22.5	47.5	30.0	24.4	69.9	5.7	1.2	55.8	43.0	0.3	43.7	56.0	0.2	6.1	93.7	—	2.3	97.7
1968	17.5	55.9	26.6	30.8	67.1	2.1	0.7	62.2	37.1	—	45.4	54.6	0.1	8.9	91.0	—	4.8	95.2
1969	16.9	52.1	31.0	50.7	48.9	0.4	0.2	61.8	38.0	0.2	42.3	57.5	0.1	5.6	94.3	—	3.7	96.3
1970	4.5	55.8	39.7	37.5	53.4	9.1	0.1	67.5	32.4	0.2	35.8	64.0	0.2	6.0	93.8	—	2.8	97.2
1971	11.9	45.5	42.6	34.3	43.9	21.8	0.1	65.3	34.6	—	17.4	82.6	0.2	5.7	94.1	—	2.0	98.0
1972	3.6	77.4†	19.0	48.5	46.2	5.3	0.1	46.7	53.2	—	16.0	84.0	0.1	5.3	94.6	0.1	2.6	97.3

*Nominal holdings. For a full discussion of sources and definitions see the notes accompanying the annual tables published in the *Bank of England Quarterly Bulletin* (March issues, 1964—73).
†For an explanation of this large increase see the *Bank of England Quarterly Bulletin* (March 1973) p. 39.

Treasury bills, an amount declining so that by 1972 it had reached insignificant proportions. Except for 1970 and 1971 they held a greater proportion of their government debt portfolio in medium-/long-term bonds than did the banks or the discount houses: the societies seem to shift about between short- and long-term stock.

The savings banks maturity composition ratios show wide variation over the period, the holdings of medium/long stock going down year by year from 1963 to 1968 and rising thereafter year by year, the opposite movement occurring in short bonds since their holdings of Treasury bills were usually zero. But these institutions seem to indicate that they have a preference for medium/long stock, and one that is stronger than that of the banking sector or the building societies; and also that they are prepared to shift between investing in the one bond market to investing in the other.

Finally, we may take pension funds and insurance companies together. They appear to have a marked preference for medium/long bonds, and a preference that has not changed over the years, the proportion of their government debt portfolio held in those bonds remaining fairly constant. For pension funds it looks as though the slight movements that have taken place in their 'liquid debt' holdings indicate some — very slight — willingness to move from bills into short bonds and vice-versa.

The changes in these ratios, or the constancy in them, for these institutions have taken place against a backcloth of movements in interest rates and interest rate differentials. They suggest that for some institutions movements in the compositions of their portfolios might have been induced by movements in interest rates, while for others, such as pension funds and insurance companies, portfolios have remained impervious to changes in interest rates and their differentials.

Such evidence is only suggestive. It ignores many things, which we may just list here since these and other relevant considerations have been dealt with *passim* in this chapter. Thus it ignores:

(i) the liabilities side of each sector;
(ii) the supply side of the market;
(iii) the fact that actual interest rates may not be the expected rates formulated by each sector, upon which its behaviour will be based, if it should regard one length-of-life bond as being a substitute for some, or any, other length-of-life bond;
(iv) an extension of (iii), the possibility that even if expected rates can be proxied (for all sectors) by actual rates, those interest rates may not adequately reflect expected *returns* on government debt.

To which we might append the more general point that the sectors discussed above are still founded on a degree of aggregation — even though the latter is less than it is in tables 6.4.1 and 6.4.2. Therefore, even if we discount (iii) and (iv) the kind of statistical data contained in table 6.4.3, looked at in the light of interest-rate changes, can lead us to make false deductions concerning the market behaviour of the financial institutions and hence about the appropriateness of any one hypothesis in explaining the term structure of interest rates, because the observed movements, or lack of movement, in the debt ratios could have arisen because of changes in the liabilities structure and/or because of the debt policy of the monetary authorities.

However, if we additionally, ignore (ii), suppose that (i) has been constant, and make a few *a priori* judgements concerning the liabilities structures of the financial institutions, as Malkiel and Terrell and Frazer have done, we can take some view from this *prima facie* evidence on the likely relevance of the Hedging Pressure Theory. Different institutions dominate the different parts of the market: those with relatively short-term liabilities tend to dominate the short end of the market, those with relatively long-term liabilities (i.e. pension funds and life insurance companies) tend to dominate the long end of the market. However, most of the institutions, save for pension funds and insurance companies, appear to move about in the bond market. Even so, institutions such as banks have a government debt portfolio which is biased towards the short end of the market. So there appears to be some switching between maturities, but with most institutions having a preference, in one degree or another, for bonds that have some relationship to their liabilities. For some institutions this preference is very marked, especially at the long end of the market, where again we cite the example of pension funds and life insurance companies.

So though the government debt market *can* be divided into segments according to the information portrayed in table 6.4.1, because parts of it are dominated by certain institutions, and though each segment would seem, *a priori*, to be dominated by institutions whose liabilities would largely square with the length of life of bonds in each appropriate segment, we have seen from table 6.4.3 that institutions seem to be willing to shift between segments, except for those sectors whose liabilities are virtually all known and are long-term. We would conclude that the *extreme* version of the Hedging Pressure Theory is not tenable on this kind of evidence; however, the weaker form of it cannot be ruled out. On the other hand, it is equally feasible to say that the evidence is not inconsistent with a Liquidity/Risk Premium Theory, suitably interpreted.

Given the difficulties surrounding the making of even a judgement of this somewhat loose nature from this kind of evidence, we suggested in earlier sections of this chapter that one possible next step would be to take each type of investor group on the market with the object of explaining and analysing the financial behaviour of each group, with particular reference of course to its activities on the government debt market. This exercise would help in determining which, if any, types of debt were substitutes, and the extent of the substitution between them. It is highly unlikely that we would find that each investor group had a sole preference for one part of the maturity spectrum, and that each of the preferred segments were different, and that the preferences were solely a function of the structure of the liabilities of each of the investor groups. It is equally likely that, even if certain investor groups have the same preference on the maturity spectrum, the market will divide neatly into unique segments. Though this is naturally a value judgement on the extreme version of the Hedging Pressure Theory, despite the weakness of the evidence given above for the U.K., it does suggest that this is a reasonable empirical statement to make. What studies of individual investor groups will show is that some do match assets and liabilities, some do to some extent, and so on. There will be overlaps between segments of the market for most investor groups, and the overlapping will, therefore, not be identical for all investor groups. It may seem advisable to put together the financial behaviour of all the investor groups into a model to see the effect on the *market* of the slightly diverse and 'overlapping' behaviour.

While constructing models of the U.K. financial sector (see section 6.5 below), we have been working on individual sectors of the financial market, mainly with a view to using the specifications of financial behaviour obtained at the partial level in the model *per se*. Although it is easier on some counts to experiment on a partial basis than in terms of large detailed models, because of time limitations, and because we are going to have to aggregate over investor groups to some extent in the formulation of a finite-sized model, we have been experimenting with the specification of behaviouristic equations at the model level. However, we are working through all the groupings named in table 6.4.3 together with finance houses, investment trusts and unit trusts, so that on a partial basis we have covered the portfolio and debt behaviour of all the major domestic financial institutions investing on the U.K. bond market.

At the time of writing it is possible to give only a brief statement of the work that has been done to date: the work is to be published as a book entitled *Studies in the Behaviour of Financial Institutions in the U.K. and the Effectiveness of Monetary Policy*, where full details will be found. But that will not appear before 1975, for some theoretical work and a substantial amount of econometric work yet remains to be done on these partial studies.

At this time most of the theoretical work has been completed on the banking sector. In particular, two models have been constructed for the commercial banks and another model, which is a slight variant of that of J. M. Parkin (104), has been developed for the discount houses.[3] Models are at present under construction for life insurance companies (which we suppose will apply to pension funds), and these are looking into the question of specifying the asset choice of these companies by means of a principle akin to the safety-first notion that has been systematised by A. D. Roy (83).[4] Unfortunately, at this juncture the econometric testing of all of these models is only just getting under way, and it is not possible to make any statements about the substitutability of different kinds of assets, and especially of bonds, in which we would have much confidence at the moment. The only results available at this stage that we should publicise here are themselves of a somewhat superficial nature, since they arise from the preliminary runs on models for insurance companies.

And yet more caveats: the data we have used for the U.K. life assurance industry are for the industry *per se*, and do not cover the structure of liabilities on their balance sheets. So on these two counts our inquiry into the behaviour of the industry on the government debt market does not represent a case study, in the conventional meaning of that term.

Insurance companies *in toto* play a significant role in that debt market. Including the general funds, they account for over twenty per cent of the total of government stock in non-official hands, and over fifty per cent of the total holdings of stock held by other financial institutions. As we have already noted, their spread of holdings reflects a marked disposition for stock over five years. In terms of their assets and liabilities, life offices dominate the insurance sector, and our comments are restricted to this part of the industry. Tables 6.4.4a and b illustrate their holdings by maturity for the years 1961—72 — where the maturity split is more detailed than that which we had to adopt earlier in this section. Table 6.4.4a depicts holdings of government debt in terms of total assets, whilst table 6.4.4b presents those holdings in the context of the total holdings of that kind of debt.

Table 6.4.4a indicates a *tendency* for the proportion of the total portfolio to be placed in medium-term stock (five to fifteen years) to

Table 6.4.4a British government securities — life assurance companies maturities as a percentage of total assets (balance sheet values)

	1961	1962	1963	1964	1965	1966	1967	1968	1969	1970	1971	1972
Up to 5 years	0.1	0.1	0.5	0.5	0.4	0.3	0.9	0.6	0.4	0.3	0.4	0.5
Over 5 up to 10 years	2.3	1.1	1.3	0.9	1.6	0.9	0.9	0.6	0.6	1.0	1.1	1.0
Over 10 up to 15 years	3.9	2.9	2.5	2.1	2.1	2.1	1.8	1.6	1.7	1.3	0.9	0.9
Over 15 years	13.7	16.0	15.5	15.7	14.2	13.9	15.8	15.9	16.0	15.3	16.9	16.8
Undated	5.5	5.5	5.6	5.4	5.3	5.2	5.0	4.8	4.4	4.3	4.4	3.6
Total assets (£m)	6253	6785	7425	8143	8826	9514	10,626	11,830	12,741	13,781	15,011	16,574

Source: Trade and Industry London, H.M.S.O. (formerly *Board of Trade Journal*).

Table 6.4.4b British government securities — life assurance companies maturities as a percentage of total holdings

	1961	1962	1963	1964	1965	1966	1967	1968	1969	1970	1971	1972
Up to 5 years	0.5	0.6	2.0	1.8	1.8	1.3	3.6	2.5	1.7	1.4	1.6	2.3
Over 5 up to 10 years	8.8	4.2	5.0	3.7	6.8	3.8	3.6	2.7	2.7	4.6	4.7	4.4
Over 10 up to 15 years	15.2	11.4	10.0	8.6	8.8	9.4	7.3	6.7	7.5	6.0	3.6	3.9
Over 15 years	53.8	62.5	61.0	63.9	60.0	62.2	64.8	67.7	69.2	68.9	71.5	73.5
Undated	21.7	21.3	22.0	22.0	22.6	23.3	30.7	20.4	18.9	19.1	18.6	15.8
Total holdings (£m)	1594	1742	1882	2001	2086	2132	2584	2782	2952	3069	3542	3791

Source: Trade and Industry London, H.M.S.O. (formerly *Board of Trade Journal*).

decline, with evidence of a far less discernible decline in the proportion invested in undated stocks. Those in long-term and short-term stocks have not changed significantly. However, if we look at government debt holdings in terms of the total of those holdings the picture changes somewhat. For we now observe that there is a very marked decline in the proportion held in medium stocks, and with some minor fluctuations there is a marked increase in the relative holdings of long stock; for short-term stock and for undated the impression generated by the two tables is very similar.

The data conveyed in these tables point to the importance of obtaining a sufficiently detailed maturity split of bond holdings. For though they support the observations made on the basis of the statistical data presented in the earlier tables of this section, they do make it possible to see more clearly the preference for long stocks and the (apparent) willingness of life companies to shift about in the bond market. But it is possible to argue that these movements may have occurred because of the changes in the structure of liabilities and so on, and they may not represent speculative behaviour. It is also possible to suggest that some changes in the portfolio composition have taken place merely by the 'rolling on process' — that is, a bond that is held year by year shifts naturally with the passage of time from being a long to being a medium and then a short bond.

But ignoring matters such as these, the kind of data given in tables 6.4.4a and b are not ideal for looking at the switching that has taken place between maturity segments, especially if it is hoped to draw conclusions on asset-switching without carrying out any formal statistical testing. If it can be shown that the life companies have, during a time period, both bought *and* sold a given stock, then this is evidence of a willingness to go for a better bargain (if not to speculate): the fact that they sell particular stocks indicates naturally that these are not automatically held until maturity. Data are available on purchases and sales for the industry and flow-of-funds data are available for it on a *net* acquisition basis. Those data show not only that life companies do shift about within the bond market — though still having a preference for longs — but that they are also prepared on occasion to switch out of fixed-interest securities into other earning assets such as equities and property.

To carry out statistical testing of the responsiveness of asset-switching to changes in 'expected returns' on alternative assets, either models can be constructed on a forward basis to explain the desired demand function of the life companies for assets in their choice set, or simple regressions can be performed on the data given in the tables above, or on net acquisition data, and on the data on interest rates (as proxies for expected returns). As we noted earlier we have done some work on building models for life companies but have to hand at this time only those results that we based on the 'regression' approach, which are used as dummy runs for the model, in order to give us pointers as to how particular variables should be specified (e.g. if there is need for a disequilibrium structure). These specifications are not entirely *ad hoc*, for the arguments in the equations (e.g. levels of, or changes in 'expected rates') will figure in the demand equation derived from the development of a portfolio choice model; and the use of portfolio proportions as dependent variables can be rationalised by making reasoned assumptions about the response of life companies to a change in their 'income'.

However, the 'regression' approach, though far less sophisticated, is not devoid of difficulties. Not the least of these is the question of how to proxy expected returns by actual interest rates. Whatever method is used, the problem is that all actual rates move together — even though there have been changes in interest-rate differentials. An added difficulty is that returns on all assets in the choice set should be included in the equations: here we face the problem of how to quantify the expected return from property investment. The upshot of all this is that we have found some of these problems to be insuperable at the time of writing. The collinearity of interest rates has proved the major difficulty, though no set of equations, no matter how close in form they were to what emerges from a properly specified portfolio choice model, performed well in 'explaining' bond holdings. The best equations were those that contained only 'expected returns'; but even here holdings of undated stock could not be accounted for, and only 30% of other bond holdings could be explained. The multicollinearity (which did not disappear when first-difference specifications and the like were employed) makes it really impossible to put any faith in the separate interest rate effects. What happened, in fact, was that the medium-term stock turned out to be a significant *complement* for short-term stock, long-term stock likewise had the same role with respect to medium-term stock, and undated stock had the same role in regard to long stock.

Rather odd findings indeed! But the implications they would have, at least as far as the life insurance industry is concerned, for theories of the term structure must be discounted. It looks, in fact, as though expected return effects are of some importance in affecting the asset choice of life companies, but how, and to what extent, we cannot really say until we have done more (true) econometric work. Again, by implication, it would appear that other factors account for the greater part of bond holdings and any shifts that occur within those holdings. Better specifications of the behaviour of life companies via the portfolio model might help unravel those factors, but it is unlikely, because it is difficult to specify the liabilities side of the balance sheet, and this is also important in specifying their expected 'cash-drain'.

What kind of conclusions can be drawn from all these observations about the bond market behaviour of the life companies? Perhaps the following might not be judged too outrageous, given the qualifications and reservations noted above about the evidence we have adduced. They seem to have a preference for long-term stock; they are prepared, not merely as Culbertson argued on the U.S. evidence, in the short run to speculate, that is to move into and out of particular maturities of bonds; they are willing to switch out of bonds into other assets. Some of these asset switches could be attributed to interest-rate effects, so that we can use the word 'speculate'; some, however, will be due to the structure of their liabilities — this could be particularly true with respect to the movement into equities and property, though there again casual empiricism would suggest that this is not the whole of the answer.

On balance, this evidence is suggestive (again we must use this by now over-used word) of the Risk Premium Theory; it does not support the Hedging Pressure Theory, though neither does it refute the Expectations Theory (we disregard the complementarity between bonds that we have found). If all other institutions behaved in the same way as life companies, so that they were prepared to indulge in asset-switching, and in asset-switching that involved their 'preferred habitat', while those other institutions had preferred habitats along the rest of the maturity spectrum, then we would be getting near to a situation in which we could reject both the Hedging Pressure Theory and the Expectations Theory.

We might expect that debt supplies had some influence on the whole of the term structure, so lending support to the Risk Premium Theory or to the Market Segmentation Theory. The 'aggregate view' equations that we have run for the U.K. bond market over the period 1954—72 lend some support to that contention. The equations run included the reduced-form kind developed by de Leeuw, the Modigliani—Sutch equations, the Okun equation and other specifications similar to those which can be derived from equations for short rates and long rates that have arisen from a general equilibrium model of the financial sector. They included equations wherein the maturity of the debt structure was represented by the 'average maturity of the debt' rather than just by the outstanding stock of 'shorts' (0—5 years) and 'longs' (over 15 years).

The best results, having regard to multicollinearity, the serial correlation in the residuals and so on, as well as goodness-of-fit, were obtained from a simple regression of the yield-gap ('long rate' minus 'short rate') on the supplies of short and long stock outstanding. This kind of equation is part of those of Scott, de Leeuw *et al.* that we have discussed in section 6.3 above; on an equilibrium specification it also contains only two out of many variables that would occur in a yield-gap equation solved for out of a general equilibrium model of the financial sector. Even so, though, in this regard it tells us only part of the picture, over 50% of the movement in the yield-gap in the U.K. during our sample period appears to be accounted for by movements in the supplies of short- and long-term stocks. Even applying the *ceteris paribus* caveat to this conclusion, it is still quite a significant one. Though we were not as successful in accounting for the yield-gap by movements in supplies as Okun was, for example, we find that their *numerical* influence on the term structure is far higher than he found — despite the fact that (with the help of an average maturity of the debt variable, which we found to be of no help) his long-rate and short-rate equations had $\bar{R}^2$ s in the nineties. The coefficient on the short debt and the long debt were respectively, —0.0008 and 0.0004, both being statistically speaking highly significant (and the value of the Durbin—Watson was 1.80). The short and long debt supplies are measured in millions of pounds. An increase in short-term stock of one thousand million pounds (U.S. billion) accompanied by an equivalent decrease in the long-term stock will decrease the yield gap by 0.4% in that year. For the U.S. Okun calculates the effect of such changes as 0.03%.

We have emphasised the dangers inherent in attempts to draw conclusions from such aggregate view results. They are based on ill specified, at times *ad hoc*, equations, and the importance of debt supplies changes as the specification of the yield-gap equation changes. But as a first step in the search for equations to examine the effect of debt supplies on the term structure they have some value, and they do suggest that those supplies can be important, as our earlier observations on the government debt portfolios of financial institutions led us to believe that they might be. Perhaps we should be more conservative, and as cautious as we have been up to this point in the book, and put the matter another way. The evidence does not offer strong support for the Hedging Pressure (Market Segmentation) or the Risk Premium Theories, but it does not refute them and it points in the same direction as the other empirical observations developed in section 6.3 of the chapter.

6.5

In this section we discuss the general equilibrium, or model, attack on the term structure, and especially on the Hedging Pressure (Market Segmentation) Theory. We have suggested in section 6.2, and *passim* in this chapter, that the most satisfactory way to tackle the question of the determination of the term structure is to construct a fully fledged model of the financial sector of a given economy, where possible giving that model links with the real sector of the economy.

The original Clayton—Dodds—Ford—Ghosh paper (84) was a primitive attempt to construct a (static) quarterly model for the U.K. financial sector for (2)1964 to (1)1970. That model — despite its many drawbacks, and despite its simplicity — was the first to appear for the U.K. One of its many deficiencies (most of which were duly acknowledged at the time!) was that it left out one of the monetary authorities' possible instruments, changes in debt supplies, since it aggregated over all government bonds. The model contained only Treasury bills and 'government stock'. Work on the model since, among many other things, has endeavoured to split government debt by maturity. What will be reported on below is the first results that have been obtained from completely re-specifying the model so that it is dynamic, etc., and includes some kind of maturity split for government debt. The results reported here come from one of two re-specifications of the size of the original model; on the one hand we have aggregated over sectors in the original model, so as to make it smaller, and on the other hand we have disaggregated the earlier model to see if we can capture more details of the causal mechanisms. Here we refer to the smaller model, which has 55 equations compared with 85 in the pilot model and 115 in the larger model.

We have already seen how difficult it is to undertake satisfactory analysis of the Hedging Pressure Theory even on a partial basis, and though conceptually it seems more appropriate, indeed ideal, to build a model to examine the theory, it is apparent, as we have partly conceded earlier on, that the difficulties increase almost exponentially as soon as we do try to construct a model *and* test it. There is what we can describe at the very least as a mountain of work to be done in this area, and in particular on the model we summarise below. We are fully alive to that fact: but we offer some of the initial results we have obtained from what amounts to the earliest estimates of what is still a pilot model, since they are the first of their kind;

also, though the caveats that must be entered in respect of our observations on the term structure theories are stronger than those that apply to the other studies we have referred to, they are perhaps not all that much stronger. So some kind of (initial) comparison can be made of our results and those reported on earlier in this chapter.

We must now say something about the model from which we are going to derive the preliminary findings on the term structure. It is founded on 'the portfolio balance approach', the theory of which has been developed most fully by J. Tobin and W. C. Brainard ((96), (97) and (98). The fundamental idea is to look at the choice of a portfolio by a given decision-maker at stated points in time, wherein he will be faced with a range of assets, his choice amongst which, given his objective function, will, *ceteris paribus*, depend upon the expected returns on the various assets in the range and on the *constraints* on his choice. Those constraints can be of different kinds. For example, there will be the usual scalar or quality-limiting variables such as 'wealth' or 'net worth' which make the balance sheet balance.

Other constraints that affect the choice of, say, assets and impose a limit on the holding of particular assets can be imposed by the investor and the nature of his activities or by some outside agent, such as the monetary authority. Official constraints, as it were, affect institutions; and we think here of controls on commercial banks, who have to have a certain percentage of their total deposits in liquid assets, which in the U.K.'s case for example, are now specified more than they used to be before the Bank of England's 1971 paper on 'Competition and Credit Control' (99). Constraints imposed from within institutions often reflect the existence of official controls or the nature of the attitude of the given institutions. As an example, in the U.K. we may look at the Building Societies. These societies have to keep a minimum ratio of 7.5 per cent of 'liquid assets'. What in fact has tended to happen over recent years is that they have consistently maintained a liquid assets ratio of twice the official figure (see D. Ghosh and J. M. Parkin (100)). This seems to reflect their own view that their objective is to maximise the rate of growth of their medium-/long-term assets while maintaining some degree of withdrawability of deposits. Their 'utility function' prescribes their holding liquid assets in greater proportions than the authorities would otherwise require. So they do have a liquidity constraint on their behaviour but it is a *self-imposed* one. If they were to follow the authorities' guide-line, then they could put proportionately more of their funds into assets that earn more than liquid assets do. But their behaviour reflects to some degree their liability to withdrawal of funds deposited with them on one month's notice.

The idea is, then, that any given investor has a certain objective in mind which he endeavours to fulfil at each decision point, subject to the relevant constraints that impinge upon his behaviour. In meeting his objective, which may be to maximise his expected utility, there will be a set of assets and liabilities which seem appropriate to that objective in the surrounding circumstances. There will emerge (*desired*) demand functions for and supply functions of various financial items. These will be of the kind we have met in chapter 2 and in de Leeuw's equation (6.3.1), where the demand/supply functions that are appropriate to the portfolio of any investor will contain as arguments in them own-rates of return, returns on the other assets/liabilities in the optimum portfolio, a wealth variable, and 'other influences'. The latter may come from constraints, and may include variables such as income; for example, the speculative behaviour individuals can undertake will be affected by their liquidity constraint, or their need for funds for transactions and maybe for precautionary purposes, which will be related in some way to some measure of their income, e.g. measured or permanent income.

Those equations are of the kind met in conventional demand theory, and are derived, of course, in the same way. The difference between that theory and the present framework of analysis is that in some degree or other we are dealing with an uncertain, rather than a certain, world. The uncertainty will relate to the returns expected from investment in particular financial assets, and to the drain of cash that will take place over the holding-period. The preferences of the given investors will indicate to what degree, if any, they are prepared to accept different kinds of 'risk'. This itself will reflect the choice of assets they ultimately make, and for how long they decide to keep them.

It is therefore possible to impute specific objective functions to investors such that, with given constraints, the kind of demand/supply functions emerge that we have just outlined. Some of those objective functions will produce non-linear asset/liability functions, while others will produce linear functions that in addition are estimatable econometrically.[5] Also, those functions will introduce 'risk' into the picture — the riskiness 'incorporated' in a given security, and the total risk regarded as being implied by a given portfolio *per se*. But if we make the assumption — an heroic assumption it is true — that risk on any given security is constant over time, it becomes subsumed in the parameters of the demand/supply functions that emerge from the process of maximising the objective function: so in terms of the statistical testing of the demand/supply equations we may ignore it.

So we can invoke the formal apparatus of economic theory to help us deduce the type of asset/liability equations delineated above, if we require to do so. Those equations will initially be equations concerned with the *desired*, or the *optimum*, quantities of the relevant assets/liabilities in the particular portfolio. They will, as far as possible, incorporate information of an institutional nature, via the relevant objective function and constraints.

Though we can argue in this open-ended and implicit fashion, we do, in fact, have to make some specific assumptions to enable the equations so derived to be operationally valuable. There is no necessity for us to go through each and every one of these assumptions, but we note one or two of them. Since it is impossible, for very obvious reasons, to construct a model that includes information on the demands/supplies of all transactors as separate transactors, some *aggregation* of information becomes the *sine qua non* for the formulation of the model into a shape suitable for econometric analysis. We shall say a little more about aggregation in relation to the model of the U.K. under discussion here shortly, but now we can just say that, apart from assuming that the appropriate functions are linear, it has to be assumed that all the agents whose functions are being aggregated behave in the same way and form the *same expectations* of the returns likely to ensue from investing in the (relevant) securities.

There is the question of where the data come from against which the model can be tested. The behaviouristic equations represent specifications to determine the *desired*, optimum, holding/provision of the relevant asset/liability. The data available will be basically time series data and they will be *observed* or *actual* data. To regard these kind of data as synonymous with the *desired* values, it is of course necessary to make the additional assumption that each sector of the model, and hence the model *per* model, is in equilibrium, and continually so in fact.

The *a priori* expectation must surely be that the model will not be in such a state of equilibrium. We could support this innocuous contention in a variety of ways. But, given the way that we have conceptualised the framework of a model, this would manifest itself in the existence of a *constraint*, which impinges upon the activity of a given sector in the model, which comes from, or is imposed by, another sector (or sectors) in the model, which constitutes the other side of the market, as it were. So, in the normal way of things, both sides of the market find that actual holdings/supplies do not equal desired holdings/supplies—expectations are in error with actual rates of interest deviating from expected rates.

The presumption that disequilibrium exists in the model will make it dynamic. There are various ways in which we can allow for this presumption — and hence in which we can set up the process by which (and the time lag with which) equilibrium is attained. The simplest way is to adopt the partial stock adjustment mechanism, where, for example, the change in the effective (actual) demand for an asset depends upon there being a difference between what the investor desires to hold of that asset at t and the holdings that he inherits from the previous period $t-1$. This latter we can best regard as his endowment with the stock of the particular asset at the outset of period t. Any difference between his desired holdings and his endowment will cause him to change his holdings. The standard 'partial stock adjustment' mechanism is of this type:

$$A_t^a = A_{t-1}^a + \alpha(A_t^* - A_{t-1}^a) \qquad (6.5.1)$$

where A^a represents the actual demand for asset A, and A^* is the desired holding of that asset. If we take A_{t-1}^a to the left-hand side of equation (6.5.1) we have an expression explaining the change in the holding of asset A period by period. Should equation (6.5.1) be in logarithms, α would represent the elasticity of adjustment, of actual to desired asset holdings. With a value of unity for α desired positions are always reached, the holdings of the asset always being in equilibrium. With a value of α that is positive but less than unity it takes some time for the actual holdings to adjust to the desired holdings: the smaller is α, naturally, the longer it takes to attain the equilibrium position.

In the conventional presentation of equation (6.5.1) A_t^* is portrayed as the desired 'long-run' holdings of asset A. We are concerned with desired holdings of assets that could be regarded in this way, but that can be changed period by period, depending upon circumstances. We can, however, use a specification such as equation (6.5.1) to relate actual and desired values. From this equation we have actual, observed, values of assets (or liabilities), depending upon immediately preceding actual values of assets and the desired holdings of assets. Here we have a simple dynamic relationship.

This relationship is in actual values, which we can measure, and the desired values, which are provided for us by the desired demand/supply functions. So, if we use equation (6.5.1) and we have those functions, all that we need do is to insert the right-hand side of them into it as appropriate. From the equation with actual values as the dependent variable, we can see immediately that since A_t^a is presumed to be a function of A_{t-1}^a we could experiment with the time series on A to discover the lag structure that is contained within it. If it should be different from the first-order difference equation form, then for given A_t^* we would have a different equation from (6.5.1). It is possible to try numerous alternative expressions of, say, the 'normal' rate; likewise, several forms of the adjustment mechanism can be tried, and the dynamic properties of any of these forms also can be changed in many ways.

In the results on the term structure given here the model has been dynamised by use of equation (6.5.1), and by assuming that this equation is relevant to all assets/liabilities for each and every sector in the model. This is a very strong assumption, but the studies that are being undertaken at the sector/institution level are beginning to experiment with alternative dynamic specifications for the assets/liabilities in the relevant sector.

We can rationalise an hypothesis such as (6.5.1) in a number of ways, by asking ourselves: why could a situation arise in which an investor does not hold the desired quantity of an asset at a point in time? One possible answer has been provided by the work on the demand for money. In that work it has proved possible to show that transaction costs, both monetary and psychic (e.g., convenience costs) could account for inertia in the adjustment process.[6] This kind of explanation of delay in the adjustment to desired positions could also be adopted here. But a strong reason — perhaps a stronger one in reality, though we cannot tell — will probably be the existence of a constraint on asset holding and liability provision that comes from the other side of the market, which we have noted previously.

We can now summarise the framework of the model of the U.K. financial sector. The sectors in the model that we are to report on here are: the banking sector; other financial institutions; industrial and commercial; personal sector; the overseas sector. The government (public) sector plays an important role in the model, naturally, but in this model (contrary to our pilot model (84)) we make no attempt to estimate the asset/liability equations for the government sector. The model also has (tenuous) links with the real sector, which are more detailed in our larger-scale model. The assets and liabilities for each sector are set out in table 6.5.1. There, a minus sign by a symbol indicates that the item is a liability (supply variable) for that sector. The notation is such that the first subscript refers to the sector and the second to the asset/liability; thus, as an example, $a_{2,10}$ is the banking sector's holdings of local authority debt. A bar

Table 6.5.1 Model of the U.K. financial system

	Sectors / Assets/liabilities	1 Public Sector	2 Banking Sector	3 O.F.I.s	4 Industrial and Commercial	5 Personal Sector	6 Overseas	Rates
1	Notes and Coin	$-\overline{a}_{1,1}$	$a_{2,1}$		$a_{4,1}$	$a_{5,1}$		$\overline{r}_1$
2	Bank deposits	$\overline{a}_{1,2}$	$-a_{2,2}$	$a_{3,2}$	$a_{4,2}$	$a_{5,2}$	$a_{6,2}$	$\overline{r}_2$
3	Deposits with O.F.I.s			$-a_{3,3}$	$a_{4,3}$	$a_{5,3}$	$a_{6,3}$	$\overline{r}_3$
4	National savings	$-a_{1,4}$				$a_{5,4}$		$\overline{r}_4$
5	Bank lending	$-\overline{a}_{1,5}$	$a_{2,5}$	$-a_{3,5}$	$-a_{4,5}$	$-a_{5,5}$	$-a_{6,5}$	$\overline{r}_5$
6	Loans for house purchase	$\overline{a}_{1,6}$	$a_{2,6}$	$a_{3,6}$		$-a_{5,6}$		r_6
7	Treasury bills	$-\overline{a}_{1,7}$	$a_{2,7}$	$a_{3,7}$	$a_{4,7}$		$a_{6,7}$	r_7
8	Govt. bonds, short	$-\overline{a}_{1,8}$	$a_{2,8}$	$a_{3,8}$		$a_{5,8}$	$a_{6,8}$	r_8
9	Govt. bonds, long	$-\overline{a}_{1,9}$	$a_{2,9}$	$a_{3,9}$		$a_{5,9}$	$a_{6,9}$	r_9
10	Local authority debt	$-\overline{a}_{1,10}$	$a_{2,10}$	$a_{3,10}$	$a_{4,10}$	$a_{5,10}$	$a_{6,10}$	r_{10}
11	Company securities	$\overline{a}_{1,11}$	$a_{2,11}$	$a_{3,11}$	$-a_{4,11}$	$a_{5,11}$	$a_{6,11}$	r_{11}
12	Unidentified	$\overline{a}_{1,12}$	$a_{2,12}$	$a_{3,12}$	$a_{4,12}$	$a_{5,12}$	$a_{6,12}$	r_{12}
13	GDFCF* + inventory				$\overline{K}_4$	$\overline{K}_5$		
14	Net worth		$\overline{W}'_2$	$\overline{W}'_3$	$\overline{W}_4$	$\overline{W}_5$	$\overline{W}'_6$	
15	Income				$\overline{Y}_4$	$\overline{Y}_5$		

*Gross Domestic Fixed Capital Formation

over an item indicates that it is exogenous to the system. For some sectors, as we shall see, there are financial assets/liabilities in table 6.5.1 that are exogenous as far as it is concerned but which, in terms of the model *per* model, have to be envisaged as endogenous variables.

The rates that are inserted in the table are the market rates that will be determined at each point in time on each of the assets/ liabilities. There is an empty box for item 13, gross plus inventory investment in the economy, as this model does not contain data on, and about the influence of, the 'marginal efficiency of capital', although this would be taken as a predetermined variable for the financial system. But real-sector variables do have a part to play in the model; apart from aspects of the capital stock (K), there are income variables (Y) for the industrial—commercial and the personal sectors. It will also be seen from table 6.5.1 that we have entered 'net worth' variables for five sectors, two of which we have posited to be determined by the system and three of which we have regarded as being exogenous to it.

We should perhaps comment briefly on the financial claims and interest rates used in the model. Considerable aggregation has had to occur on the assets/liabilities covered, but the classifications are broadly in line with those used in the official sources (see n. 9). Thus, bank deposits are not separated into demand and time deposits, national savings include savings certificates, premium bonds and the like but not the investment accounts of savings banks. The maturity split for government bonds is only 0—5 years for shorts and over 5 years for longs. As we indicated in our discussion on the aggregate data for the U.K. (section 6.4), ideally we would prefer a greater split but this is all the data can allow. Additionally, quarterly data are not available for the bondholdings of the industrial and commercial sector, even though the annual stock register figures do indicate such holdings. Consequently we have had to assume holdings are zero. Local authority debt is an amalgam of temporary money, bills and stocks. In the case of the rates used, $\bar{r}_1$ is the negative rate of inflation proxying the opportunity cost of holding cash. For the rate on bank deposits we have taken this as 2% below bank rate; r_3 has been proxied by the use of the building societies' share rate, and in the case of national savings it was difficult to arrive at a single rate to be used with the static 2½% paid on the ordinary accounts and the higher rate paid on savings bonds, so we selected instead the implicit rate on premium bonds. For $\bar{r}_5$ the variance was the same as for $\bar{r}_2$ so only one rate was used in the equations. The building societies' mortgage rate was used for $\bar{r}_6$. Rates for government debt, treasury bills, short and long bonds were freely available in published statistics but for local authority debt some representative rate had to be found to cover the heterogeneous nature of this financial claim, and so we took the rate on three month deposits; r_{11} was proxied by use of an earnings yield for the industrial sector (Actuaries 500 share index). For the unidentified we were uncertain about what rate to use for such a residual sector. We chose finally to use the rate on the special investment account of trustee savings banks. This is calculated semi-annually, so we felt that it would not bias the results for interest-rate effects. Although our use of rates may appear arbitrary we are in the process of running the model with a series of different rates to assess the present results.

Before dealing with the results on page 283 et seq, we should discuss the behaviour of each of the sectors in the model and the means by which the model has been estimated. Since their discussion is a rather technical one on aspects of financial model-building, some readers may find it more appropriate to proceed to the presentation and discussion of the results on the term structure. In discussing the details of the model we shall find it convenient to consider each sector separately; and we shall do so by taking them in the order in which they appear in table 6.5.1.

We are not explaining the public sector's behaviour in this model, and all its liabilities are taken to be exogenous to the system; consequently we do not require information on its capital stock, net worth and income. With the inclusion of the Bank of England's Banking Department in the banking sector of the model it is not possible therefore for us to separate out special deposits as an instrument of monetary policy.

The liabilities that are identified in the model, with the exception of bank lending ($-\bar{a}_{1,5}$), represent the *supplies* to the financial sector of notes and coin and of the various items of public sector debt we have been able to take account of, given the data at our disposal. The supplies then of the term structure variables, very short-term debt, short-term and long-term debt, are determined by the public sector. To some degree this assumption is a debatable one, and it could be contended, on the basis of the (apparent) policy of the U.K. monetary authorities, that at certain periods certain debt instruments have been exogenous while at other periods they have been endogenous. There have been times (in the sixties, up to 1969) when the authorities were prepared to let the market have whatever it demanded of certain maturities of debt to stabilise interest rates; at other times they have been prepared to play an active, as opposed to a passive, role on the market by attempting to influence the structure of interest rates through their open-market operations. In the former situation we would have to conclude that the supply of debt was determined by the system itself; and in the second situation we would be entitled to regard debt supplies as partly exogenous and partly endogenous. The latter classification arises from the fact that it is the structure of rates generated — or likely to be generated — by the system which causes the authorities to intervene on the debt market by altering the available supplies of debt. The authorities, that is, have a reaction function based upon their desired term structure: this could well take the form of equations relating the changes in the relative stocks of debt instruments to the previous period's relative interest rates.

But none of this can detract from the fact that it is the monetary authorities who decide, by whatever means are open to them (such as releasing stock on their register, actually issuing new stock, etc.), the change in the amount of debt that is made available to the non-official purchasers of that debt. We do not have the type of situation, for example, which is equivalent to that wherein the banks have to accept as liabilities any deposits that other sectors wish to lodge with them. Also, we must remember two additional factors: (1) the government sector does have a borrowing requirement, and this may have to dominate its thinking on the appropriate size and structure of the debt; we know that the supply of Treasury bills is important in this context and that they are without any question exogenous to the financial sector; (2) our observation points will not be on a day-to-day basis, when the attempts by the authorities to influence interest rates, to 'nudge' them in this direction or that, will be most relevant or discernible. In fact, our data are on a quarterly time period.

So debt supplies are exogenous: for econometric purposes some decision has to be taken. There is not enough evidence to make us believe that such an assumption is so wide of the mark. In any case, given the shortage of observation points on the data, it is not such an easy matter to try out alternatives to defining the debt supplies as being of this form.

The supply of notes and coin raises more difficulties than do debt supplies: but we have let it be exogenous. The other items in the balance sheet cause no problems, except that we should note that for this sector, and for all sectors, we have incorporated the items 'unidentified'. On occasions this is a large item; but it should figure in the balance sheet even though it must cover a number of financial items that cannot be identified and separated out from it. This makes it difficult to fix an expected return on it; we just have to impute one, We might just also mention the item $-\bar{a}_{1,4}$: this is regarded as being endogenous *for the system* (and hence exogenous for the public sector considered in isolation), for this is a variable of which we can say that whatever is demanded (by the system) is supplied (by the system itself).

We would willingly concede that it is possible to specify some equations for the public sector that would still make the supplies of debt exogenous, rather than just stating that the supplies are exogenous. Remembering that debt supplies are a direct reflection of the government's borrowing requirement, this latter could be specified in terms of variables that are exogenous for the system, e.g. the level of income in the economy, the average tax rate, etc. But in practice it is not as easy as one might believe to incorporate such equations into the model; and for our present purposes we leave this matter here.

It is best if we consider the remaining sectors of the model by listing their behaviouristic equations, which are of the form we have discussed already in this and in the preceding section. We begin with the banking sector.

In terms of table 6.5.1 the only item that we need pause over *per* item is that for net worth. This is not, strictly speaking, a net worth variable: it is a variable that comes from summing the items across the balance sheet; so it is, therefore, a kind of residual item, which includes such things as capital stock (the physical premises of the banking sector) and reserves. We cannot identify these items in sufficient detail from our data (which we shall discuss presently), since these are partly lumped together with the same items for other financial institutions. We have decided to let this 'net worth' variable be exogenous.

For this sector the endogenous variables are items 1, and 5—12. The desired quantities are functions of the expected returns on those items of total assets, of 'net worth' and of the major factor imposing on their behaviour the level of deposits that the other sectors in the economy make with them. As far as they are concerned this is exogenous: but in terms of the whole financial sector the level of deposits is endogenous. If the banking sector was disaggregated, so that one segment of it dealt solely with the commercial banks, then it would be possible to take account of the liquidity constraints imposed upon them by the monetary authorities. In that case, it can be shown that it is possible to split the assets held by the banks into two distinct categories; on the one hand there is a set consisting solely of liquid assets, and on the other hand there is a set composed entirely of 'speculative' assets. In either set the only expected returns that are relevant are the returns on the items contained within each set.[7] However, in this model we have all the banks and discount houses lumped together, so that we have to lose some of the institutional flavour of each of the institutions within the banking sector. As general hypotheses, the desired asset functions as assumed here do not lose too much of that flavour.

For the 'other financial institutions' the same kind of considerations apply with respect to the items in their balance sheets, the nature of their behaviouristic functions and so on. However, when we come to the question of the aggregation of the institutions that make up this sector, we are doing more violence to the facts than we are for the banking sector. In this sector the institutions are: finance houses, investment accounts of savings banks, building societies, pension funds, insurance companies, and unit and investment trusts. Our earlier observations on the way that some of these institutions appear to behave would lead us to feel that we should reconstitute this sector. We should perhaps, for instance, have finance houses and building societies as separate sectors; and have pension funds and insurance companies as another, joint, sector. We have attempted such disaggregation in the larger model, but again this is easier said than done, for the data on finance houses are not as good as they could be for our purposes. But for now we have a group of institutions which we have aggregated to form the 'other financial institutions' sector.

We turn now to the industrial and commercial sector. The demand/supply variables for this sector, items 1—3, 5, 7, 10 and 12, are suggested to be functions of the expected returns on those items, together with income, net worth and company securities issued. The explanatory variable is regarded as being exogenous for the *system*; so too is the total of company securities issued at a point in time. *For the sector*, though it is an explanatory variable, it is possible that it is an endogenous variable. The net worth variable is a proper net worth figure, because it is the sum of financial items and fixed capital. The latter is taken to be exogenous and, given that fact, we regard net worth as endogenously determined by the system. The same considerations apply to the 'personal' sector.

For the overseas sector, which is probably the least well specified sector, the asset/liabilities given for it in table 6.5.1 depend on the expected return variables and a 'net worth' item. The latter again is a residual item, the data at our command not being detailed enough to allow us to do anything other than to have a proxy for net worth. We have let this be exogenous to the system: in any case this seems a justifiable assumption.

To repeat the point, each set of equations for the sectors in the model can be rationalised using standard portfolio theory. The equations are for desired quantities and they are assumed to be linear — or to be produced from the kind of objective function that will produce such relationships between the variables. The model contains 45 such behaviouristic equations; it also contains 8 market clearing equations to determine the 8 jointly-determined interest rates; and 2 balance equations for the net worth of the industrial and commercial and the 'personal' sectors, making 55 (independent) equations in all. There are also 55 variables that have to be determined by the model.[8] Since we have assumed that the equations are linear in the variables, a solution can exist to the system, and this solution will be unique.

The behaviouristic equations referred to in the above represent desired relationships. To estimate those equations we have to do two things; (1) allow for the existence of disequilibrium behaviour; (2) measure expected returns. From what we have said in other chapters of this book, it can be appreciated that we could use several methods, based on past returns, to assess expected returns on them. For our present purposes we have all expected returns formed in the same way for all sectors — formed, in fact, by an inertia hypothesis; thus the expected future return on an asset is proxied by the present (spot) rate of return (interest) on it. The dynamising of the model comes from (1) where, for the term structure results we report here, we follow the scheme given in equation (6.5.1).

This brings us to a point at which we must say something more detailed and specific than we have done so far on the data we have used for the current model. These are quarterly data, based on the flow-of-funds accounts for the U.K.[9] from 1963(1) to 1972(3). We cannot get stock data for the majority of the financial items in the balance sheets of the various financial sectors in the models, so we have to use flow-of-funds data, but the use of such a term is in a way a little misleading. They are effectively net acquisitions data (officially labelled 'transactions in financial assets'), and they consist of both stock changes and changes due to 'income flows'. We have interpreted the data somewhat loosely by regarding them as first differences: at times, because of the method of evaluating assets, this will not be strictly correct.[10] If the data were pure flow-of-funds data then it might be argued that the behaviouristic equations of each sector should be formulated with this fact in mind, and that as a consequence those equations should contain *levels* of expected returns in the set of explanatory variables, just as the stock (or 'level') equations do.[11]

The (behaviouristic) stock equations discussed above for each of the sectors are then transformed into change-in-level equations. This necessitates translating equation (6.5.1) in similar fashion. On certain assumptions this allows us to include a lagged dependent variable in each of the desired demand/supply equations.[12]

So *in toto* we have 66 *predetermined* variables, and since we have several jointly determined variables we need to use a technique for estimating the set of behaviouristic equations simultaneously. It is readily seen that each of those equations is identified in terms of the order condition.[13] But if we are to estimate the equation by, say, two-stage least squares or three-stage least squares we immediately face a difficulty. There are only 38 observations that we can draw on (not 39, because of the lag). So at the first stage we cannot run the jointly determined variables on the set of predetermined variables. We need to use an instrumental variable technique of one kind or another if we are to use a simultaneous estimator. Here the results we quote rely on the use of principal components rather than, say, on the perhaps more scientific method introduced by F. M. Fisher (112) of structurally ordered instrumental variables.[14] The first 25 components of the set of predetermined variables were selected to use as the set of explanatory variables at the first stage of two-stage least squares; to calculate, that is, the 'predicted' values of the jointly determined variables (the eight rates of interest, etc.) for use in the second stage, wherein the behaviouristic equations themselves were run against the data.

It is possible to extend and vary the econometric estimation of even this simple model. We have already mentioned the question of extending it by using three-stage least squares, which, since it is a truly simultaneous technique, is perhaps more ideal than two-stage least squares. Also, it is possible to select the set of predetermined variables — if we may still loosely call them that — to run the first stage of either two- or three-stage least squares by other methods, one of which we have noted above. But whichever instrumental variable technique is used at the pre-first stage, it is possible at the second and third stages to impose some special restrictions on the estimates of the coefficients in the behaviouristic equations for each sector.

These kinds of restrictions are similar to those used by de Leeuw which we have noted earlier in this chapter. Thus, if we take any one sector, we can impose upon the desired demand/supply equations for that sector, if we are arguing that they have been implicitly derived from standard portfolio theory, the fact that they should exhibit symmetry. Therefore the effect on, say, asset i of a change in the (expected) return on asset j, everything else being constant, should be equivalent to the effect on asset j of a *ceteris paribus* change in the (expected) return on asset i, these interest rate effects being the analogue of the price effects in conventional consumer demand theory. These (linear) restrictions on the relationship between the parameters in the equation for each sector can be imposed, although not so straightforwardly, on the disequilibrium specification of those equations. Additionally we can impose the restriction that the coefficient on an interest rate must sum to zero across the balance sheet. A sector's scalar variable (net worth, etc.) also has a parallel with the income, or budget restraint, variable in consumer demand theory, and it is possible to impose constraints on the parameters on that scalar variable that follow from conventional demand theory; that is, they should all sum to unity, on a *ceteris paribus* assumption. The use of these restrictions has figured in recent work on the portfolio behaviour of financial institutions, though not with much success. So far we also have not been able to record any success for such restrictions; the data do not support them.[15]

The results on the model presented below do not contain these restrictions and they are based on two-stage least squares estimated with principal components having been used as the way round an under-sized sample at the first stage. There are other ways, then, in which the results could be obtained, some of which have no value (such as the imposition of the symmetry and aggregation restrictions). Others might give better results; but the main improvement seems likely to come from the re-specification of some of the sectors, and of their dynamic structure.[16]

We come now, after all this preamble, to the results themselves and what they mean, on the assumptions we have made, about the term structure. We do not have room to quote all of the results for the model: so what we have done is to tabulate those for the items in which we are interested, namely Treasury bills, short-term and long-term government bonds. These are given in tables 6.5.2 to 6.5.6. Even with these results, which are the best we have been able to produce with this specification of the model, it is readily apparent that, while some of the government debt equations are very good indeed, some are extremely poor. One of the problems that highlights itself is the lack of degrees of freedom; another is the extremely high degree of multicollinearity that exists in the equations. (This is indicated by det. C in the tables, where this is the determinant of the zero-order correlation matrix of the explanatory variables in each equation.) This does present difficulties, since one of the objectives is to see which assets are substitutes for each other,

Table 6.5.2

Banking Sector			Coefficients on											
			Rates[1] relating to											
			Notes and coin	Bank lending	Loans for house purchase	Treasury bills	Govt bonds short	Govt bonds long	Local authority debt	Company securities	Unidentified	Bank deposits (including public sector)	Net assets of banking sector	
Holdings of		Constant	$\bar{r}_1$	$\bar{r}_5$	r_6	r_7	r_8	r_9	r_{10}	r_{11}	r_{12}	$\bar{a}_{12} + \hat{a}_{22}$[2]	$\bar{W}'_2$	Lag of dependent variable
Treasury bills	a_{27}	-0.87 (0.69)	-140.9 (99.3)	-191.9 (338.8)	-265.9 (208.7)	213.3 (413.9)	2.33 (150.4)	191.6 (211.8)	-99.9 (81.0)	-16.34 (77.4)	-291.4 (463.3)	-0.0002 (0.0006)	0.034* (0.008)	-0.147 (0.14)
Govt bonds short	a_{28}	1.07 (0.63)	-133.2 (81.8)	98.9 (282.1)	-9.76 (203.2)	-188.4 (352.7)	23.0 (131.0)	-415*5 (176.2)	55.6 (70.6)	-35.9 (64.6)	-582.4 (435.1)	-0.0005 (0.0005)	0.006 (0.006)	-0.38 (0.19)
Govt bonds long	a_{29}	0.06 (0.31)	46.1 (44.2)	-40.9 (157.8)	-34.2 (97.7)	56.8 (194.8)	-120.1 (91.6)	-22.0 (127.1)	-0.72 (40.22)	3.65 (35.9)	-21.3 (218.7)	-0.0001 (0.0003)	0.0003 (0.003)	-0.29 (0.31)

		R^2	$\bar{R}^2$	F	det. C
Treasury bills	a_{27}	0.74	0.61	5.83	0.0002
Govt bonds short	a_{28}	0.56	0.35	2.69	0.0002
Govt bonds long	a_{29}	0.34	0.02	1.06	0.00009

[1] Those rates that are not exogenous are predicted values obtained at the first stage.
[2] $\hat{a}_{22}$ is the predicted value of all bank deposits held outside the public sector.

Table 6.5.3

Other Financial Institutions		Coefficients on: Rates[1] relating to: Bank lending	Loans for house purchase	Treasury bills	Govt bonds short	Govt bonds long	Local authority debt	Company securities	Unidentified	Deposits with 'other financial institutions'	Net assets of 'other financial institutions'	
Holdings of	Constant	$\bar{r}_5$	r_6	r_7	r_8	r_9	r_{10}	r_{11}	r_{12}	$-a_{33}$	$\bar{W}'_3$	Lag of dependent variable
Treasury bills a_{37}	−0.005 (0.058)	−3.95 (11.23)	−11.00 (8.84)	3.29 (13.84)	0.319 (6.01)	6.46 (7.96)	−0.773 (3.31)	0.92 (3.17)	−9.43 (18.91)	0.00007 (0.0074)	0.00042 (0.027)	−0.262 (0.165)
Govt bonds short a_{38}	−0.005 (0.163)	27.47 (31.07)	−48.07 (25.25)	−55.83 (37.84)	−4.517 (17.69)	44.72 (22.42)	6.77 (9.51)	7.50 (8.99)	−43.85 (53.83)	0.005 (0.021)	−0.014 (0.074)	−0.258 (0.165)
Govt bonds long a_{39}	−0.318 (0.339)	−95.64 (63.42)	73.35 (58.45)	98.70 (79.00)	−19.20 (37.25)	−264.0* (48.96)	45.33 (23.24)	−33.61 (18.49)	−461.13* (116.90)	−0.268* (0.054)	−0.412* (0.152)	−0.0591 (0.147)

		R^2	$\bar{R}^2$	F	det. C
Treasury bills	a_{37}	0.209	−0.125	0.626	0.0007
Govt bonds short	a_{38}	0.369	0.102	1.38	0.00086
Govt bonds long	a_{39}	0.849	0.785	13.31	0.00026

[1] Footnote as for table 6.5.2.

Table 6.5.4

Industrial and commercial			Coefficients on										
			Rates[1] relating to										
			Notes and coin	Deposits with other financial institutions	Bank lending	Treasury bills	Local authority debt	Unidentified	Income	Company securities	Net assets		
Holdings of		Constant	$\bar{r}_1$	r_3	$\bar{r}_5$	r_7	r_{10}	r_{12}	$\overline{Y}_4$	$-\bar{a}_{4,11}$	W_4	$a_{4},(t-1)$
Treasury bills	a_{47}	−0.389 (0.265)	−11.54 (5.96)	−5.72 (27.3)	30.14 (20.4)	−37.5 (23.1)	−3.81 (5.39)	48.8 (36.9)	0.013 (0.024)	−0.071 (0.075)	0.011 (0.011)	−0.60* (0.106)

		R^2	$\overline{R}^2$	F	det. C
Treasury bills	a_{47}	0.631	0.494	4.62	0.004

[1] Footnote as for table 6.5.2.

Table 6.5.5

Personal sector			Coefficients on												
			Rates[1] relating to												
			Notes and coin	Deposits with other financial institutions	National savings	Bank lending	Loans for house purchase	Govt bonds short	Govt bonds long	Local authority debt	Company securities	Unidentified	Income	Net assets	
Holdings of		Constant	$\bar{r}_1$	r_3	$\bar{r}_4$	$\bar{r}_5$	r_6	r_8	r_9	r_{10}	r_{11}	r_{12}	$\bar{Y}_5$	W_5	Lag of dependent variable
Govt bonds short	a_{58}	0.297 (1.174)	72.23 (46.5)	155.91 (365.9)	-222.4 (309.5)	26.97 (50.05)	-61.71 (194.9)	-111.90 (96.0)	141.13 (119.09)	-10.79 (46.8)	61.22 (60.4)	205.36 (293.46)	-0.033 (0.0198)	-0.0095 (0.175)	-0.455 (0.240)
Govt bonds long	a_{59}	-1.894* (0.841)	-48.43 (32.26)	-6.83 (262.9)	160.59 (215.7)	-45.87 (158.8)	-82.24 (158.8)	76.87 (63.88)	-291.6* (52.96)	31.01 (33.49)	-2.159 (40.31)	-442.1 (227.7)	0.049* (0.015)	0.038 (0.122)	-0.509* (0.192)

		R^2	$\bar{R}^2$	F	det. C
Govt bonds short	a_{58}	0.319	-0.049	0.87	0.0028
Govt bonds long	a_{59}	0.690	0.522	4.10	0.0020

[1] Footnote as for table 6.5.2.

Table 6.5.6

Overseas Sector			Coefficients on									
			Rates[1] relating to									
			Deposits with 'other financial institutions	Bank lending	Treasury bills	Govt bonds short	Govt bonds long	Local authority debt	Company securities	Unidentified	Net assets	
Holdings of		Constant	r_3	$\bar{r}_5$	r_7	r_8	r_9	r_{10}	r_{11}	r_{12}	$\bar{W}'_6$	Lag of dependent variable
Treasury bills	a_{67}	0.161 (0.61)	-543.2 (441.9)	-379.5 (303.9)	263.2 (372.6)	550.2* (169.7)	-390.0 (212.8)	103.3 (102.1)	-105.7 (106.7)	56.5 (525.7)	0.46 (0.39)	-0.42 (0.21)
Govt bonds short	a_{68}	0.079 (0.04)	-52.5 (29.6)	9.07 (20.4)	-13.7 (25.3)	-20.6 (11.0)	14.7 (14.6)	12.4 (6.6)	3.52 (6.6)	-12.9 (35.3)	-0.018 (0.03)	-0.27 (0.21)
Govt bonds long	a_{69}	0.134* (0.063)	-85.9 (45.0)	20.4 (30.9)	-33.2 (38.4)	-27.8 (16.7)	19.8 (21.9)	20.7* (10.1)	4.72 (9.99)	-36.1 (53.3)	-0.012 (0.04)	-0.23 (0.21)

		R^2	$\bar{R}^2$	F	det. C
Treasury bills	a_{67}	0.515	0.336	2.87	0.0004
Govt bonds short	a_{68}	0.262	-0.011	0.959	0.0005
Govt bonds long	a_{69}	0.272	0.0021	1.008	0.0005

[1] Footnote as for table 6.5.2.

and to what extent they are substitutes. Just taking the coefficients on the interest rates at their face value, in terms of those on the interest rates on Treasury bills, short bonds and long bonds, (r_7, r_8 and r_9 in the tables) we may comment on the substitutability of one kind of debt for another in the light of each of the tables 6.5.2 to 6.5.6.

For the banking sector we find that Treasury bills are complements for short and long bonds, and that their own-rate coefficient is also positive. Short bonds, however, are gross substitutes for Treasury bills and long bonds with the coefficient on the short-bond rate being positive. Long bonds are gross substitutes for short bonds, complements for Treasury bills: but their own-rate coefficient is negative. It is clear from the results given in table 6.5.2 that the data do not support the presumption that symmetry holds; though we cannot test for this, the data are also likely to confirm the fact that in all equations the assets are gross substitutes for each other, given the sign-switching of coefficients that occurs between equations. These considerations apply to all the tables, in fact.

Exactly the same statements can be made about the substitutability of government debt for the 'other financial institutions' as were made for the banking sector. For the industrial and commercial sector, of course, we only have an equation for Treasury bills: there the coefficient on the own-rate of interest is negative. The personal sector holds both short- and long-term bonds and the results for those bond holdings are particularly odd: the own-rate responses are negative, while the bonds are complements for each other in both equations. Finally, the results for the overseas sector reveal the following: apart from the short-bond equation, the own-rate coefficients are positive; in the Treasury bill and long-bond equations these items of debt are gross substitutes; Treasury bills are complements for short bonds, whilst the latter are substitutes for the former; long bonds are complements for short bonds, but short bonds are gross substitutes for long bonds.

From the present model, given the estimated stochastic equations, it is possible to calculate — from the total model where the market-clearing and balance equations are taken in conjunction with the stochastic equations, of course — the multiplier effects, both static and dynamic, on the endogenous variables in the model of changes in any of the variables that are exogenous to it.[17] So, for example, for any of the monetary authorities' instruments in the model (e.g. changes in debt supplies, changes in bank rate), we can calculate its effect on the financial system. It is also possible to select a set of targets for the authorities (e.g. to make the long rate stand above the short rate, to change the money supply) and derive the optimum vector of instruments it should use. As an extension of the exercise we could see what kind of trade-offs exist for the monetary authorities in the execution of monetary policies or in the formulation of new strategies. For example they may have to accept an x per cent increase in the long over the short rate if they want to reduce the money supply by y per cent. To provide this kind of information, and particularly to see if the non-bank financial intermediaries can play a countervailing role in regard to monetary policy, is one of the main reasons for our attempting to build a workable model of the U.K. financial sector.

Here we must keep solely to the effects on the term structure in the model of changes in government debt supplies. From the static or impact multiplier it is found that a *unit* change in the supplies of Treasury bills, short bonds and long bonds causes the changes in the rates of interest on those items of debt given in table 6.5.7. There are several things we should say about these multiplier effects.

Table 6.5.7 Static Interest Rate Multiplier Effects

Debt variables	Interest rates		
	r_7	r_8	r_9
$-\bar{a}_{1\,7}$	0.0014823	0.000805	0.0001226
$-\bar{a}_{1\,8}$	−0.0013107	0.0009684	−0.0008926
$-\bar{a}_{1\,9}$	−0.0008643	−0.0010251	0.0108006

The static multiplier effects give us the immediate (hence impact) effects on the system of a unit change in a particular exogenous variable, all other variables remaining constant. There is a once-and-for-all unit change in the relevant exogenous variable. In gauging the effects of the latter on the financial system we assume the coefficients on the 'first difference' stochastic equations, which naturally figure so prominently in the total model, to be the coefficients in the stock or level version of those equations.

In interpreting the results presented in table 6.5.7 we must bear in mind the point that these come from (one million pound) unit changes in debt supplies; and we have to scale up appropriately the numbers recorded there. To keep the results comparable with those quoted earlier on the aggregate view approach to the term structure by Okun and ourselves, we may convert the numbers in table 6.5.7 so that they depict the effects of a thousand-million-pound change in the three items of government debt. On that basis the outcome is eminently sensible and provides more support for the view that relative debt supply changes affect the structure of interest rates.

Suppose we look at a change in the supply of Treasury bills, *everything* else staying constant in the system at the moment the supply changes. The immediate effect is for the rates on all three items of debt to rise, the rises declining as we proceed from the short to the long end of the market. The effects of the change in the supply of Treasury bills on the other endogenous variables in the system, besides its effect on the bill rate, have been to cause investors to move out of both short and long bonds. In terms of the government debt market *per se* there is a substitution of Treasury bills for short and long bonds, and the degree of substitution increases the shorter is the bond, although some of the immediate effects on interest rates in the government debt market will have arisen from the changes in other endogenous interest rates in the system. The impact effect, then, of an increase in Treasury bill supply is to lower the yield gap between longer and shorter stocks; an increase of £1,000 million in that supply raises the Treasury bill rate by 1.48%, raises the short bond rate by 0.8% and the long bond rate by 0.123%.

If we consider a *ceteris paribus* increase in the supply of short bonds the effect is to raise the own-rate and to lower the two other rates of interest. Given the other effects of changes in the supply of government bonds on the other interest rates, and so on, in the system, we have a movement into Treasury bills and long bonds which suggests that these are complements for short bonds when the market is looked at *in toto*. The results for the individual sectors considered in isolation would not lead us to that conclusion. What happens now is that the gap between the long rate and the short rate declines; the gap between the short rate and the Treasury bill rate increases.

We see that an increase in the supply of long bonds is accompanied by an increase in the long bond rate. There is a fall in the other two rates. *Ceteris paribus*, Treasury bills and short bonds are complements for long bonds. The yield-gaps, long-rate less short-rate or Treasury bill rate, both increase.

The present form of the model, then, shows that changes in debt supplies in the U.K. can have effects on the term structure of interest rates. It also indicates that interest-rate changes in one part of the bond market can influence those in another part, and that some forms of government debt are substitutes for each other.

At the sector level the model does not give any clear indication of substitution between financial claims, but if the results are taken at their face value they reveal that demands for claims, and for the different types of government debt, are sensitive to interest-rate changes. But what is relevant is the combined effect of each sector's behaviour on the market.

Our findings on the portfolio behaviour of the various sectors in the financial system and on the effect of their combined behaviour lend support to the Risk Premium Theory or the weaker form of the Hedging Pressure Theory. However, our findings do have limitations and it must be remembered that there is a great deal of multicollinearity in each of the stochastic equations in the model. Though the collinearity can be reduced by the imposition of the restrictions on the portfolio and debt behaviour of the institutions that follow the theory of choice under uncertainty, those restrictions do not hold for the model as now specified and for the data used. These considerations mean that some of the estimates at the sector level look rather odd, are not significantly different from zero, and do not produce enough clear evidence on the responsiveness of financial claims to returns on (potential) alternative claims.

As with any of the econometric studies contained within this book, our results also depend, or could depend, upon any one or several of the assumptions contained within the model. Bearing this in mind, the model does give us some information on the term structure in the U.K., and it can tell us many other things about monetary policy when it is fully processed.[18]

6.6

The discourse in this chapter has been lengthy, and it has covered a great quantity of empirical evidence of varying kinds. We must accordingly attempt to summarise that evidence, and do so briefly so that our discussion is not extended unduly.

We begin with the partial studies for the U.S.A. These studies have not been rigorous attempts to specify the portfolio and debt behaviour of investors and to test resulting specifications econometrically. For the most part they looked at the portfolio composition of particular classes of investors, especially the larger financial institutions. On the whole the evidence, though it is only *prima facie* evidence, pointed to a situation where investors are influenced by the Hedging Pressure Theory or the Risk/Liquidity Premium Theory. Terrell and Frazer's evidence can be classified in this category despite the fact that they suggested that their evidence strongly supported the Hedging Pressure (Market Segmentation) Theory.

The aggregate view approach, as we denote it for the U.S.A., did not support the Hedging Pressure Theory, in that changes in debt supplies were found not to have much influence on the term structure. The only exception to this is provided by the study of Terrell and Frazer, although their evidence, and particularly their interpretation of it, is open to doubt.

This contradictory evidence comes from studies that were undertaken largely on the basis of the same kind of data over the same type of data periods. Several reasons could be advanced for the conflicting conclusion. For example, the partial studies are only suggestive of portfolio behaviour and they look at institutions mainly on a partial basis, out of the context of the market, and out of context of the market for all (appropriate) financial claims. But from all other sides the aggregate view approach is itself suspect and open to criticism of one kind or another.

If we turn to the U.K. and concentrate on our own findings we have a slightly different picture. The partial studies, of the portfolio composition type, support the Hedging Pressure Theory or the Risk Premium Theory. The examination of the portfolio behaviour of life companies that we have done to date and reported on above suggests that some speculative behaviour seems to take place but that there is a strong element of hedging that occurs.[19] The aggregate view equations and the financial model both confirm the findings of the partial studies. Supplies of debt have an influence on the term structure, but so too do expectations if the returns are high enough.

What emerges from our deliberations in this chapter is that it is desirable where possible to investigate fully the portfolio and debt behaviour of as many institutions and other investors in the economy as possible, then, to see how they interact and overlap in the environment of the market, and finally to put the information gained into a model framework, as far as it is feasible to do so.

Notes to Chapter 6

1. We are assuming that bonds of the appropriate lengths of life are available and that, additionally, the return on them meets the minimum specifications required by the given institutional investor. If the latter should happen to be a life insurance company its obligations might be various. Some of these will perforce take that company into the equity market, because they are explicitly equity-linked. The policies it writes might, in addition to guaranteeing the full repayment of the premiums paid into the company by the policy-holders, commit the company to payment of a certain minimum return on the money invested by the policy-holders. In such a case, naturally, the company will be concerned with capital and income certainty. But our brief is not wide enough to enable us to consider these matters, nor can we bring the equity market into our discussion.

2. We might here have put hypothesis in inverted commas; for what Michaelsen has put forward should not perhaps be given such a grandiose title. For it *is* an identity: the only element of conjecture in it that would enable it to begin to be considered an hypothesis is that concerning the error term. But here again, we come back to the old question as to what we can say about that variable. Whatever we assume about it implies something about our conception of the Traditional Theory. Michaelsen's interpretation of it is that that theory requires expectations to be fulfilled on the average, but not necessarily all of the time.

If Michaelsen's equation is to be taken as an hypothesis and tested, some independent estimate of expected holding-period returns has to be arrived at. It is not much value using only *ex post* data and investigating the properties of the error term in the equation for the given bonds. Culbertson rejected Michaelsen's equation because it could not be used without some measure of, *inter alia*, *ex ante* holding-period return. In his later and more detailed paper Michaelsen (87) attempted to meet this point, and to test his hypothesis using data other than those of Culbertson. But the method of measuring expected holding-period yields seems open to question, and, of course, there is the perennial problem that different ways of formulating a variable which we cannot observe leave the final outcome of any testing open to doubt.

3. This research is being carried out by our colleague, Mr D. G. McEnhill, who has to date produced two working papers on this research ((105), (106)).

4. These models form part of a wider piece of research being undertaken by J. C. Dodds into the activities of insurance companies.

5. As an illustration of the former type of objective function we may note that put forward by A. D. Roy (83).

There are a number of functions that produce linear asset/liability equations, and equations that can be readily subjected to economic testing. Here we might mention that advanced by R. J. Freund (101), whose utility function has figured prominently in recent work on the portfolio selection and debt behaviour of financial institutions, particularly in that of J. M. Parkin ((104), (100)). In its original specification that utility function does not meet the Pratt–Arrow condition of decreasing absolute risk aversion (see n. 12, chapter 2).

6. On this topic see E. Feige (36), where references can be found to the early work in this area.

7. This has been demonstrated by D. G. McEnhill (105).

8. It is the number of *independent* equations that is relevant here; and there are 55 such equations, even though *prima facie* it might seem that we have

double-counted a stochastic equation from some of the sectors because of the nature of the 'net worth' variables.

9. The data for the model have been obtained mainly from standard U.K. sources such as: The Bank of England *Quarterly Bulletin*; *Financial Statistics*; The Bank of England *Statistical Abstract*; and *The Board of Trade Journal*. Some data have also been obtained privately from the Bank of England.

10. This allows us to bypass the 'stock-flow' controversy over the determination of bond prices and hence yields that raged from the early 1950s to the 1960s (see G. L. S. Shackle (121)).

11. Some might argue that the nature of the data should determine the formal specification of the model and that 'flow-of-funds' data require a different set of behaviouristic equations from those we have developed. If the data were as precise as the term 'flow of funds' would imply there might indeed be a case for changing the equations in the model. We might have each dependent variable as some function of the flow of funds into the investors' exchequer, that is his 'income', and of the levels of the rates of interest on the own-asset and alternative assets. Income would determine the amount of money to be dispensed, and relative rates of return, given risk, would determine to which assets the money was allocated. Any adjustments in stocks of assets would come about through the attempt to adjust the portfolio period by period to some 'long-run desired position'. We see many drawbacks, both conceptual and empirical, to the employment of such largely flow equations. One obvious obstacle to their adoption is a mundane one: the data are not available in stock form for enough financial claims to make it possible to include the stock-adjustment mechanism.

12. We assume that equation (6.5.1) can hold for all time periods and that the desired quantities of assets/liabilities can change, even though they might turn out to be 'long-run' quantities. If we take a first difference of equation (6.5.1) we have the dynamic adjustment mechanisms we require:

$$\Delta A_t^{\mathrm{a}} = \Delta A_{t-1}^{\mathrm{a}} + \alpha(\Delta A_t^* - \Delta A_{t-1}^{\mathrm{a}}) \tag{1}$$

from which we have:

$$\Delta A_t^{\mathrm{a}} = \alpha \Delta A_t^* + (1-\alpha)\Delta A_{t-1}^{\mathrm{a}} \tag{2}$$

and with the equations for ΔA_t^* we have the new form of the stochastic equation.

That this specification is consistent with equation (6.5.1) can easily be demonstrated. From that equation:

$$A_t^{\mathrm{a}} = \alpha(A_t^* - A_{t-1}^{\mathrm{a}}). \tag{3}$$

If we set equations (1) and (3) equal to each other we find, upon simplifying, that this relationship emerges:

$$A_{t-1}^{\mathrm{a}} = A_{t-2}^{\mathrm{a}} + \alpha(A_{t-1}^* - A_{t-2}^{\mathrm{a}}) \tag{4}$$

which is nothing other than equation (6.5.1), lagged one period. The two equations are consistent and so we may use (2).

13. On identifiability see, for example, Theil (72), pp. 489—97. We have not done any *a posteriori* testing to see if the rank condition is satisfied.

14. On the use of principal components for under-sized samples see B. M. Mitchell (113).

15. A theoretical discussion of these types of restrictions can be found in the paper by S. Royana and K. Hamada (see (116)). See also J. M. Parkin (104), who provides an illustration of how to apply these restrictions in econometric work. We found (84) that *F*-tests on the restrictions, taken either individually or collectively, indicated that they be rejected at acceptable levels of significance. This is the case with the present model also, although the restrictions (other than the symmetry restriction) were not so far off being relevant. Imposing such restrictions reduces the multicollinearity problem, and if they work it makes it easier to disentangle the results and to draw some positive conclusions from them.

16. In fact, where there is an under-sized sample (of observations) as here, Theil ((72), pp. 533–5) has shown that two-stage least squares defined by the generalised inverse reduces to ordinary least squares; and that three-stage least squares reduces to Zellner's technique (26) for estimating seemingly unrelated regressions. So the amount of experimentation with alternative estimating techniques that may be necessary or worth while is small, at least theoretically speaking; for there is always the gap between the mathematical theory and the, as it were, numerical exercise of fitting the equations to the data. Depending upon the sample size and the nature of the data (e.g. the degree of collinearity between the variables in the data set), the results could vary from using, say, single-equation least squares and two-stage least squares. We have, in fact, used Zellner's technique in imposing the restrictions on the stochastic equations for the sectors in the model.

17. The technical details on the calculation of static and dynamic multipliers can be found in Theil (72) pp. 463–8. We should perhaps note here that, in inverting the matrix of coefficients on the jointly determined variables in the model (which is required to calculate the multiplier effects), we have written a special partitioned inversion programme to minimise the rounding error that could appear because of the large number of zeros in the matrix coupled with the high numbers for some of the coefficients caused by multicollinearity.

18. These depend also upon the dynamic structure of the various multipliers in the model, which we cannot discuss here. Neither can we go into the interim multiplier's effect of changes in government debt.

19. One of the general comments that Charles F. Carter made to us is well worth quoting in full here:

> If I may speak as director of an insurance company, part of our fixed interest portfolio is set against 'high income bonds', or policies maturing at a fixed date, or other obligations which are substantially foreseeable in amount and timing. If one wants £1 mn. in 1990, the circumstances in which one would want to get there by a chain of short-term investments are, though conceivable, distinctly unlikely. But another (and greater) part of the portfolio is simply part of the general corpus of investment — equities, mortgages, property interests, debentures, gilt-edged. Here it is very present to our minds that, at any time beyond the next few months, we might want to vary the proportion of gilt-edged: so that, if we buy long, we take a considerable risk of capital loss (i.e. suffer a loss of liquidity). With long-term gilt-edged yielding 10–11%, we take this risk; but there is no doubt that the high yield is necessary to persuade us to this course.

7 A Perspective: Suggestions for Further Research

Our deliberations on the term structure of interest rates have put into sharp relief the kind of major problems by which economics as a discipline is continually confronted when it is striving both to propound testable hypotheses of some substance on particular issues and to subject them to empirical inquiry. Bonds, or financial claims, are intrinsically concerned with *time*. *Ipso facto*, any attempt to analyse the trading activity on the bond market, and hence any attempt to unearth the nature of the forces which determine the exchange ratios that are established between bonds of differing lengths, must grapple with the ineluctable questions of uncertainty and of expectations. *Time* and *Knowledge* are inseparable.

In some way the (elusive) concepts of uncertainty and expectations have to be given some shape both for the individuals on the bond market, whether they be borrowers or lenders, and for the market, since it is the market situation that determines the bond prices and their yields. Each of the theories we have considered has dealt in its own way with uncertainty and expectations in formulating the characteristics of the demand and supply functions for the various kinds of bonds or financial claims. For lenders, for example, given their endowments (or 'net worth'), the theories make different assumptions about their preferences, or objective functions, which contain suppositions about investors' attitudes to the existence of uncertainty or 'risk'. Those preferences may be regarded as being innate, so that the 'psyche' of an individual investor is such that he is a risk-averter or a risk-lover, or they may have arisen because of the nature of the commitments of the investor; for example, the investor may be an insurance company, in which case its liabilities may determine its attitude in regard to 'risk'.

Conjectures of one form or another, conjectures which are usually bold in their nature, are made to enable the time dimension to be handled in one way or another. The interaction of the conjectures produces a particular view of the financial market and hence a particular hypothesis on how any stated relationship between long and short bond yields can materialise, and can change from one moment to another.

The Expectations Theory has the simplest answer to the problem posed by the presence of time: it effectively assumes time away. Uncertainty disappears from the world. Knowledge is gained before its time, as it were — or is believed to be so gained. The commitments of individuals might be dissimilar; so too might their wealth positions: but these differences have no effect on bond yields with uncertainty ruled out and replaced by perfect foresight, or subjective certainty — at worst they could only affect the maturity distribution of the bonds actually traded (though whether they will we cannot tell *a priori*).

The Hedging Pressure Theory, to take another example, in its extreme format assumes that all investors are (complete) risk-averters. They react to the presence of 'risk' in the face of their (largely assumed to be known) obligations by seeking out that strategy which will enable them to meet their obligations with certainty. They *avoid* accepting risk (as far as they are able to by the activities of borrowers).

Once a theory of the term structure has been formulated, there remains the formidable task of subjecting it to empirical scrutiny, a task that can require some measurement of expectations for individuals or for the market to be made, even though the theory itself denies any role to expectations. In testing the Traditional Theory nothing can be accomplished without full information on (market) expected short-term rates of interest. This is not surprising, given the tenor of the theory. But to refute the Hedging Pressure Theory the expectations of individual investors also have to be quantified so that tests can be undertaken to show if those expectations do affect the demands of investors for the financial claims that are traded on the market.

Testing the theories of the term structure has meant that several conjectures have been placed under the microscope simultaneously, such as:

(a) the assumptions of a theory;
(b) the hypotheses(is) that emerge(s) from a theory;
(c) the methods that have been employed to quantify expected interest rates.
(d) the nature of the procedures by which the underlying data have been derived (if they have not been given by 'the market' itself).

All of the empirical studies we have discussed, be they those of others or of our devising, bear witness to this.

The development of a theory to account for the structure of interest rates requires assumptions to be made, and the testing of the resulting theory necessitates the making of further suppositions. We cannot escape from these facts. Though we might quibble with the analytical constructs that go to make up the theories we have discussed, there can be no denying that in some measure they each have something to commend them. They all have the attribute that they try to handle the issues of uncertainty and expectations by incisive steps which produce, out of an intimate skein of complexities that threatens to engulf us as we endeavour to unravel it, remarkably straightforward and striking theories. They have certainly cut the Gordian Knot!

Each theory produces hypotheses that given 'adequate data' are testable, or, if we like, are refutable. Each one drops out different aspects of the complexities that surround the choice process under uncertainty. For example, the Expectations Theory sifts out the difficulties in such a way that investors' preferences, commitments and risk itself are discounted. The Hedging Pressure Theory, in contrast, gives preferences and commitments the major role: risk is there and investors act in an extreme way in response to its presence. Expectations are irrelevant to them, whereas in the Expectations Theory risk is absent, and expectations can play a full role in determining the behaviour of market participants. Each theory stresses varying aspects of the issues that (could) become relevant when individuals have to choose financial assets under a state of ignorance of some degree or another.

The greatest difficulties attach to the testing of the theories, so that it is not always possible to say whether the empirical data support the theory or refute it, because of points such as (a)—(d) listed above. Consequently we are often not in a position where we can judge whether the one theory is 'better' than another, or any other theory. Though it is therefore no straightforward task to take an overview of what we have said, we can make some observations on our findings and especially give some pointers to further work in this area.

The Expectations Theory, more perhaps than the other theories, requires adequate, market-given, data on expected short-term rates of interest before it can be tested. The tests of the theory *per se* to date suffer from the inherent weakness that they rely on the market making accurate forecasts of future one-year spot interest rates. Any testing related to the ethos of the Expectations Theory has to be performed in the context of the Meiselman Hypothesis. We have raised doubts about the analytical value of that hypothesis, but this should not allow us to detract from the originality of Meiselman's work, which has had such an impact on research in this field of inquiry.

However, on the basis of the evidence we have considered that has been brought to bear on the hypothesis both by other researchers and by ourselves, we would at least have to put a question mark by both the short-rate and the long-rate versions of that hypothesis. We have already noted the likely importance of the data for the success or otherwise of the hypotheses under test and we may recall an oft-used catch-phrase, 'an hypothesis (theory) is as good as the data'. There are elements of all four items ((a) — (d)) referred to earlier involved in the empirical evaluation of the Meiselman hypothesis — apart from the question of the econometric testing of the hypothesis. But the *nature* of the data does seem to play a fundamental role in determining whether or not the hypothesis has empirical content. If the data have been smoothed from observed yields-to-maturity, the hypothesis has high explanatory power, at least for a few years into the future. Thereafter it is not so powerful. Where data derived by linear interpolation or other methods are employed the outcome is not that favourable to the hypothesis: for some types of data, especially indeed those based on linear interpolation, the results are decidedly poor. Though, we cannot be too dogmatic about all the characteristics of the data; for the quality of the results is not a unique function of the country of origin of the data or of the time period on which the data are based (e.g. annual, quarterly).

If we are to persist with studies of the Meiselman kind we would think that the theoretical base of the hypothesis should be developed and that we should make more detailed attempts to wrestle with the problems of calculating more perfect yield-to-maturity data (here use might be made of the researches of Brew (119) and Pepper (120)). Yet errors there still will be if we rely on the Hicksian and Lutzian formulae to obtain our sets of forward rates from the yield data. If it should ever happen that we can obtain enough data on expected short rates from the market, this is the kind of data that might rescue the Meiselman Hypothesis and show it to be a good indicator of changes in expected short rates on the market. But as useful as such data would be, for the Expectations Theory as well, it is highly unlikely that we shall have enough data, of a usable form, to enable us to perform a 'fair' test on the hypothesis.

There is plenty of work, then, that could be done on yield curves, which could prove profitable in view of the (virtual) certainty that we shall have to rely on those curves for further work on the term structure.

The other theories, such as the Malkiel Theory and the Hedging Pressure Theory, appear to open up useful avenues for exploration. But again these suffer from the standard problems. The Risk

Premium Theory also seems to have some part to play in the real world, from the tests undertaken of the Meiselman Hypothesis, the Malkiel Theory and the Hedging Pressure Theory, but it is extremely difficult to test *per se* — the data problems are too immense.

Because of data problems it could be suggested that we might as well work with a relatively simple and direct hypothesis on the term structure, something of the aggregate view 'predictive' type. The evidence that we have assembled here would suggest that we should make use of something like the (Keynesian) Malkiel Theory. True, that theory is inevitably based on a particular view of the market, and it contains measurement problems (of the expected normal rate) just like other theories. Be that as it may, the theory would be worth persisting with if a straightforward equation is being sought. There are ways in which it can be developed to produce good results though those results do depend somewhat on the specification of the hypothesis and on the data. But it is worth working on and it is an appealing theory in its own right.

Even though it entails far more work of both a theoretical and econometric nature, our preference is for studies to be undertaken of the individual investor on the bond market. These can be by groups of investors, split into smaller categories than we have them at present in our model of the U.K. financial sector, and the studies would involve analysis of the portfolio behaviour of a sample of investors in each group, an analysis of the type used by Wehrle (94) and Malkiel (11), based on interviews with the appropriate investment fund managers. This method of approach enables us to specify with more accuracy the objective functions of investors, their commitments/obligations, the relevance to them of expectations, and the way in which they form expectations.

Though this might cause difficulties of aggregation, we would be beginning to get to grips with the fundamental issues. We could then see if certain factors were important to particular investors in influencing their activity on the bond market. We could allow ourselves more degrees of freedom in testing the various theories of the term structure, both at the individual investor group level and at the aggregate, market, level. We could, that is, make fewer assumptions, or let the empirical results tell us what factors are relevant. To judge these issues *in toto* we would need to put the individual information back into the confines of some kind of model.

Despite the immensity and complexity of the problems involved in exercises such as these, we believe this is the sensible way to proceed. This is the direction in which we have been going in our current work, developing the material in chapter 6. If insurmountable obstacles should arise to the formulation of a full-scale, and what will be large, model of the financial sector, the individual studies should begin to tell us what we want to know. It is highly likely that they will confirm the general view that emerges from our work on the U.K. to date, namely that the Hedging Pressure Theory in its weaker form, or the Risk Premium Theory, dominate the activities of those trading on the bond market. It may also turn out that the final model we need to use is no bigger than the 115-equation disaggregated model we are now developing out of the model discussed in chapter 6: for the studies of individual behaviour may show us that we need not disaggregate indefinitely.

References

1. J. R. Hicks *Value and Capital* 2nd edition Oxford, Clarendon Press (1946).
2. F. A. Lutz 'The Structure of Interest Rates. *Quarterly Journal of Economics* (November 1940) pp. 36–63. Reprinted in American Economic Association *Readings in the Theory of Income Distribution* Homewood, R. D. Irwin (1946) pp. 499–529. References are to this reprint.
3. D. G. Luckett 'Professor Lutz and the Structure of Interest Rates' *Quarterly Journal of Economics* (February 1959) pp. 131–44
4. J. L. Ford and T. Stark *Long- and Short-Term Interest Rates* Oxford, Blackwell (1967)
5. J. L. Ford and J. C. Dodds essay in C. F. Carter and J. L. Ford (eds) *Uncertainty and Expectations in Economics: Essays in Honour of G. L. S. Shackle* Oxford, Blackwell (1972)
6 I. Fisher *The Theory of Interest* New York, Macmillan (1930)
7. J. M. Keynes *A Treatise on Money* Vol. II London, Macmillan (1930)
8. D. Meiselman *The Term Structure of Interest Rates* Englewood Cliffs, New Jersey, Prentice-Hall (1962)
9. R. S. Masera 'Least-Squares Construction of the Yield Curves for Italian Government Securities 1957–1967' *Banca Nazionale del Lavoro* Part 1 (December 1969) pp. 347–71 and Part 2 (March 1970) pp 82–102
10. A. Buse 'Hicks, Lutz, Meiselman and the Expectations Theory' *Review of Economic Studies* (July 1970) pp. 395–406
11. B. G. Malkiel *The Term Structure of Interest Rates* Princeton, New Jersey, Princeton University Press (1966)
12. J. R. Hicks *Critical Essays in Monetary Theory* Oxford, Clarendon Press (1967)
13. K. H. Borch *The Economics of Uncertainty* Princeton, New Jersey, Princeton University Press (1968)
14. D. G. Champernowne *Uncertainty and Estimation in Economics* Vol. III Edinburgh, Oliver and Boyd (1969)
15. F. A. Lutz *The Theory of Interest* Dordrecht-Holland, D. Reidel (1966)
16. J. Von Neumann and O. Morgenstern *Theory of Games, and Economic Behaviour* 3rd edition, Princeton, New Jersey, Princeton University Press (1953)
17. H. Markowitz *Portfolio Selection; Efficient Diversification of Investments* New York, John Wiley (1959)
18. J. Tobin 'Liquidity Preference as Behavior Towards Risk' *Review of Economic Studies* (February 1958) pp. 65–86
19. K. J. Arrow *Aspects of the Theory of Risk-Bearing* Helsinki, YRJO Jahnssonin Saatio (1965)
20. J. W. Pratt 'Risk Aversion in the Small and in the Large', *Econometrica* (January-April 1964) pp. 122–136
21. J. Mossin 'Optimal Multiperiod Portfolio Policies'. *Journal of Business* (April 1968) pp. 215–29

22. J. R. Hicks 'Liquidity' *Economic Journal* (December 1962) pp. 787–802
23. J. W. Conard *An Introduction to the Theory of Interest* Berkeley, California, University of California Press (1959)
24. M. Friedman *Essays in Positive Economics* Chicago, Chicago University Press (1953)
25. A. S. Goldberger *Econometric Theory* New York, John Wiley (1964)
26. A. Zellner 'An Efficient Method of Estimating Seemingly Unrelated Regressions and Tests for Aggregation Bias' *Journal of the American Statistical Association* (June 1962)
27. W. B. Hickman 'The Term Structure of Interest Rates: An Exploratory Analysis' (mimeographed pamphlet) New York, National Bureau of Economic Research (1943)
28a. J. M. Culbertson 'The Term Structure of Interest Rates' *Quarterly Journal of Economics* (November 1957) pp. 485–517
28b. J. M. Culbertson 'The Interest Rate Structure: Towards Completion of the Classical System' in F. H. Hahn and F. P. R. Brechling (eds) *The Theory of Interest Rates* London, Macmillan (1965)
29. C. Walker 'Federal Reserve Policy and the Structure of Interest Rates on Government Securities' *Quarterly Journal of Economics* (February 1954) pp. 19–42
30. R. A. Kessel *Cyclical Behaviour of the Term Structure of Interest Rates* New York, National Bureau of Economic Research (1965)
31. A. Griliches 'Distributed Lags: A Survey' *Econometrica* (January 1967) pp. 16–49
32. L. A. Koyck *Distributed Lags and Investment Analysis* Amsterdam, North-Holland (1954)
33. M. Nerlove *Distributed Lags and Demand Analysis for Agricultural and other Commodities* Washington D.C., U.S. Department of Agriculture, Agriculture Handbook No. 141 (1958)
34. R. Solow 'On a Family of Lag Distributions' *Econometrica* (April 1960) pp. 393–406
35. S. Almon 'The Distributed Lag between Capital Appropriations and Expenditures' *Econometrica* (January 1965) pp. 178–96
36. E. Feige 'Expectations and Adjustments in the Monetary Sector' *American Economic Association Papers and Proceedings* (May 1967) pp. 462–73
37. F. de Leeuw 'A Model of Financial Behaviour' in J. S. Duesenberry, G. Fromm, L. R. Klein and E. Kuh (eds) *The Brookings Quarterly Econometric Model of the U.S.* Chicago, Rand McNally (1965)
38. M. Friedman *A Theory of the Consumption Function* Princeton, New Jersey, Princeton University Press (1957)
39. J. A. G. Grant 'Meiselman on the Structure of Interest Rates: A British Test' *Econometrica* (February 1964) pp. 51–71
40. D. Durand *Basic Yields of Corporate Bonds, 1900–1942* New York, National Bureau of Economic Research (1942)
41. D. Durand 'A Quarterly Series of Corporate Basic Yields 1952–1957; and some Attendant Reservations' *Journal of Finance* (September 1958) pp. 348–56
42. S. Homer *A History of Interest Rates* New Brunswick, New Jersey, Rutgers University Press (1963)
43. E. Malinvaud *Statistical Methods of Econometrics* Amsterdam, North-Holland (1966)

44. N. R. Draper and H. Smith *Applied Regression Analysis* New York, John Wiley (1966)
45. F. R. Macaulay *The Movements of Interest Rates, Bond Yields, and Stock Prices in the United States since 1856* New York, National Bureau of Economic Research (1938)
46. L. G. Telser 'A Critique of some Recent Empirical Research on the Explanation of the Term Structure of Interest Rates' *Journal of Political Economy* (December 1967) pp. 546–61
47. P. Cagan chapter II in M. Friedman (ed.) *Studies in the Quantity Theory of Money* Chicago, University of Chicago Press (1956)
48. H. G. Johnson *Essays on Monetary Economics* London, Allen and Unwin (1968)
49. C. F. Carter 'On Degrees Shackle: or, the Making of Business Decisions' in C. F. Carter and J. L. Ford (eds), referred to in 5 above
50. G. L. S. Shackle 'The Nature of Interest Rates' *Oxford Economic Papers* New Series (January 1949) pp. 99–120
51. A. Koestler *The Ghost in The Machine* London, Pan (1970)
52. G. L. S. Shackle *Expectations in Economics* Cambridge, Cambridge University Press (1949)
53. G. L. S. Shackle *Decision, Order and Time in Human Affairs* 1st edition Cambridge, Cambridge University Press (1961)
54. R. Solow *Price Expectations and the Behaviour of the Price Level* Manchester, Manchester University Press (1969)
55. D. Fisher 'The Structure of Interest Rates: A Comment' *Economica* (November 1964) pp. 412–19
56. D. Fisher 'Expectations, the Term Structure of Interest Rates, and Recent British Experience' *Economica* (August 1966) pp. 319–29
57. A. Buse 'Interest Rates, The Meiselman Model and Random Numbers' *Journal of Political Economy* (February 1967) pp. 49–62
58. G. O. Bierwag and M. A. Grove 'A Model of the Term Structure of Interest Rates' *Review of Economics and Statistics* (February 1967) pp. 50–62
59. J. Van Horne 'Interest-Rate Risk and the Term Structure of Interest Rates' *Journal of Political Economy* (August 1965) pp. 344–51
60. T. E. Holland 'A Note on the Traditional Theory of the Term Structure of Interest Rates and Rates on Three and Six-month Treasury Bills' *International Economic Review* (September 1965) pp. 330–6
61. R. Roll 'Interest-Rate Risk and the Term Structure of Interest Rates' *Journal of Political Economy* (December 1966) pp. 629–31
62. J. H. Wood 'Expectations, Errors and the Term Structure of Interest Rates' *Journal of Political Economy* (April 1963) pp. 160–71 (Review article of Meiselman (8))
63. J. H. Wood 'The Expectation Hypothesis, the Yield Curve, and Monetary Policy' *Quarterly Journal of Economics* (August 1964) pp. 457–70
64. J. A. G. Grant 'Structure of Interest Rates, A Reply to Douglas Fisher' *Economica* (November 1964) pp. 419–22
65. J. Robinson 'The Rate of Interest' *Econometrica* (April 1951) pp. 92–111
66. D. H. Robertson *Essays in Money and Interest* London, Collins (1966)
67. N. Kaldor 'Speculation and Economic Stability' *Review of Economic Studies* (1939–40) pp. 12–16
68. C. Nelson *The Term Structure of Interest Rates* London, Basic Books (1973)

69. C. A. E. Goodhart chapter 1 in H. G. Johnson *et al.* (eds) *Readings in British Monetary Economics* Oxford, Clarendon Press (1972)
70. N. Wallace 'The Term Structure of Interest Rates and the Maturity Composition of the Federal Debt' Ph.D. dissertation, University of Chicago (1964)
71. G. L. S. Shackle *A Scheme of Economic Theory* Cambridge, Cambridge University Press (1965)
72. H. Theil *Principles of Econometrics* Amsterdam, North-Holland (1971)
73. J. Stewart and A. J. Rayner 'Qualitative Factors in Linear Regression Analysis' *Manchester School* (December 1970) pp. 339–58
74. N. Liviatan 'Consistent Estimation of Distributed Lags' *International Economic Review* (January 1963) pp. 44–52
75. L. R. Klein 'The Estimation of Distributed Lags' *Econometrica* (October 1958) pp. 553–65
76. D. H. Robertson *Lectures on Economic Principles* London, Collins (1963)
77. B. A. Goss *The Theory of Futures Trading* London and Boston, Routledge and Kegan Paul (1972)
78. J. W. Conard *The Behaviour of Interest Rates* New York, National Bureau of Economic Research (1966)
79. G. C. Chow 'Tests of Equality Between Sets of Coefficients in Two Linear Regressions' *Econometrica* (July 1960) pp. 591–605
80. J. P. Burman and W. R. White 'Yield curves for gilt-edged stocks' *Bank of England Quarterly Bulletin* Vol. 12 Number 4 (December 1972)
81. J. M. Keynes *The General Theory of Employment Interest and Money* London, Macmillan (1936)
82. J. M. Keynes *A Treatise on Money* Vol. I London, Macmillan (1930)
83. A. D. Roy 'Safety First and the Holding of Assets' *Econometrica* (July 1952) pp.431–49
84. G. Clayton, J. C. Dodds, J. L. Ford and D. Ghosh 'An Econometric Model of the U.K. Financial Sector: Some Preliminary Findings' essay in H. G. Johnson and A. R. Nobay (eds) *Issues in Monetary Economics* Oxford, Clarendon Press (1974)
85. J. B. Michaelsen 'The Term Structure of Interest Rates: Comment' *Quarterly Journal of Economics* (February 1963) pp. 166–74
86. J. M. Culbertson 'The Term Structure of Interest Rates: Reply' *Quarterly Journal of Economics* (November 1963) pp. 691–96
87. J. B. Michaelsen 'The Term Structure of Interest Rates and Holding-Period Yields on Government Securities' *Journal of Finance* (September 1965) pp. 444–63
88. E. J. Kane and B. G. Malkiel 'The Term Structure of Interest Rates: An Analysis of a Survey of Interest Rate Expectations' *Review of Economics and Statistics* (August 1967) pp. 343–55
89. J. H. Wood 'An Econometric Model of the Term Structure of Interest Rates' a paper presented to the Econometric Society, Pittsburgh (December 1962, revised March 1964) unpublished. Referred to in B. G. Malkiel (11)
90. W. T. Terrell and W. J. Frazer 'Interest Rates, Portfolio Behaviour and Marketable Government Securities' *The Journal of Finance* (March 1972) pp. 1–35
91. A. M. Okun 'Monetary Policy, Debt Management, and Interest Rates: A

Quantitative Appraisal, in Stabilization Policies' *Commission on Money and Credit* Englewood Cliffs, New Jersey, Prentice-Hall (1963) pp. 331–80

92. R. H. Scott 'Liquidity and the Term Structure of Interest Rates' *Quarterly Journal of Economics* (February 1965) pp. 135–45
93. F. Modigliani and R. Sutch 'Innovations in Interest Rate Policy' *American Economic Association Papers and Proceedings* (May 1966) pp. 178–97
94. L. S. Wehrle 'Life Insurance Investment: The Experience of Four Companies' (chapter 6) in *Studies of Portfolio Behaviour* Cowles Foundation Monograph 20 New York, John Wiley (1967)
95. J. Duesenberry *Business Cycles and Economic Growth* New York, McGraw-Hill (1958)
96. J. Tobin and W. C. Brainard 'Financial Intermediaries and the Effectiveness of Monetary Controls' *American Economic Review* (May 1963) pp. 383–400
97. W. C. Brainard and J. Tobin 'Econometric Models: Their Problems and Usefulness' *American Economic Association Papers and Proceedings* (May 1968) pp. 99–149
98. W. C. Brainard 'Financial Intermediaries and a Theory of Monetary Control' chapter 4 in D. Hester and J. Tobin (eds) *Financial Markets and Economic Activity* Cowles Foundation Monograph 21 New York, John Wiley (1967)
99. 'Competition and Credit Control' *Bank of England Quarterly Bulletin* (June 1971) pp. 189–93
100. D. Ghosh and J. M. Parkin 'A Theoretical and Empirical Analysis of the Portfolio, Debt and Interest Rate Behaviour of Building Societies' *Manchester School* (September 1972) pp. 231–44
101. R. J. Freund 'The Introduction of Risk into a Programming Model' *Econometrica* (July 1956) pp. 253–63
102. J. Hirshleifer 'Liquidity, Uncertainty, and the Accumulation of Information' in C. F. Carter and J. L. Ford (eds) referred to in (5) above
103. H. A. J. Green 'Uncertainty and the Expectations Hypothesis' *Review of Economic Studies* (October 1967) pp. 387–98
104. J. M. Parkin 'Discount House Portfolio and Debt Selection Behaviour' *Review of Economic Studies* (October 1970) pp. 469–97
105. D. G. McEnhill 'A Discussion of the Constraints Affecting U.K. Commercial Bank Behaviour' (January 1973) (mimeographed)
106. D. G. McEnhill 'The Objective Function of the Commercial Banks – A Discussion' (November 1972) (mimeographed)
107. A. Buse 'The Structure of Interest Rates and Recent British Experience: A Comment' *Economica* (August 1967) pp. 298–313
108. P. J. Dhrymes *Distributed Lags, Problems of Estimation and Formulation* San Francisco, Holden-Day, and Edinburgh, Oliver and Boyd (1971)
109. G. L. S. Shackle *Epistemics and Economics: A Critique of Economic Doctrines* Cambridge, Cambridge University Press (1972)
110. A. J. Ayer *The Problem of Knowledge* Harmondsworth, Penguin (1956)
111. D. W. Jorgenson 'Rational Distributed Lag Functions' *Econometrica* (January 1966) pp 135–49
112. F. M. Fisher 'Dynamic Structure and Estimation in Economy-wide Econometric Models' in *The Brookings Quarterly Econometric Model of the United States* referred to in (37) above, pp. 589–635

113. B. M. Mitchell 'Estimation of Large Econometric Models by Principal Component and Instrumental Variable Methods' *The Review of Economics and Statistics* (May 1971) pp. 140-6
114. R. V. Roosa *The Place of Monetary Policy in the Economic Policy of the United States* Washington D.C., Per Jacobsson Foundation (1965)
115. *Linked Life Assurance* Report of the Committee on Property Bonds and Equity-Linked Life Assurance, Cmnd. 5281 London, H.M.S.O. (1973)
116. D. D. Hester and J. Tobin (eds) *Risk Aversion and Portfolio Choice* Cowles Foundation Monograph 19 New York, John Wiley (1967)
117. 'Yield curves and representative yields on British Government securities' *Bank of England Quarterly Bulletin* (March 1967) pp. 52—6
118. J. P. Burman 'Yield curves for gilt-edged stocks: further investigation' *Bank of England Quarterly Bulletin* (September 1973) pp. 315—26
119. J. M. Brew 'Gilt-Edged Yield Curves' *Investment Analyst* (December 1966) pp. 3—23
120. G. T. Pepper 'Selection and Maintenance of a Gilt Edged Portfolio' *Journal of the Institute of Actuaries* Vol. 90 (1964) pp. 88—93
121. G. L. S. Shackle 'Recent Theories Concerning the Nature and Role of Interest' *Economic Journal* (June 1961) pp. 209—54

Index